Freedom's Prophet

Freedom's Prophet

*Bishop Richard Allen, the AME Church,
and the Black Founding Fathers*

Richard S. Newman

NEW YORK UNIVERSITY PRESS

New York and London

NEW YORK UNIVERSITY PRESS
New York and London
www.nyupress.org

Library of Congress Cataloging-in-Publication Data
Newman, Richard S.
Freedom's prophet : Bishop Richard Allen, the AME Church,
and the Black founding fathers / Richard S. Newman.
p.   cm.
Includes bibliographical references and index.
ISBN-13: 978-0-8147-5826-7 (cl : alk. paper)
ISBN-10: 0-8147-5826-6 (cl : alk. paper)
1. Allen, Richard, 1760–1831. 2. African Methodist Episcopal
Church—Bishops—Biography. 3. Bishops—United States—
Biography. 4. African Methodist Episcopal Church—History.
I. Title.
BX8459.A4N49 2008
287'.83—dc22   2007043259
[B]

New York University Press books are printed on acid-free paper,
and their binding materials are chosen for strength and durability.

Manufactured in the United States of America
10 9 8 7 6 5 4 3 2 1

For Lisa

Contents

Preface and Acknowledgments

"Brave!" "Ingenious!" "Tactical!" "Brilliant!" High school students were shouting out words that best described Richard Allen's 1799 eulogy of George Washington. I had asked them to pick just one word to characterize Allen's speech, hoping that this little task would create the beginnings of a broader discussion on African American protesters during the American Revolutionary era. A graduate-school friend who directed a wonderful program of one-day sessions at Strong Museum in Rochester for advanced-placement high school students had put me in front of the group of about sixty kids from different schools. I handed out my document, crossed my fingers, and hoped that someone would raise a hand to start the discussion. About forty-five minutes later, I could barely get them to stop debating Allen's ideology, strategy, literary style, and political goals. "You should write a book about him," one of the teachers whispered to me as the students filed out of the room. This book is my attempt to build on that wonderful discussion about a black founder and his world a few years ago in a Rochester classroom.

"I was afraid this would happen." Now the words came from my great editor at NYU Press, Deborah Gershenowitz, who had to put up with yet another request for an extension on the book. "Why can't biographers just let go of their subjects?!" She laughed when she said it, but Deb was right: it's tough to spend years with a biographical subject and then let go. I always had great excuses—I found a new source, I faced a new question, I just wanted to tweak a chapter one last time. One of the best things about finishing a book, of course, is the opportunity to thank the many people who helped make it possible. Learning about Richard Allen and his world has been revelatory. But working in some of America's best research libraries, and getting savvy advice from great friends and scholars, has been similarly fulfilling. It is a pleasure to say thank you in print.

Let me begin by offering thanks to the people who helped get *Freedom's Prophet* off the ground. John Paul Dyson and Joan Hoffman at Rochester's Strong Museum allowed me to teach in their amazing AP history program several times, including that first session on Richard Allen. Students and teachers from several Rochester high schools helped me to see that a broader audience might be interested in Allen's story. My editors at NYU Press quickly and enthusiastically agreed to the proposed biography, for which I'm grateful. Once again, Allison Waldenberg got me started before leaving for greener pastures. Deb Gershenowitz seamlessly assumed control of the project, waited patiently as I did more research, prodded me to finish at the right moment, and then offered an exacting but encouraging reading of the entire manuscript. She's been a terrific editor and now friend. Andrew Katz copyedited the manuscript with care and kindness, and Despina Papazoglou Gimbel expertly saw the project through production.

Several institutions and organizations offered critical financial support. The National Endowment for the Humanities provided a "We the People" Summer Stipend that facilitated research and writing at a key moment. A short-term fellowship at the American Philosophical Society allowed me to study the Wesley Church breakaway movement in depth. An associate fellowship at Yale's Gilder Lehrman Center allowed me to examine Allen's emigrationist thought in more detail. That fellowship also introduced me to one of the most collegial and important scholarly environments for the study of race and slavery that I have ever had the pleasure of being around. Thanks to Rob Forbes, Tom Thurston, and Dana Schaffer for many fine conversations there. A special thanks to the GLC's directors, past and present: David Brion Davis and David Blight, respectively, each of whom proved gracious and intellectually welcoming on my several visits to New Haven.

The Library Company of Philadelphia remains my scholarly home away from home—and one of my favorite places in the world. Since I began working on *Freedom's Prophet*, I've spent a considerable amount of time there, first as a Society for Early American Historians short-term fellow, then as director of an NEH Summer Seminar for School Teachers on Abolitionism, and most recently as co-organizer of a major conference on Atlantic Emancipations. Every time I return, I'm reminded of the Library Company's extraordinary and extraordinarily helpful staff and scholars. A hearty thank-you to Connie King, Linda August, Charlene Peacock, Jennie Ambrose, Wendy Wolofson, and Debbie Schapiro for help and advice on any range of subjects. As usual, Jim Green provided bonhomie and critical readings—formal and informal—of work relating to Richard Allen, particularly the black founder's world of print. Phil Lapsansky has already been described by Shane White as "incomparable," so I will merely say that he is beyond compare as archivist and interpreter of early black life. Without him, *Freedom's Prophet* would be a much thinner and less ramifying study. It has been a real pleasure to get to know John Van Horne, a great scholar in his own right, over the past several years. He has become a friend and advocate in so many ways that I'm not sure a simple thank-you is enough.

The manuscript has benefited from commentary by numerous friends and colleagues at conferences, workshops, beer halls, coffeeshops, and myriad other venues. Again, a simple thank-you seems too slight for the time they've taken to make this a better book. Needless to say, I remain responsible for any mistakes and provocative interpretations contained in the book. In the beginning, Graham Hodges, Roy Finkenbine, Julie Winch, William Freehling, Jim Stewart, Doug Egerton, Patrick Rael, John Stauffer, and Erik Seeman provided encouraging commentary on, and readings of, chapters. Liz Varon, Manisha Sinha, Ira Berlin, Mia Bay, Joanne Melish, Wilson Moses, Clint Rodreick, David Waldstreicher, and Donald Yacovone offered, at various times, both formal and informal commentary on parts of the book, for which I remain in their debt. After we worked together on a Philadelphia project, Gary Nash literally handed me his notes on Allen, meticulously saved from work on his monumental study of black Philadelphia, *Forging Freedom*; I remain grateful for his aid and support. Dee Andrews provided a thorough and challenging reading of the penultimate version of the manuscript—heroic work indeed! At lunch one day, Steve Hahn offered encouraging words about the project that helped push me in new directions. Derek Krissoff, an old friend and editor in another connection, continues to make me smile with his words of wisdom. Kathryn Ostrofsky, a Penn graduate student in history and one of the best researchers I've ever met, has been an invaluable source of information. At Howard University's Moorland-Springam Research Center, Donna M. Wells provided access to Allen's first portrait.

Several people at the National Parks Service in Philadelphia have helped me conceptualize Allen's founding world through their amazing tours of city streets and artful research in dusty archives. Steve Sitarski, Joe Becton, Jim Mueller, Doris Fanelli, and Anna Coxe Toogood have been amazing friends of the project as it's developed over the past few years. Douglass Mooney, an inveterate historical consultant and amazing researcher, generously provided information on blacks' earliest petition effort to Congress.

At Cliveden, the summer estate of Allen's first master, Benjamin Chew, just outside Philadelphia, I was lucky to meet scholars and museum professionals who remain interested in linking their story to African American history. Dave Young, Phillip Seitz, and Ann Roller have generously shared research and opened Cliveden's doors as a testing ground for ideas that made their way into the book.

One of the great joys of learning about Richard Allen has been spending time at Mother Bethel Church in Philadelphia. A historical, cultural, and architectural gem, the church always inspires. I've been lucky to know pastor Jeffrey Leath, who never fails to be welcoming in a way that would make Richard Allen himself smile. Amen! I'll never forget taking a group of NEH teachers to Sunday services at Bethel. Pastor Leath generously acknowledged us and then gave a rousing sermon. "Wow. That's the most amazing religious experience I've ever had," one teacher beamed on the way out. Richard Allen's lineal descendent Katherine Dockens, retired now, was a warm and welcoming presence on my many visits to her ancestor's church. I consider it a privilege to have met and learned from her.

The fifteen members of my NEH summer seminar on abolitionism in 2006 helped me get over the hump and think about finishing *Freedom's Prophet*. Though we studied many other reformers, Richard Allen took center stage on more than one occasion—so much so that the teachers clandestinely purchased a Richard Allen action figure for me at the end of the summer! I'm thinking of Britt, Diana, Michael, Sharon, Jerome, Abby, Melissa, Nina, Rebekah, Alexandria, Jim, Darren, Andy, Marc, and Malcolm. I can't thank them enough for their collective insights and good cheer. Special thanks to the great Jim Stewart for suggesting the NEH.

At Rochester Institute of Technology, I'd like to thank former dean Andrew Moore and interim dean Glenn Kist for providing incredible financial support for the completion of *Freedom's Prophet*. In addition, the College of Liberal Arts Faculty Research Fund generously offered short-term grants to facilitate early travel to archives in Philadelphia. Finally, the Department of History, especially its fabulous chair, Rebecca

Edwards, always offered (extra) funding for conference travel that allowed me to present papers several times a year without worry.

Portions of the introduction and chapter 5 appeared previously in book and journal form. I'm grateful to the New Press for permission to reprint selections from my essay "A Chosen Generation," in McCarthy and Stauffer, eds., *Prophets of Protest,* and to the *William and Mary Quarterly,* for permission to reprint material from both "Black Founders in the New Republic: An Introduction" and "We Participate in Common," which appeared in the January 2007 issue.

Finally, thanks to the people who have mattered most—family and loved ones. As always, I want to express my love and gratitude to family members—my brother and sister, Eric and Ruth, and my parents, Bob and Milda Newman. Thanks for always being there (and for watching the house and animals when I was out researching Allen). Lisa Hermsen has lived with Allen over the past several years, visiting Philadelphia archives and Mother Bethel Church on more than one occasion. Though a fine scholar in her own right, she loves a good sermon and never seems to mind my (endless) Allen stories. "One with another," Allen would often say. *One with another.*

With those words, I lovingly dedicate this book to Lisa.

Introduction

A Black Founder's Many Worlds

If I could write but a part of my labors, it would fill a volume.
—Richard Allen, *Life, Experience, and Gospel Labours*

If you go to Philadelphia today and stop at the corner of Sixth and Lombard streets, you stand on hallowed ground. Here one of early America's leading reformers built an internationally famous church, wrote pamphlets of protest that served as models for generations to come, and championed liberty and justice for all. "He was one of the most talented people of his generation," a distinguished scholar of the American Revolution has written; he was a true "Apostle of Freedom," an early biographer declared. His name was Richard Allen. He was a black founder.[1]

For those who visit "Mother Bethel," as his South Philadelphia church is still called, objects big and small commemorate Allen as a black founder. A hand-fan informs its holders that the church "stands on the oldest parcel of ground continuously owned by blacks." The simple object—made of the thinnest cardboard material but deceptively useful during the sweltering Philadelphia summers—also highlights Allen's organization of the first black reform society in America (the Free African Society) during the magical year of 1787. Knowing that many modern-day visitors will already have taken in the Liberty Bell and Independence Mall (where white American founders attempted to craft "a more perfect union"), the Mother Bethel fan implies that the formation of the Constitution was but one of the many key events occurring in Philadelphia that year. Black founder Richard Allen led another critical event less than a mile from where Washington, Franklin, Hamilton, and Adams once stood.

In his hometown, as one might suspect, Allen's legacy remains strong. The Philadelphia phone book lists the number for "Mother Bethel" and then adds that the church sits on land "purchased by Richard Allen" in 1791. Guided tours roll past Mother Bethel on most days, and Sunday services at Allen's magnificently rebuilt church (refashioned in 1889 in the Romanesque style favored by late-nineteenth-century American architects like Henry Hobson Richardson) find visitors attending from all over the world. "Welcome, Bienvenue, Welcommen," the church hymnal says. "No institution allows deeper insight to the heart and soul of African Americans than the church," AME pastor Jeffrey Leath has written, and "Mother Bethel . . . has been a shining star for African Americans for over two hundred years." (Today, the broader AME Church boasts a global membership of over two million people.) "The courage and compassion of her founder, Bishop Richard Allen," he continues, "set a tone for succeeding generations."[2]

Allen's contemporaries agreed. "Richard Allen! Oh my God!!" celebrated Boston activist David Walker wrote in 1829. "The bare recollection of the labors of this man fills my soul with all those very high emotions which would take the pen of Addison to portray." Allen's admirers constitute a who's who of African American life: celebrated reformer Frederick Douglass, black physician James McCune Smith, famed female preacher Jarena Lee, the pathbreaking urban sociologist W. E. B. Du Bois. "If true greatness consists in self-sacrificing heroism and devotion," African American preacher John Palmer told a gathering at Allen Chapel in Philadelphia at the close of the nineteenth century, "if again, greatness consists in that manifest patriotism which yearns to strike the blow which results in bringing freedom and liberty to an oppressed people . . . then Richard Allen was great."[3]

White reformers celebrated Allen's founding credentials as well. He was, one commentator wrote of an 1813 engraving of the Rev. Richard Allen, "the first black Bishop in the United States and perhaps the world!"[4] During the 1790s, Quaker abolitionist Warner Mifflin roamed the mid-Atlantic countryside touting Allen's pamphlets of protest, telling whoever would listen that this man—yes, an African American writer!—must be studied. A decade prior to Mifflin's clarion call, the young and recently freed Richard Allen had so impressed the country's leading Methodist missionary, Francis Asbury, that the white chaplain asked the prodigy preacher to be his special assistant in saving American souls. And before even this, Allen gained renown around his childhood home of Dover, Delaware, for using a white preacher to finagle freedom from his second master. Allen always behaved "honestly," wrote Stokeley Sturgis, Allen's former master, in 1783. Though a young man and enslaved, Allen seemed destined for big things.[5]

For many of his admirers, Allen was not simply a great black man—a significant achievement itself in an age that equated blackness with enslavement—but a man who belonged to the ages. "There is one man whom our people should never forget," Philadelphia's Bishop A. W. Wyman told a crowd at an Allen birthday celebration in February 1865. "Rome had her Caesar . . . Germany her illustrious Luther . . . America her Washington, Jefferson and Abraham Lincoln." African Americans could proudly offer their own "illustrious hero" in the vaunted Allen.[6] Delaware pastor N. H. Turpin went a step further: Allen was "truly a Moses." Allen, Turpin wrote at the end of the Civil War, was one of the first Americans to call for universal brotherhood in this world while knowing deep in his bones that it existed in the next one. Americans black and white should offer thanks and praise to "the sainted Richard Allen and his noble soul and spirit [for] laying so firm a foundation [of liberty] for his sons to build upon."[7]

For whatever reason they celebrated him, black communities came to commemorate Allen's birthday—February 14—as a day of black pride. (In what may have been the sincerest form of flattery, Frederick Douglass even claimed it as his own birthday.) One of the most memorable "Allen Day" events occurred in Philadelphia in February 1865, when a small gathering honored Allen's heroic deeds alongside Lincoln's Emancipation Proclamation.[8] As the choir sang "beautiful hymns," worshipers conjured not only Lincoln's visage but Allen's too. The memory of Allen, a man who fought slavery before Lincoln was even born, appeared more saintly than ever. A tireless abolitionist, community activist, and minister, Richard Allen would always be remembered as a black founder.

Despite his many achievements and towering reputation, no modern biography of Richard Allen exists. The last major study of Allen was produced by African American scholar Charles Wesley in the 1930s. Written during an era that treated black history as secondary to the nation's main themes, Wesley's book pictured Allen as both an American and an African American hero. (Unsurprisingly, Allen's emigrationist musings found little space in Wesley's fine book). Historian Carol George's stirring monograph of Allen's central role in the formation of the African Methodist Episcopal Church was one of the few post-civil-rights-era biographies of a black founder, though it has been over thirty years since that volume's publication. More recently, Dee Andrews, Gary Nash, and Albert Raboteau, among others, have made Allen a key figure in their artful examinations of Methodism, black community building, and Afro-Christianity, respectively. But there is still no authoritative biography of Allen's long and ramifying life.[9]

Freedom's Prophet attempts to recapture Allen's key role in post-Revolutionary American and African American life. Indeed, borrowing a phrase from David Levering Lewis's monumental work on Du Bois, one might say that Allen's story provides a "biography of his race" during the early republic—and a biography of race as a lived experience in early national America. Although biography remains a cornerstone of history writing, there are still relatively few books dedicated to examining the lives of African-descended people in the eighteenth-century Western world.[10] Allen's seven decades on American soil illuminate, among other key issues, race relations in the late-eighteenth and early-nineteenth centuries, the advent of the black church and black abolitionism, the rise of black leadership traditions and print culture, the varieties of black nationalism and political discourse espoused by African American reformers through time, and the ever-expanding debates over black identity in the Atlantic world.[11] Above all else, this book poses a simple question: what happens if we put Richard Allen into the hallowed American founding generation? The text then considers Allen as essentially the forerunner of modern civil rights activists, for his belief in nonviolent but confrontational reform offered lessons for virtually every black leader who followed in his wake.

It is important at the outset to underscore the momentous age in which this black founder lived. Born a slave in a colonial American world that barely questioned bondage, Allen grew up to see slavery crack in Western culture. He also lived to see racial subjugation revivified through waves of discriminatory codes and practices, from segregated seating in most Northern churches (inequality in the House of the Lord! Allen would exclaim) to rescinded black voting rights in most Northern states. Indeed, except among academic specialists, it is all too easy to forget that black founders like Allen lived through a tumultuous era of American race relations. Historians formerly referred to this time period as "the first emancipation"; it might be better understood as America's first Reconstruction.[12] Not only was the American Revolution a fresh event in the minds of both black and white Americans—not least because the War of Independence prompted between sixty thousand and one hundred thousand slaves to flee bondage[13]—so too was the nation's first experiment with emancipation: the ending of slavery by Northern states between 1780 (when Pennsylvania passed the first gradual abolition act) and 1804 (when New Jersey passed the last such bill).[14] In addition, the Chesapeake states of Delaware, Maryland, and Virginia eased emancipation restrictions, prompting thousands of manumissions by the early 1800s. Black freedom was no longer a rumor. On top of this, Allen witnessed the ending of the slave trade in America and England, the massive growth of slavery in the South and Southwest (a doubling of enslaved populations over Allen's life), the rise of the domestic slave trade between Northern and Southern locales, and the advent of the world's first black republic, Haiti. Richard Allen's world was filled with high hopes and dashing disappointments.

Yet Allen did not live through these immense changes passively, a black man adrift in a sea of impersonal and malevolent forces. Rather, he shaped, and was in turn shaped by, the events swirling around him. As the most prominent black preacher of his era, he helped inaugurate a moral critique of slavery and slaveholding that shaped abolitionism for years to come. As one of the first black pamphleteers, he pushed not only for slavery's demise but also for black equality. As a black institution builder, he spurred the creation of autonomous organizations and churches that nurtured African American struggles for justice throughout the nineteenth century. As a sometime doubter of American racial equality, he participated in black emigration to Haiti. As a leader of the first national black convention, he defined continent-wide protest tactics and strategies for a new generation of activists.

Bishop Allen's lifelong struggle for racial justice makes for a compelling and illuminating story—a tale about a black founder and African Americans in the early American republic.

1. Richard Allen beyond the Myth: "Modest without Timidity"

Just who was Richard Allen? Though he left no personal papers or scholarly archive, we know a good deal about him. He married twice and claimed in his last will to love "his beloved [second] wife," Sarah. He had six children—Richard, Peter, John, James, Sarah, and Ann—

and is remembered in Allen family lore as a kind and loving parent. He owned several properties, worked a host of jobs (from skilled trades to unskilled day jobs), and tried at least once in his life to start a major business. Though a proponent of black autonomy, he had many white friends, from the celebrated (Benjamin Rush and Francis Asbury) to the unheralded (antislavery activist Warner Mifflin). One of Allen's prized possessions was a seventeenth-century Bible given him by white abolitionist Thomas Garrett. The tattered book still sits safely behind a pane of protective glass in the Richard Allen Museum below Bethel Church. Allen could be kindly: he bequeathed his famed walking cane—willed to him by Absalom Jones—to a fellow black preacher. He could also be shrewd, as in 1830 when he maneuvered the first black convention to Philadelphia rather than let New York City's or Baltimore's black reformers claim the honor of hosting the event.

"Modest without timidity" is the way AME Bishop Daniel Payne described Allen's personality. That phrase characterized Allen's physical presence too: he was of average height for his time and locale, a modest five foot seven or five foot eight. The fiery black Presbyterian orator Henry Highland Garnet later described Allen as "a little below the middle size, roundly built, with a frame that indicated endurance and strength." Garnet called Allen "a beautiful Negro," for his dark complexion and tightly curled hair. In his later years, according to Garnet, Allen's hair took on a "beautiful silver gray" color—nearly biblical in its shimmering tones. For the young Garnet (who was just a boy when he encountered Allen), the Bishop's wonderfully silvery mane accented his chocolate brown skin, making Garnet forever proud of his African ancestry. Garnet perhaps read a little too much into Allen's complexion, for the black founder had (like Frederick Douglass later) a multiracial ancestry. Family lore says that his mother was mixed race (and his father African).[15]

Allen's less than imposing physical size did not in any way detract from his commanding stature. Virtually everyone who knew the preacher commented on his incredibly strong will and palpable sense of certitude. Indeed, to gauge Allen's character and inner drive, all one had to do was peer into his dazzling eyes. Garnet's words are again instructive. He met the distinguished preacher in the late 1820s on one of Allen's trips to New York City, where Garnet's family had settled after a daring escape from Maryland slavery. Garnet's father was a religious man and knew well of Allen. When Allen came to Manhattan for Methodist revivals, Garnet recalled that he always took time to visit the flock of kids who ran to the preacher's side as he entered the room or disembarked from a boat. Children called him "Papa" Allen, and he seemed as gentle and kind as anyone could possibly be. Garnet had the most wonderful memory of "standing between" the great preacher's creaking knees, listening to the "venerable" man gently instructing the lad to "be a good boy, and serve, honor and obey the Lord."[16]

When preaching, however, or when his ire had been raised, Allen's eyes flashed, commanding the respect of everyone around him. "They seemed to blaze with a fire that attracted the attention of all who beheld them," Garnet wrote after the Civil War, nearly forty years removed from his time with "Papa" Allen. But he vividly remembered Allen's piercing gaze as an emblem of black confidence and pride.[17]

Perhaps Allen's most important trait was his rigid determination, some would say obstinacy. Allen was *stubborn* in an era when many black people learned to dissemble, defer, and concede to white authority in order to survive. Even black comrades learned about Allen's stubbornness. When the Free African Society refused to follow Methodist principles, Allen balked. Then he left the group he helped organize. "No religious sect," he explained, "would suit the capacity of the coloured people as well as the Methodist."[18] When whites criticized African Americans during the yellow-fever epidemic, Allen wasted little time in calling them hypocritical and racist—doing it in print and having that printed work sent up and down the Atlantic coast and even off to Great Britain.

Allen was a man for whom propriety and dignity remained key parts of his identity. At the celebration of his sixty-eighth birthday in 1828, "a number of respectable ladies and gentlemen met at the right Rev. Richard Allen's" longtime Philadelphia home. Yet, as a black newspaper reported, they did not engage in an evening of dancing and revelry. Allen would not have it. "The entertainment," as *Freedom's Journal* put it, "was intermingled with singing and prayer."[19] Allen sang his favorite hymns and gave thanks to the Lord for seeing him through another year. One just cannot imagine this man, this superserious personality, being caricatured in any way.

Allen's famous 1813 portrait, commissioned by the black preacher himself, displayed his dignified persona. His already-graying hair topped a rounded face with a prominent forehead, a flat nose and dimpled chin, and those deep-set yet piercing eyes. Dressed appropriately in the

"Rev. Richard Allen," artist unknown, 1813. The second of three portraits drawn of Allen during his lifetime, this remains perhaps the most famous image of the black founder. Allen's piercing eyes, celebrated black abolitionist Henry Highland Garnet recalled, "seemed to blaze with a fire that attracted the attention of all who beheld them." (Courtesy of the Library Company of Philadelphia)

day's formal garb—a dark, heavy vest and long suitcoat with a white cravat—Allen puts on no airs. Just as important, his pose refuses to let viewers condescend to or pity an African American figure. In fact, Allen turned the tables on those who would look his way, shooting a piercing glance outward while pointing his finger firmly downward toward a Bible on his lap. It is a striking position, for Allen is not a passive subject in the least, a man content simply to have his portrait painted. Richard Allen, everyone knew from one look at him, was literate, moral, and upright—and he was in control of how people saw him.

Most people knew Allen as a religious man, a minister of the gospel, and eventually the nation's first black bishop. As a pious Methodist (he converted in 1777, at age seventeen), Allen's theology revolved around two key beliefs: Christian moralism and liberation theology. As a devout evangelical, Allen believed that the Christian religion defined the essential elements of daily life for every American, black or white: piety, sobriety, cleanliness, humility, and charity. Quoting the Bible, Allen implored black and white Americans to "do good and . . . hope for nothing" in return, except heavenly reward. Christianity also taught Americans to love one another no matter the class, ethnic, or racial lines seemingly dividing them. "Love your enemies," Allen preached throughout his life, "do good and lend, hoping for nothing again, and your reward shall be great."[20] Not only would faith and good works guarantee one's entry into heaven, they would also ensure harmony of the disparate souls composing the American nation. In other words, true Christian morality served as a delicate bridge of understanding between white and black Americans. Whites needed to heed God's word and emancipate enslaved people. But Afro-Christian freemen, Allen lectured, had to live by the Golden Rule: treat others as you would be treated. Liberated black Christians could not seek to settle scores with cruel former masters through violence; rather, they had to exemplify Christian charity and forgiveness. In this manner, he believed, African Americans would move from outsiders to fellow believers to equal citizens. Allen's was truly a theology of inclusiveness.

His Christian moralism notwithstanding, Allen also helped define the meaning of liberation theology, the notion that God sided with oppressed people.[21] In his first major statement on American bondage, penned in 1794, Allen reminded slaveholders that God almighty had obliterated unrepentant Egyptian slaveholders. As the story of Exodus foretold, the Lord would again wreak divine vengeance on recalcitrant American masters. "We do not wish to make you angry," Allen argued, "but excite your attention to consider how hateful slavery is in the sight of that God who hath destroyed kings and princes for their oppression of slaves."[22] Emancipation and renunciation of racial superiority could, however, salvage one's soul. But destroying slavery was only part of Allen's liberation theology. A corollary came from Psalm 68: "Princes shall come out of Egypt," Allen declared, and "Ethiopia shall stretch forth its hand to God." Like other black founders and activists after him, Allen believed that Psalm 68 established a moral foundation for black freedom, including black citizenship in the American republic. Once freed from bondage—and the stigma of slavery—African Americans would redeem both themselves and the nation by emphasizing equality of the races. They would be the people on whom the great experiment in liberty depended, for African Americans would lead the charge against bondage. In this sense, Allen's liberation theology offered not merely a warning to American slaveholders but hope: by embracing true Christianity, and liberating bondpeople, they could avert the terrible fate awaiting all sinners. But that fate would indeed come to those who ignored God's sympathy with oppressed people.[23]

As his antislavery sermonizing and pamphleteering efforts illustrate, Allen adhered to the principles of nonviolent protest throughout his life. Even in an age of great slave revolts, from Gabriel's Rebellion in Virginia to the Haitian Revolution in the Caribbean, Allen's ideology was perhaps the norm. Most slaves in the Atlantic world did not, and could not, successfully rebel; most enslaved people had to endure. But what did that actually mean? For Allen and black founders, it meant turning nonviolent protest—enduring over the long haul—into a moral and political weapon. By marshaling the tools of modernity (institution building and mass organizing, print culture and public demonstration, the deployment of democratic ideals and nationalist ideologies), they sought to refute the notion that blacks were either subhuman, political outsiders, or nothing better than maroons at the edges of Western society.[24] For Allen, black abolitionism (which espoused full equality for African Americans beyond slavery) was the heart and soul of America's future. He and other black founders still do not get enough credit for developing this idea, or for creating a tradition of public protest that undermined notions of racial superiority every bit as much as Atlantic-world slave rebellions.[25] Indeed, down to the American Civil War, many slaveholders' greatest fear was not massive slave rebellion but the specter of a "blackened" republic via universal emancipation and African American equality.[26] In Lincoln's day, these fears took the rather infamous name of "Black Republicanism." But they harked all the way back to black founders' vision of revolutionizing the white republic from within.

Obviously, Allen's Christian faith informed his understanding of nonviolent protest. He read Psalm 37 as the keynote to his activism. Famous for its prophecy that "the meek shall inherit the earth" (37:11), the Psalm also instructs Christians to "Rest in the Lord, and wait patiently for him" (37:7). "Mark the perfect *man,* and behold the upright: for the end of *that* man is peace," it concludes (37:37). Allen loved this reference so much that he used it as the epigraph to his autobiography. Like Frederick Douglass, he may have believed that blacks could never win a violent uprising in America anyway. More probably, his temperament and deep faith made him believe that black endurance would, as the biblical story of Exodus and Psalms 37 and 68 prophesied, eventually win out and transform the Western world.[27]

Often depicted as unschooled, Allen nevertheless mastered literacy, largely through religious instruction and Bible study while in his late teens and early twenties.[28] Literacy served as a critical platform for Allen's faith ever after. Allen began and ended each and every day with prayer. Although he favored "extempore" preaching—speaking off the cuff rather than writing out (and reading) sermons—Allen vigorously studied biblical exegesis. He owned two big sets of biblical commentaries. He studied them not merely for ministerial purposes but to defend the black community. On one striking occasion in 1802, Allen jumped in front of a drunken white soldier who had accosted his black congregation on the street. As the threatening white figure receded into the Philadelphia night still screaming, Allen whipped around and told his parishioners that Satan frequently worked this way, testing God's followers by raising up wicked men. "That was a lesson worthy of the greatest preacher," a white female itinerant visiting from England gushed after witnessing Allen in action.[29]

As much as these details about Allen's physical appearance, theology, and preaching style amuse, delight, and inform, they also beg questions. How did Allen approach fatherhood as a black parent in the early republic? Did he ever cast a vote in any civic election? And, perhaps most important, what were his deepest feelings about the struggle for racial justice in America? Unfortunately, when one digs deeper into his personal thoughts and emotions, Allen becomes like the overwhelming majority of African Americans before the Civil War—a bit harder to track. Allen did not leave a voluminous private correspondence, nor did he leave a daily journal or diary of his thoughts for later scholars to mine.

The novelist John Edgar Wideman provides a hypothetical example of the type of personal source unavailable to Allen biographers. In his stunning novel *The Cattle Killing*, Wideman uses African American figures during the Philadelphia yellow-fever epidemic of 1793 to examine issues of race and identity in the African American past—issues Allen himself grappled with in his own autobiography. But Wideman goes further than Allen ever did. In one key scene, based on Allen's real-life departure from a segregated white church, Wideman imagines Richard Allen interrogating himself. "When you marched out," Wideman writes, "marched away, admit, Allen, in your secret heart you hoped the entire congregation, black and white, would rise and march out with you in affirmation of God's law." This is not supposed to be Wideman's voice but Bishop Allen's, "on the edge of his bed thinking these thoughts."[30]

Allen penned no such thoughts. And so one is left with basic questions about one of the most important African American leaders of his or any other era. This problem is quite familiar to scholars of black life. Even at the turn of the twentieth century, when black literacy rates had increased dramatically and slavery itself had faded into memory, it was difficult to find the types of primary sources for black private life that one could locate with relative ease for many white figures. The scholar and biographer Paula Giddings has written that uncovering the details of even one of the most prominent black couples of the industrial age —the poet Paul Laurence Dunbar and his wife, Alice Ruth Moore— proved elusive, for "such primary sources are understandably rare, even among educated blacks."[31] Why? Racial fears, for one thing: black Americans have often veiled their feelings for fear of repercussions by white figures. Lack of educational resources and leisure time might be another explanation. But there it is: a paucity of source material on early black thought.

Allen's autobiography, dictated to his son near the end of his life around 1830, is quite stunning for what it left out. Allen stated at the very outset of his narrative that "slavery is a bitter pill," a lesson he learned early (as a slave separated from his family) and often (Allen was mistakenly grabbed as a runaway slave in the early 1800s).[32] But Allen stopped there, telling readers merely that he eventually purchased his freedom. What happened to his mother? How did he react when informed that he would be separated from his parents? Did he ever attempt to reconnect with lost family members? Allen's reticence on such matters is interesting when one considers that he died just prior to a literary revolution: the advent of antebellum slave narratives. Befitting a romantic, confessional, highly emotional age, with a more literate reading public than ever before, these new-style autobiographies of the 1840s and 1850 revealed slaves' innermost thoughts to a largely white, Northern, middle-class audience hungry for tales of injustice in the South. Frederick Douglass and Harriet Jacobs remain the model slave narrators, telling white readers their feelings about being sold, whipped, humiliated, and ultimately freed.

That was not Allen's time and certainly not Allen's style. In fact, his reticence about detailing personal emotions may explain a bit more about his own personality (modest but stubborn) and the time in which he matured (America's founding era, a time dominated by dour federalist mentalities preaching about a virtuous citizenry). He may very well have believed that veiling one's deeper thoughts was critical to black survival. There may also be more to the story. Consider again Allen's autobiography. Like Thomas Jefferson's frustrating personal history, it is epistolary and instructional rather than confessional and revelatory. Neither Allen nor Jefferson explained their incredible lives in any probing manner. In true Enlightenment fashion both Allen and Jefferson hoped that their public deeds (and for Allen, his religious journey) would instruct readers about how to lead a moral, upright life in America. Another model in this regard may have been even closer to Allen—his fellow Pennsylvanian Ben Franklin's instructional autobiography.[33]

In this sense, Allen (like Jefferson and Franklin) remained very much a man of the eighteenth century. He took cues from the world he grew up in—founding fathers discussing liberty and virtuous public service, Americans debating the meaning of constitutions and moral citizenship, slaveholders walking around Philadelphia defending bondage. Allen also meditated on what was missing from that world: black commentary, black insight on public duty, a black man's vigorous though nonviolent response to racial oppression. Allen truly believed that public work revealed one's inner character, that *his own* public work would reveal *his* character. Both Allen and Jefferson lived in a world that valued the public over the private. Jefferson's tombstone merely asks people to remember his three great public accomplishments—writing the Declaration of Independence, ensuring religious liberty in the Virginia constitution, and launching the University of Virginia. No one asked him, but Allen chose to be buried beneath Bethel Church, and that must be his view on the matter of his own legacy: public accomplishment is all that need be remembered of this black founder's life.

2. *Allen and Black Founders*

Founders build things—nations, constitutions, institutions of governance and learning, belief systems that open unto worlds others scarcely knew existed. It is hard, according to David McCulloch, to underestimate the importance of a white founding figure like John Adams, who helped win the American Revolution, craft the federal Constitution and build a nation that stood tall in the Atlantic world. We can never know enough about him, McCulloch wistfully comments.[34] What exactly did Allen and black founders do? And what happens when you attempt to define them into the broader pantheon of American founders?

For answers, we must begin with Allen's church. In Mother Bethel, Allen built a physical edifice that defined African American Christianity and black autonomy for years to come. Here, ideas preceded bricks and mortar, for before Allen literally built his church in the 1790s he envisioned an autonomous black religious institution where none had previously existed. Allen once recalled that even local blacks doubted the efficacy of an independent black church in Philadelphia, so fearful were they of a white backlash. But after segregated seating policies were instituted at white churches, Allen appeared to be a visionary, and many blacks soon joined his exodus from segregated Northern pews and galleries for independent black churches. For subsequent generations, Allen's act of defiance had all the meaning and power of Rosa Parks's sit-in during the mid-twentieth century. The comparison is not superficial. For while both events—Parks's sit-in and Allen's walkout of segregated pews—were courageous nonviolent acts in and of themselves, they also set the stage for new black freedom struggles.

Indeed, after Allen's exit from a segregated white church, the young preacher had to build an autonomous black church with his own money and hands. In 1794, Allen bought an old blacksmith shop and hauled it to Bethel's present location, a spot of land he had purchased just a few years earlier beyond Philadelphia's more saturated urban grid. Honing skills learned both at his second master's Delaware home and along the mid-Atlantic coast during his first few years of freedom, Allen crafted a pulpit, arranged the pews, and whitewashed the walls of his new church. After being inaugurated in July 1794, Bethel Church, as it was soon known, became identified with black abolitionism and the dream of black redemption.

Allen's founding status rested on other constructions too. As *Free-*

dom's Journal reported in February 1828, Allen was "the first person that established a Benevolent Society among us for the grand purpose of relieving one another in time of duress."[35] The Free African Society, which Allen created with Absalom Jones in 1787, spawned dozens of "African Benevolent Societies" over the years, including over forty such institutions in Philadelphia alone.[36] Allen (again with Jones) also published the first copyrighted document by a black author in the United States: "A Narrative of the Black People," printed in January 1794. Right up to his death, Allen used print to publicize an impressive array of topics, including black church politics, the memory of slavery in eighteenth-century society, Canadian emigration, and the need for black unity in the face of continued white hostility. For example, in 1817 he helped draft a petition against the American Colonization Society that firmly asserted Northern black leaders' intimate bond—intellectually and ideologically—with Southern slaves. "Resolved, That, we never will separate ourselves voluntarily from [you]," the petition told enslaved people, for "[you] are our brethren."[37] The document quickly assumed an iconic status in black communities, underscoring racial unity across lines of status, geography, and condition.

There is a note of exceptionalism in Allen's early and consistent emphasis on racial unity. Indeed, free black Northerners were unique in the late-eighteenth-century Atlantic world for their steady allegiance to enslaved people. As David Brion Davis has intriguingly explained, in many parts of the Caribbean free blacks and enslaved Africans were often divided by lines of status, racial complexion, and even ideology. "One point that historians of black abolitionism have mostly overlooked is that free blacks in the West Indies generally supported the slave system," Davis has observed, "and the more successful ones became owners of slaves and even of large plantations." Only after the Haitian Revolution began did free and enslaved Caribbean people of color join forces under a unified racial banner. But before that, Richard Allen had insisted that free and enslaved African Americans belonged to the same community.[38]

Allen's ability to build autonomous black institutions and inaugurate a printed discourse among free people of color propelled him into the upper echelons of black leadership by the early nineteenth century. In this sense, Allen's very leadership position heralded something new, for it skillfully blended African traditions with American political practices. Traditionally, African leadership flowed from priests and medicine men. Because they were "considered intermediaries between the gods and members of the community," these respected figures (particularly priests) "assumed the task of interpreting the universe and codifying and rationalizing cultural values."[39] Following the American Revolution, black leaders' task of explaining, codifying, and rationalizing values and events shifted in key ways. Now they interjected black voices into societal debates over racial justice and attempted to explain to white citizens African American claims to equality. To project their voices, black founders used print as well as the pulpit, republican theory as well as African communal traditions.

In the broadest sense, black founders included men and women who fought against racial oppression in some public way, shape, or form during the early republic and thereby set models of public protest for later activists. Thus, rabble-rousers and revolutionaries like Virginia slave rebel "Gabriel," born in 1776 and put to death in 1800 after his slave rebellion failed before even getting started, must be considered key members of the black founding generation. But for every Sam Adams there was a John Adams, and so the black founding generation might also claim brash but bookish personas like Phyllis Wheatley, the prodigy poet and Massachusetts slave whose literary exploits confounded racial assumptions in Revolutionary America (even the worthiest of worthies, from Ben Franklin to George Washington, found themselves wondering about black freedom claims when reading her poems). Unheralded names could be added to the list of black founders too—the four Massachusetts slaves who in 1773 petitioned the colonial assembly for liberty before America had even claimed its independence, the band of South Carolina slaves who marched through Charleston's streets in 1776 verbally demanding their freedom, and countless other black men and women whose struggles for liberty and equality are all but lost to history but still inspired others.

Black founders might also be defined as the rising generation of race leaders who built autonomous institutions—churches, schools, benevolent groups—in locales transiting from slavery to freedom.[40] Like Allen, they moved from local to national and even global politics by establishing a broader nonviolent movement capable of challenging slavery and racial discrimination. In Philadelphia, Absalom Jones and James Forten joined Allen to form the great triumvirate of African American reform. For decades, they gave shape to black leadership, arguing that America

"Distinguished Colored Men," artist unknown, 1883. This post-Reconstruction poster placed Allen in the company of the nineteenth century's most distinguished black activists and politicians, including Frederick Douglass, whose image is in the center of the poster. Allen is to his immediate right. (Courtesy of the Library Company of Philadelphia)

was a black homeland and that African Americans had a vital role to play in redeeming the American republic.

Both in Philadelphia and nationally, black founders matured in a dynamic community context. Before he became "Richard Allen," celebrated black leader, the young itinerant minister lived among Afro-Philadelphians who shared his ambition of racial—not merely individual—uplift. For example, Allen shared much with a black man a generation older named James Dexter. Like the famous Allen, the less-famous Dexter was a one-time colonial slave who secured his freedom (in 1767), probably by saving money to pay off his deceased master's estate. The industrious Dexter then worked as a coachman for several years before becoming a "fruitier" in the 1790s. Well-known to white abolitionists, he eventually bought property, married, and turned to racial-uplift projects in the last two decades of the eighteenth century. Dexter joined Allen's Free African Society, which developed the art of community organizing by borrowing from Dexter's 1782 campaign to secure black burial grounds in Philadelphia's potter's field. Dexter and Allen also became church builders at roughly the same time. While Allen created the AME Church, Dexter hosted founding meetings of St. Thomas's African Episcopal Church.[41]

Intriguingly, Allen's and Dexter's community-building and racial-uplift initiatives did not develop out of blacks' segregated living arrangements. Allen and Dexter lived a mile apart from each another in diverse neighborhoods during the 1780s and 1790s. (Rigid segregation would become a feature of antebellum and industrial Philadelphia.) Dexter resided in a predominantly German-Quaker enclave where only 5 to 10 percent of the population was African American. Located almost directly on the site of the present-day National Constitution Center near Arch and Fifth streets, Dexter's home sat in a neighborhood where black laboring people rubbed elbows with elite white men. The same held true for Allen: his longtime Spruce Street home was one of only six black residences on a street of white laborers, merchants, doctors, and gentlemen.

Allen's and Dexter's residential stories tell us that black community building in many Northern locales remained very much a product of imagination and hard work—it was not a fait accompli simply because free black men (and women) were clustered tightly in an urban environment. Just as slaves throughout the Atlantic world had to forge slave cultures out of diverse backgrounds, so too did Allen and other black community leaders combine ties of kinship and color with those of persuasion and craftiness to build durable free black institutions. This included finding public meeting spaces for black reformers who were spread out geographically; articulating goals that cut across lines of status, color, and disparate religious beliefs; and sustaining membership rolls amid the economic crosscurrents taking black people to jobs throughout an ever-expanding commercial city.

Up and down the Atlantic seaboard, free black communities coalesced not so much around single leaders but around churches, reform institutions, and kinship networks that included visible saints like Allen, less visible saints like Dexter, and truly unheralded community activists like Allen's first and second wives, Flora and Sarah Allen, who followed him out of a segregated white church and supported the creation of Mother Bethel (Allen's first wife, Flora, was married to the preacher at the time, while his future second wife, Sarah Bass, attended the same Methodist meeting). In New England, the talented quartet of black leaders that burst forth in the last years of the eighteenth century—Prince Hall, Paul Cuffee, Lemuel Haynes, and Hosea Easton—relied on the community- and family-uplift initiatives of a coterie of less visible men and women. Hall, perhaps the best known of these figures (he started the first Masonic Lodge in black America in 1784 and used his home and meetinghouse over the next three decades as a base for black political activity until his death in 1807), relied on the support of members of the African Meeting House. Easton, perhaps the least known of New England's black leaders, learned the art of protest in a white republic from his father, a former slave who worked to secure his freedom. When black Baltimorean Daniel Coker surveyed free African American culture in 1810, he celebrated not merely great black men like Allen but the rise of entire free black communities, free black churches, and free black reform groups. Quoting from the Bible (1 Peter 2:9–10), Coker declared, "Ye are a chosen generation," with black founders serving as "a royal priesthood" to "an holy nation, a peculiar people." Before the Revolution, the overwhelming majority of blacks in colonial America were slaves; in the nineteenth century, free black communities thrived along the Atlantic coast, and black founders envisioned themselves as a rising moral force in American culture.[42]

Perhaps the most intriguing aspect of Allen's and black founders' activism, then, was their increasing cynicism about achieving racial justice in America. By the second decade of the nineteenth century, Allen grew so doubtful that he flirted with various Atlantic-world emigration plans. No fleeting consideration for him, Allen meditated on black removal for the last fifteen years of his life. He supported black-led African-colonization schemes before becoming one of the most forceful African American proponents of Haitian emigration. America, he told Haitian president Jean-Pierre Boyer in 1824, is a land of oppression, whereas the great black republic of Haiti promised "freedom and equality."[43] Allen even headed the Haitian Emigration Society of Philadelphia, helping hundreds of black émigrés set sail for the Caribbean. Still later, he supported emigration to Canada.

In making such pronouncements, Allen participated in a great wave of black Atlantic reform. Soon after the Haitian revolution ended with the creation of the first black republic in the Western Hemisphere, African-descended people in the Americas reconceived the very basis of their antiracist struggle. Perhaps, black leaders in Boston, New York, Philadelphia, and Baltimore argued, African Americans did not have to remain in the United States to achieve true liberty. Rather, they could join people of color throughout the Atlantic world to build a new Zion in Haiti or Canada or Africa. Though not often thought of as a black nationalist, Allen came to believe in the utility of building a black nation in the Western Hemisphere—as long as Christian piety served as a foundation of that black nation. Like countless other black reformers and intellectuals after him, Allen came to see racism as America's original sin. Black redemptive suffering could only go so far before Allen, again like countless other black leaders after him, decided to explore some form of black nationalism.

In this manner, Allen's life exemplified one of the defining characteristics of black activism before the Civil War: the movement from integrationist to nationalist beliefs. Perhaps because most scholars have viewed Allen as primarily a religious figure, his radical side has not garnered much attention (beyond the obviously radical act of starting a black church in the 1790s). Yet like so many black leaders following in his wake, Allen's concern with achieving racial justice compelled him to consider the efficacy of a variety of tactical and strategic imperatives, including schemes that we would now define as part of a black-nationalist agenda like emigrationism. Allen's willingness to consider black emigrationism was part and parcel of a larger series of strategic questions that he wrestled with throughout his life—and that generations of black leaders continue to consider in our time: Would interracial activism ever lead to black equality, or was black autonomy an end in and of itself? Was the American nation a vessel of freedom for people of color or an iron cage of oppression? Were people of African descent destined to return to Africa, or would they redeem any and all nations they touched in the Western Hemisphere?

In reconsidering the meaning of African identity and national allegiance in the age of democratic revolutions, Allen was one of the earliest black leaders to express publicly the feelings of "double consciousness" that W. E. B. Du Bois famously articulated later—a division between his African and American identities. Early in his protest career, Allen expressed great confidence in American society's ability to achieve racial reform. "We pray to the same God," he wrote in 1794, and that fact alone should lead to emancipation and racial equality in the United States. By the late 1820s, however, as slavery grew both demographically and geographically, and as Northern racism intensified, Allen grew pessimistic. At the 1830 free black convention, he emphasized the need for a black safety valve beyond American shores.[44]

Yet despite his divided consciousness, Allen never left the United States. Instead, like other black founders, he redoubled his protest efforts domestically by seeking to influence the rising generation of abolitionists during the 1820s and 1830s, by supporting the first black newspapers, by raising consciousness about non-slave-derived products, and by inaugurating the black convention movement.

3. An Integrated Founding Generation

As a *black* founder, Richard Allen's credentials are secure. But Allen believed himself to be a member of two founding generations. He was a black leader who built reform institutions to redeem African Americans, and he was a broader moral leader who wanted to redeem the American republic from the sin of racial subjugation. The nation was incomplete, Allen argued over and over again, as long as the American people accepted slavery and racial exclusion. Allen's many pamphlets of protest prodded American statesmen to banish bondage. Their refusal to do so compelled Allen to think of himself as a moral leader who discussed topics that timid or self-interested statesmen avoided.

And as far as Allen was concerned, many white founders did scrupulously avoid the slavery issue. In his award-winning book *Founding*

Brothers, the modern historian Joseph Ellis agrees, calling this "the silence": early white leaders' conscious strategy of avoiding discussion of bondage (for fear it would sunder the young nation and foment slave rebellion).[45] Black founders like Allen provided what can only be called "the reply," a collective attempt to discuss publicly slavery and racial injustice. Allen's artful eulogy of George Washington—whose house he visited as a master chimney sweep in Philadelphia—remains the black bishop's boldest attempt to build an abolitionist republic through images and words. Allen's speech, delivered initially at his church and then reprinted in Baltimore, New York, and Philadelphia newspapers, praised Washington for emancipating his slaves (after his wife's death) and critiqued Americans who retained bondage. "May a double portion of his [emancipatory] spirit rest on all the officers of the Government of the United States," he called out, "and the whole of the American people."[46] Abolitionism was not subversion (as many white commentators feared) but patriotism, as Washington (according to Allen) had finally demonstrated.

In this sense, we might call Richard Allen an African American "republican."[47] Far from a mere party label, the postrevolutionary republican was the American equivalent of the English Commonwealthman—the consummate advocate of the nation's greater good. A republican believed that building and maintaining a democratic republic required moral rectitude on the part of the citizenry. Because there was no monarchy or aristocracy, republicanism held, American citizens had to sacrifice personal good for the nation's betterment, to think of national rather than local interests, to ground American identity in concepts of public duty, civic virtue, and equality. No mere Spartan code of behavior, republicanism was at its heart "nothing less than a utopian hope for a new moral and social order led by enlightened and virtuous men," in the words of historian Gordon Wood.[48] Because the American Revolution had been viewed as a radical experiment in representative government, Wood argues, it tore apart traditional modes of society—monarchy, patronage, hereditary political privilege.

Richard Allen believed that he participated in this radical experiment of nation-building and republican citizenship. America, Allen argued, was more than the sum of its local, state, and federal governments. Rather, it was an ideal: universal freedom. Unless and until the founding generation rectified the racial wrongs that undermined that ideal, the American experiment would fail. The nation therefore required men of faith to step forward and defend both abolitionism and equality. If, as a black man, he could not vote—and thereby participate in what scholars refer to as the "deliberative" rights of citizenship—then Allen would become a passionate dissenter from the racial status quo. His dissent became part of an emerging tradition (scholars call it "persuasive politics") that influenced subsequent generations of radical abolitionists, civil rights reformers, and antislavery statesmen.[49]

At the heart of Allen's moral vision was an evangelical religion—Methodism—that promised equality to all believers in Christ. Indeed, one of Allen's best claims to equal founding status was his attempt to merge faith and racial politics in the young republic. His constant sermonizing on slavery's evil was (in theory) perfectly pitched to men and women who viewed faith as a key part of the American character. Jon Meacham has perceptively noted that several leading white founders "came to believe that religion, for all its faults, was an essential foundation for a people's moral conduct." Although many of these men were deists who believed in a distant God of reason and not revelation, Allen hoped that they would nevertheless listen to black freedom appeals steeped in religious understandings of morality. After all, many white Americans saw the Revolutionary War through the lens of Exodus (with the British playing Pharaoh). Moreover, Allen knew that below elite founders, a host of local leaders believed deeply in the Christian gospel. In Allen's eyes, black Christians would be the prophets of a new American morality promising not just spiritual liberty but universal freedom.[50]

But Allen's vision of a moral republic had a secular corollary: the Declaration of Independence. That document, he believed, was a covenant binding Americans of all races, classes, and religions into a nation of equal citizens. On more than one occasion, Allen spoke in the "name of the laws of the commonwealth of Pennsylvania" and as a "fellow citizen" of the United States. In merely making such claims, Allen hoped to challenge the notion that America was, and would forever be, a white man's republic.[51]

Of course, most white founders vehemently disagreed. As Jefferson sneered, African Americans had never produced great art or rhetoric—how could they possibly be considered equal citizens?[52] To judge from the massive resurgence of literature focusing solely on white founders—a trend labeled "founders chic" by one iconoclastic group of scholars[53]—many popular historians agree. The founders, whether defined as political men, religious leaders, or moral reformers, remain white men in wigs.

Black founders' exclusion from the broader pantheon of early American heroes is certainly ironic when one considers just how much men like Franklin, Jefferson, Madison, and Washington shared with Allen, Forten, and Jones. Although there are obvious differences (the former group was never literally enslaved), both black and white founders were often self-made men. During the 1820s, a white commentator called Richard Allen "a self-created Bishop," a man "whose importance is measured by the fact that he probably created 100 [black] ministers by his ordination."[54] In addition, both sets of founders were often the first in their families to gain some sort of advanced education: for white leaders like Madison, this meant college; for Revolutionary-era blacks like Allen, literacy skills.

Finally, both groups of founders had their creative imaginations stirred by outsider status. This point is perhaps the most underappreciated link between white and black men of Allen's generation. White revolutionaries received little respect within the British Empire. As Bernard Bailyn has reminded us, colonial men existed on the periphery of British power—they were not privy to the inner workings of English politics, nor did they have access to colonial circles of power, where status and personal connections reigned supreme. Because they felt so politically marginalized, white colonials even took to calling themselves "slaves" to Mother England. British exclusionary treatment spurred colonial imaginations on such things as the right of revolution, human liberty, and the fundamental necessity of written constitutionalism.[55] Similarly, black founders often fell outside white definitions of citizenship and public standing in the new republic. But their marginalization did not prevent them from seeking to expand the discourse of American rights. Indeed, like white revolutionaries during the colonial crisis with Britain, black founders desperately sought an audience with their oppressors.

Allen's virtual dialogue with Benjamin Franklin illustrates the point. Franklin and Allen briefly lived together in early national Philadelphia during the nation's founding era. Although they never actually corresponded with each other, Franklin and Allen began their public considerations of American race relations at virtually the same time, the years following the ratification of the federal Constitution. In November 1789, Franklin, the one-time slaveholder and late convert to abolitionism, signed two messages on the broader meaning of black freedom in

America. He did so as president of the Pennsylvania Abolition Society. Delighted that Pennsylvania had issued the world's first gradual abolition act just a few years before, Franklin nevertheless expressed the concerns of many white citizens when he labeled black freedom a potential problem. "Slavery," the normally irrepressible Franklin observed in uncharacteristically pessimistic tones, "is such an atrocious debasement of human nature, that its very extirpation, if not performed with solicitous care, may sometimes open a source of serious evils." Long treated as "a brute animal," freed blacks became "machines" unused to reasonable reflection who posed a great risk to the American citizenry. Indeed, Franklin warned, "under such circumstances, freedom may often prove a misfortune to [former slaves], and prejudicial to society."[56] To guard against what he believed would be blacks' natural tendency toward social disruption (and dissension from whites), Franklin and the Pennsylvania Abolition Society proposed becoming African Americans' moral guardians. Committees would watch after their moral, economic, and social well-being and report to Pennsylvania citizens on the prospects and perils of a biracial social order. Without such white oversight, Franklin feared, there could be no black freedom.

A former slave now in the capital of free black life, Richard Allen publicly challenged Franklin's line of thinking. The problem, he commented in 1794, lay not in blacks' essentially subversive nature but in white society's consistent failure to nurture African American equality. Allen condemned not only slavery but also the racialist beliefs underpinning slavery and black inequality. He then proposed his own solutions in very Franklinesque language. Whites, Allen suggested, might try the "experiment" of treating black people as they would members of their own family. Next, he wrote in an almost direct reply to Franklin's fears of black equality, white citizens must believe in their own Christian and republican language. It was a message he returned to again and again: liberate blacks, teach them scripture and principles of good citizenship, and watch them become pious and respectable members of the American republic. Allen repeated these thoughts in his eulogy of Washington, when he told free blacks that their public mourning of the sainted Washington demonstrated their ability to sacrifice personal animosity for national good. As he put it, such actions "will make you good citizens."

Reading Allen's thoughts next to Franklin's, one is struck not only by the public dialogue in which these two founding figures engaged but by how much of a difference Allen's ideas have made over the long term. Racial equality is now part of Americans' innermost sense of nationhood. What, after all, was Abraham Lincoln's call for a "new birth of freedom" during the Civil War other than a rousing resuscitation of black founders'—of Allen's—original creed? What is modern Americans' faith in multiracial democracy other than a ratification of Allen's vision—people of all races and ethnicities can live together peaceably in American culture. Thomas Jefferson never thought so, Washington did not want to talk about it, and even the elder abolitionist Franklin had his doubts. We must then turn to Allen and black founders to understand the genealogy of multiracial democracy. As Allen put it in Jefferson's day and age, "if you love your children, if you love your country, if you love the God of love, clear your hands from slaves, burden not your children or country with them."[57] That Allen's language conjures images of none other than Martin Luther King, Jr.—the modern hero of civil rights and the man who spoke of the civil rights struggle as a "loving" movement—speaks volumes about the potency of his ideas and claims to founding status.

1

"For Zion's Sake . . .
I Will Not Rest"

As the new year opened, a comet streaked across the Philadelphia sky. While scientific observers methodically plotted its "very
swift" movement, commoners wondered what omen this cosmic event
heralded. A few weeks later, on February 14, 1760, at two o'clock in
the morning, an enslaved child was born to a woman in the possession
of a prosperous local attorney. Surely, no one could have predicted that
the black babe, who later took the name Richard Allen, was what the
comet had heralded. And yet, for African Americans over the next two
centuries, Richard Allen's birthday carried all the significance of prophecy. Lines from Isaiah 62:1, which a Philadelphia printer published on
that very day—February 14, 1760—seemed tailor-made for Allen's future: "For Zion's sake, I will not hold my peace, and for Jerusalem's
sake I will not rest, until the righteousness thereof go forth as bright-
ness, and the salvation thereof as a lamp that burneth."[1]

For the moment, Allen's birth occurred in what to most contemporary observers would have been mundane circumstances. Philadelphia
sat contentedly in the British Empire, colonial trade filled the city's merchant shops with the finest goods the world had to offer, and slavery
was a normal part of colonial life in the City of Brotherly Love. "To be
sold," an ad proclaimed in the *Pennsylvania Gazette* the day Allen came
into the world, "a young healthy Negro fellow, country born, about 20
years old, has had the smallpox and measles, was brought up to country
work. Enquire at the new printing office."[2] The big news of the day was
the progress of what became known as the French and Indian War,
which recently turned in favor of British forces. Other than intriguing
occurrences (a comet, prophetic lines from the Bible) and news of another war between ancient rivals France and Great Britain, there was
nothing auspicious about Allen's birth year. If the biographer Douglas
Egerton could write of Virginia slave rebel "Gabriel's" nativity, "in the

year 1776, a slave child was born to a lie," the best one can say of Allen is that his birth year revealed a hard truth: servitude remained the lot for most blacks.[3]

Allen would spend the rest of his life overturning that supposed maxim.

1. *"I Was Born"*

Neither Allen nor any of his biographers have had much to say about his earliest years. "I was born," Allen matter-of-factly began his autobiography, "a slave to Benjamin Chew, of Philadelphia. My mother and father and four of us children were then sold into Delaware state."[4] Allen said little about childhood slavery, the memory of being sold, or what his parents thought of bondage. But all his life, Allen recalled the constant struggle of bondpeople like himself to live, love, and somehow survive. Even after he secured his own freedom, Allen could not forget how horrible slavery had been. "I address you with an affectionate sympathy," he wrote as a free man of thirty-four making his first public pronouncement to enslaved African Americans, "having been a slave and desirous of freedom as any of you." Before he gained that freedom, Allen underscored just how "impatient" and even "discouraged" slaves might become over their servile status.[5] The daily drudgery of bondage tried his patience; separation from family members—which occurred when his second master ran into financial difficulty later on—tried his soul. "Slavery is a bitter pill," he famously wrote at the end of his life.[6] No mere rhetorical flourish, Allen knew precisely the meaning of those words.

Beyond his bitter memory of bondage, Allen's unwillingness to elaborate on his youth has proved vexing to historians. The simplest details remain obscure. Was Allen born in Philadelphia, as his autobiography suggested, or in Delaware, as new evidence might indicate? Both scenarios seem plausible, though neither is definitive.

Allen's first master, Benjamin Chew (1722–1810), was a prominent attorney and magistrate who settled in Philadelphia in 1754 after having lived in Maryland and Delaware. Chew eventually became chief justice of colonial Pennsylvania. A gentleman of property and standing, he was what people in colonial society referred to as a "worthy." Wealthy enough to own several impressive properties in both Delaware and

Pennsylvania, Chew called an elegant mansion on Front Street his main Philadelphia home. Located just off the Delaware River, Front Street bustled with shops, merchants, and slaves. The London Coffeehouse, just down the street from Chew's home and a prominent meeting place, served as an outdoor slave market. Chew and other prominent officials conducted business there, from buying and selling land to buying and selling slaves. If born in Philadelphia, a young Allen would have been familiar with the London Coffeehouse's slave auction blocks. If he went by them, then like other members of the city's black community he probably observed harrowing scenes—public slave sales, families being separated, slave shackles protecting masters from slaves' tendency to run.[7]

Chew's slaveholdings varied, but, as one historian has put it, he "bought and sold slaves" his entire life.[8] Like other worthies, he viewed slave labor as a critical part of estate building, no matter the size or locale. In urban areas like Philadelphia, this meant utilizing slaves as porters, butlers, cooks, and laborers in fancy homes. In the Pennsylvania (and Delaware) countryside, this meant using slaves to clear the land, build houses and barns, and tend to crops. Richard Allen and his family were thus bound to a man who viewed bondage as vital to business, society, and culture in a place already known as the City of Brotherly Love.

Because Pennsylvania did not ban bondage until after American independence—and because Allen claimed to be born "a slave *to* Benjamin Chew, of Philadelphia" and then "sold *into* Delaware state" (emphasis added)—it is not hard to imagine Allen's enslaved family roots beginning in colonial Philadelphia. Yet a compelling case can also be made for Allen's Delaware birth. In this scenario, he was born in Kent County, Delaware, on one of Benjamin Chew's three plantations. All of Chew's Delaware properties contained sizable numbers of enslaved people, and only a small number of the over three hundred known Chew slaves ever resided (or were born) in the Philadelphia area. Perhaps Whitehall plantation, one of Delaware's largest, was Allen's first home. According to Phillip Seitz, curator of history at Cliveden, Benjamin Chew's one-time summer home in Germantown, Pennsylvania (and now a nicely restored National Trust Historic Site), Allen may have been born of a fieldhand at Whitehall. Indeed, Allen's autobiography never mentioned his parents' or his own domestic service under Chew, a possible sign that he was not born of a house servant in Philadelphia

(Chew rarely moved house servants from Philadelphia to Delaware or fieldhands from Delaware to Philadelphia). So Allen's Delaware birth is possible.[9]

The major problem with this scenario is documentation. There were a few male slaves born on Chew plantations in 1760—there was a "Cato" at Whitehall and another "Cato" at a nearby plantation—but no enslaved person named "Negro Richard" or anyone with Allen's exact birthday of February 14.[10] Was Allen misremembering things and actually born in 1757 or 1762, dates corresponding to other male slave births on Chew properties in Delaware? This is unlikely, for Richard Allen's second master, Stokeley Sturgis, also claimed that Allen was born on February 14, 1760.[11] So perhaps Allen was an anomaly in Chew's holdings and was born in Philadelphia, beyond the more rigorous plantation documentation of Chew's Delaware properties.

For the Allen biographer, this is only the first of many such quandaries. Where was the great preacher born? When did he leave a segregated Philadelphia church and inaugurate Bethel? Why did he rename himself "Richard Allen" upon gaining freedom? Allen never offered insightful answers to any of these queries. Taken together, these gaps underline the problem of deciphering the life of any African American person of that time, even so vaunted a figure as Allen. Lacking control of their own bodies, and denied information about their surroundings, enslaved people like Allen could scarcely be expected to track their own lives with precision. Then, too, there is the matter of Allen's personality. He was convinced that private details mattered little in one's life—only the public man, and good works, could fully measure one's worth. Allen's autobiography, conceived in the early nineteenth century after the former slave became the nation's first black bishop, focused little on the gaps in his historical record and more on his historic accomplishments beyond bondage.

Despite a paucity of conclusive evidence, we can reconstruct parts of Allen's youth in colonial and then Revolutionary Philadelphia and Delaware, not to mention the world as it then existed for an enslaved person in both urban and rural bondage. Let us begin by placing Allen with his first master, Benjamin Chew, in Philadelphia during the early 1760s, as Allen himself would have it. Allen lived with Chew until perhaps the age of eight, which means that he may have resided in Philadelphia during the 1760s, a key era for enslaved people in this mid-Atlantic locale. Within the British Empire, Philadelphia stood tall: it was the third-largest city under British rule, not to mention one of colonial North America's financial hubs and an intellectual capital as well. On any day of the week, a person visiting Philadelphia's wharves would find ships from around the world—Antigua and Barbados in the Caribbean, London and Belfast in the British Isles, Charleston and Boston in the colonies. One could purchase fine linens from the mother country; teas from the Dutch East Indies; books, pamphlets, and newspapers from most other parts of the world; and just about anything else one could want.[12]

For a short period of time in the 1760s, Philadelphians desired African slaves. Philadelphia was not colonial America's central slave-trading port—that honor went to Charleston, South Carolina—but it did serve as a slave depot for the middle-Atlantic region, stretching from southern New Jersey and southeastern Pennsylvania through Delaware and Maryland. Between 1759 and 1766, Philadelphia merchants and slave owners imported the largest number of slaves in the city's history—over one thousand Africans. This trend, prompted by a shortage of white indentured servants following the Seven Years' War between England and France, did not last. By the 1770s, slave imports trickled to a near halt. Still, by 1767, the city contained roughly fifteen hundred people of African descent, or roughly 7.5 percent of colonial Philadelphia. Fewer then one hundred black persons (just fifty-seven) could call themselves free. So Allen and his family would have been like the majority of Philadelphia blacks: they belonged to someone else.[13]

Although Pennsylvania had a reputation as a liberal colony, slavery had deep roots. Like colonies southward, Pennsylvania laws clearly defined bondage: only black colonials could be slaves for life. Richard Allen was born a slave because his mother had been enslaved. And so it was for thousands of other enslaved blacks, in the colonial North as well as the colonial South.

Just how many enslaved people existed in the Quaker State? Exact numbers remain difficult to come by, but at the time of Allen's birth the colony contained perhaps as many as fifteen thousand slaves (a number that fell drastically by the 1780s). In the Pennsylvania countryside, slaves worked wheat fields, cleared land, and labored at countless miscellaneous activities. A visitor from, say, colonial Virginia or South Carolina (or from the British Caribbean) would not have been surprised to find slaves in Pennsylvania; such a visitor would have noticed, however, that few of rural Pennsylvania's slaveholders owned great numbers of bondpeople. Whereas South Carolina rice plantations could hold hundreds of slaves, a large Pennsylvania plantation might contain only seven.[14]

Richard Allen was born into, and matured in, a world that accepted slavery. Massachusetts, Connecticut, and New Jersey embraced bondage; so too did Rhode Island and New York, colonies that contained the highest percentages of slaves above the Mason-Dixon line.[15] In Allen's Philadelphia, artisans, not merely wealthy men like Benjamin Chew, owned slaves. In fact, roughly one of every five families had slaves. But per capita slave holdings remained relatively low: urban dwellers owned fewer than five and quite often only one or two slaves. In this regard, slaves were indicators of status. We know that wealthy folks like Chew used slaves in a variety of ways, from launderers to laborers. But what did slaves do for artisans and merchants? They did nearly everything— loaded wagons, built homes and storefronts, cut wood, served as cooks, cartmen, and cleaners. Absalom Jones, a Delaware slave who journeyed to Philadelphia with his master during the second half of the eighteenth century, worked in a dry-goods store, filling stock, hauling goods, and generally doing as told. Jones was quite lucky, though, for his master allowed him to attain literacy skills and attend Anthony Benezet's Quaker school.[16]

Despite slavery's legal and cultural standing, some Pennsylvania masters were haunted by a looming idea: bondage was a sin. Pennsylvania Quakers took the first antislavery measures on the North American continent in 1758 by banning slave trading; they subsequently banned slaveholding too. The Society of Friends formed an antislavery vanguard thereafter, providing the foundation of the world's first organized antislavery group, the Pennsylvania Abolition Society. During Allen's youth, however, Quakers remained a minority of slavery's critics.[17]

The eighteenth century also witnessed a flowering of black resistance and achievement, as enslaved people ran away in increasing numbers, mastered literacy, and sought to redeem the very word "African." Phyllis Wheatley, John Marrant, Olaudah Equiano, Agrippa Hull, Prince Hall—this new generation of African-descended people began building a trans-Atlantic freedom struggle centered on the notion of black humanity. Take Venture Smith: born in 1729 in Africa, Smith was captured and sold into New World bondage while just a boy. He purchased his freedom in 1765, having chopped so much wood, threshed so much grain, and labored so hard that he could also set his sights on buying his wife and two sons. But Smith was not content with his own freedom.

To prove bondage was thievery, he wrote one of the first American-style slave narratives during the 1790s. "I've made considerable money," Smith recalled bitterly, "and paid an enormous sum for my freedom."[18]

Allen imbibed strength from nascent black-freedom movements. As a free man, Allen incorporated the term "African" into a host of fledgling black enterprises: the "Free African Society," a black mutual-aid group formed in 1787; the "African Methodist Episcopal Church," an autonomous African American religious organization, formed in the early 1790s; the "African Society for the Education of Youth," formed in 1804. When Allen discovered in 1807 that white religious leaders had craftily conceived legal documents undermining his own church's autonomy, he wrote a rebuttal of their actions entitled simply the "African Supplement." Like Venture Smith, Allen's belief in African redemption was fueled at an early age.

Despite the heroic struggles of black activists in Allen's time, and the humanitarian inroads of antislavery Quakers, bondage was still nasty, brutish, and anything but short for Pennsylvania's enslaved population. For most white colonials, the word "African" still connoted slavery. And before Allen made it out of his youth, he discovered another of slavery's wicked little rules: he was chattel—a movable commodity.

2. Delaware

Around 1768, Allen and his family were sold south to one of Benjamin Chew's Delaware neighbors, a middling farmer named Stokeley Sturgis. Located in Dover, in the fertile Delaware River Valley, Sturgis's farm was part of a thriving agricultural economy that included not only the cash crop of tobacco but also a range of staple products like wheat, rye, and corn. Farmers in the Delaware Valley enjoyed ready river access to the principal urban market in the area (Philadelphia), not to mention parts of Maryland and Virginia. Abundant forest products (timber for barrel staves) supplemented Delawareans' agricultural production.[19]

The archives are silent on why Benjamin Chew sold the Allens. We know that he ran into financial troubles and, further, that he had no moral qualms about selling slaves to replenish his financial stocks. Moreover, Chew owned Delaware land next to Sturgis; it was a quick and easy deal. Whatever the reason, Allen spent over a decade on Sturgis's farm.

Allen's Delaware was awash in paradoxes. Slavery had been a prominent feature of the state's landscape since the early 1700s, when farmers turned to bondage to maximize tobacco, wheat, and corn yields. Yet Delaware masters also were the least tied to a single cash crop (such as Virginia's tobacco barons or South Carolina's rice moguls). In Kent County, by the Revolutionary era, historian William H. Williams writes, "slaveholders and other farmers concentrated on growing wheat and corn," rather than building the larger tobacco plantations found elsewhere in the Chesapeake. As a result, many enslaved people—like Allen and his family—found themselves on smaller plantations, with much closer proximity to masters. As in the case of Pennsylvania, colonial Delaware's slave demographics must remain estimates. But by the 1770s, Delaware contained roughly eleven thousand slaves. The average Delaware slave lived on a farm of ten persons or fewer—that is, ten persons in all, master, mistress, their children, and a few slaves.[20]

It was hard to maintain a stable black family life anywhere in the South. Allen found this out when Sturgis sold the young boy's mother and three of his siblings to cover debts. Now, as Allen put it, "three of us children remained" with Sturgis, while four family members scattered like the winds.[21] Allen suggested that he still visited his mother, noting in his autobiography that she became "a very pious woman" after the sale.[22] But Allen did not elaborate, indicating that he could not visit as much as he wanted or that the subject remained a sore one. William Williams makes the striking claim that, despite the state's small geographic size, "most bondsmen did not have an easy commute" if they wanted to maintain contact with relatives "and could [therefore] make only sporadic visits." Virginia and Maryland slaves faced similar problems, but, ironically, these more densely settled slave locales provided marginally more access to separated husbands and fathers. Delaware's "generally smaller and more thinly scattered" slave settlements meant that only a "small percentage of male slaves lived with and therefore had daily contact with their wives and children."[23]

Slaves' living arrangements were equally makeshift: they lived in attics, basements, and sometimes barns or sheds if masters were wealthy enough. Although some larger plantations had slave cabins, most Delaware slaveholders did not erect separate quarters for their chattels. Sturgis owned a fairly typical Delaware dwelling, what might be described by a modern real-estate broker as a "colonial-style" house. Allen lived with the Sturgis family, either in a small cabin or in some corner space in the house itself. As was the custom, Sturgis would have supplied basic living material to his slaves, although as a middling master he probably did not provide more than was absolutely necessary.

Allen did not discuss his daily working life on Sturgis's plantation, but it involved "putting crops forward."[24] This meant planting corn, wheat, and flax—there is little record of tobacco on Sturgis's farm. No tobacco, no toil? Not so, for even these staple products translated into well-regulated work shifts for slaves like Allen. Corn required intense labor to get successful yields in the days before modern fertilization techniques and machinery. Prior to the Revolution, Delaware slaves used farm implements (hoes) to till the soil, working the land foot by foot (only after the Revolution came the ox and plow). Corn was planted in the spring and harvested in late summer. Working corn crops taught slaves like Allen hard life-lessons: you worked the land as soon as your master told you to, and even after the crop had been "put forward" you moved on to a succession of other tasks demanded by your master—clearing wheat fields, tending livestock, hauling crops to and from storage areas. "Shuck corn, shell corn, carry corn to mill," a slave song went, "grind de meal, gimme de husk; bake de bread, gimme de crus'."[25] A rough translation: a slave's work was never done, and you got only crumbs in return.

So life was never easy for an enslaved person, no matter the locale. If Delaware did not have massive plantations dedicated to big-time cash crops, it offered land to be cleared and waterways connecting its corn and wheat yields to the Atlantic world. Land sales boomed around Allen's Dover home. For sale, ad after ad declared in Philadelphia papers, one hundred, five hundred, one thousand acres of great Delaware land. The ads did not say so explicitly, but it was a given that slaves (or less likely but still an option, white tenants) would do the clearing, the planting, the building on all these properties. Richard Allen probably did all of these chores on Sturgis's farm. After Allen left Sturgis's home in the 1780s, he worked as a sawyer, butcher, mason, and cartman, which indicates familiarity with each job.

Clearly, Allen's memories of slavery as "a bitter pill" meant more than spiritual anguish—bondage was hard labor. Unsurprisingly, enslaved people escaped whenever possible. Kent County masters were no strangers to fugitives in their midst. "Ranaway from the subscriber," one fugitive-slave ad read in 1765, "a mulatoe [*sic*] slave, named Joe." This runaway "can read print and will try to pass for a freeman," the ad warned.[26] Similar ads placed in Baltimore and Philadelphia newspapers told the tale of black resistance spreading beyond Allen's Delaware home.

Though they did masters' work all day and into the night, enslaved blacks worked after-hours to gain extra funds for various pursuits, from contributing money to roaming preachers (which Allen said cost "a quarter" during the Revolutionary War) to buying one's freedom. "The slaves would toil in their little [garden] patches many a night until midnight," Allen recalled as an old man. Putting in their own crops was also a way of creating autonomy from masters. Sundown to sunup was enslaved people's time. They used it not only to supplement their diet through personal gardens (Allen noted that he and other slaves had to do this "to support them[selves] with more than their masters gave them") but also to hold prayer meetings in the woods, tell stories of ancestors and family members sold to other plantations, and pass on literacy skills and African traditions.[27]

Land, labor, and slaves' struggle for autonomy—these were not the only things that framed Allen's Delaware years. Indeed, the historian's eye returns once again to paradoxes swirling around him. Although Allen's Delaware was viewed as a part of the Chesapeake through much of the eighteenth and nineteenth centuries, it had important connections to Pennsylvania. As such, Delaware had a more vibrant manumission tradition than any other Southern state by the close of the eighteenth century. By 1800, according to one estimate, an incredible 50 percent of Delaware's black population was free, a much higher percentage than any other Southern locale.[28] Furthermore, Delaware's proximity and connections to liberal Pennsylvania (with its large Quaker population) influenced enslaved blacks, many of whom traveled from Delaware to Pennsylvania after manumission.

Allen recognized Delaware's unique status. When he had earned his liberty and begun traveling the evangelical circuit, Allen refused to travel to the Carolinas with Methodist preacher Francis Asbury. Those "slave countries," as he put it, scared the hell out of him.[29] Life was nowhere easy for a slave, Allen already knew. But nowhere in the South was slave life more conducive to black freedom than in Delaware following the Revolution—especially if a slave was focused on liberty.

3. Redemption

By his teenage years, Allen had learned some of the ultimate lessons slavery had to offer. Sold once himself, he had also been separated from his mother and three of his siblings; sunup to sundown belonged to his master's many chores; on the vertical ladder of colonial society, he occupied the bottom-most rung. Although he referred to Sturgis as a kind man and, in the absence of his own father (whom he never discussed in his autobiography), very nearly a parental figure, Allen felt remarkably like Frederick Douglass did in his teenage years on a Maryland plantation. "I am," Douglass wrote of his feelings at age seventeen, "but the sport of a power which makes no account either of my welfare or my happiness." Separated from family members and told again and again that he was essentially "a wild young working animal," Douglass feared that he would spend the rest of his life in "bitter and lifelong bondage."[30] Allen knew the same despair:

> When we would think that our day's work was never done, we often thought that after our master's death we were liable to be sold to the highest bidder, as [Sturgis] was much in debt; and thus my troubles were increased, and I was often brought to weep between the porch and the altar.[31]

Yet by the time he turned twenty, Allen had secured a freedom agreement. It all began in 1777, when the teenager was "born again" after hearing a revival sermon preached near Sturgis's home. "The genesis of the African Methodist Episcopal Church (AME)," the Mother Bethel website grandly informs modern-day Internet browsers, "which today numbers over 2.5 million members, can be traced to a clearing in the Delaware woods in the year 1777. To that sylvan setting an itinerant Methodist preacher came, spreading the gospel to a group of slaves, among whom was a seventeen-year-old fieldhand named Richard Allen."[32] The newly converted young man soon brought a revivalist preacher to Sturgis's home (making the planter feel the guilt of slaveholding), had a manumission agreement drawn up, and began planning a life of liberty. There was no way that Allen would spend the rest of his days in "bitter bondage"! Thankfully, he observed, "a door was open unexpectedly for me to buy my time and enjoy my liberty." Allen refused to let the door close without sneaking through.[33]

It is important to examine the details of Allen's remarkable six-year journey from slave to born-again Christian to free person of color. For one thing, it highlights at an early age one of Allen's most distinguishing characteristics: his incredible will, stubbornness, and focus on a singular goal. As friend and foe, white as well as black, would ever discover, Allen could not be moved from his goals. He was, wrote Daniel Payne in the 1890s, a "master-spirit"—a man who exuded a firm belief in his objectives.[34] That unshakable sense of mission gave even the young Allen a sense that he could shape events seemingly beyond his control.

Moreover, Allen's spiritual journey to Christianity and his secular journey to freedom occurred at a critical time in North America. Around him swirled the events of a revolutionary war, trans-Atlantic revivalism, and the first antislavery movement in Western culture. Each of these broader forces swept down in some way to touch Allen's life.

The war between the American colonies and Britain reverberated in many ways, from establishing the nation of which Allen would try so hard to become a part to establishing liberty as the American lingua franca. The Revolution also unleashed the first sustained public attack on the institution of slavery in Western culture. Just as many colonials had accused Britain of oppressing them as virtual slaves (with no rights and liberties), so too did black slaves tell American masters that they were unjustly held in true bondage. (In Charleston, South Carolina, slaves famously marched through the city streets in the summer of '76 with a banner declaring, "Liberty!") The American Revolution's intense focus on rights and liberties shattered the institution's standing. Slavery, quite simply, became a dirty word. One fact illuminates this mighty transformation: in 1776, every one of the new thirteen American states sanctioned slavery; by the turn of the century, however, every Northern state had adopted gradual abolition plans, and Southern states like Virginia had removed many restrictions on private manumissions.[35]

There were two key parts to this antislavery surge: the rise of secular abolitionist movements, centered in Allen's hometown of Philadelphia; and the rise of evangelical antislavery, which touched Allen directly when he converted to Methodism in the 1770s. The Pennsylvania Abolition Society (PAS) was formed in Philadelphia in 1775, and it dedicated itself to the proposition that slavery must be publicly challenged. Composed of some of the new nation's ablest legal and political minds —just before his death, Benjamin Franklin served as the group's president—the PAS advocated gradual abolitionism. It considered the Penn-

sylvania Abolition Act of 1780 a model for Atlantic-world slavery re-
gimes. The act declared that all Pennsylvania slaves born after 1780
must be registered with state officials; they would then be emancipated
at age twenty-eight.[36] By 1804, the legislature of every American state
north of Pennsylvania had gradually abolished bondage (save Massachusetts and Vermont, which did so by judicial and constitutional de-
crees, respectively).

By the Revolutionary War, trans-Atlantic religious itinerants also began arguing that slavery was a sin. Besides Quakers, no group was more
fervently antislavery than Methodists. A dissenting religion founded in
the 1730s by former Anglican John Wesley, Methodism emphasized
class meetings (with rigorous attention paid to biblical texts rather than
ministers' erudition), camp revivals (where congregants visually displayed the power of God's saving grace), and expansive preaching circuits (which extended deep into the North American countryside). For
Methodists, the Lord was not some distant and angry figure but a palpable and healing presence in people's lives. Anyone could alter his or
her destiny, Methodists claimed, by embracing God through a conversion experience. Though opponents derided Methodist claims that Bible
study and conversion outweighed the significance of formal schooling
(or predestination), they could not deny the group's appeal among average folks, from the growing British working class to slaves in British
colonies. Wesley furthered Methodism's appeal by emphasizing charity
in daily life. He visited prisoners and spread the gospel among workers
and farmers beyond the reach of the Anglican Church. By the Revolution, Methodist itinerants in America alone had carried Wesley's movement to thousands and thousands of people, including increasing numbers of African Americans.[37]

One Methodist hot spot was Allen's boyhood home, the mid-Atlantic
region of Pennsylvania, Delaware, Maryland, and Virginia. Itinerant
Francis Asbury, who had trained with Wesley in England before coming
to America, encouraged black colonials (and then Americans) to embrace Methodism. "The poor Negroes have been deeply affected with
the power of God," he wrote his parents after one Baltimore revival in
January 1773. He kept his eye out for notable black worshipers, like an
unidentified man who might "be fit to send to England soon to preach"
(surely not Allen, who was still too young for such work). Asbury marveled at blacks' "astonishing" preaching abilities.[38]

For his part, Allen marveled at Methodism's unadulterated appeal to enslaved people. Methodists were plain and simple, he recalled; they emphasized "extempore preaching," and they eagerly spoke before black audiences. "I am well convinced that the Methodist has proved beneficial to thousands and ten times thousands," Allen said.[39]

Although American Methodism would eventually split into northern and southern branches during antebellum debates over slavery's sinfulness, in Allen's day Methodists were not shy about their antislavery commitments. This early "antislavery militancy," as Dee Andrews calls it, flowed from John Wesley himself.[40] "Have you, has any man living, a right to use another as a slave?" Wesley wondered in his famous denunciation of British bondage, "Thoughts upon Slavery" (1774). "It cannot be."[41] Wesley remained interested in trans-Atlantic antislavery movements, even going so far as to encourage famed British abolitionist William Wilberforce to read the latest abolitionist publications from black authors like Olaudah Equiano.[42] Allen may not have read Wesley's antislavery pronouncements until later, but Wesley's itinerants surely told the young convert that Methodists believed in the spiritual (and sometimes social) equality of blacks. And that news inspired him.

Allen "got religion" in 1777. The memory of his conversion experience stayed with him until the day he died. Indeed, Allen's autobiography trumpeted two birthdays: the one that put him on earth in 1760 and his rebirth, or conversion experience, as a teenager, "during which time I was awakened and brought to see myself poor, wretched and undone, and without the mercy of God must be lost." But Allen saw the light. "One night I thought Hell would be my portion," he went on, and "I cried to the Lord both night and day. . . . I cried unto him who delighted to hear the prayers of a poor sinner." Speaking figuratively, Allen then famously exclaimed, "all of a sudden my dungeon shook, my chains flew off, and, glory to God, I cried."[43]

Gary Nash has surmised that young Allen experienced a spiritual crisis after Sturgis sold his mother.[44] Religion became the balm for the reeling teenager. Allen's siblings helped him discover a religious community that embraced all souls. "My oldest brother embraced religion, and my sister," he wrote in the 1830s.[45] From them, Allen learned that Methodist preachers had come into Kent County in the summer of 1777. Led by former slaveholder Freeborn Garrettson, they initiated a series of revivals at homes surrounding Sturgis's property. One such event occurred at Benjamin Wells's place, the next farm over. Allen may indeed have had his first encounter in the forest, where revivals often occurred; or he might have seen a traveling preacher outside Sturgis's home or in town on market day. On receiving the word of God, Allen confessed his sins and endured a brief period of "doubt," before finding "the Lord afresh."[46] From that moment onward, one might say, Allen's career as a slave was never the same. He now attended Methodist class meetings, led exhortation sessions in and around Sturgis's farm, and became a reliable, even trusted, member of Delaware's revivalist world.

Allen's quick mastery of, and dedication to, Methodism was incontestable. Each day began and ended with prayers. Few who met the young preacher came away doubting his sincerity. Allen believed "in the unity of the Godhead, a trinity of persons," believed "O blessed Jesus, that thou art of one substance with the Father, the very and eternal God," and believed "that thou didst truly suffer, and was crucified . . . to reconcile us to thy Father and to be sacrificed for sin." And, crucially, Allen now believed that he had an important place on God's earth. "Thou has not only given thyself to die for me," he prayed, "but to be my spiritual food and sustenance . . . and endless comfort." The Lord looked out for young Richard Allen, a slave ("Thou hast not abandoned me," he said), and Allen professed to be the Lord's undying servant.[47]

Why did the young enslaved man become a true believer and not a revolutionary? Part of the answer is temperamental. Allen simply took to the Methodist faith. Beyond this, though, Allen appreciated the sense of security—of belonging—he felt in God's arms. "I entered life without acknowledging Thee," he relayed in one section of his autobiography. "Let me therefore finish it in loving Thee." "God is Love," he also proclaimed, clueing readers in to another rationale for his deep sense of faith: there was an eternal power beyond his master who treated him not as an object but as a person to be loved. Instead of eternal bondage, Allen came to believe that his destiny was in the care of a benevolent force. The Lord, he wrote, "from time to time raised up instruments" of revelation, reconciliation, and justice. Allen now saw himself as just such a figure. His life had a noble purpose, a benevolent end, a supreme sanction. As he put it, slavery taxed the soul as much as it depleted the body. "The love of God" brought renewal and a sense of "hope," "confidence," and direction of which "no master can deprive you."[48]

Aside from spiritual blessings, Allen found that Methodism allowed him to become an antislavery spokesman. The Revolutionary period is often remembered as a triumph of reason over emotion, with Enlightenment precepts embraced by skeptical men producing a democratic culture. This picture obscures the significance of religion as a revolutionary force. Roaming preachers attacked more than generic sin in Allen's youth; they railed against centralized authority and hierarchies in the house of the Lord. Black evangelicals joined this crusade, forming a formidable challenge to an institutional status quo that viewed slavery as acceptable and descendants of Africa as inferior. Methodism "appealed to ambitious, intelligent, young African Americans," historian Graham Hodges argues, because "many Methodist ministers were openly antislavery."[49] The church also actively recruited blacks like Allen, offering them organizational duties as exhorters and preachers. In the upper Chesapeake, Francis Asbury relied on Allen to spread the gospel to people of color. But he was not the only black preacher to gain notoriety during the Revolutionary era. His generation included a half-dozen major black ministers, many of whom had Methodist connections: John Jea, Absalom Jones, Boston King, John Marrant, George White, and Peter Williams. For them, as for Allen, the light of revelation was powerful enough to destroy the shackles of slavery.[50]

4. Everybody Say Freedom

Methodism brought Allen freedom. Or rather, Allen shrewdly used Methodist preaching to shame his master into bargaining slavery down into a contract for freedom. He moved tactically and in stages. But for the first time in his life, Allen manipulated events to his benefit.[51] "He who would be free must strike the first blow," an African American aphorism stated.[52] Allen struck with the word of God.

Allen first had to prove to his master that religion did not make for recalcitrant slaves. Masters' preferred biblical text was "servants will obey masters" (1 Peter 2:18). Allen assured Sturgis that he would not disobey while attending Methodist worship. This was a critical maneuver: with revival preachers working the Dover area, Sturgis was ridiculed by his neighbors for allowing Allen to so openly embrace Methodism. Wouldn't even a meeting every other week "ruin [his] Negroes"? they chided. Allen and his brother resolved to work harder, giving Sturgis no excuse for cracking down on their pious observances. They even missed a few meetings as a show of loyalty. "Is this not your meeting day?" a surprised Sturgis might ask on the Thursday that Allen was supposed to attend Bible study. "No sir," came Allen's reply, "we would rather stay at home and get our work done." With this, Sturgis was convinced that religion made excellent servants.[53]

Allen then worked on longer-range plans. Not content to be an enslaved believer, he plotted to bring revivalist preachers into Sturgis's house. According to Allen, Sturgis and his wife "being old and infirm," and doubtless thinking of the afterlife, "asked some of the Methodist preachers to come and preach at his house." Actually, the thought did not just suddenly come to Sturgis; Allen put it there, asking if the "preachers [could] come and preach at" the Sturgis home someday. Indeed, Allen's leadership in the episode is underscored by what happened next. Knowing that preachers had been accused of interceding between masters and slaves, Allen asked Sturgis for a note to his class leader (a man named John Gray), who feared attending Sturgis's house without a formal request from Allen's master. Sturgis refused to write a note but sanctioned Allen's invitation. White preachers went to Sturgis's home knowing they had the slave master's blessing.[54]

Meetings occurred in and around Sturgis's home during the summer of 1779 (including visits by Francis Asbury). Then came Freeborn Garrettson's visit, perhaps in September 1779. "Thou art weighed in the balance," Garrettson lectured a shaking Sturgis, "and found wanting" (Daniel 5:27). Sturgis wilted when the Word of the Lord was revealed to him. "After that," Allen wrote, "he could not be satisfied to hold slaves." The two soon struck a deal for Allen and his brother's freedom.[55] "I had it often impressed on my mind that I should one day enjoy my freedom," Allen recalled thinking at the time.[56] That time was now, for he had just shaped the course of his own emancipation.

By January 25, 1780, the twenty-year-old Allen had a written agreement with his master: he would pay two thousand dollars over the next five years for his freedom. So nice did that word "freedom" sound that Allen paid his first installment—$150—early.[57] Allen worked feverishly over the next several years to bring his agreement with Sturgis to fruition. How hard did Richard Allen work? He claimed to have cut so much wood on his first day alone that "it was only with difficulty I could open or close [my] hands." He actually prayed for a cure. Then Allen rested for a few days, doing other chores while his blistered and bleeding hands healed. Driven by fears that "after our master's death we were liable to be sold to the highest bidder," Allen eagerly returned to what he referred to as "his work" of gaining freedom. He cut more wood, took on more odd jobs, and refused to pause for anything but prayer, food, and fellowship.[58]

We can approximate Allen's workload by consulting various sources. Allen recalled earning fifty Continental dollars per month at a Delaware brickyard. Debt to his master amounted to two thousand Continental dollars. This translated into roughly three and half years of hauling bricks to secure his freedom, with no external expenditures. Another, perhaps more telling, indicator was Allen's woodcutting work. Pay scales instituted well after the Revolutionary War set rates for what sawyers could charge. Cutting oak or hickory was rated at two to three Pennsylvania schillings per cord (one dollar in Continental currency was roughly seven and a half Pennsylvania schillings). Allen observed that he could cut "a cord and half to two cords per day." If you do the math, that means it would have taken three thousand to four thousand cords of wood and, at Allen's hard-working rate of one and a half to two cords a day, fifteen hundred days, or roughly five years, of cutting wood for Allen to pay off his agreement with Sturgis.[59]

Allen would have had to work all day every day at the single chore of cutting wood—an activity that made his hands blister and bleed—for five years straight. And that did not include money for food, clothing, transportation, or any other miscellaneous cost. Considering Stokeley Sturgis's already weakened financial state, Allen was now responsible for such items. Add to this the shaky state of the American economy and it is clear that Allen worked like hell to gain his freedom. Indeed, pray though he might for deliverance, Allen left nothing to God or fate —he was going to gain his freedom as quickly as possible.

The record shows that Richard Allen made good on his freedom agreement a year and half early. He signed his contract with Stokeley Sturgis in 1780; he paid the last installment of debt in August 1783, providing Sturgis not only with the necessary funds for his liberty but also with bushels of corn, wheat, and salt. The piece of paper that Allen took away from Sturgis (when he was twenty-three years old) assured that nobody would call Richard Allen a slave anymore. As Sturgis's deed put it, "I do hereby for myself, my heirs, executors, administrators or assigns manumit, exonerate, release and forever discharge and set at full liberty said Negro man named Richard quitting all claim that I were they in my right may or might have to him by virtue of any law, custom or usage whatsoever."[60]

Allen was right to take no chances with his freedom. Many blacks became entrapped in dubious emancipation schemes of one sort or another, particularly as the Revolutionary War ended and slaveholders came to view bondmen as still-vital commodities in a reconstructing economy. Some Northern masters deviously used the promise of emancipation to lull slaves into a false sense of security, only to sell them south before their liberty date approached. In New York City (which adopted a gradual abolition law in 1799), according to one scholar's estimate, perhaps one-third of the enslaved population was sold south before gaining liberty. Allen did everything he could to avoid such a fate.[61] He paid his debt early, got that freedom paper, and eventually had it deposited in the master files of the Pennsylvania Abolition Society for future reference. It sits there today as the very first manumission agreement on file.

5. The Name Game

After gaining his independence, another matter weighed heavily on the newly freed Richard Allen. What would he call himself? His emancipation agreement refers merely to a man called "Negro Richard." But names meant a lot to enslaved people. Out of the reach of masters' ears, they would sometimes use different names to refer to one another.

The story of how "Negro Richard" took the name "Richard Allen" went to the grave with the man himself. He never explained his reasons in public, and no family member or acquaintance left any insights. Gary Nash has suggested that the liberated slave took the last name "Allen" to honor a well-regarded Pennsylvania jurist (named William Allen) who had been Benjamin Chew's neighbor.[62] If this is true, then perhaps Allen was also paying homage to his home state, which in the exact same year that he signed a manumission deal with Sturgis had passed the world's first gradual abolition law. Whatever the reason, Allen's renaming constituted the first act of self-possession in his life.

Taking a name and making a name for himself were not necessarily the same thing. After securing his freedom and renaming himself, Allen set off on the Methodist preaching circuit. Ever cautious and calculating, Allen took no chances when he hit the road. He made sure he had a pass, or a letter of testimonial, allowing him unfettered movement. This recently discovered document shows just how important mobility was to the young Allen. On August 27, 1783, his former master Stokeley

Sturgis penned a six-line pass for Allen, telling anyone who would challenge the young black man that he was indeed "free" and that Allen "intends to travel some ways abroad from this [place?] to work where it suits him." Sturgis added that Allen always "behaved himself . . . honestly when he wrought about this place."[63] Clearly, Allen had made his grand intentions known to those closest to him, including his former master. Far from being content with mere freedom, Allen dreamed of traveling far and wide, of working where he wanted, of spreading the gospel to all who would receive it, of settling in a place he decided to call home. Sturgis's evident desire to vouch for Allen's character, not to mention his concern with Allen's dream of traveling "abroad," is almost touching. That little document conveyed Allen's biggest desires (his wanderlust) to anyone who would read it. He carried it wherever he went and made sure to pass it along to posterity.[64]

In no time at all, the wandering Allen became a familiar figure at camp meetings and revivals. "Come unto me, all ye that are weary and heavy laden," he would call out, "Glory be to God!" "This man must be a man of God!" people replied upon hearing Allen's voice. "I have never heard such preaching before."[65] So dedicated was he to the evangelical circuit that even while tracking cartloads of salt between Delaware and Pennsylvania during the Revolution—Allen made deliveries to American forces—he held "church" at the side of the road. "I never forgot to serve my Lord," Allen said. "I used oft-times to pray, sitting, standing or lying."[66]

Word of Allen's circuit preaching eventually made it to Pennsylvania abolitionists, who used his story as a model of black uplift in the new republic. In a pamphlet prepared in 1787 for distribution among British abolitionists (who wanted the information as fodder for their own anti-slave-trading campaigns), Pennsylvania reformers compiled stories of free black preachers, workers, and community builders who exemplified black achievement. This first-ever group portrait of African Americans in the emancipating North celebrated the possibilities of abolitionism in trans-Atlantic culture. That Allen became the very first subject of these testimonials speaks volumes about his renown as a black minister of the gospel. "He believed it to be his duty to Travel abroad as a Preacher of Righteousness," the pamphlet declared, noting that Allen paid out of pocket to be a Methodist itinerant. His extensive "religious journeys" were so impressive, however, that white officials soon paid his expenses. (Allen's dedication extended to "Indian natives," among whom he spent nearly two months preaching.) Allen distinguished himself as a businessman too, abolitionists continued, for his dry-goods operations gained him both "money and reputation." Only four years removed from paying off his freedom dues, the former slave was now known on both side of the Atlantic.[67]

Allen's first base of operations was Wilmington, Delaware, in 1783. Allen then moved northward to New Jersey, where he spent several weeks preaching the gospel. In the spring of 1784, Allen arrived at the home of well-known preacher Benjamin Abbott, who lived on the western edge of New Jersey. Quickly impressing the white cleric, Allen preached with Abbott at several local meetings. Allen then moved to the other side of New Jersey, living briefly with Joseph Budd (another white acquaintance), before going to Bennington, New Jersey, and finally Pennsylvania. "I walked until my feet became so sore I blistered," he recalled of this one year of itinerant activity. "I could scarcely bear them to the ground."[68]

Despite bouts of illness, Allen kept moving and preaching. Between 1784 and 1785, he worked on circuits in southeastern Pennsylvania; Baltimore, Maryland; and Kent County, Delaware. By the time he finished his itinerancy in early 1786 and moved back to Philadelphia, Allen had traveled several hundred miles and impressed thousands of worshipers, many of whom were white. In his autobiography, Allen named nearly two dozen people with whom he stayed and prayed on his mid-Atlantic sojourns. The majority of his contacts were white people. This fact underscored the young black man's early belief that religion could form a bridge of understanding between the races. In his first published attack on bondage in 1794, Allen challenged masters to end slavery lest they face eternal damnation. If guilty masters like Thomas Jefferson balked at this notion and worried about slaves' vengeance, then Allen perceptively pointed to the Bible. Christianizing slaves and emancipating masters prayed to the same God, he lectured; neither party would dare treat the other wrongly, lest they be eternally condemned. Indeed, freed blacks would live under the same Golden Rule as former slaveholders: they must treat others as they would be treated. For Allen, this was no mere parlor philosophizing. His revivalist experience was proof positive that black and white could pray together, eat together, and live together as equals in the new American republic.[69]

His optimism notwithstanding, Allen recognized the dangers of black itinerancy, particularly in Southern states. In 1785, the great Methodist itinerant Francis Asbury (1745–1816) asked the talented and increasingly well-known black exhorter to "travel abroad" with him. They would visit slavery's heartland, Maryland and Virginia, before traveling to both North and South Carolina. Asbury warned Allen that he must not "intermix with slaves" in the Deep South and that he would "have to sleep in his carriage" at nights. "I would not travel on these conditions," Allen replied firmly. Why not? Asbury wondered. "If I was taken sick," the free-speaking Allen countered, "who would support me?"[70]

Asbury apparently did not understand Allen's concern, for he told the young man that he would provide adequate food and clothing. Allen repeated his fears, again telling Asbury plainly, "I would not travel on these conditions." Allen simply doubted that he would be treated as a free man in the heavily enslaved South. He envisioned a scenario in which he was left to the kindness of locals, who already made clear their doubts about black equality and abolitionism. Worse, he suffered from rheumatoid arthritis. What if he could not travel for a while? No, Allen could not imagine risking his freedom in the Deep South. He told Asbury no and headed north again.[71]

Allen's reluctance to travel with Asbury did not prevent these Methodist itinerants of the gospel from forming a great interracial friendship —a relatively uncommon thing in late-eighteenth-century America. In 1803, Allen celebrated their two decades of fellowship by purchasing a horse for Asbury (for the not-unsubstantial sum of ninety dollars). That token of gratitude, gladly accepted by Asbury (who had worn out his own mare), was but a small repayment for Asbury's longtime assistance to Allen. When Allen broke from white Methodists at St. George's in the early 1790s, Asbury gave the inaugural address to the new black church. It was Asbury too who ordained Allen as the first black Methodist deacon in 1799. And of course, in 1785, only a bit removed from slavery and just beginning his own itinerancy, Allen received his first major boost from Asbury, who had actually called for the talented young exhorter by name. Come and help me save souls, he asked Allen. Here, Allen recalled, was a bishop who not only recalled a black man's full name but wanted his help.

Allen and Asbury had good reason to become friends. Like Allen, Asbury was attracted to the bare-bones aspects of Methodism. Nothing pleased Asbury more than "serious" prayers and "serious" congregations. Also like Allen, Asbury relished discipline—regular prayer, prayer as a daily ritual and not a weekly obligation, prayer as a mode of living and working. Why were people mired in hypocrisy and sin? "Neglect of Prayer," Asbury declared. And Asbury surely won favor with Allen for speaking directly, truthfully, even painfully about God's word. Sin was sin, there could be no way around it, both Allen and Asbury believed. At the start of 1778, Asbury preached to a large crowd in Allen's Dover. "The people felt the weight of Divine truths," he noted of that day. He did what he called "plain-dealing" at other prayer meetings in the weeks that followed. "What shall it profit a man if he gain the whole world and lose his soul?" Asbury prodded his listeners. Was an eternity of hell worth ignoring righteousness? Asbury "spoke searchingly" about sin, even if it did not endear him to religious and political authorities. That was a man after Allen's heart.[72]

Allen and Asbury shared something else, for religion offered both a route out of a grinding existence. Asbury was born in England only a few years prior to Allen. He worked as a blacksmith before becoming a traveling lecturer. In 1771, he answered Methodist calls to work as an itinerant in the American colonies. He spent the next several decades building Methodism in the American countryside. According to one estimate, he traveled over one hundred thousand miles to spread the Word. Asbury also demonstrated that he could look beyond race. In Maryland in 1773, he recalled a wonderful "public worship" session at which "a serious Negro was powerfully struck" by the Word. The man did not say much, but he "trembled" as the conversion experience enveloped his entire body. "The very house shook," Asbury wrote.[73]

Allen's itinerant work fostered other memorable meetings. At the end of 1784, for example, he made his way from New Jersey to Pennsylvania, settling in a small town called Radnor, located just a dozen miles from Philadelphia. His feet bloodied from miles of walking, he came to the home of Caesar Waters and his wife, a black couple eager for Allen's companionship. After chatting awhile, they asked the young preacher to stay for tea. A delighted but weary Allen agreed to stay but found that he could not move from his chair to the dinner table. "They brought the table to me," a grateful Allen remembered. When later at night Allen finally hobbled out of his chair, Mrs. Waters "bathed my feet with warm water and bran." Restored and revitalized, Allen awoke the next morning ready to preach. "We had a glorious meeting!" he glowed. The couple asked him to stay a few days more, to share food and the love of God. Days turned into weeks at the couple's insistence. Around Radnor, Allen preached to groups large and small. Word spread about the black preacher's commanding presence. "How can we be saved?" people asked him. "Prayer and supplication to the throne of Grace," he told them. Allen's meetings bore all the signs of a good old revival, with shouting and hollering in the name of the Lord. "Many souls were awakened," as he put it, "and cried aloud to the Lord to have mercy upon them."[74]

Allen called the Waterses the "kindest" people he had ever met. But something else occurred to him while in Pennsylvania: there were relatively "few colored people" like the Waterses to preach to. Perhaps, Allen thought, he should now dedicate time to building a black Methodist constituency.[75]

That opportunity came in February 1786, when he accepted the invitation of a white Methodist elder to come to Philadelphia and minister to black congregants in the burgeoning city he once called home.

6. Portrait of a Man Named Allen

For anyone of the Revolutionary era, much less a black man and former slave, Allen had lived an amazing life by 1786. He had been sold by his first master and separated from his mother by his second master; he had been born again; he chartered his own ticket to freedom and earned more as a laborer than most people of the time, white or black; he had been anointed as an up-and-coming exhorter on the Methodist circuit.

Allen even had his portrait painted, probably after attending the inaugural Methodist conference in Baltimore in December 1784. This organizational meeting created the structures that defined the Methodist Episcopal Church in America: the office of bishop, the powers of the presiding elder in congregational life, the continuing importance of conversion experiences and itinerant work. The "Christmas Conference" also created "a new and detailed antislavery rule": Methodists must liberate their slaves lest they be denied the Lord's Supper and expelled from the church. Although the Methodist Church subsequently retreated from such antislavery orthodoxy, in the 1780s it appeared to be part of the abolitionist vanguard. Allen may have been the picture of Methodists' great antislavery future.[76]

Indeed, Allen so impressed the many white preachers who gathered in Baltimore that he became the subject of a magnificent portrait, the earliest rendition we have of him. Dressed in the simple but dignified

Allen's first portrait, c. 1784–85. This is the first likeness of Allen—
and among the first of black founders. Recently liberated and gaining fame as an itinerant Methodist preacher on the mid-Atlantic
revival circuit at the time of this sitting, Allen soon after settled in
Philadelphia, where he founded the African Methodist Episcopal
Church. (Courtesy of Howard University)

garb of a roaming preacher—Allen wore a black waistcoat with a white
scarf tied into a cravat—he forthrightly faces his viewers, the smallest of
smiles forming above his chin. Allen appears absolutely unfazed by his
portrait; he does not frown or clench his jaw in the least. He is amiable,
confident, assured. His winning personality must have influenced the
artist, for Allen's portrait is set against a rather cheery blue-white background, rather than the weighty and severe backdrops (deep velvety
reds or chocolate browns) of most other Enlightenment portraiture.

Still, the unidentified artist captured perfectly Allen's piercing gaze—the intensity of those eyes that Henry Highland Garnet would later recall as Allen's essential (and most unforgettable) physical feature.[77]

Allen's portrait was painted before he celebrated his twenty-fifth birthday. This fact alone says something rather remarkable. People knew him not by generic racial features (a black man, a slave) but by name and accomplishment. His name was Richard Allen, and few people who met him over the next few decades ever forgot that.

2

Gospel Labors

When Richard Allen journeyed to his boyhood home of Philadelphia in 1786, he had just turned twenty-six. Since his manumission, he had traveled to a half-dozen states in the new American nation and worked at well over half a dozen different jobs too. Stability would now become Allen's primary concern. After settling in the City of Brotherly Love, he sought to build institutional homes for the burgeoning free black community—churches, reform groups, educational societies. He also struggled to secure equality for African Americans in the new republic. "Whoever hopes for great things in this world," Allen wrote, "takes pains to attain them."[1] He went to great lengths to achieve his dreams.

Allen's efforts soon paid off, as he helped inaugurate two of the most revered black-led institutions in early national America: the Free African Society, a benevolent organization, and Bethel Church, which would become one of the most powerful African American churches in the United States. Achieving equality proved decidedly more difficult, however. The black founder's antislavery sermonizing met with apathy and even anger. But Allen was not deterred. Indeed, he knew that hardship was part of the long, hard road a prophet traveled.

1. Church Roots

Allen's church dated to his itinerant work in Delaware, Maryland, New Jersey, and Pennsylvania. He recalled that few free blacks attended services in Northern locales and that Southern masters tried to keep roaming preachers away from slaves.[2] Yet experience as a Methodist class leader told Allen that both free blacks and enslaved people hungered for the Word. Soon after attending the inaugural Methodist conference in Baltimore in 1784, Allen decided that someone must convert blacks into a powerful Afro-Christian constituency.

In what initially appeared to be a happy coincidence, Philadelphia's Methodist elder pressed Allen to preach to local blacks at St. George's Church. Allen traveled to the Quaker City in February 1786 and began holding services at the very early hour of 5 a.m. The itinerant bug briefly bit, but rising attendance compelled Allen to stay put. "I soon saw a large field open in seeking and instructing my African brethren," he recalled.[3] Allen remained in Philadelphia the rest of his life.

The city that Allen inhabited was not that of his youth. In the 1760s, Allen had been like the majority of his black brethren in British Philadelphia, where perhaps 90 percent of the roughly eighteen hundred blacks were slaves. By the 1790s, black Philadelphians were overwhelming free, and the City of Brotherly Love had become a capital of free black life. When Pennsylvania abolitionists did the first of several census-style reports on black Philadelphians in the early 1790s, they visited roughly four hundred free families representing nearly thirteen hundred people of color, including ninety-nine homeowners. These numbers grew markedly by the early nineteenth century, when free blacks represented roughly 10 percent of the overall population. Most free blacks, the PAS noted, referring to the rising Allens of the world, "conduct [their lives] reputably and . . . some are very worthy citizens."[4] A sizable contingent of Philadelphia blacks came from outside the city, including those from the Pennsylvania countryside who traded rural life in slavery for urban life in freedom. Others migrated from Chesapeake locales, including runaway slaves who settled in a known abolitionist state with a known abolitionist society (the PAS) ready to aid them.[5]

Philadelphia's growing reputation as an abolitionist capital beckoned blacks along the Atlantic seaboard. The PAS had initially organized as a lobbying group that protested bondage sporadically in legislative halls and courts of law. By 1789, endangered blacks from rural Pennsylvania, Maryland, New Jersey, and Virginia had flooded the group with so many appeals for legal aid that the PAS shifted tactics. It hired more lawyers and represented more blacks in court at the close of the eighteenth century than any other abolitionist organization. Some black litigants were the victims of recalcitrant Pennsylvania masters. No sooner had the state's gradual abolition law been passed in 1780 than slaveholders sought to evade it. The PAS intervened for black freedom. Devious masters beyond Pennsylvania also brought slaves into the state without registering them properly—another violation of the abolitionist law. The PAS again intervened for black freedom (prompting, in some cases, immediate liberation followed by apprenticeship for formerly enslaved people).[6]

Blacks took strong action themselves, both by running *away* from masters and by running *to* white abolitionists for legal aid. In some cases, black runaways proved so irritating and costly to slaveholders inside and outside Pennsylvania that masters ended up striking bargains with slaves. In exchange for pledges against running away again, blacks would turn slavery for life into an indenture contract for a shorter number of years (often seven). White abolitionists officiated many of these indentures, further ensuring black freedom. Of course, PAS members could be paternalistic too—and they certainly did not win every case. They even refused to take some cases involving fugitive slaves for fear of offending Southern masters. But in a new American nation dedicated to liberty for some, and to slaveholders' property rights in man, the PAS was indeed a beacon of hope. In 1790, for instance, the group successfully blocked a proposed revision in the new state constitution separating whites' from blacks' rights. Abolitionist activism ensured that Pennsylvania citizens collectively had only one set of rights. Many freed blacks, as James Forten would later declare, came to view Pennsylvania "as the only state in the union wherein the black man is treated equally to the white."[7]

Allen made his own abolitionist contributions by working as a go-between for PAS activists. On several occasions, endangered blacks contacted the rising black preacher for help. Allen contacted abolitionist lawyers who investigated African Americans' freedom claims. In 1788, Allen and the PAS sued a white coachmaker who illegally sold his slave to a non-Pennsylvanian.[8] African Americans who claimed to be kidnapping victims or wrongly enslaved former residents of Pennsylvania contacted Allen from as far away as Mississippi.[9] By aiding threatened blacks, Allen helped define the Quaker State as a Northern antislavery borderland that chipped away at slavery's national status.

Philadelphia was no heaven, Allen already knew, but it still proved to be a haven of sorts. Had not Allen himself come north to abolition's home instead of traveling south through the slave countries when he gained his own freedom? Like other people of color, he believed that Philadelphia—and, by extension, the abolitionizing state of Pennsylvania—offered a measure of hope for racial redemption in the new nation.

2. *Industry and Uplift*

From the moment he arrived in Philadelphia, Allen worked feverishly. "Idle hands do the Devil's work," Poor Richard once told Pennsylvanians. Ben Franklin would have been proud of Allen's work ethic. He did anything to rise in Philadelphia society, laboring as a whitewasher, dry-goods dealer, and cobbler on his way to becoming a master chimney sweep, entrepreneur, and minister supported by his congregation. Allen's chimney-sweeping business was particularly profitable. Ever known as a dangerous trade, chimney sweeps stuffed themselves into the narrowest fireplace chutes, danced on top of sharply slanted roofs, and spent their days face-to-face with ashes and soot. "The business was crowded, unhealthy and dangerous," two modern labor scholars have commented. But free blacks rose in a profession many whites preferred to avoid.[10] Indeed, whereas black sailors in Philadelphia rarely became masters of their own ships, several African Americans became master chimney sweeps.[11]

Allen recognized the potential profitability of chimney sweeping when he started his business in 1789. Philadelphians had established a price index that paid chimney sweepers according to risk—the higher the chimney, the greater the wages. Because Philadelphia was the nation's largest urban center, not to mention a trans-Atlantic trading hub and soon-to-be federal capital, it contained a sizable number of homes with lucrative—or dangerously high—chimneys. And Philadelphia's chimneys had to be cleaned from September through May, when chilly days and nights kept home fires burning. Allen met this demand by doing some of the best and toughest work in the city.

Allen was evidently a tough mastersweep. In 1790 a "boy [named] . . . Tilghman Fitzgerald" complained to white abolitionists about working with the rising black preacher. The PAS sought to investigate the matter but had trouble locating the young lad, "owing to his being employed [by Allen so far] from home." White abolitionists eventually determined that although Allen's mastery did not seriously harm Tilghman Fitzgerald, it did pose risks. The PAS therefore assumed the boy's indenture.[12]

This was not Allen's first problem with an apprentice. In 1789 he placed the first of two runaway ads in the *Pennsylvania Gazette* seeking the return of "an indented Indian mulatto boy named Israel Tolman, whose father was a white man and mother an Indian."[13] Born around

1773, Tolman (alias Tallman) allegedly hailed from Allentown, Pennsylvania. Allen may have acquired Tolman as part of a PAS plan to bind out young people of color. Tolman evidently bolted to escape not only the drudgery of chimney sweeping but Allen's fearsome work ethic. Allen twice offered a reward of four dollars for Tolman's return, indicating his firm belief in the sanctity of indenture work.

These ads tell us something else too: Allen was rising economically. Though no great sum when compared to recapture rewards offered by other masters (escaped slaves fetched up to twenty dollars), four dollars was a significant sum for Afro-Philadelphians. Hiring apprentices like Tolman also meant outlays of capital for food, lodging, tools, and eventually freedom dues. That Allen had disposable income to reclaim an apprentice is therefore revealing. In fact, Allen employed a steady number of apprentices during the 1790s. In February 1793, for instance, he signed an agreement with a young man named Paris. The indenture lasted four years and six months (ending in August 1797), with Allen agreeing to teach Paris the craft of chimney sweep and providing "freedom dues" (perhaps a new suit or some tools).[14] In the late summer of 1793, Allen took on more apprentices for a business he planned with fellow black preacher Absalom Jones: a nail factory. In 1795, he helped several former Jamaican slaves find indenture opportunities in Philadelphia.

Beyond serving as a symbol of his rising status, the practice of apprenticing marked Allen as a black leader in the eyes of many white Philadelphians. Despite Allen's troubles with two indentures, the PAS still viewed him as a key contact in the black community precisely because he could hire young people of color. The 1790s witnessed a brief burst in white demands for apprenticed black labor (European immigrants would cut into this need during the 1800s). Allen and other black leaders worked with the PAS to find apprenticing opportunities for black men and women transiting from slavery to freedom.

Apprenticing also gave Allen an early forum for espousing uplift schemes. According to Allen, by working hard, learning a craft, and remaining humble and pious, freed blacks would rise in American culture. Interestingly, his uplift ideology might have had as much to do with notions of nation-building prevalent in early national Philadelphia as his own religious scruples. For like other working Americans, Allen hoped that his exertions would contribute to the rebuilding of a shattered economy. Pennsylvania abolitionists certainly echoed this line of thinking, noting that black industry and uplift were part and parcel of a national effort to perfect American economies, politics, and the social order itself (albeit with white abolitionists' paternalistic eyes constantly watching them).[15] By the early nineteenth century, Allen's visions of moral uplift seemed a bit didactic to the rising generations of free blacks who encountered more-virulent forms of racism.

For the moment, though, Allen was concerned with rising. By working hard, acquiring land and money, and serving as a master of young apprentices, Allen did just that, and he was undisputedly among black Philadelphia's leadership class by the early 1790s. He soon took that leadership position in challenging new directions.

3. The FAS

Plus ça change: the more things change, the more they stay the same. The French phrase captures perfectly what many black people, including Allen, felt upon arriving in Philadelphia. Slavery might have been on the decline in Pennsylvania, but whites' negative racial attitudes remained entrenched. In fact, emancipation was less a single wave washing over the Quaker State and more an ebb and flow of tides slowly eradicating racial subjugation. For every step forward (the passage of a gradual abolition law), liberated blacks experienced several steps backward: discrimination in the workplace, inadequate public schooling (though free blacks paid equal taxes), and, most seriously for Allen, segregated church pews.

Allen believed that free blacks needed religious guidance to navigate through the rough waters of freedom in late-eighteenth-century Philadelphia. Religion, he argued fiercely, provided the moral discipline necessary to survive white prejudice. Christianity taught piety and compassion, not to mention industriousness and perseverance. Indeed, Allen believed that piety and industriousness went hand in hand—and both were tied to abolitionism's ultimate success. "To you who are favored with freedom," he sermonized, "let your conduct manifest your gratitude toward the compassionate masters who have set you free." Do not be perceived as "lazy and idle," Allen warned, for "the enemies of freedom plead it as a cause why we ought not to be free." Like other black itinerants of the gospel, Allen remained confident that those who followed the pious path of Afro-Christianity—by working hard, forgiving whites' transgressions, and praying daily—would achieve much in American (and Atlantic-world) culture.[16]

Allen's optimism was a vital quality during these years, and it is rather striking considering the small number of black congregants that he initially encountered at St. George's Church: there were five African Americans there when Allen arrived. As even the most naive Sunday-schooler knew, the original Apostles more than doubled that contingent! Black congregants were simply too few to build anything like a black church. According to Allen, black Philadelphians were "long forgotten" by white clerics. In response, he not only increased his preaching activities within the church but also sought out black communities south of Philadelphia's market center, where a vibrant community of former slaves was beginning to rise. He preached up to "five times a day"—in St. George's, on street corners, "wherever I could find an opening," as he put it. The eager Allen also created prayer meetings for black congregants. His incessant activity paid off. Within a year of coming to Philadelphia, he had built "a society of forty-two [black] members" at St. George's.[17]

By 1787, Allen's thoughts turned to finding "a place of worship for the colored people," or perhaps even building an independent "African church." He found a few allies but more skeptics. "Respectable" blacks resisted Allen's overtures about a separate church, possibly for fear of offending white leaders. For their part, white clerics adamantly opposed an autonomous black church. When Allen, Absalom Jones, William White, and Darius Grinnings raised the idea at St. George's, they were lectured and harangued by white leaders who "used very degrading and insulting language to us," as Allen vividly remembered.[18]

From 1787 through 1792, Allen bided his time by further building a black niche within St. George's. He also led "meetings of exhortation" beyond church walls—ecstatic, emotional minirevivals reminiscent of circuit preaching. White elders viewed this rising black presence "as a nuisance," in Allen's words.[19] White derision was a backhanded compliment to a gifted black organizer, for few could deny Allen's key role in attracting more blacks—and thereby, more congregants—to St. George's. In fact, St. George's overall membership grew while Allen was there, and church elders soon planned a second story to accommodate the swelling numbers. Construction of a new wing was funded, in part, by monies collected from Allen's adherents.

Meanwhile, white elders began to circumscribe Allen's activity: he was forbidden to exhort in an ecstatic manner and instructed to give services in a sober, deferential, quiet way. On the surface, Allen complied. In his mind, though, he let the dream of an African church take flight. Just imagine an independent black church not beholden to white officials! "The Lord is with us," Allen told his brethren about the future of this gleaming, autonomous church. "If it was His will, the work would go on." Perhaps someday very soon, black Philadelphians would build their own house of the Lord.[20]

Although he only whispered about it, Allen had planted the idea of an African church in 1787. In that year, Allen and seven other men turned to a related concern: creating a black mutual-aid society. Characterized as a quasi-religious but nondenominational organization from its very inception in April 1787, the Free African Society (FAS) expanded Allen's vision beyond religion.[21] Just as he came to see blacks as an underserved (and often despised) minority within Philadelphia's religious landscape, so too did Allen view them as socially bereft. In a racially prejudiced society, he wondered, where could free blacks turn for financial or educational support? Not to former masters, or to the city council, or even to white abolitionists who scrutinized all loan requests with great rigor. In a time when Philadelphia was turning into a free black capital, mutual aid among blacks assumed particular significance.

The Free African Society was dedicated to community action "without regard to religious tenets," as the group's preamble put it. "We, the Free Africans of the city of Philadelphia and their descendants," the founding document continued, "do unanimously agree for the benefit of each other to advance one shilling . . . monthly . . . to hand forth to the needy of this society." Members would "support one another in sickness, and for the benefit of their widows and fatherless children," provided they live "an orderly and sober life."[22]

Beyond providing financial support to member families, the FAS epitomized black independence in the post-Revolutionary period. Blacks would be known as self-sufficient and prudent, black leaders proclaimed. This was a particularly important statement for Allen and his brethren to make, for a majority of the Free African Society's eight founding members had once been enslaved. Yet the word "slave" never appeared in the Society's early records. These men did not wish to be known as "former slaves," a term that set them apart from the rest of society, but as "free Africans." White abolitionists hailed the organization's self-help initiatives. The Free African Society became a model institution, not just for Afro-Philadelphians but for black communities around the country.[23]

Indeed, although the FAS formed out of the friendship between "Absalom Jones and Richard Allen, two men of the African race, who . . . have obtained a good report among men,"[24] it owed as much to a strong sense of communalism among Afro-Philadelphians. One of the most important social characteristics of African society, communalism served as the foundation for free black culture in early national America. Connections between past and present, between African heritage and American realities, remained omnipresent to black founders like Allen. Nearly every major free black institution created in the urban North following the American Revolution had the word "African" affixed to it, from Masonic lodges to educational groups to benevolent societies. Even though a decreasing number of Northern African Americans had direct contact with African culture by the closing decades of the eighteenth century, emerging black leaders desperately wanted to link their collective uplift to a glorious African past. "The Communal ethic of mutual responsibility that was part of blacks' African heritage," James Horton and Lois Horton observe, "made such cooperative organization a cultural imperative." When combined with the fact that "most white communities denied blacks access to public graveyards," or education, or any number of civic opportunities, communalism became absolutely critical to free blacks.[25]

Yet there is also a distinctly modern political tone in the group's formation. For the Free African Society was not merely a benevolent communal organization but a lobbying group. Created at a moment of political ferment in American society, and taking shape against the backdrop of "nationalist" movements in Western culture, the FAS offers one of the first examples of the idea that free blacks were a nation within a nation. Though diverse, one of the hallmarks of black nationalist thought, according to political scientist Michael Dawson, is the "time-tested skepticism in black communities that, when it comes to race, America will live up to its liberal values."[26] In this sense, the FAS exemplified nationalist as well as Africanist sentiments. In 1790, for example, the group petitioned city leaders for a plot of land in the common cemetery, or Potter's Field. Located southwest of present-day Independence Hall, the African burial ground, as it became known, served as a key

site of black communal gatherings and mourning rituals for the following several decades. The lesson for Allen and his brethren was that
black organization and politicking got results.

Black leaders in other cities formed similar benevolent organizations
by the close of the eighteenth century. The FAS corresponded with
groups in Boston and Newport, helping to establish the first national
dialogue among free black leaders. As the FAS discovered, free blacks
were not a monolithic entity. In the fall of 1789, for example, the Newport Free African Union Society in Rhode Island pledged to support African emigration schemes as a means of repudiating American racism.
The FAS countered that peaceable protest *within* America would work
better than physical departure. Still, the FAS did not lecture Newport
blacks about the folly of their ways. They agreed to disagree.[27]

Despite the FAS's importance, it could not hold Allen's interest. By
mid-1789, he had formally departed the group, though evidence indicates that Allen still worked with FAS members on key black initiatives
in Philadelphia. Indeed, that Allen spent so little time recounting the
successes and failures of the FAS in his autobiography signifies his own
devotion to forming a black church. Evidence of Allen's differences with
the FAS came in the form of disciplinary action: the FAS accused him of
trying to "sow division among us" by politicking for a black church.[28]
Allen had attended the group's monthly meetings and given money to
the benevolence fund as prescribed by FAS policy. But he also attempted
to hold separate religious meetings with an eye toward forming a black
Methodist church. Allen's compatriots then learned of his legendary
will, for any attempts to reason with him failed. He would not adhere
to the FAS's nonsectarian doctrine if it interfered with his attempts to
build black Methodism. And so, Allen stopped attending FAS monthly
meetings after November 1788. By June 1789, the FAS had actually
ejected him from the organization.[29]

Allen's departure from the FAS did not lessen his sense of accomplishment. Every day blacks seemed less dependent on white good will
and more confident about voicing their opposition to white prejudice.
Indeed, Allen himself was emboldened, particularly about building a
free black church. Between 1790 and 1792, he helped raise money for
an African church from black as well as white figures. Allen recalled
that he and Absalom Jones raised $360 in one day alone, "the great-
est day's collection that we [ever] met with!"[30] Although the young
preacher gave no date, historians estimate that it must have been some-

time in 1791. For in the summer of that year, roughly a dozen black men—including both Allen and Jones—met with Benjamin Rush to craft an "Articles of Faith" for the black church. While Jones led a group of black men who addressed wealthy and well-placed white leaders about larger donations to a future African church (none other than George Washington donated money to the cause),[31] Allen negotiated for church land in south Philadelphia.[32]

Talk, hope, endorsements, even money—despite all this, at the start of 1792, black Philadelphians still had no church of their own, nor had they separated from white denominations like St. George's, which increasingly sought to put "uppity" blacks in their segregated place. What would have to be done to make the African church a reality? Allen was done waiting for answers.

4. *Head Up, Eyes Open, Fist Clenched*

When one sits down to write Allen's life, a single event stands above all others: the founding of the African Methodist Episcopal (AME) Church. Allen certainly thought so, highlighting the AME's establishment as his most cherished accomplishment.[33] Many others have agreed. The distinguished scholar of black religion Albert Raboteau has called the AME "the most important denomination and arguably the most important African-American institution for most of the nineteenth century."[34] Beyond America, the AME has served as a model for black independence movements. When in the 1890s "black Christians in Pretoria, South Africa withdrew from the [white] Wesleyan Methodist Missionary Society," James Campbell writes in his international history of the AME, they joined forces with "the oldest and largest church in black America," the very one founded by Allen a century before.[35]

The signal event of Allen's life also featured one of the great moments of African American reform: black exodus from a segregated white church.[36] One of the first "back of the bus" moments, blacks' departure from St. George's served as an early version of Rosa Parks sitting down on a Montgomery bus in 1955 and standing up to racial injustice. The story began sometime in the early 1790s, when Allen and other black members learned that they could not sit in their normal pews. Rather than comply with what the historian Carol George has called "segregated sabbaths," they bolted.[37] "Here was the beginning and rise of the first African church in America," Allen himself wrote of the walkout.[38] The incident served as a biblical parable. The Reverend Henry McNeil Turner even called it a march to the Promised Land.

Allen's retelling of the incident has become legendary. "A number of us usually attended St. George's church," Allen wrote in both the AME *Doctrines and Discipline* (1817) and his autobiography (1833), "and when the colored people began to get numerous in attending the church, they moved us from the seats we usually sat on, and placed us around the wall." It got worse: blacks were informed one Sunday morning that they must sit in a segregated balcony. Because services had already begun, Allen claimed that blacks misunderstood the hastily given directive and went to the seats on the main floor, "not knowing any better." "Just as we got to the seats," Allen continued, "the elder said 'let us pray.'" Kneeling as they had done countless times before, black parishioners thought only about the Word of the Lord. But, Allen explained, this morning's prayers were drowned out by "considerable scuffling and low talking." Lifting his head, Allen's eyes focused not on the throne of grace at the head of the church but on an unbelievable sight just a few feet away: white trustees "having hold of the Rev. Absalom Jones, pulling him off of his knees, and saying, 'you must get up—you must not kneel here.'" An incredulous Jones admonished the man to "wait until prayer is over."[39]

The commotion intensified. "No," the white official insisted, his hands still clutching Absalom Jones's shoulders, "you must get up now or I will call for aid and force you away." "Wait until prayer is over," Jones pleaded, refusing to rise. "With that," Allen explained, white officials moved in, attempting to banish African Americans to the segregated balconies.[40]

They need not have bothered. According to Allen, "by this time prayer was over," and blacks "all went out of the church in a body." What must have been going through the minds of white ministers and parishioners as this phalanx of blacks marched en masse out of St. George's? "It raised a great excitement and inquiry among the citizens," Allen commented. But white responses mattered little to him. As far as he was concerned, black parishioners now saw that they would never be treated equally unless they formed their own congregation. In Allen's words, whites "were no more plagued with us in [their] church."[41]

If the walkout of St. George's and the subsequent founding of Mother Bethel Church remains Allen's canonical achievement, it is also the subject of a good deal of historical debate. Just when did blacks leave St. George's and form their own church? Earlier Allen scholars, such as Charles Wesley and Carol George, argued that blacks' exodus occurred in 1787, just as Richard Allen had originally claimed. More recently, historians have pushed the date forward to 1792–93, thanks in large part to the wonderful detective work of Milton Sernett of Syracuse University.[42] Sernett mined the records of St. George's for this era, discovering that a new (and therefore segregated) balcony was not even undertaken until 1792. Still, no one knows precisely when black and white parishioners squared off in the City of Brotherly Love. Indeed, one of the leading scholars on early black Philadelphia, Library Company archivist Phillip Lapsansky, wonders why Allen would misrepresent blacks' break from St. George's. It might well have happened in 1787, he claims. "Why would he lie?"[43]

Academic as it sounds, more than historical nitpicking is at stake here. On the one hand, a walkout date of 1787 would mean that racial segregation forced Richard Allen and his black brethren out of a white church before they ever had the chance to claim equality. Moreover, as William Douglass noted in the first full-scale history of independent black churches in 1862, the year 1787 has always had a magical resonance for Americans. Why wouldn't blacks want to claim that year as their own? Douglass saluted African Americans' departure from St. George's as a continuation of the revolutionary spirit that animated American independence. "The Revolutionary struggle," Douglass wrote in galloping prose, "in which was involved the great principles of human rights, was still fresh in the minds of all, from the least to the greatest"—from black leaders like Allen to white worthies like Washington. In short, Douglass believed in a 1787 exodus from the segregated church.[44]

On the other hand, a 1792–93 walkout from St. George's would mean that blacks had planned an independent church all along, with the final confrontation underscoring the predetermined need for black religious autonomy. Blacks did not wait for whites to segregate them, Gary Nash has written in support of this view; they acted boldly and self-assertively in the years leading up to the confrontation with whites to form their own church. The keys to this early black action, according to Nash, were "dignity, self-generated power," and "positive" identifications with an African past.[45]

So were black Philadelphians forced to form their own church after being treated unequally in 1787 or did they seek independence in 1792–93 because they wanted their own church? Beyond this chicken-and-egg question, though, an equally important question lurks: just what was Richard Allen's role in the black exodus? Did he premeditate a confrontation with whites, whenever it occurred? Although many scholars have toyed with this notion, few would answer with an unequivocal yes. There is, however, more than enough evidence to support the claim. To begin, Allen's conspiratorial role in leaving St. George's bears much resemblance to the episode in which he convinced his Delaware master to hear a guilt-producing sermon from Freeborn Garrettson—the same episode that eventually brought Allen his freedom. Recall that Allen basically tricked his master into attending that meeting. Far from demanding freedom, Allen worked behind the scenes to get the same result. He did not even give the fateful sermon that scared his master so. But he knew in advance what his master would do when he heard God calling slaveholders to account.

Likewise, in the St. George's walkout, Allen was no simple bystander. He had been aware of white complaints about blacks' intermingling in so-called white pews for some time. He may have *precipitated* a confrontation in which blacks would either, one, gain acceptance as equals or, two, see once and for all the necessity of an independent church. This was precisely the story passed on by a correspondent to a New York paper, the *Colored American,* in 1837. In an unheralded article entitled "The History of Churches and Ecclesiastical Organization among the People of Color," the unnamed writer described Allen fomenting a rebellion against racial exclusion. "The colored members of [St. George's] Church and congregation had up to that time occupied a seat in the principle floor with white people," he commented. This presumed equality soon gave way to resentment among whites. Didn't blacks know their place? Whites wanted black parishioners pressed against the wall in the back of the church or, even better, planted in the new balcony planned for the second floor. These antiblack "murmurings" predated the formal building of a "Negro pew" but reached a zenith when whites "determined to remove the people of color to the Gallery."[46]

In this version of events—which the correspondent interestingly dates to "1792 or 1793, I forget which"—Allen and black congregants are fully aware of plans to segregate them, not to mention the deeper anxieties over blacks sitting next to whites. Knowing full well that whites might rebuke them, Allen led his people into the main pews. When told to go to "blacks-only" seats in the balcony, Allen then triumphantly led his brethren out of the church. As the correspondent to the *Colored American* put it, despite "hearing of" the proposed seating arrangement, Allen and his congregants still "went into the gallery of their own mind." They sat intently, waiting for services to begin and, when they did, prayed devoutly. "Devotion" gave way to protocol, and blacks were asked to leave. Absalom Jones "begged that the colored people might remain unmolested till the close of services." The white officer only demanded Jones's removal more loudly.[47]

Then the key moment arrived. As soon as the "prayer ceased," the correspondent wrote, "the colored people," led by the wonderfully sure Richard Allen, "got up and left the Church." Fittingly, in the 1837 report, Allen is given the final words upon leaving segregated St. George's: "Said the Bishop—'We never entered it again!'"[48]

Allen's own description of events is much more famous than this one. But tellingly, for he often refrained from trumpeting his own accomplishments, Allen himself assumes a less central role in his own story. Events occur, and he is there to react. In the 1837 history of the incident, however, Allen essentially plots a confrontation with whites over unfair seating practices. The 1837 writer does not say so, but his tale might have been accented by hearing Allen in the confines of the AME Church, a space where Allen felt free to speak more plainly. "Heaven is free for all who worship in spirit and truth," Allen once said.[49] He might have added, as the 1837 correspondent implied, the Lord helps those who help themselves.

But just why would Allen need to work in so crafty a manner to push for a black church? As for his black brethren, Allen knew that some members of the community still hesitated to support an independent black church. True, blacks had held separate services in the Quakers' African School between 1788 and 1791; and by February 1792, black leaders had also negotiated for land dedicated to a future African church. But no structure had since been completed, and Allen surely felt that black Philadelphians needed a galvanizing event to spur independent action. Perhaps, he surmised, blacks moved carefully for fear of white retaliation. Even discussion about creating an independent black church worried some Quakers, traditional friends of black Philadelphians. Decades after blacks walked out of St. George's, Allen could still recall that until that very moment few African Americans felt as strongly as he did about completing an African church. But, as he so wonderfully put it, the walkout of segregated pews "filled" the black community "with fresh vigor to get a house erected to worship God in."[50] Here Allen could essentially say "I told you so" to Philadelphia blacks without actually having to say the words.

As for the white community, the exodus from St. George's provided cover to black actions. No sooner had Allen marched black parishioners out of the segregated church than he and other blacks renewed their efforts to gain white supporters. If he had departed St. George's before any serious conflict arose, then white authorities (friends of Benjamin Rush, say) would likely have refused to help him build a black church. But whites landed the first blow. Shrewd through and through, Allen realized that many white citizens, as he wrote, "were [now] ashamed of their conduct."[51] In other words, Allen's actions made blacks the injured party. And what a difference this made! When Allen, Jones, and others began soliciting white support in 1791, William White, head of Christ Church, derided the cause. He even hectored Benjamin Rush about it. The African church, he told Rush one morning on a Philadelphia Street, was the worst example yet of blacks' newfound sense of racial "pride."[52] But after the St. George's incident, Rush told white benefactor John Nicholson (who provided two thousand dollars in loans to Philadelphia blacks), "you will not—you *cannot* refuse their request for the sake of religion & Christianity."[53]

Seeing Allen as a stealth operator (the architect of blacks' exodus from St. George's Church) perhaps helps us understand why he never set the record straight about the official origination date of the black church. All journeys begin in the mind. Allen may have first envisioned a black church in 1787. After running into opposition from black as well as white figures, he searched for an event that would reinvigorate blacks, put whites on the defensive, and make Allen himself appear to be the visionary that he was. That final confrontation occurred later, sometime in 1792 or 1793. As far as Allen was concerned, though, that five-year period (from first thought until the final break from white Methodists) formed one great episode. In 1837, The *Colored American* put Allen's walkout more boldly in perspective: "By the character of this act, it is unnecessary to speak."[54] But the act did speak, about Allen's incredible head as well as his heart.

5. An African Church

Having left St. George's, black Philadelphians focused on building an African church. They had to stand firm against white backlash. As perhaps the key leader of the St. George's walkout, Allen would bear the brunt of Philadelphians' criticisms. While some whites felt shame over their treatment of black parishioners, others fumed at Allen's actions. When blacks "hired a storefront, and held worship by ourselves," Allen remembered, "we were pursued with threats of being disowned." When "we got subscription papers out to raise money to build the house of the Lord" and received financial and moral support from two distinguished white Philadelphians (one of whom, Benjamin Rush, was a signer of the Declaration of Independence), "the elder of the [Methodist] Church still pursued us." Why, he asked Allen, did black Philadelphians insist on building their own church? A stubborn Allen refused to yield on any point, infuriating the elder. "I have the charge given to me by the [Methodist] Conference," he sternly lectured Allen, "and unless you submit, I will read you publicly out of the Meeting!" "Show us where we have violated any law," the black preacher shot back, and "then we will submit."[55]

Submit! That was a keyword for both Allen and the elder, although each camp viewed the word from diametrically opposed perspectives. For many whites, blacks were supposed to submit to white wills beyond bondage. Slavery may have been a grievous wrong, but postemancipation whites still believed themselves to be "the dominant culture."[56] For black Philadelphians, race-based deference had seen its final days. Allen thus displayed black pride when he replied to a white elder attempting to put the young black preacher in his place. In leaving segregated St. George's and building a black church, Allen knew that no church doctrine had been breached—only the custom of racial exclusion. So when the elder threatened to read Allen "out" of the Methodist Conference, Allen retorted that "we should seek further redress." After all, he continued, "we were dragged off our knees in St. George's Church . . . and treated worse than heathens." After facing such humiliations in a so-called House of the Lord, Philadelphia blacks "were determined," as Allen put it to the elder, "to seek out for ourselves" a true house of worship. Then "you are not Methodists!" the elder bawled before departing in a huff.[57]

Any remaining doubts about the viability of an independent black church must have been quashed when the elder asked for a second meeting with African Methodists. Why would white officials call for another meeting unless they feared that blacks could, and now would, build their own church? This time the white cleric tried a softer appeal. "He told us that he wished us well," Allen observed, "that he was a friend to us." The elder appealed to blacks' sense of propriety, religious scruples, and deference. "He used many arguments to convince us that we were in the wrong in building a church," Allen wrote. Stop raising money for your own church, the elder told blacks, his tone rising; use your funds for the greater glory of St. George's.[58] The appeal went nowhere. African Methodists would not return to St. George's.

Once again, a meeting between the white elder and Allen turned confrontational. Allen now spoke from a position of strength. "If you deny us your name [as Methodists]," he sternly lectured the elder, "remember that 'you cannot seal up the Scriptures from us, and deny us a name in heaven.'" "We will disown you all," the elder yelled, once again leaving in anger. Allen was somewhat shaken. "This was a trial I never had to pass through before," he admitted. Still, he remained sure that Methodist leaders beyond St. George's (such as Francis Asbury) would "support us." And as Allen gathered his brethren, who focused not on "if" a black church could be completed but "when" the first services would be held, his confidence returned. "We met with great success," Allen commented with characteristic understatement.[59]

6. Two Churches

Sometime in March 1793, Richard Allen awoke before dawn, prayed to the Lord, and then prepared to dig the foundation of an African church. Recognizing all Allen had done, the elder Absalom Jones deferred to the younger Allen. "As I was the first proposer of the African church," Allen himself noted with a rare but evident sense of pride, "I put the first spade in the ground to dig a celler for [that church]. This was the first African church or meetinghouse that was erected in the United States of America."[60]

This was not, however, the foundation of Allen's Bethel Church. The ground cleared that day became St. Thomas's African Episcopal Church, located on Fifth between Walnut and Locust streets. Allen's African

Methodist Episcopal Church would rise just a few blocks away. Allen's sense of religious certitude led to the division of the two new churches. For the question that once occupied his mind at the Free African Society arose again: which denomination would the African church follow—Methodism or another sect, say, Episcopalianism? Allen said Methodism. His great friend Absalom Jones agreed, though many black parishioners refused to align themselves with Methodism after St. George's. Allen felt that Methodism transcended a segregated church. Methodists often embraced antislavery, affected no airs, and committed themselves fully to the Lord. Conversely, the Episcopal Church had a reputation as being ostentatious and concerned with adornments. For Allen, Methodism was the religion for "plain and simple" (even unlettered) people. "The reason that the Methodist is so successful in the awakening and conversion of the colored people," he explained, was the church's "plain doctrine." It had also been the denomination associated with his liberation. Allen refused to submit to the black majority's wishes.[61]

Allen formed the AME Church, while Jones accepted the offer to head St. Thomas's African Episcopal Church, which did not claim complete independence from the white Episcopal hierarchy. Allen's congregation took root on land he had originally purchased in 1791, thus giving Bethelites legitimate claim to holding "the oldest plot of land continuously owned by blacks" in Philadelphia: the lot at Sixth and Lombard streets. By the summer of 1794, a pack of mules had dragged to that site the physical edifice of what would become Richard Allen's spiritual home: a former blacksmith's shop he had converted into a church. Allen loved this idea of conversion: instead of a nonbelieving bondperson, he became a Christian convert; instead of a suffering slave, he became a successful free person of color; instead of a deferential black man, he become an independent citizen. As Dee Andrews nicely points out, Allen's belief in black uplift may have added fuel to the church-building fire, for he realized that white Methodists would never let black preachers rise in the church hierarchy. Trapped in a middling position, he decided that building an African Methodist church was his only true option.[62]

The church's official dedication occurred on July 29, 1794. White dignitaries, including Methodist bishop Francis Asbury, joined black congregants for the special occasion. Asbury had known Allen for a decade and was glad to give the opening sermon. "Our colored brethren," Asbury excitedly scribbled in his journal that night, "are to be governed by the doctrine and discipline of the Methodists."[63] The name "Bethel" came from a prayer offered by the Reverend John Dickins, another well-known white Methodist whom Allen had known for several years (Dickins officiated at Allen's first marriage).[64] Speaking from the Book of Genesis (28:19), Dickins told black parishioners that the AME Church would serve as a beacon for saving souls. "Amens" echoed throughout the tiny church.

Allen may have liked the name "Bethel" because of its allusion to spiritual destiny. "This is the gate of heaven / And Jacob rose up early in the morning, and took the stone that he had put for his pillows, and set it up for a pillar, and poured oil on the top of it / And he called the name of that place Beth-el" (Genesis 28:17–19). In this section of the biblical story of Genesis, according to a modern scholarly exegesis, the Lord "renews his promise to Jacob as previously he has given it to Abraham (13:14–17) and Isaac (26:1–5)": there is one true God who has anointed a chosen people on earth. Bethel, meaning "temple" in Hebrew, "marked the place where Jacob saw in a dream the gate of heaven and received a manifestation of God. Jacob's great strength, attested in his single-handed erection of this monolith, must have been legendary."[65] Perhaps Allen saw himself as a modern-day Jacob, a "pious, honest" man who carries forth biblical destinies of a chosen people.[66]

Within a year, Allen had attracted over one hundred congregants (at St. Thomas's, congregants initially numbered almost 250 before rising to over 400). By 1796, the savvy preacher sought to solidify the young congregation's future by securing a state incorporation for Bethel Church. On August 23, nine Bethel trustees signed the "Articles of Association of the African Methodist Episcopal Church, of the City of Philadelphia, in the Commonwealth of Pennsylvania."[67] On September 12, 1796, state officials granted corporate status to Bethel AME Church. Joining Allen were trustees John Morris, William Hogan, Peter Lux (each of whom could not sign his own name), Robert Green, Jupiter Gibson, William Jones, Jonathan Trusty, and Prince Pruine (all literate). Few of these men had achieved Allen's economic success, though Green and Trusty had risen above laboring ranks (the former was a waiter and property holder, the latter a mastersweep). While Absalom Jones's St. Thomas's African Episcopal Church attracted some of Afro-Philadelphia's wealthiest families, including black sailmaker and financier James Forten, Allen's AME appealed to a wider cross-section of folks (from day laborers to middling black merchants). By Allen's death in 1831, his AME Church had exploded in membership, claiming over three thousand parishioners in Philadelphia alone.

7. *Flora Allen and Sarah Allen*

Allen initially counted on forty congregants, a respectable number but barely enough to keep any fledgling church going. Bethelites persevered and then grew, not merely because of a daunting founding figure such as Allen. They also relied on an unheralded band of pious women. With an incident as famous as Allen's walkout from St. George's (including the memorable image of black men being pulled from the pews by white officials), it is easy to lose sight of black women's signal role as church builders. Allen's autobiography does not even mention women's exertions at Bethel.

But soon after Allen departed segregated St. George's, he was joined by perhaps as many as thirteen women whose names are buried deep in dusty church archives. The list includes Allen's first wife, Flora, as well as a young Methodist named Sarah Bass, who later became Allen's second wife (after Flora passed away).[68] Not much is known about these women, save that they usually joined Allen's new church as part of a family network (Esther Trusty, like Flora Allen, followed her husband, Jonathan, to Bethel, where they became longtime congregants). They remained at the church through lean times, filling the pews on Sunday mornings, raising money for church repairs, and spreading the word about the glories of Bethel Church.

The nature of black women's founding role is best illuminated by Flora Allen and Sarah Bass. Richard Allen was a most eligible bachelor by the early 1790s. Pushing into his thirties when he began building African Methodism brick by brick, he was financially secure. Many of his great compatriots were already married. Obviously, Allen's peripatetic nature and deep dedication to an independent black church posed problems for any would-be partner. A potential spouse would have to honor Allen's deepest religious commitments and passions as her own.

His first wife, Flora, was just such a person: a helpmate who assumed his innermost burdens as her own. A former slave who settled in the

City of Brotherly Love during the final decades of the eighteenth century, she attended class meetings run by black as well as white preachers. Selfless and dedicated to community uplift, she shared Allen's vision of creating a strong and independent free black church. Indeed, after they wed in October 1790, Flora aided Allen's leadership ascent not only by abiding her husband's commitment to African Methodism but also by establishing a respectable home.[69] For any public persona of this era—a rising black preacher no less than a white politician—there was just no underestimating the importance of having a respectable house for visitors, friends, and the community at large. Creating a virtuous domestic image was especially important for African American leaders, shadowed as they were by stereotypical images as beasts of burden. A stable house registered in the public mind with order and respectability. Before marrying, Allen's compatriot James Forten relied on his mother to keep a respectable home. So too did Absalom Jones's wife guard her husband's image in the public realm.

Flora Allen made sure that Richard Allen appeared to friends and foes alike as a settled and suitable black public man. Visiting white preachers duly took note. "I dined with my good black friend Richard Allen's wife," the Reverend George Cuthbert wrote in his diary in 1797, after a stopover at the Allen residence. "I believe if there is a Christian in Philadelphia this old black woman is one."[70] As Cuthbert's rather blunt prose suggests, he was a white minister dining with Allen and his wife, a quite radical thing to do in early national Philadelphia. Just think back to the incident a few years earlier at St. George's, when white parishioners refused to pray next to black congregants. Now here was a liberal-thinking minister breaking bread with a black founding family. Cuthbert's praise of Flora Allen's piety also conveyed her status as an emerging icon of black virtue. Outside the home, Flora Allen demonstrated her commitment to black church building by praying with her husband at class meetings and Sunday services, cosigning property deeds (indicating that she may have used her own laboring wages for church-building initiatives), and participating in benevolent activities in the black community.[71]

Sadly, on March 11, 1801, Flora Allen died after a nine-month illness. A death notice in *Poulson's Daily Advertiser* the following day indicated her significance to both her husband and a rising Bethel Church.[72] Nevertheless, when Richard Allen married Sarah Bass that same year, the legend of strong black women in the church continued.

"The life of Sarah [Allen]," Hallie Brown wrote in her instructional collection of stories of important black women, *Homespun Heroines* (1926), "is indissolubly linked with that of her husband." Like Flora, Sarah Allen was a helpmate and confidante. She too hosted guests, cosigned property deeds, and allowed Allen to serve as a distinguished black public man. "She grieved with him in sorrow and rejoiced with him in the day of his victory and success," Brown observed of Sarah Allen's continuing role as helpmate.[73]

Also like Flora, Sarah Bass had been a slave (she was born in Virginia in 1764) before attaining freedom and settling in Philadelphia. After attending services at St. George's (she sat in Methodist class meetings with her future husband), she became a founding congregant of Bethel Church. Her charitable work during the yellow-fever epidemic of 1793 impressed Richard Allen so much that he highlighted it in a subsequent pamphlet. "Sarah Bass," he observed, is "a coloured widow woman, [who] gave all the assistance she could, in several families, for which she did not receive any thing; and when any thing was offered her, she left it to the option of those she served."[74] After they wed, Sarah Allen became "a household word in the homes of African Methodism." To a growing legion of admirers, she represented black religiosity, virtue, and kindness. As a tribute to her caregiving role at Bethel Church, black Methodists soon took to calling her "Mother Allen."[75] "Her house was the resort of the brethren who labored in the ministry," AME bishop Daniel Payne stated. "Long will her motherly counsel be remembered."[76]

In both Flora and Sarah Allen, one sees the creation of the "black republican mother": the iconic black woman whose domestic-sphere work, religious piety, and self-sacrificing dedication to communal uplift symbolized early African American femininity.[77] Because blackness and hypersexuality were often intertwined in the eyes of many white citizens, the black republican mother was an idealized countertype—a paragon of black virtue. In one sense, the black republican mother functioned very much like her white counterparts. She was responsible for bringing dignity, piety, and moral culture to the home. Bishop Payne would later assert that black women must ever remain in the domestic sphere, for black uplift depended on the proliferation of virtuous black homes.[78]

But in Allen's time, the black republican mother also worked beyond the home for the greater good of black uplift. Church and community

"Early Days of African Methodism," in John H. W. Burley's "Bishops of the AME Church," 1876. Bethel Church's humble beginnings in a former blacksmith's shop known affectionately as "The Roughcast" are rendered in this image from 1876, the year that African Americans around the country pledged money to an Allen monument in Philadelphia. The preacher depicted here may represent Allen, though in 1816 (the date next to this figure) he was a bit older. (Courtesy of the Library Company of Philadelphia)

building demanded that black women pitch in where they could, either by garnering wages that underwrote church activities or by getting more directly involved in church politics (women helped safeguard Bethel Church during nineteenth-century confrontations with bullying white Methodist officials and rabble-rousing white rioters). Sarah Allen later collected rents from Allen family properties and, in a more daring role, aided fugitive slaves traveling through Philadelphia. "Thoroughly anti-slavery, [the Allens'] house was never shut against 'the friendless, the homeless, the penniless fugitives from the House of Bondage,'" Bishop Payne once commented.[79] Against the opposition of male church leaders, Sarah Allen even helped female preachers like Jarena Lee speak publicly in the black church.

In short, black founding women did not have the luxury of simply tending home. They worked alongside Richard Allen in any way they could. Without the selfless actions of Sarah and Flora Allen, not to mention countless other black women, Bethel Church may not have survived its rough beginnings.

8. Always Return Home

"Always return home," an African proverb declares. For the rest of his life, Richard Allen's true home remained Bethel Church. Although seemingly the result of a simple dispute over segregated seating at a white church, the formation of Allen's congregation represented a big leap forward in his reform ideology. To redeem African Americans, Allen realized that he would need more than his deep-felt Christian faith. He would need the memory of African communalism and the tools of modernity (in the form of political mobilization and even nationalist thinking) to build an institution capable of galvanizing and protecting free blacks for the duration of their freedom struggle. At this point in his life, Allen did not yet believe that black exodus—that black nationalism—required international migrations. Rather, he was confident that organizing free blacks as a nation within a nation, what we might think of as a nonviolent but confrontational lobbying group, could yield significant results in the American civic realm.

Failing that, Bethel would welcome oppressed blacks in an autonomous space free from white control. As Allen himself called out shortly before his death, "Bethel [was] surrounded by her foes, but not yet in despair."[80] Since that time—save for a short period when Bethel was being rebuilt—Allen's body has resided underneath his beloved Bethel home.

3

The Year of the Fever, Part 1

A (Deceptively) Simple Narrative
of the Black People

We have many unprovoked enemies, who begrudge us the liberty
we enjoy, and are glad to hear of any complaint against our color,
be it just or unjust; in consequence of which we are more earnestly
endeavoring all in our power to warn, rebuke and exhort our
African friends, to keep a conscience void of offense towards God
and man; and, at the same time, would not be backward to inter-
fere, when stigmas or oppression appear pointed at, or attempted
against them, unjustly; and we are confident, we shall stand
justified in the sight of the candid and judicious for such
conduct.

—Richard Allen and Absalom Jones, "A Narrative of the
Proceedings of the Black People"

In 1794, Richard Allen published his first pamphlet. A relatively short work, the document had a long and (for the time) standard
title: "A Narrative of the Proceedings of the Black People during the
Late Awful Calamity in Philadelphia, in the Year 1793; and a Refuta-
tion of Some Censures Thrown upon Them in Some Late Publications."
Beneath the pamphlet's baroque exterior, Allen and his coauthor, Absalom Jones, packed a powerful message: black leaders would protest racial stereotyping in print. Although white leaders had certainly glimpsed
black protest throughout the Revolutionary era—in freedom petitions
to state legislatures and protest marches in city streets—Allen and
Jones's document would be the first federally copyrighted essay by African American writers. For this reason, the legendary black historian
Charles Wesley once hailed Allen as "a pioneer Negro publicist."[1]

Allen and Jones's "Narrative" served several functions. First, it attacked racist accusations hurled by celebrated printer Mathew Carey, who labeled the black masses villainous during Philadelphia's devastating yellow-fever epidemic of 1793. Second, the document established Allen's leadership position well beyond local black and abolitionist communities. Third, it represented yet a further maturation of Allen's reform politics. Like other black leaders emerging in the age of democratic revolutions, Afro-Philadelphians relied increasingly on print to wage struggles against both slavery and racial injustice. Prince Hall, William Hamilton, Peter Williams, John Marrant, Olaudah Equiano—every one of these figures produced pamphlets of protest. More explicitly political than antebellum slave narratives (and less devoted to personal reminiscences), pamphlets nevertheless made African American voices a key part of trans-Atlantic abolitionism. Allen and Jones's literary production was a critical part of this movement.

In a more personal sense, Allen's literary turn provided a key outlet for his frustrations and aspirations. As he later recalled, friends often begged him "to leave a small detail of [his] life and proceedings," so that after he was "dead and in the grave" others could study the great preacher's life.[2] Well before publishing his autobiography, Allen met this demand by producing a steady stream of pamphlets. Beginning with the yellow-fever narrative, and its various addenda (including Allen's individually authored antislavery appeal), these documents formed a running, if episodic, commentary on early American society from a black man's perspective. From 1794 onward, nearly everything Allen did had an analog in print, from declaring Mother Bethel independent of white Methodists and eulogizing white antislavery figures to quelling an attempted secession movement at his church and supporting Canadian migration. Few of Allen's black abolitionist peers provided so consistent a printed trail to follow.

There was a final reason for Allen's increasing emphasis on print culture. Allen believed that print made visible black founders' moral critique of, and political claims on, the American republic. If white citizens could not hear his commanding words in Bethel Church, they must read them in pamphlets, newspaper articles, and broadsides. For Allen, printed protest created a potential bridge to white leaders and citizens. He would use that connection to claim equality and justice for all.

It all began with that first document.

1. Dreams to Remember

Allen's yellow-fever pamphlet focused on an issue he had already encountered at St. George's Church: racial prejudice. That was not the issue he had been thinking about months before the yellow-fever attack. During the summer of 1793, Philadelphia was in the midst of a mini golden age, and Richard Allen hoped to bask in the rays of economic prosperity shining all around him. With the financial and social disruptions of the Revolutionary War long gone, Philadelphia reassumed its place at the head of American economic and cultural life. A bustling port made it the new nation's wealthiest city, as ships from all over the world choked the Delaware River. Philadelphia was also the nation's largest city (New York City overtook it only in the 1820s). The federal government called the city home during the 1790s, and so locals grew familiar with the famous faces traipsing about. There is George Washington's carriage, they might matter-of-factly tell visitors. The Bank of North America, the American Philosophical Society, the Library Company (the nation's first lending library), and Charles Wilson Peale's brand-new museum of natural history were all situated in the City of Brotherly Love as well.[3]

Philadelphia was also a veritable urban stew. Although it has long had a reputation as a blueblood capital—composed of wealthy families of homogeneous background—during the 1790s it was a city "marked by remarkable ethnic and racial variety, swimming with natives from Northern Europe, Africa, the West Indies, and various parts of North America," in the words of historian Billy G. Smith. The decade saw smaller "waves of migrants" wash over Philadelphia, particularly French and German émigrés. Also prominent among 1790s newcomers were former slaves, some from the Pennsylvania countryside, some from southern locales, and some from the revolutionary island of Haiti.[4]

Big, bustling, and diverse, Philadelphia somehow remained compact. While the urban grid expanded both northward and southward, the city proper comprised a few dozen blocks. No great distance separated squalor from splendor. One of the most opulent estates of the day—William Bingham's magnificent home at Third and Spruce streets—sat just south of the main town square. Called "too rich for any man in this country," the estate was fronted by magnificent brick fences, and splendid formal gardens appeared in back.[5] Bingham's block also housed grocers, tailors, cabinetmakers, and other middling types. On some streets, commoners, transients, and day-laborers lived side by side with gentlemen, bankers, and politicians. Although this physical layout made visions of the poor easy to conjure, it also facilitated big dreams.

Richard Allen was a dreamer. From 1788 through 1791, he resided at 59 Dock Street (near present-day South 2nd Street), a diverse, crowded neighborhood.[6] A former inlet filled by colonial authorities, Dock Street looked like a paved-over river—crooked and winding. Dr. Benjamin Rush had other ideas about the neighborhood, calling it filthy. That fetid area, fed by slaughter pens, once let loose yellow fever in the 1760s. Why would anyone like it?

Allen probably rented his Dock Street property. But he was not content to stay there. By January 1791 Allen had purchased a house at 150 Spruce Street, a place he would call home for the rest of his life. Although the address suggested close proximity to the Delaware waterfront, Philadelphia's quirky numbering system put Allen's house at the edge of Philadelphia's growth. On the property deed, Allen's home was listed as "a tenement and lot . . . between fourth and fifth street."[7] Allen bought the house and land for 250 Pennsylvania pounds from a farmer named John Willson. By the mid-1790s, he was one of just seven blacks out of a street population of 110 people. Allen's neighbors on either side were white: shoemaker Daniel Kuhn on his right side (as Allen looked out of his front room) and scrivener Edward Lane on his left. Across the street lived Richard Butcher, a black laborer, and down the street lived two black grocers, two black mariners, and a black confectioner. Allen took in a boarder, a white laborer named Nicholas Fulkers.[8]

Because rigid racial segregation was not yet in vogue, Allen's living arrangements paralleled those of many other Afro-Philadelphians: he lived closely among whites. Absalom Jones, who lived a few blocks away from Allen at 165 South Third Street, could count only one other African American resident on his block (a fruitier several houses down). James Dexter, the former slave turned coachman and friend of both Allen and Jones who lived on the other side of town at 84 North Fifth Street, counted white neighbors as acquaintances.[9] Other than Welsh's Court, a very small all-black enclave several blocks from Allen's home, most Afro-Philadelphians lived in a majority-white environment.[10]

From his home, Allen could see Philadelphia's many strivers milling about, from tavern keepers, tailors, and carpenters to merchants, sea captains, and "gentlewomen." From the evidence of his land deals, Allen hoped to join the more successful of them. After purchasing his

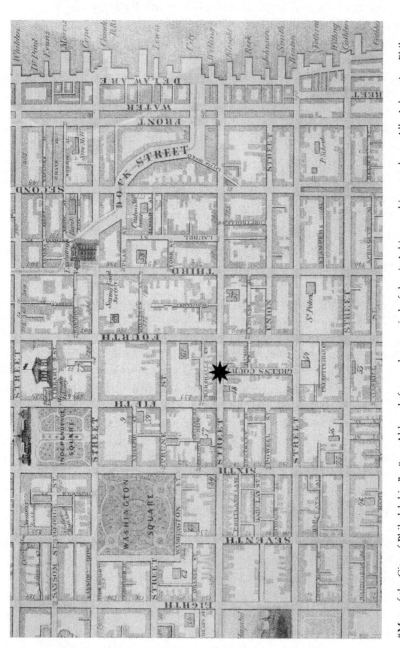

"Map of the City of Philadelphia," 1849. Although from a later period of the city's history, this map shows Allen's longtime Philadelphia home at 150 Spruce Street, indicated on the map with an asterisk. Note how close Allen lived to Independence Square (home of the Constitutional Convention of 1787 and the Liberty Bell), which served as the epicenter of the federal government—and the haunt of white founders like Washington, Jefferson, Hamilton, and Madison—between 1790 and 1800. (Courtesy of the Library Company of Philadelphia)

home, Allen called himself a trader, grocer, dry-goods dealer, and mastersweep before finally settling on the more respectable label of "minister" in the early nineteenth century. He was not just a black man hoping
to get by. Rather, like the city pulsating around him, he was a man of
driving ambition, a black man looking forward to—no, banking on—
upward mobility.

He already demonstrated a certain enterprising spirit when he led
blacks out of a segregated church and helped plan Bethel. Now in the
summer of 1793, Allen planned an enterprise that fit the spirit of the
times: a nail factory. What better way to build a thriving business than
by producing the very ligaments of the building trade! Allen had two
black partners: Absalom Jones and Caesar Whittington, a member of
St. Thomas's African Episcopal Church. Allen also took out a fifty-
pound loan from the whites-only Pennsylvania Abolition Society. The
note was payable in eighteen months. Whatever anger he may have felt
at white Philadelphians after his battle over segregated seating policies
at St. George's, Allen did not let it erase his sense of interracial potential. Wary though he might have been of white prejudice, Allen refused
to believe that white and black men could never live together, work
together, pray together—or secure money from one another. And so, together, black entrepreneurs and white reformers helped launch "Absalom Jones and Co." (it was natural to put the elder Jones's name on the
enterprise). A brave new world of black-white interaction seemed to
have arrived in Philadelphia.[11]

So confident was Allen in the venture that he put up his recently purchased home as collateral. What was a little short-term debt on the road
to economic success? The new business partners also agreed to take on
black apprentices to facilitate the business. Allen wrote to "a Mr. Townsend, of Baltimore (a white person) . . . to procure a large number of
colored boys, and send them to Philadelphia, in order that they might
be apprenticed to learn the art of manufacturing nails."[12] Once again a
master of young men, Allen provided housing, food, and freedom dues
to his charges. This meant more outlays of capital in the near future.
Clearly, he was not a man to doubt himself.

Approaching white abolitionists for a major loan was itself a display
of self-confidence. Allen knew he would have to make a good case, for
white reformers remained scrupulous businessmen. They also put African Americans under intense inspection. When PASers visited African
American families, they noted "with pleasure" how free blacks lived,

acted, worked, and prayed (or not). Nothing brought abolitionist approbation more quickly than men and women who worked "industriously" or conducted their affairs "in an orderly fashion."[13] Furthermore, fifty dollars was a lot of money to white reformers, who could use those funds to hire a black schoolteacher (which the group did in 1793 for less than Allen's loan) or buy a new school property for the growing number of black pupils in their care.[14] Allen had to be worthy.

It says a lot about the black preacher's winning ways that the PAS approved the loan. On July 6, 1793, the group called a special meeting to officially consider Allen's (and Jones's) loan request. Abolitionists thought this "a subject of importance," and they dutifully appointed a select committee to examine the matter. Four men were charged with surveying "the expenses [abolitionists] shall incur, [and] also the sufficiency of the proposed security[,] as well as the probability of being repaid the money at the time mentioned." Four days later, on July 10, the committee provided an answer: Allen was golden. "The security offered by Richard Allen," the committee told a special meeting of the PAS, "appeared to be amply sufficient." By the end of July, the fifty pounds had been "loaned as directed," with "a bond warranted . . . from Richard Allen."[15]

Thus, as another sweltering Philadelphia summer plodded on, Allen, Jones, and Co. prepared to launch their nail factory. With prayers to the almighty, and a nod to abolitionist money lenders, Allen dreamed about a great future. The business appeared to get off on the right foot too. In September, an abolitionist committee reported that "Jones & Co." was "likely to prove useful" to the black community. Indeed, abolitionists' only surprise came when Allen did not approach them for "interference and assistance"—that is, business advice—"as might have been expected."[16]

Didn't abolitionists know that Richard Allen's predictions of success, like his collateral, were "amply sufficient"?

2. The Dreaded Fever

It all came to the proverbial crashing halt when an epidemic hit town. The late summer of 1793 found Allen's Philadelphia gripped by perhaps the worst yellow-fever outbreak ever. Citizens fled the sickened metropolis, infected homes were barricaded, and city fathers worried that the

City of Brotherly Love would disintegrate amid death, disease, and distrust. By mid-September, one man observed, "terror now became universal."[17] As ever more citizens died or departed Philadelphia, the city seemed to deflate. Anxious officials up and down the Atlantic seaboard worried at the very mention of the city's name. "I have a patient in the Yellow Fever from your city," a doctor in Baltimore wrote to friends in Philadelphia. "He arrived here yesterday . . . [and] is as yellow as saffron."[18] Baltimore actually banned Philadelphians unless they could prove they had been out of the fever's vicinity for seven days. Virginia quarantined Philadelphia ships. New York sent five hundred dollars to the Quaker City, hoping to save America's "seat of empire" from this "pestilential disease."[19] Perhaps the most alarming sign: the usually punctual Pennsylvania Abolition Society stopped meeting for over two months!

From the moment it began, the yellow-fever epidemic was a public-health crisis. Thousands of citizens fled, hospitals became overwhelmed, and dead bodies rotted in homes. Thomas Jefferson, always itching to return to his beloved Monticello, wasted little time in leaving the temporary federal capital in mid-September. Though he had resided on the less densely packed Schuylkill River side of town, he kept abreast of the fever's relentless progress. Philadelphia was in the grip of this "nondescript disease," Jefferson informed James Madison, and neither physicians nor healers could conceive a cure.[20]

Among the infected was Allen himself, who came down with the fever in late September. He was admitted to Bush Hill, a former mansion turned hospital northwest of Philadelphia that was commandeered by city fathers after its owner did not return from Europe.[21] Here he stayed from September 29 until November 20. Allen was lucky to survive. His Spruce Street neighborhood was devastated by the disease, with fifty-five residents dead by the end of the year (out of 708 people), while over 250 fled their homes. Of the 117 houses on Spruce Street, nearly half (54) were shuttered and empty. Black residents were particularly vulnerable because they did not have the money or means to leave the infected area. Forty percent of white Spruce Street residents left, as opposed to only 15 percent of black residents.[22]

Part of the problem was diagnosis.[23] Eighteenth-century doctors had not yet determined yellow fever's cause (the disease is spread by mosquitoes). Most people believed that it spread via miasmas, or polluted fogs. Thus, one fought yellow fever by clearing the air. One of the best, if unintended, remedies was a cigar or pipe—the smoke chased away infected mosquitoes.

Allen vividly remembered the dreaded disease taking over his body. Headaches, chills, and sharp pains in the chest were often followed by an upset stomach. Was this a garden-variety cold or flu? Not if it morphed into raging fevers and yellowish complexions. When these more serious symptoms occurred, Allen reported, hysteria and even lunacy might follow. "Some [patients] lost their reason and raged with the fury madness could produce," he recalled.[24] If they did not go mad, yellow-fever victims might experience a painful and often lonely death. Even if one survived, the fever took a toll, what with prescriptions of bleeding, "evacuating the bowels," and drugs like laudanum administered regularly to survivors. In Philadelphia, America's medical capital, doctors like Benjamin Rush were overwhelmed with patients pleading for the latest cure science could muster. Every day brought dozens of new cases. The situation seemed hopeless.[25]

Ironically, international trade—Philadelphia's lifeline—had brought the sickness in the first place. A ship from the West Indies docked in the Delaware River let loose mosquitoes with the deadly germ. For years afterward, alarm bells rang when overstuffed ships loomed on Philadelphia's wharves. In August 1794, a ship from New Orleans came up the Delaware River with "Putrid Hides," which, many Philadelphians believed, might cause another outbreak. The *Philadelphia Gazette* urged readers to be vigilant. Not just this vessel but every ship arriving in port should undergo "the most precise examination." It was a "duty we owe to humanity."[26]

The final numbers of the 1793 epidemic were grisly. Historians estimate that four thousand to five thousand people perished, among them roughly four hundred African Americans.[27] That figure would be disturbing enough in the twenty-first century; in Richard Allen's time, the number of the dead amounted to a large town or small city. It was a catastrophe of the first order. And yet the death toll was only part of the story. The epidemic challenged the very foundations of American virtue and citizenship. Philadelphia, the nation's leading city and its governmental center, seemed to be falling apart. One symptom of civic malaise: every one of Philadelphia's newspapers shut down, save Andrew Brown's *Federal Gazette*. "The present crisis," the paper pleaded, "is a period of difficulty and distress in this metropolis." Citizens must remain not only calm, Brown continued, but virtuous. Because his Federalist-backed newspaper remained the only journal in operation, Brown told Philadelphians that the *Gazette* would become a nonpartisan clearinghouse of information. "The means to communicate information," he told readers, "especially with regard to the prevailing disorder, is of great importance." Brown would not let his city down.[28]

Brown underscored the moral obligations of the citizenry at large in a story from nearby New Jersey. Writing to a friend in Philadelphia, a Trenton commentator told the sad tale of a local man "cruelly starved" by friends and family because he might have contracted yellow fever—*might have*. This story "arouses all our indignation and feeling against men so devoid of principle and humanity," the New Jersey man stated. "And yet, of such men our own state . . . contains too many."[29] And what of Philadelphia, the fabled City of Brotherly Love now in the death grip of yellow fever? Were its citizens worthy or licentious? "Remember the Golden Rule," the *Gazette* informed readers. As a correspondent added, Philadelphians should "visit the abodes of wretchedness, to enter into the feelings of the unfortunate, to sympathize with their sorrows and relieve their distresses." These actions, the writer commented, "are truly elevating and ennobling" and they put do-gooders "above the rest of mankind."[30]

Alexander Hamilton agreed. While other members of Washington's famed first cabinet had escaped Philadelphia, Hamilton contracted yellow fever. Under the personal care of a doctor, Hamilton recovered. While doing so, this white founding figure watched Philadelphia nearly crumble. In September, he wrote to the *Gazette* from his convalescent home at Spruce Street and Third, only a few blocks from Richard Allen's house. The present epidemic demanded benevolent attitudes and moral action, he argued. If the people devolved into anarchy and hysteria, then the republic could not survive.[31]

Out of this catastrophe came a single ray of hope, at least according to Benjamin Rush, the famed physician and signer of the Declaration of Independence. Rush mistakenly believed that blacks had an immunity to the cursed fever. After all, he ventured, no black Philadelphian had contracted the disease by early September. So he wrote to Allen, asking blacks to serve as nurses to the sick and dying. "My dear friend," he petitioned,

> It has pleased god to visit the city with a malignant & contagious fever, which infects white people of all ranks, but passes by persons of your

color. I have therefore taken the liberty of suggesting to you whether this important exemption which God has granted to you from a dangerous & fatal disorder does not lay you under an obligation to offer your services to attend the sick who are aff[licted] with this malady. Such an act in your society will [crossed out: render you acceptable to] be very grateful to the citizens, and I hope pleasing in the light of that god who will see every act of kindness done to creatures whom he calls his brethren, as if done to himself.[32]

The Lord Almighty, Rush thought, had created public sickness so that black Philadelphians might leap over racial hurdles and convince white Americans to support abolitionism. Never mind that his reasoning rested on faulty assumptions and racial stereotypes. Rush knew he was right.

Time proved Rush wrong, of course. Blacks died in roughly the same proportion as whites. The fever merely took a bit longer to be diagnosed in the black community. Yet Allen and Jones listened to Rush. "Early in September [1793]," they later wrote, "a solicitation appeared . . . to the people of colour to come forward and assist the distressed, perishing and neglected sick." Black leaders met this civic challenge, they observed, "sensible that it was our duty to do all the good we could to our suffering fellow mortals."[33]

Just why did black leaders act? It is certainly true, as scholars have often pointed out, that Rush pushed the right buttons. He personally informed Allen and Jones that God had intervened on blacks' behalf. He also prodded the black community by issuing an anonymous public challenge in the paper: blacks must aid whites because whites had long supported blacks through abolitionism.

But Allen and Jones also believed that black aid to white citizens would help the cause of racial justice. Aiding infirm whites would prove black civic-mindedness and even enhance abolitionism in the nation's capital city. Indeed, Allen and Jones played up black civic virtue when they recounted African American responses to the yellow fever, leaving out Benjamin Rush's personal appeal.

Allen and Jones acted for another reason. They hoped yellow-fever benevolence would mend fences with members of the white community still upset over the St. George's walkout. Allen and Jones had already relied on white figures for financial support of their autonomous black churches (Rush had helped secure money for them). And the black duo had also utilized the PAS for a start-up loan. They might not be in business but for white reformers! Finally, the black community relied on white reformers for legal aid to runaways and kidnapping victims. The PAS made its abolitionist reputation by doing legal scutwork for blacks: visiting local jails to see if free blacks had been kidnapped or if fugitive slaves needed advice, checking ships on the docks to make sure slaves were imported legally, providing legal representation to blacks bargaining with masters over an indenture agreement or manumission document.

No emigrationist at this time, Richard Allen cast his lot with Philadelphia, a majority-white community where he would marry, raise a family, work, and probably die. The white community was in need of help. The yellow fever offered blacks a chance to aid the ailing city and, perhaps too, redeem African Americans in the public eye. "Our services" during the fever, Allen and Jones told the public, "were the production of real sensibility."[34]

In this sense, Allen and Jones acted as fellow citizens who not only felt a certain pull in Rush's appeals but who also understood public discourse about a virtuous citizenry. Clearly, they read Brown's and Hamilton's appeals to civic virtue in the *Gazette*. Just as clearly, they hoped that white Philadelphians would, in turn, work for black justice. In early September, Mayor Thomas Clarkson thankfully informed the public of African American leaders' benevolent actions. "It is with peculiar satisfaction," he stated, "that the African society . . . touched with distress have voluntarily undertaken to be nurses to attend to the afflicted."[35] Together, black and white leaders attempted to solve a public-health crisis and maintain civic order.

From September through November, when the fever finally subsided, black leaders marshaled a dynamic force of black aid workers, including women (though Allen was incapacitated for much of October and November, friends kept him updated on black benevolent work). The contingent included Allen's older brother, John, who remained in Philadelphia during the 1790s. Though not as famous as his sibling, John Allen was a committed Methodist who became a trustee of Bethel Church. He also served as a valued part of Richard Allen's inner circle, particularly during the yellow-fever crisis. With his brother in the hospital, fate unknown, John Allen worked as a nurse and laborer, perhaps bringing in funds for the Allen family.[36]

Walking the gloomy streets of Philadelphia, black aid workers visited hundreds of yellow-fever victims and their families. A writer in Boston, hearing of Allen and Jones's civic benevolence, scribbled a celebratory poem in their honor. "Brethren of Man and friends of fairer clay!" it went, "God Almighty would ever recall Your Godlike Zeal in Death and triumphant day."[37] Allen, Jones, and their assistants visited roughly twenty families per day (that is, when Allen himself was not in the hospital). The first case that the black duo attended to was a dying husband and wife whose two children remained uninfected. Allen's team nursed the man to health but saw to it that his deceased wife received a proper burial. Such fearful sights weighed heavily on them, Allen and Jones recalled, but prayer "strengthened us." Another belief kept them going: that blacks were being "as useful as possible" to whites, and not as slaves or servants but as fellow citizens.[38]

Black aid workers did jobs that white citizens could or would not do. "It was very uncommon," Allen and Jones remembered, "to find anyone that would go near, much more handle, a sick or dead person."[39] They not only attended to the sick but also carried out the dead and served as gravediggers (burying not just bodies but infected beds, linens, and clothes as well). As leaders of the black community, Allen, Jones, and William Gray coordinated benevolent work, hiring laborers and reporting to city officials on a day-to-day basis. Though his church was not officially operating yet (that would occur in the summer of 1794), Allen probably made announcements about benevolent work to congregants who had followed him out of St. George's and still met with the black preacher regularly. If Allen and Jones did as much benevolent work as they claim, other black congregants must have been involved too.

Allen and Jones portrayed their nursing chores as highly intimate and even physical activities. Illness shattered walls between blacks and whites. "Perhaps it may be acceptable to the reader," they offered, "to know how we found the sick," for "our opportunities of hearing and seeing them have been very great." Called to private homes, black medical aides cautiously entered doorways that had been shuttered tight to keep infected people isolated. They found patients in various states of illness. Sometimes, when a victim was literally mad with the fever, he or she would flail violently or attempt to "runaway"—which meant that black nurses had to grab a hold of the patient (sometimes two nurses were required to hold back a single person). Some nurses reported finding victims sprawled on the floor, screaming in agony, and covered in blood. Whatever happened, black nurses were often the ones to deal with it. And they often attended to the sick and dying for days at a time.

In this manner, Allen and Jones engaged in blatantly physical contact with ill patients, bleeding them, feeding them, sometimes even restraining them physically. When Benjamin Rush deputized Allen and Jones to initiate his bleeding remedies on whites (Rush was too busy to deal with every case), he reported that they visited hundreds of families. Allen and Jones put the number at roughly eight hundred. Treatment might begin by gently touching white bodies to calm or soothe scared patients. If they resisted, however, clutching or grabbing was called for simply to restrain these potential madcaps.

Then came what must have been an intense moment, one filled with anxiety, dread, and a number of complex emotions for black nurses as well as white patients: the bleeding procedure itself. Imagine Richard Allen sitting beside a deathly ill white man or woman, close enough for both parties to smell each other's breath, look deep into each other's eyes, and sense fear. Allen helps the patient expose an area of skin just beneath the shoulder; he pulls out a sharp instrument with one hand while steadying the patient's arm with his other hand. An incision is made, and blood begins to pour out. White family members may stand around Allen, nervously wondering if he knows what he is doing. Or no one may be there, save Allen and his patient, a black man holding the hand and the life of a white man (or woman?) in his own. Death has no mercy, an old song says. People had to confront their racial fears to survive, even if that meant letting free black men cut into their skin to (allegedly) bleed away the cursed disease raging through their bodies.

Beyond these physical procedures, African Americans were de facto medical examiners and notaries, telling city authorities about each day's run of dead and ill patients. For a brief period of time, black Philadelphians seemed to have real power over white citizens' lives. In one moving case, Allen and Jones reported that a man called on them to prepare for his death. The calm gentleman laid on the ground while his two black nurses took measurements for a coffin. The dying man then instructed Allen and Jones "to superintend his funeral," which they did. "Truly our task was hard," they commented. Some white authorities agreed. According to Philadelphia's mayor, black nurses and laborers attended to their "hard" public chores with mercy and rigor. They were saviors.[40]

3. Racial Vectors

The yellow fever was many things: a public-health crisis, business buster, test of civic mindedness, and proving ground of medical theories (Benjamin Rush's remedy of bleeding and "evacuating the bowels" was said to be nearly as bad as yellow fever itself). It also became a vector of racial fears. Indeed, as the fever got worse, and blacks became even more indispensable, racial fears escalated. If things were stolen from a home, for example, many white citizens blamed blacks. Some whites also felt that black nurses were price gouging.

Allen and Jones were incredulous. "We feel ourselves sensibly aggrieved by the censorious epithets of many, who did not render the least assistance in the time of necessity," they blasted after the fever had subsided and racial accusations spiked. Before most of the newspapers closed down briefly, many of them skewed racial perceptions by reporting only white deaths. "Even to this day," the black duo fumed in 1794, it is "generally received opinion in this city, that our color was not so liable to the sickness as the whites."[41]

Many whites feared that African Americans would literally overrun a hollowed-out Philadelphia. White flight magnified blacks' civic role and presence to something rare in Northern locales: a black presence approaching a quarter of the population. Of Philadelphia's pre-epidemic population of roughly fifty thousand persons, perhaps half fled the city before November, most if not all white citizens. Another five thousand people perished during that time, again mostly white citizens in raw numerical terms. The City of Brotherly Love was reduced to a population of around twenty thousand. African Americans had totaled five thousand persons, or just over 10 percent of the city's original population. All of a sudden, the black population seemed to double, an effect magnified by black runaways hiding out in Philadelphia. No Northern state had more than 15 percent of its population composed of either enslaved persons or free blacks. Only New York City surpassed a 20 percent black population. Thus, Philadelphia's racial composition momentarily approached, if it did not entirely equal, that of Chesapeake locales—the slave South—with their much heavier concentrations of African Americans (30 to 60 percent of the population in many places, the majority of whom were enslaved).[42]

Philadelphians reacted by releasing some of their innermost racial fears. Recall that in many white Philadelphians' lifetime slavery had been the normal lot of the black populace. And slavery remained technically legal in Pennsylvania in the 1790s, gradual abolition schemes working slowly but surely (but slowly) to drain slavery from the Quaker State. Indeed, one sad irony of the yellow-fever epidemic was that an immediate emancipation bill brought before the Pennsylvania legislature was not passed because the statehouse recessed to deal with the disease. For many whites, the very mention of the word "black" still conveyed something different and unequal. Andrew Brown's *Federal Gazette* relayed an alleged discussion between two New Jersey farmers visiting Philadelphia that perfectly captured white citizens' racial fears. Having come to the infected city to sell their precious goods at inflated prices, the men eventually notice the sizable black presence.

> *Farmer 1*: Did you learn any news [of the epidemic]?
> *Farmer 2*: The best of news, and that from the Negroes, for they only come to market now! They told me 14,200 have already died—2900 have gone out of town—so that only 1425 people remain!
> *Farmer 1*: Why George, your account is indeed a *black one*![43]

Appreciative though many white citizens were, many others proved outright hostile to black civic action. Reports of rude behavior and even violence against black pallbearers accumulated. White citizens' complaints had an undeniable economic edge. Despite the fact that relatively few white citizens dared expose themselves to yellow-fever victims, some wondered why black nurses and laborers received equal wages. Interestingly, Allen and Jones did not initially charge money for their services (the city reimbursed tradesmen, including some blacks, who aided sick people). They asked for money only when nursing tasks became financially draining. Nevertheless, like other blacks, they could become targets of white rage.[44]

Mayor Thomas Clarkson may have provided unwitting fuel to the fire in a public missive designed to protect black nurses and pallbearers. "The persons who are employed to remove the dead," Clarkson nobly told Philadelphia citizens in September 1793, "have been frequently interrupted, insulted and threatened whilst performing their business by persons who appeared to possess no sentiment of humanity."[45]

Persons? The locution is interesting: Clarkson directed his words at Philadelphia "citizens," but his message implied that African Americans claimed no such status. Blacks were "the persons who are employed to remove the dead"; whites, the citizens benefiting from such humane action. Clarkson undoubtedly meant to offer Richard Allen, Absalom Jones, and countless other free blacks protection. Moreover, Clarkson remained a steadfast ally of the two black leaders, graciously permitting them to republish his public commendation of their work. Finally, Clarkson made no bones about whites who refused to act benevolently or humanely during the crisis—they were devoid of humanity. Still, Clarkson made equally clear that the general citizenry did not necessarily include free blacks. Not once did he say blacks were "fellow citizens," "citizens of color," or anything other than "persons."

Instead, here is precisely what he said of Richard Allen and free blacks: "the public safety requires that protection be given to *these useful persons*." And here is what he said to whites: "good citizens are called upon to afford it to them." Blacks: useful persons. Whites: citizens. Just what was the future of blacks in the state of Pennsylvania, Allen and Jones wondered later on, when free blacks could not claim the rights they deserved? Precious few voices considered blacks full and equal members of the body politic, their arduous, even death-defying yellow-fever work (recall Allen's sickness) notwithstanding.

Then came the final blow: Mathew Carey's best-selling pamphlet of the event, which in one notorious section blamed many blacks for exploiting whites during the catastrophe. The first edition came out in November 1793; over the next two months, this medium-sized pamphlet (no more than one hundred pages long) went through four editions and sold ten thousand copies, according to one estimate. Nearly a year later, advertisements heralded new editions.[46] Citizens poured into Carey's printing office—located in the heart of the business district—to get each new edition and learn what the distinguished man had discovered about one of the worst epidemics in the city's history. In other words, people would long remember what Carey had to say.

Although he praised "the elders of the African church" for their honorable aid to enfeebled whites, Carey also lambasted the black masses for acting intolerably. He identified no one in particular; rather, Carey referred to groups of "the vilest blacks" roaming city streets, causing trouble, and ripping off helpless whites. "Some of them," he charged, "were even detected in plundering." Again, Carey offered few specifics. He didn't have to; his accusation rested on public stereotypes easily conjured: blacks ransacking abandoned white homes, struggles between shifty former slaves and weakened whites over money pouches, blacks laughing at white illness.[47]

Needless to say, Allen and Jones bristled at Carey's "partial relation of our conduct." They worried that, worse than mere words that would disappear into the wind, Carey's comments would become a fixed part of white minds. His words "will prejudice the minds of the people in general against us," they feared. Suppose that one of the so-called honorable blacks came to work in a white home, the duo conjectured— would even this "virtuous" black person be viewed as a "stigmatized wretch," "abused, despised, and perhaps dismissed from employment" because of Carey's careless comments? Free blacks had been stigmatized with the broadest possible stroke of Carey's pen. Now white citizens would assume that all blacks belonged to "the vilest class."[48]

Whites would assume this, Allen and Jones believed, unless black leaders issued their own printed rebuttal.

4. *It Might Have Been*

By mid-November 1793, the yellow fever had abated. By the end of the year, the entire episode belonged to the history books. In a perfect world, Allen and Jones might have read about their own civic high-mindedness in a grand historical narrative. They might have read about black leaders' mobilization for civic good. They might have read about the blow Allen and Jones had dealt to racial stereotypes. Alas, it was only a tale that might have been.

Instead of conquering heroes, Allen and Jones found themselves in the middle of a nasty public battle over racial accusations and stereotypes. For this reason, as Phil Lapsansky has put it, "there is a certain pissed-off quality" running through Allen and Jones's pamphlet, written and published in January 1794.[49] "We apprehend it necessary to publish our thoughts on the occasion," they began, calling their pamphlet a community reply to Carey. "We are solicited," Allen and Jones made clear, "by a number of those who feel injured . . . to step forward and declare facts as they really were." Carey's "partial representation," as they put it, made it too easy to forget about the heroism of countless black Philadelphians, such as an obscure figure named Lampton, "a poor black man . . . [who] went constantly from house to house where distress was and gave assistance without fee or reward." Or there was the example of Allen's future wife, Sarah Bass, a black woman who lost her own husband but "gave all the assistance she could, . . . for which she did not receive anything."[50]

The problem, as Allen and Jones quickly foresaw, was much broader than correcting one man's errors of fact. Carey's published remarks would forever stigmatize free black Philadelphians as villainous and therefore incapable of becoming good citizens. "Mr. Carey's first, second, and third editions are gone forth into the world," Allen and Jones wrote, "and in all probability have been read by thousands." Even if Carey published a corrected edition, people would recall his initial accusations. A Poor Richard–style aphorism sprang to mind: "An ill name is easier given than taken away." Nevertheless, they resolved to publish a broader attack on Carey's prejudicial account.[51]

By turning to print as a key means of prosecuting the struggle for justice, Allen and Jones participated in the making of black modernity. One of the defining elements of modern democratic culture is the existence of a vibrant public sphere where citizens debate a range of issues relevant to the civic order. The expansion of print during the eighteenth and nineteenth centuries funneled new voices into the American public sphere, prompting wide-ranging discussion of just which voices were legitimate in the public realm. On top of that, both print culture and literacy were associated with modernity itself. Jefferson linked a group's potential humanity to the literary arts, and many Enlightenment thinkers linked the production of national historical narratives—and therefore historical consciousness—to the superiority of certain (read: Western) cultures. In modern nations, ran the wisdom, citizens read widely, exchanged views in the public sphere, and produced narratives that exemplified the brilliance of their national culture.[52]

Defined outside of mainstream political institutions, and derided by many white figures as beyond the pale of literary ability or incapable of creating narratives of their own history, black founders like Allen and Jones determined to invade the public sphere. For them, literary production legitimized a broader "black" identity in American political culture and redefined black uplift for a new, democratic age. African American pamphleteers could utilize print culture to expose the limits of American democracy, challenge the boundaries of proslavery ideology, and critique race-based thinking in postemancipation societies.

Allen and Jones's pamphlet made clear that, even in emancipating

Pennsylvania, race thinking continued to be the major barrier to black equality. As they explained, African Americans had acted benevolently throughout the yellow-fever crisis, thinking not of their own health but of the broader importance of rendering civic aid to would-be fellow citizens. Black leaders were shocked, therefore, to read critiques not of individuals but of African Americans as a racial class. America's original sin, they seemed to be saying, was indeed race.

There were other concerns too. On the matter of usurious prices allegedly charged by black nurses, Allen and Jones countered that most African Americans took minimal compensation. Some black laborers took nothing at all. If anything, Allen and Jones maintained, blacks as a class acted more heroically than whites. "We can with certainty assure the public that we have seen more humanity, more sensibility from the poor blacks than the poor whites." Did not many whites (like Mathew Carey himself) flee Philadelphia? Did not others simply hide in Philadelphia to prevent exposure to illness? African Americans, such as Allen and Jones themselves, "have buried several hundreds of poor persons and strangers, for which we have never received, nor never asked any compensation."[53]

As to the charge of black insolence, Allen and Jones recounted several stories of black sacrifice. Whereas Carey offered innuendo and generalizations about black conduct, Allen and Jones provided details, names, quotes. There was, for example, the story of "Caesar Cranchal, a black man, [who] offered his services to attend the sick and said, I will not take your money, I will not sell my life for money." He contracted the dreaded fever and died for his noble deed. There was Mary Scott, who cared for a small family until the father and child perished. The widow worried that Mary Scott would ask for exorbitant wages. Yet Scott asked for a half dollar per day, terms that the widow refused to accept on grounds that it was too small a sum. She granted Scott an annuity of "Six pounds a year . . . for LIFE." Stories of black sacrifice went on and on, the duo sighed. And still African Americans faced abuse and slanders.[54]

Allen and Jones also discussed their own financial sacrifices. Although both men claimed to have given roughly seventy days to yellow-fever activities, Richard Allen could not have matched Absalom Jones's work schedule for the simple fact that he contracted the sickness himself. Allen probably worked half as long as Jones did. Nevertheless, the black duo lost roughly two months of working time. In addition, yellow-fever work took time and money away from family. To attend sick people, cart the dead bodies away, and, in compliance with city codes, "bury beds" left by infected folks, Allen and Jones had to hire their own assistants (they had five men under them) and purchase or rent carriages, coffins, and other items. When the balance sheet had been finalized, the two men found that costs exceeded receipts. "We are out-of-pocket 178.98 pounds."[55]

As successful and even rising black men, they could perhaps afford such a net loss of income. But could other blacks? Their pamphlet wanted whites to remember the very specific sacrifices blacks of all social stations had made—blacks as a community—and not generic stereotypes of blacks plundering and raiding white homes.

What Allen and Jones did not explain to the public was that their own business had been crippled by the yellow fever. Not only did the fever scare away business, but it also took away start-up funds from Allen and Jones. In short, they had no money to pump into their fledgling nail factory. Far from an economic success, all that remained of the nail company was the hope that had once conjured it into being.

And the debt. Allen was still responsible for the fifty pounds he borrowed from the PAS. To put that amount in proper perspective, consider that the average Philadelphia household made roughly 125 Pennsylvania pounds per year in the early 1790s. Thus, Allen had to pay roughly one-quarter to one-third the amount of the average person's salary to the PAS (without the benefit of extra income from the nail factory) *over and above his own living expenses.* Remember too that Allen's own property was at stake as collateral for the debt. Add to that the money that Allen and other black leaders used to cover the cost of their yellow-fever work ("for coffins, . . . hearses, . . . the support of five hired men"), for which they did not receive adequate reimbursement, and the economic tale of woe multiplied greatly.

Debt in Allen's day translated into more than a legal responsibility for monies owed. For Americans of the late eighteenth century, debt became entangled in concepts of freedom and slavery. Although credit networks expanded after the American Revolution (and therefore, so too did debt), indebtedness could still bring reproach, stigma, and a possible loss of freedom. For Allen and Jones, the nail factory was a pathway to more financial security and therefore personal independence. Having an outstanding loan threatened their stability and standing. Would Allen enter debtor's prison if he could not pay his loan? Although the

PAS would not likely have supported such action, the group may not have dealt with the black preacher on future occasions. His conduct as a businessman would have been, well, questionable. Add to all this a final (if much older) stigma—that debt was a *sin!*—and Allen and Jones could feel twice burned: the yellow fever brought a generic rebuke on Philadelphia blacks, and the failed business brought the payment of their own loan into doubt, threatening two rising black men's reputations.[56]

The loan became worrisome enough that the black duo approached white abolitionists in March 1794.[57] Did they seek forbearance or merely a restructuring of the debt? Neither Allen nor Jones ever discussed their visit to the PAS. Abolitionist records indicate that the two men met with PAS officials on at least two occasions, once explaining "the loss sustained by them on account of their services during the late sickness in this city" and a subsequent time laying out all their accounts for reformers to examine. With the loan coming due, Allen and Jones probably explained to the PAS that they had a number of their own outstanding bills but, as yet, very little cash. And since they had been active as nurses and laborers, they had not been able to earn money on their own. Thus, when they said "we are out-of-pocket" nearly two hundred pounds, Allen and Jones were not merely saying goodbye to disposable income—they spoke from the position of businessmen caught short and with some explaining to do. Wouldn't abolitionists understand?[58]

Abolitionists did indeed take the matter seriously, considering the "case of Allen and Jones" at four meetings spread over three months. A select committee was appointed to see if the black duo's claims had merit. The PAS would decide whether or not Allen and Jones were "sufferers" and what remedies, or "relief," would be appropriate.[59]

Allen and Jones dealt with the PAS Committee on Inspection. One of four subcommittees established by white abolitionists to "improve the condition of the free blacks," the inspection committee was charged with "superintending the morals . . . of the free Negroes." As broadsides explained to the public, the inspection committee's members would gladly offer blacks "advice and instruction, protection from wrongs and other friendly offices." When Allen and Jones appeared before the group, hoping to persuade them to grant Allen some form of "relief," inspection officers confessed that they could offer much in the way of friendly offices but no more. The loan must be repaid.[60] Because Allen had worked with white reformers to guard free blacks from the vices of freedom, it must have been a humbling experience for him to be lectured by the inspection committee.

Although the PAS did not forgive the debt, it approved "an essay," or certificate, explaining that Allen and Jones had been public servants during the yellow-fever crisis and deserved monetary recompense from those they aided. The language is fascinating, for at one and the same time the PAS note sympathized with Allen and Jones's plight while providing no hard and fast relief. "It having been represented to the committee of the abolition society," the note stated,

> that Absalom Jones and Richard Allen were like to be sufferers in point of interest for the relief of the sick and internment of the dead during the prevalence of the fever in 1793, said committee having been appointed to examine such vouchers as they might be able to produce it appears to us that they are in the whole losers by the same over and above the want of compensation for their own personal services as well as the employee of two bound servants.

This finely honed and neatly presented report told Allen and Jones what they themselves already knew: they had lost money from people who did not pay them for yellow-fever aid.[61]

The abolitionist essay differed markedly from Allen and Jones's yellow-fever pamphlet. Whereas the abolitionist note was rather disinterested and bureaucratic, Allen and Jones's document captured black outrage in a perfectly controlled way. Here one glimpses the divergence of black and white abolitionism in the early republic. The PAS did not think it important to examine racial stereotyping (did Allen and Jones receive less money for yellow-fever work because of racism?). Moreover, abolitionists did not make the matter public, either by reprinting their note in newspapers or by circulating Allen and Jones's own pamphlet to business and political leaders. Allen and Jones, on the other hand, published a fierce denunciation of racism in late-eighteenth-century Philadelphia, hoping to clear not only their own names but the honor of the black community as a whole. If nothing else, their dialogue with white reformers proved that black leaders were right to march off on their own and publish a black-authored account of the yellow fever.

To be fair, the yellow fever compelled white abolitionists to reckon with their own finances. At roughly the same time that Allen and Jones requested relief, the committee on education reported that subscriptions to black schools ran perilously low. The group hastily appointed two members to chase down new pledges. In addition, the winter and spring of 1794 found the PAS inundated with "many requests for relief from free blacks," including legal aid for kidnapping victims. For the PAS, forgiving Allen and Jones's debt meant taking funds from black educational endeavors or legal-aid coffers, and this in a time of reduced abolitionist reserves.[62]

What ultimately became of the loan? Richard Allen, so determined to succeed, eventually paid off his debt to white abolitionists. More poignantly, he soon purchased a country home that removed him from Philadelphia's feverish summers and all the trouble they brought. Well into the twentieth century, in fact, Allen family members journeyed out of the City of Brotherly Love during the summer and vividly recalled their founding father's need for country respite.

5. The First Copyrighted Black Authors

Having written an essay that vigorously defended black Philadelphians from slander, Allen and Jones had to publish their document. Although a seemingly mundane procedure, the yellow-fever narrative would be the first black political pamphlet signed by Afro-Philadelphians in the new republic (an anonymous pamphlet appeared in the 1780s ostensibly authored by a person of color).[63] Their pamphlet would be a bold declaration of black civic standing. But would anyone publish it, especially considering Allen and Jones's counterattack on Mathew Carey?

For printers, all the world is a page. Although print—like the modern-day Internet—was a quite revolutionary medium in the 1700s, printers worked in a highly businesslike manner. They printed countless "day jobs" to keep coffers filled, mixing and matching mundane work (broadsides and other ephemera) with literary masterpieces. Printers rarely missed an opportunity to make money. Benjamin Franklin, who owned at least five bondpeople during his life, banked on fugitive-slave ads for a steady revenue stream during the 1730s and 1740s, and his successor, Mathew Carey, published these ads well into the 1790s.

Despite the free advertising opportunity, some printers refused to be publicly associated with black printed protest. In Boston, Allen correspondent Prince Hall published two important addresses during the

1790s without white printers' names affixed to the documents (well-known proprietors Thomas Fleet and Benjamin Edes). Why? The black Bostonian challenged white ruffians to come to his front door if they opposed his right to publish. This challenge worried white printers. Hall distributed the pamphlets on his own. He also forwarded copies to Allen and Jones, making them aware of the problems black writers faced.

Of course, white printers might very well publish a pamphlet of protest if its black author(s) included an explanatory introduction by a white editor. The vice in this virtue, as slave narrators knew well, was white oversight. New Yorker Jupiter Hammon, a former slave who published both poetry and prose in the 1780s, let his printers insert introductions informing white readers that, yes indeed, a black man could write! Hammon counseled slaves to obey their masters, which his white editors further applauded. Would Hammon's sponsors have gushed "about the genuineness of the production" before them if he had forthrightly attacked white racism à la Allen and Jones? Perhaps not.[64]

So when the black duo marched into Philadelphia streets in January 1794, manuscript in hand, they had to be vigilant. Who was aligned with, or scared of, Mathew Carey? Who would buck convention and affix his name to a vigorous black-authored assault on racial prejudice? Perhaps the easiest way for Allen and Jones to publish their pamphlet would have been to consult white abolitionists. In 1794, the PAS hired Zachariah Poulson, a respected name in print circles who had already published the group's anti-slave-trading petitions to Congress. Poulson's shop was at 80 Chestnut Street, just a few city blocks from Allen's home.

Allen and Jones instead approached William Woodward, a young printer who had only recently come to Philadelphia. They recognized him as a man without connections to either the PAS or Mathew Carey. In addition, Woodward had already published edgy productions (pamphlets praising the French Revolution, for example)—he was not worried about supporting black authorship. The choice of Woodward thus made a strong statement about black editorial autonomy.[65]

After Woodward printed the pamphlet—in a run of 250–500 copies —Allen and Jones marched over to the clerk in charge of federal copyright for the District of Pennsylvania. The officer, a man named Samuel Caldwell, worked out of his home at 54 Chestnut Street. On January 23, 1794, Caldwell assigned the pamphlet copyright number 55, affix-

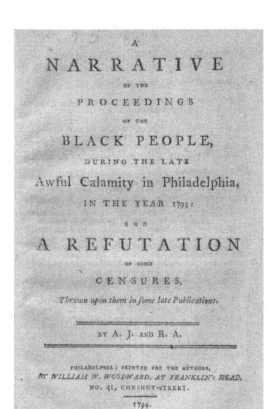

"A Narrative of the Proceedings of the Black People
during the Late Awful Calamity in Philadelphia,"
1794. The title page of Allen and Jones's fierce pamphlet denouncing antiblack accusations in yellow-fever
Philadelphia. The black duo secured federal copyright
number 55 in the District of Pennsylvania, making
them the first African American writers to attain official recognition as authors. (Courtesy of the Library
Company of Philadelphia)

ing an official seal to the document. Now Allen and Jones would be enshrined as the first copyrighted black authors in the United States.[66]
There can be little doubt that Allen led the copyright charge, for he
subsequently secured copyright for other pamphlets (whereas Jones did
not). Why was this so important to the young black preacher? According to Article I, Section 8 of the Constitution, Congress had the right to

"promote the progress of science and useful arts by securing for limited times to authors and inventors the exclusive right to their respective writings and discoveries." With a federal copyright, the former slave could call himself an "author and inventor." And he had just helped invent the modern black political pamphlet.

4

The Year of the Fever, Part 2
Allen's Antislavery Appeal

God knows the hearts of all men.
—Richard Allen, "An Address to Those Who
Keep Slaves and Approve the Practice"

With his coauthorship of the yellow-fever pamphlet, Richard Allen entered national and international reform circles. Confirmation came from Allen's nemesis, Mathew Carey, who found himself in the surprising position of having to reply to "Richard Allen and Absalom Jones, two free Africans" whose "publication ushered to the world . . . abuse . . . on *me*." Carey's concern stemmed from the distribution of the black duo's pamphlet in both America and Britain. Though he brushed aside their work as "undeserving of notice," Carey was stung. He explained that he had originally praised Allen and Jones's benevolent work and only chastised "the vilest blacks" for "extorting" money. He did not "cast a censure on the whole" black community. Allen and Jones's services "demand public gratitude," he exclaimed. "I would ask the reader, is this the language of an enemy?" Is it, he finished, "honorable for Jones and Allen to repay evil for good?"[1]

Because antiblack thinking transcended Carey, Allen was not content merely to critique a celebrated printer's problematic production. He also wanted to attack the foundation of American race prejudice: slavery. At the end of Allen and Jones's yellow-fever narrative, Allen inserted his own antislavery missive—the first public challenge to bondage by a black founder since Congress moved to Philadelphia. "We do not wish to make you angry," he proclaimed, "but excite your attention to consider how hateful slavery is in the sight of that God, who hath destroyed kings and princes for their oppression of the poor slaves."[2] American masters must heed God's word or face divine punishment.

1. An Antislavery Standard

Allen called his antislavery addendum "An Address to Those Who Keep Slaves and Approve the Practice." In crafting it, he relied not merely on biblical moralisms but on his rising sense of self. As Allen put it, the Lord "from time to time raise[s] up instruments" to spread righteousness throughout the world. Allen viewed himself as just such an instrument. And now was the time for the black preacher to plead the cause of the oppressed.[3]

Although early national Philadelphia was a far cry from pre–Civil War Washington, Allen concerned himself with an issue that had already sparked debate in the nation's capital. From 1790 to 1800, when the federal government temporarily resided in Allen's hometown, congressmen, presidents, and statesmen examined issues ranging from runaway slaves to abolitionists' political standing before the law. In 1793, for example, Congress passed the nation's first fugitive-slave law. The impetus for it may have come from Pennsylvania's borderland status. Gradual abolitionism prompted enslaved people from Delaware, Maryland, and Virginia to head for the Quaker State. While Pennsylvania abolitionists constantly boosted their lawyerly cadre to keep pace with this trend, Southern masters fumed. Congressional slaveholders became especially concerned when traveling to Philadelphia. Though they had six months to comply with the gradual abolition statute, out-of-state masters still had to worry about runaways who might find refuge among the city's vibrant free black community and/or legal support from the PAS. In one of the best-known cases, South Carolina congressman Pierce Butler sued Pennsylvania abolitionist Isaac Hopper for allegedly helping a slave to escape.[4]

On the international scene, news of the Haitian slave rebellion reached Philadelphia by the early 1790s, with escaping Haitian masters and slaves telling tales of the massive black uprising. Although Pennsylvania would not grant immunity to fleeing French masters, they sought refuge in the Quaker State anyway. Nearly a thousand Haitian slaves were gradually liberated over the following several years with Pennsylvania abolitionists' aid. Allen's Philadelphia was, in short, full of antislavery discussion, black revolutionary action, and slaveholder concern about bondage.[5]

To all of this, Allen added a black man's nonviolent call for racial justice. With the nation's best and brightest men governing from Philadelphia, he believed that he had a unique chance to propel black abolitionism nationally. While many white reformers critiqued slavery, black abolitionists like Allen condemned both bondage and racial injustice. He began by attacking slavery as an unchristian and unpatriotic institution. Allen favored both private manumission and state-sponsored abolition laws. Gradual abolitionism was the gold standard in Allen's day. But some statesmen viewed it as too radical to embrace. When Allen published his abolitionist treatise in 1794, neither New York nor New Jersey (containing an aggregate of roughly twenty-five thousand slaves) had yet passed gradualist laws.[6] No Southern state would ever pass a gradual emancipation law.

Allen's antislavery appeal combated these fears by labeling abolitionism patriotic, pious, virtuous, and thoroughly American. To those who charged that slave liberation would fail, Allen vigorously dissented. In one of his most stunning sections, he appeared to address none other than Thomas Jefferson, the slaveholding revolutionary who professed to hate slavery but to fear abolitionism even more. "If you love your children, if you love your country, if you love the God of Love," Allen declared, "clear your hands from slaves, burden not your children or country with them."[7] Roughly a decade earlier, Jefferson had published *Notes on the State of Virginia,* a survey of Virginia's political, social, and geographical makeup originally prepared for a foreign diplomat. "I tremble for my country when I reflect that God is just," Jefferson worried in one section of the document.[8] The Virginia founder referred to the slaveholder's dilemma: although the American Revolution had made slavery anathema in a nation dedicated to liberty, masters feared universal emancipation and the prospect of black equality. In subsequent years, Jefferson embraced the colonization of freed blacks as the only safe route to a liberated and lily-white America. Historian William Freehling labels this notion "Conditional Termination": slavery would go only when emancipated blacks did.[9] Until that time, Jefferson wrung his hands in guilt. Allen refused to let such apathy go unchallenged, declaring abolitionism safe and practicable in Southern as well as Northern states.

How did Allen know about Jefferson's *Notes on the State of Virginia?* Free black mathematician Benjamin Banneker's 1792 almanac reprinted Jefferson's thoughts on slavery. That very almanac was published in Philadelphia. It is not hard to imagine Allen holding a copy of *Banneker's Almanac* and finding inspiration for his own antislavery musings while reading Jefferson's theoretical condemnation of slavery. "The whole commerce between master and slave," Jefferson observed, "is a perpetual exercise of the most boisterous passions, the most un-remitting despotism on the one part, and degrading submissions on the other. Our children see this, and learn to imitate it." And so, Jefferson wondered, "can the liberties of a nation be thought secure when we have removed their only firm basis, a conviction in the minds of the people that these liberties are the gift of God? That they are not to be violated but with his wrath?"[10] That is why Jefferson trembled—the same God to whom he once appealed for revolutionary freedom might also condemn recalcitrant American masters for denying that same free-dom to black people. No matter, for like Madison, George Mason, Pat-rick Henry, and many other Virginia worthies, Jefferson's hatred of slav-ery in the abstract would not translate into freedom for slaves in his midst.

Just what was the problem with emancipation, Allen wondered, that Jefferson could so vigorously attack bondage yet remain a guilty slave-holder? Was it, as Jefferson himself had argued, that whites doubted black intellectual capabilities? If so, Allen wrote, slaveholders should re-alize that they perpetuated black ignorance and therefore their own fears about abolitionism. "Will you," Allen asked, "plead our incapac-ity for freedom, and our contented condition under oppression, as a suf-ficient cause for keeping us under the grievous yoke?" When blacks "plead with our masters" for liberty, it is "deemed insolent." Yet when blacks did not rebel en masse, whites believed they were "contented" simpletons. The matter need not be so complicated, Allen concluded, for "God himself hath pleaded [slaves'] cause." Slavery was wrong, and masters must get on with the business of emancipating their Christian brethren.[11]

This idea led to Allen's black abolitionist mantra: freed slaves could become valuable citizens if educated and treated equally. Released from the shackles of slavery, African Americans would rise as a thinking—not just a working—class. "We believe if you would try the experiment of taking a few black children, and cultivate their minds with the same care . . . as you would with your own children," he challenged, "you would find them upon trial . . . not inferior in mental endowments" to whites. Contemporary sociologists have a phrase for Allen's ideas: nur-ture over nature. African Americans were not destined to be slaves, la-borers, or "useful persons"—anything but citizens—because of some stereotypical racial makeup. Rather, Allen had the very modern idea that circumstances created a person's future. Provide equal opportunity, and most anyone would succeed. Leave people mired in educational and social wastelands, and they will sink.[12]

In making such pronouncements, Allen confronted another of white founders' fears: that race war would follow emancipation. "Why not retain and incorporate the blacks into the state?" Jefferson had mused. "Deep-rooted prejudices entertained by the whites" was only part of the answer, he concluded; perhaps more dangerous were the "10,000 recollections by the blacks of the injuries they have sustained." According to Jefferson, free blacks would exact revenge on former masters and destroy the American republic. Many white statesmen and even reformers agreed.[13]

Not so, Allen maintained. Freed slaves would be filled with gratitude toward the Christian men and women who had liberated them. "That God who knows the hearts of all men," he observed, "and the propensity of a slave to hate his oppressor hath strictly forbidden it to his chosen people." Citing Deuteronomy (23:7), Allen claimed that black Christians were commanded to "love our enemies, to do good to them that hate and despitefully use us." Just as the Lord instructed masters to liberate slaves, Allen argued, so too did He instruct liberated blacks to love their former masters. Black liberation was not dangerous in the least.[14]

Allen hoped his ideas would resonate beyond slaveholders. Though well-meaning, many white abolitionists also stumbled over the issue of race. The PAS believed that blacks needed constant paternal assistance to rise in American culture. In broadsides and pamphlets distributed throughout the black community, they established themselves as the guardians of freedom, ever ready to teach liberated slaves about morality, virtue, literacy, cleanliness, and piety. Though a late-in-life convert to gradual abolitionism, PAS president Ben Franklin expressed concerns about former slaves' collective psyche. According to a broadside posted by Franklin and the PAS, Pennsylvania blacks had come out of slavery as "machines" and "brute animals." Because of their oppressed experiences, Franklin explained, "freedom may often prove a misfortune to [the slave] himself and prejudicial to society"—unless white reformers remained their moral overseers.[15] Other PAS members explored the issue of racial difference in ways that prefigured nineteenth-century racial science. At a speech before the American Philosophical Society in 1792,

Benjamin Rush likened darkened racial pigmentation to physical illness. Ever the physician and Enlightenment taxonomist, Rush had to find a rationale for skin-color variation. To be sure, Rush wanted his distinguished audience to view blacks as fully human. But he also conjectured that leprosy had altered blacks' skin color. Whites should sympathize with their ill black brethren until medical cures neutralized the disease of color.

Rush's pronouncements were not out of the mainstream. New Jersey Presbyterian minister Samuel Stanhope Smith offered a cultural analog to Rush's bleak medical diagnosis of blackness. Like Rush, Smith believed that slavery was an evil. Also like Rush, he argued that African Americans were fully part of the human family. Unlike Rush, however, Smith believed that the problem was black culture. In his own address to the American Philosophical Society, Smith argued that global cultures had diverged over time. According to his logic, Euro-Americans mastered the arts, sciences, and literature, while Africans devolved into tribalism. Racial reform was therefore possible only if whites rescued the black masses.

When compared to these thinkers, Allen sounds refreshingly modern. For example, whereas Rush and Smith viewed African Americans as either sick or culturally stunted, Allen believed that blacks suffered because of racial stereotyping and physical oppression. Similarly, whereas Jefferson and Franklin had feared that black and white people could never live together in a world free from slavery (because manic blacks would wreak havoc on their former white rulers), Allen argued that religion would buttress racial reconciliation. On issue after issue, Allen seems to be pointing the way toward an American multiracial future.

Allen's antislavery address charted new territory for another reason: he argued that his racial status informed black abolitionism. Oppressed people, Allen and black founders argued in countless pamphlets, poems, and petitions, must be seen as legitimate agents of the abolitionist cause precisely because they understood slavery's physical and psychological abuses. Although this notion may seem obvious in the twenty-first century, it was anything but crystal clear in Allen's time. African Americans' lack of public standing as politicians or lawyers, many white reformers believed, made them ineffective abolitionists. Moreover, PASers asserted, enslaved people could not understand the broader philosophical issues flowing from abolitionism—they were too close to the oppression they experienced to articulate grievances. In fact, neither Richard

Allen nor any other black activist was invited to join the PAS during the early national period. (Robert Purvis, who was one-quarter black, became the first African-descended member of the group during the 1840s.)

Rather than distance himself from blackness, bondage, and personal experience, Allen embraced his identity as a former slave and person of color. "We can tell you," he wrote at the beginning of his antislavery appeal, "from a degree of experience, that a black man, although reduced to the most abject state human nature is capable of, short of real madness, can think, reflect and feel injuries . . . that you who have been and are our great oppressors, would manifest if reduced to the pitiable condition of a slave." By framing racial justice in personal terms—in other words, by showing how black people experienced racism—Allen hoped to inspire empathy for blacks as oppressed fellow citizens, rather than damaged objects in need of paternalistic support.[16]

As Allen's arguments suggest, early black abolitionism emphasized the significance of printed appeals to the public at large. Though written in polemical rather than narrative form, free blacks' pamphlets of protest prefigured antebellum slave narratives in several ways. First, they offered black abolitionists a vital forum for articulating grievances. There is very little evidence that Pennsylvania's black founders—Allen, Jones, Forten—ever voted or voted consistently. Although no law prevented black suffrage, custom dictated African American deference to white sensitivities. Without the right to vote, or access to formal political venues (like Congress), free blacks turned to printed protest to advocate abolitionism. Second, pamphlets of protest in Allen's era, like slave narratives in Frederick Douglass's time, engaged in consciousness-raising. Although Allen provided no details—no specific program—about how emancipation should occur, he told Americans that slavery was a monstrous wrong. He used words that would prick the ears of any Christian and/or patriot: slavery repudiated "the God of Love"; bondage was "oppression" and "dominion" of the worst sort; slaves longed for "freedom" above all else. As important, Allen let Americans know that slavery tore apart black families (like his own) and destroyed the hopes and talents of countless black individuals. "It is in our posterity enjoying the same privileges with your own," he stated, "that you ought to look for better things."[17]

By challenging slaveholders and slaveholding statesmen to embrace abolitionism as a national objective, Allen's antislavery address diverged from white abolitionist strategies. Although the PAS had submitted the nation's first abolitionist petition to Congress (then temporarily meeting in New York City) in 1790, harsh rebukes from Deep South slaveholders convinced the group to narrow its abolitionist focus in subsequent years. Whereas that first petition challenged Congress to "step to the very verge of its powers" to ban the international slave trade and institute a national gradual abolition program, subsequent memorials stressed the federal government's ability to restrict international slave trading. Though the group would continue to chip away at slavery's margins by representing blacks in Northern courts of law, its members did not think that national abolitionism should threaten the union. Tellingly, the PAS did not petition Congress on national abolitionism for the entire decade that the federal government resided in Philadelphia. Allen's abolitionist missive, aimed at both national governing officials and the public at large, was the first major attack on slavery in the nation's Northern capital. It would not be the last black abolitionist appeal to the government in Philadelphia.[18]

Nor was Allen's appeal the lone example of black activism in the North. Signs of blacks' new public protest strategy abounded in Allen's America. One of the best examples came from a black New Yorker, who made antislavery arguments quite similar to Allen's in a 1790 newspaper debate with a white writer. The unknown author, who took the pen name "Africanus," confronted a white writer who claimed that blacks were the missing link between apes and humans. "I am a woolly haired Negro," "Africanus" responded, "the son of an African man and woman. I am a master of a trade, . . . employ my time rationally, . . . and have been instructed in the Christian religion." Do not, "Africanus" stated flatly, "consider me as the link in the creation by which the monkey hangs to the gentleman." Indeed, "Africanus" claimed "myself equal to . . . any spirited, noble and generous American freeman."[19] Like Allen, "Africanus" had utilized print to project black abolitionism into the American public sphere.

Public debates over abolition during the 1790s were shaped not just by domestic concerns over American-style gradualism but by the Haitian rebellion as well. For more than a decade after it began in 1791, the Haitian revolution became the worldwide focus of black liberation. While some American newspapers respectfully reported on Haitian leader Toussaint L'Ouverture's leadership, others commented on the menace of a successful black uprising in the nearby Caribbean, even comparing slave rebels to bloodthirsty savages intent on exacting revenge against whites anywhere and everywhere. In 1791, for example, George Washington pushed Americans to "crush the alarming insurrection of the Negroes in St. Domingo" before it spun out of control. Pennsylvania congressman Albert Gallatin worried that an independent Haitian republic would be the equivalent of letting loose "so many wild tigers on [Western] society." Jefferson, who reinstituted an embargo on Haiti after assuming the presidency in 1801, called Caribbean slave rebels "the cannibals of the terrible Republic."[20]

Allen's views on the Haitian revolution, the largest slave rebellion in the Western Hemisphere (resulting in the creation of the Republic of Haiti in 1804), are not entirely clear. As an advocate of nonviolent abolitionism, he hoped that New World bondage could be dismantled peaceably. As a New Testament Christian moralist, he also believed that blacks must forgive their enemies in order to build an interracial brotherhood of equality, love, and faith. Yet as his antislavery appeal illustrated, Allen favored an early form of liberation theology: the notion that God sympathized with oppressed people. Like other members of the black founding generation (and generations of enslaved people North and South), he drew inspiration from the Old Testament story of Exodus, in which a vengeful God destroyed Egyptian slaveholders for ignoring Israelites' abolitionist pleas. Black Bostonian Prince Hall used Exodus to publicly empathize with Haitian slave rebels. "My brethren," Hall observed in 1792, "let us remember what a dark day it was with our [enslaved] African brethren six years ago, in the French West Indies." "Nothing but the snap of the whip was heard from morning to evening," he continued, "and all manner of tortures inflicted on those unhappy people for nothing else but to gratify their masters' pride." But, Hall charged, "blessed be God," liberation had gloriously arrived. Perhaps violence in the service of freedom was divine.[21]

Although Allen offered no similar public celebration of the Haitian uprising, he sympathized with enslaved peoples' plight on the deadly island. His antislavery appeal ominously alluded to Haiti as evidence that Americans had a limited amount of time to embrace universal emancipation before enslaved people would rebel. "The deadly insurrections [slaves] have made," Allen observed, are "enough to convince a reasonable man, that great uneasiness and not contentment, is the inhabitant of [slaves'] hearts."[22] The moral lesson of Haiti? American statesmen and the citizenry at large ignored black freedom struggles at their own peril.

Nevertheless, the black preacher would not explicitly condone rebellion. Bondage, Allen knew from his own experience, pushed enslaved people to the brink of despair. As he wrote in a brief address to the black community (which Allen also appended to the yellow-fever pamphlet), "I have myself been a slave and was as desirous of freedom as any of you." Slavery was synonymous with "darkness and perplexity." But, he lectured American slaves, do not "sink at the discouraging prospects" before you. "Let no rancor or ill-will lodge in your breast for any bad treatment you may have received," he flatly stated. Vengeance was for the Lord alone. "Think no more of the evil," he counseled, and instead "help forward the cause of freedom" by embracing piety, industry, sobriety, and forgiveness.[23]

Allen's belief in black piety as an antidote to racial oppression deserves a closer look, for he viewed religion as a form of intellectual resistance. Faith, he fervently believed, allowed people of color to endure "the worst condition" imaginable. Moreover, because God was a power beyond the reach of even the mightiest master, enslaved people could take solace in the notion that slaveholders would face divine retribution. Prefiguring nineteenth-century slave spirituals, Allen noted that "the power of the most cruel master ends" at death and that eternal torment awaited all recalcitrant slave owners. On the other hand, even the most lowly bondman would be "admitted to freedom which God hath prepared for those of all colors that love him." For these reasons and more, as Allen confidently put it, enslaved Christians should "value [faith in God] more than anything else." In short, Allen argued that faith helped loosen the master's iron grip on the slave's mind, thereby beginning the mental process of emancipation. For Allen, the Christian faith made enslaved people stronger and more resilient—anything but the machines or simpletons many white slaveholders and abolitionists believed them to be.[24] Like radical abolitionists of the antebellum era who based their moral suasion campaigns on Christian love and truth, Allen remained a firm believer in the power of words to foment nonviolent change.

2. Allen's Library

How did the former slave with no formal schooling produce so stirring an antislavery appeal? Though Allen never discussed his education publicly, he probably learned to read and write through religious instruction at his second master's Delaware home. Allen recalled discovering the word of God in 1777, going "from house to house, exhorting my old companions, and telling to all around what a dear Savior I had found" in the Lord. "I [then] joined the Methodist society," he finished, and "met in . . . [Bible] class for several years."[25] He honed his literacy skills on the revival circuit, studying the style of white preachers and black class leaders who had mastered the Word.

Like the majority of eighteenth-century black leaders, Allen was a self-made reader and writer. No black founder attended college, trained in a lawyer's office, or did anything resembling a political apprenticeship. (Absalom Jones and James Forten attended Quaker schools briefly, learning rudimentary literacy skills, but nothing more.) This fact raises broader questions about Allen's (and black founders') literary models, work habits, and patronage. How did they gain literacy, who did they read, and how did these things influence their pamphlets of protest?

Despite the proliferation of work on African American reform, scholars still know relatively little about black abolitionists' literary production.[26] Think of the most famous black abolitionist, Frederick Douglass. Scholars have found no working drafts of Douglass's debut book, his famous 1845 autobiography. The same is true of David Walker's 1829 "Appeal," Maria Stewart's "Productions" (1835), and countless other black-authored texts. A marginal comment from just one of those writers would be worth its weight in historical gold. Now consider the opposite: the richness of literary archives on white statesmen. Allen's fellow Philadelphian Ben Franklin produced a literary output that fills nearly fifty volumes. In the twenty-first century, it takes the best modern technology to fit Franklin's massive archives in a manageable electronic format. There is nothing even close to illuminate Allen's literary world.

Luckily, Allen left important clues about his library. Piecing them together, we can reconstruct key parts of this black founder's intellectual universe. That Allen even owned books, or a library, might be surprising. As a black preacher, Allen was best known for "extempore" preaching—or preaching from the heart without notes. Later AME ministers, like Daniel Payne, lamented Allen's lack of formal schooling, further fueling stereotypical views of the black preacher as a rather unsophisticated thinker. But as his will testified, Allen owned several sets of scholarly books. Similarly, a probate inventory of his country home (purchased by Allen in the early nineteenth century) found that Allen had "books" all around him. Just what were these books, and what did they mean?

Unsurprisingly, Allen owned several copies of the Bible. His most cherished copy, a leather-bound edition dating to colonial times, was given to him by white abolitionist Thomas Garrett in the early 1800s. Allen posed with the handsome text in his famous 1813 portrait, pointing viewers' eyes downward toward the impressive tome. Allen held on to that Bible for the rest of his life, passing it on to family members (Bethel Church proudly displays it today).[27]

The Bible was a vital text to Allen and black founders. According to religious scholar Allen Dwight Callahan, "the Bible is one of the few books of world literature that looks at life 'from below.' It is replete with upsets that flout the rules of power, privilege, and prestige."[28] Like other African American preachers, Allen was particularly enamored of Exodus, the story of ancient Jews' divinely wrought liberation from Egyptian slavery. As previously noted, Allen's antislavery appeal made a direct comparison between ancient and American bondage, arguing that God had already "destroyed kings and princes for their oppression of the poor slaves." Divine retribution of unrepentant American masters was biblically ordained.[29]

Though the former slave felt the power of biblical stories like Exodus deep in his bones, Allen's theology was also informed by scholarly exegesis. He owned two massive sets of biblical analysis. The first, *Expository notes, with practical observations upon the New Testament of our Lord and Savior Jesus Christ* by Thomas Burkitt, declared that religion was a "labour of love."[30] "All the return I desire from you," Burkitt informed readers, "is your living in a daily imitation of that grand pattern of holiness and obedience, which is here set before you, and in every page recommended to you; and that we may continue to strive together in our prayers one with another, for that grace which may enable us to the faithful discharge of our respective duties towards God, towards each other, and all mankind."[31]

The second scholarly text in Allen's library, Thomas Scott's *A Commentary on the Whole Bible,* offered similar insight on the Holy Word. "Man alone possesses the capacity of distinguishing between truth and falsehood; between moral good and evil; and of receiving instruction in social and relative duties," Scott wrote in a preface to his commentaries. "From these premises we infer, with absolute certainty, that the all-wise Creator thus constituted our minds, and conferred upon us these distinguishing powers, in order to render us capable of Religion, for the purposes of his own glory, and of our own felicity, in connection with that of our fellow-creatures."[32] Like Burkitt, Scott wanted Christians to strive for holy communion with the Savior, no matter their circumstances, color, or class. If this idea did not stir Allen's mind, then another one did: according to Burkitt and Scott (both Englishmen whose texts circulated widely in post-Revolutionary Anglo-American culture), the Lord required Christians to embrace one another as equals.

We do not know when Allen attained copies of these multivolume collections (each set ran six volumes). The Burkitt edition was reprinted in America as early as 1794, and Scott's text became available a decade later. But that Allen secured biblical commentaries and then valued them enough to bequeath copies to his heirs tells us much about his mindset. Far from a stereotypical black preacher—for whom raw feelings and emotions outweighed intellectual acumen—Allen was dead serious about attaining scholarly knowledge.

One of Allen's prized texts was a true classic: *The Whole, Genuine and Complete Works of Flavius Josephus*.[33] A Jewish scholar of Roman times (the first century A.D.), Josephus earned a decidedly mixed reputation over the next several millennia. To many, he was a traitor and scoundrel who joined a rebellion against Rome only to betray his fellow conspirators (convincing them to die fighting Roman conquerors while he capitulated). To others, Josephus was an Oracle—a man who captured the struggles of the Jewish people as few writers ever had. Some commentators believed that God had saved Josephus to tell the history of oppressed Jews. Whatever the reality, Josephus became an important scholar of the ancient world, particularly Jewish history. As a twentieth-century commentator noted, Josephus's literary work aimed at nothing less than the "exalt[ation of] the Jewish people in the eyes of the Greco-Roman world."[34]

Both Richard Allen and Absalom Jones purchased copies of Josephus's works in 1795, though it is likely they had access to the text earlier. Copies of Josephus's works were widely available in American society. As far back as the 1740s, for example, Ben Franklin's *Pennsylvania Gazette* had advertised a British edition.[35] However, because the 1795 edition was only the second Philadelphia printing (the first coming in 1774), it attracted substantial patronage from Philadelphia's moral and intellectual elite: celebrated jurist William Rawle, renowned scientist David Rittenhouse, the peripatetic Benjamin Rush. And there amid roughly five hundred names were two black men, Allen and Jones.[36] Allen lugged the giant book home, where it remained part of his personal library for nearly forty years.

Allen drew key lessons from the ancient Jewish scribe. First, he discovered that God's righteousness always shone through, especially to the patient, pious, and oppressed members of society. Second, he learned that oppressed peoples must transcribe their own versions of history, for dominant cultures expressed little interest in the lives of marginalized people in their midst. Finally, he identified with Josephus's finely wrought literary style. While some people "undertake to write histories" to flatter great men, Josephus declared in the preface to *Antiquities of the Jews,* others "are driven to write history because they are concerned in the facts." Allen and Jones's yellow-fever pamphlet, the two

"Pharaoh and His host of Egyptians Drowned in the Red Sea," from the Woodruff and Turner edition of *The Whole, Genuine and Complete Works of Flavius Josephus, the Learned and Authentic Jewish Historian* (Philadelphia, 1795). Both Allen and Jones bought this edition of Josephus's works in 1795. One of the leading sources of ancient Roman, Jewish, and early Christian history, the Jewish scholar Josephus was probably a model for Allen and Jones's yellow-fever narrative. Allen, like other black founders, may have reveled in Josephus's depictions of Exodus, particularly the image of Egyptian slaveholders being struck down by a righteous God. (Courtesy of the Library Company of Philadelphia)

men wrote, was not written to flatter anyone's ego but to "declare facts as they really were." Similarly, just as Josephus had attempted to soften the impact of his historical polemic by citing support from "learned" Roman patrons (Josephus explained that "some [well-known] persons . . . who desired to know our history . . . exhorted me to come forward with it"), so too did Allen and Jones claim that "respectable citizens" had urged them "to step forward" with their own history of blacks in the yellow fever. (Allen and Jones probably referred to Benjamin Rush.) In republican Rome as well as the early American republic, heeding such time-honored protocols of intellectual engagement could determine how marginalized authors were read and received.[37]

As these references to Josephus show, Allen thoughtfully used ancient sources to build a rhetorical persona capable of entering the world of Enlightenment-era public discourse. Well aware of stereotypes about black intellectual inferiority, he (and Jones) mined ancient sources to create a document that had not only passion but also historical solidity. Clearly, Allen saw Josephus as an insightful analyst of minority oppression in an imperial land. With Josephus as a model, Allen could produce a profound polemic against American race thinking in the age of Jefferson—a political tract exuding not merely passion but erudition and historical depth.

Like other black founders, Allen was comfortable with secular as well as sacred texts. He read not only Josephus but also works by contemporary American statesmen, including both Ben Franklin and George Washington. Recall that Allen's antislavery appeal urged Americans to engage in "an experiment" in racial equality by treating former slaves as they would their own children. Allen's Franklinesque focus on "experiments" and "trials" as a means of liberating both blacks and whites from the burden of racism reveals his familiarity with at least some of Poor Richard's writings. Similarly, Allen's eulogy of Washington (from 1799) quoted directly from the American president's "Farewell Address," warning Americans to remain patriotic by not forming foreign entanglements.[38]

Early black writers like Allen also read one another. Before producing their yellow-fever document, Allen and Jones read Prince Hall's first pamphlet, "A Charge" (1792).[39] Hall pointed them to the work of itinerant black preacher John Marrant, who had produced a spiritual autobiography in 1785 (which circulated in both London and the United States). Allen, Jones, Hall, and Marrant all claimed that blacks had an important role to play in trans-Atlantic reform culture. They would be the Redeemer People. We are the grace of God, Hall exclaimed; we are the chosen ones, Marrant echoed; we are America's abolitionist saviors, Allen and Jones added.[40]

From this assemblage of literary models—Exodus and Josephus, Franklin and Washington, Hall and Marrant—Allen learned how to fold edgy commentary into enlightened discourse. Both the yellow-fever document and the antislavery appeal critiqued white citizens' hypocrisy while simultaneously deferring to the literary conventions of gentlemanly discourse. Allen never said, for example, that masters would be vanquished by slaves—he merely pointed out that the biblical story of Exodus said so. Like the best writers and orators of the high Enlightenment era, Allen mastered the art of the literary thrust and parry.

3. Men in Wigs

Allen's search for literary inspiration among both ancient and contemporary writers signifies his desire to enter what some scholars refer to as the Republic of Letters, a classical age of American statesmanship and political rhetoric in late-eighteenth-century America. From constitutional ratification debates to the Federalist Papers, American leaders sought to create political commentary that exemplified the genius of America. They did so not just in formal political institutions but beyond Congress and state houses, producing letters, pamphlets, newspapers, and books at a dizzying rate.[41] Living in the temporary federal capital of Philadelphia, Allen was as close to the epicenter of American statecraft—and therefore to the Republic of Letters—as any free black person could be. In crafting an attack on slaveholders, as well as a broader defense of black benevolence during the yellow-fever epidemic, Allen was well aware of the need to write on an elevated plane of discourse. Righteous indignation formed only part of his message; rhetorical mastery—exemplifying a black classical style—formed the other.

Indeed, in an era when statesmen still wore powdered wigs, Allen targeted elite white statesmen. The very first lines of the antislavery appeal invite such analysis. "The judicious part of mankind," Allen wrote, "will think it unreasonable, that a superior good conduct is looked for, from our race, by those who stigmatize us as men, whose baseness is incurable, and may therefore be held in a state of servitude, that a merciful man would not deem a beast to." Allen's words—"judicious," "un-reasonable," "baseness"—were chosen with tactical precision to appeal to those men in wigs.[42] Though his point remained that African-descended people were not destined to be enslaved, Allen knew that unbridled hostility toward white attitudes would not sell in this high-Enlightenment time. He had to appear to be a reasonable, thinking critic of American race thinking.

Absalom Jones may have exerted a powerful influence on Allen's early writings. Nearly fifteen years Allen's senior, and an adult pupil at Quaker abolitionist Anthony Benezet's night school for people of color, Jones was much more familiar with the art of formal rhetorical persuasion (in schools similar to the one headed by Benezet, Pennsylvania abolitionists had young black students learn penmanship by repeatedly writing the phrase, "quote great authors").[43] He was also by nature a moderate soul—less a hotspur than Allen. He taught the young preacher to think more deeply about literary style and comportment in the Republic of Letters.

In this manner, the black duo formed one of the great African American friendships of the early republic. Was it the equivalent of Jefferson and Adams (with quarrels interrupting an otherwise long friendship?), Jefferson and Madison (with a common heritage binding the two men for decades), or Franklin and Adams (with two men bridging personal differences to get something important done)? The exact analogy may not be as important as the fact that Allen and Jones's long friendship is one of the very few early black collaborations that historians can so fully document. Their bonds of affection were threaded from similar backgrounds. Like Allen, Jones grew up enslaved in Delaware. Although born prior to Allen in 1746, Jones bought his own liberty after his future friend had done the same (Allen in 1783, Jones in 1784). Like Allen, Jones found solace in religion; like Allen, he worked hard throughout his life to achieve freedom. One of the first things he saved for was a spelling book. He continued to strive in Philadelphia, where his master had moved in the early 1760s. Jones persuaded a co-worker at a dry-goods store to teach him to read. He then attended Benezet's school. Jones secured his wife's freedom (she was a Philadelphia slave too) and then bought not one but two different homes (which he used as rental income in later years). He eventually had the honor of sitting for a portrait of himself. Like Allen, his portrait displayed a sober black Christian holding the Holy Bible. "Made of that blood which flowed in

Adam's vein!" a Boston poet wrote of Jones and Allen, as if they were a single entity, "who rates not colour, but th' immortal mind."[44]

Allen and Jones quickly felt kinship upon Allen's arrival in Philadelphia in 1786. After their initial meeting, these "two men of the African race," as the preamble to the Free African Society stated, "often communed together," prayed together, and fell into "conversation" about boyhoods spent in Delaware bondage and a new future for free blacks in Philadelphia.[45] Both men led exemplary public lives that demolished stereotypes of African Americans as potentially problematic citizens. Not only did they start the Free African Society and Philadelphia's inaugural African churches, the duo co-organized the city's first African Masonic Lodge in 1797 (and the second black Lodge in America organized under Prince Hall). Allen served as the group's treasurer.[46] Under their leadership, black masonry provided yet another organizational home from which Afro-Philadelphia's growing leadership class could meet for fellowship, conduct business in and beyond the black community, and engage in both benevolent reform and consciousness-raising (Freemasons abetted black abolitionism by believing in the universal fellowship of all men; black Masons also celebrated ancient Africa as the birthplace of Freemasonry itself).[47]

Allen could not fail to be impressed by Jones's seriousness and sense of purpose. Jones returned Allen's regard, imbibing the young preacher's organizational energy and drive. Like apostles, they pledged "to support one another" no matter the religious, philosophical, or personal disputes they might endure. "From virtually the moment they met in Philadelphia in 1786," the historian Sydney Kaplan once put it, "Richard Allen and Absalom Jones would be co-workers and leaders in the striving of black people to achieve justice and equality." That friendship lasted for "thirty-odd years," until Absalom Jones passed away in 1817.[48]

Still, questions have arisen about the depths of Jones and Allen's friendship. They disagreed on the degree of autonomy black churches should seek (the AME wanted complete freedom, but Jones's St. Thomas's Episcopal was satisfied to concede some authority to white bishops), they appear not to have corresponded much during their lives, and they even went to court over their failed business partnership.

Whatever disputes they endured, both Allen and Jones recognized that the growth of Philadelphia's free black community required a new brand of black leadership, one centered in diverse community groups and multiple leadership figures rather than a single man. Here, seeming division became strength. Thus, although Allen eventually broke from Jones and the Free African Society to form an African Methodist Church, he realized he could still work with Jones on the broader cause of racial justice. In other words, Allen and Jones learned that they could disagree and still respect each other. Allen was certainly more impassioned, as his departure from the FAS indicated. Though much younger, he had also achieved freedom before Jones. The more moderate Jones, on the other hand, waited patiently to acquire property while in bondage and even secured his wife's liberation prior to his own. He knew he would gain freedom and rise; time was on his side.[49]

None of these temperamental differences mattered when Allen and Jones joined forces to combat Northern racism and slavery's Southern expansion.[50] And when years later Absalom Jones gently laid his aging fingers on Richard Allen's shoulders in the symbolic "laying of hands" necessary to crown Allen the inaugural bishop of the AME Church, he could only have smiled. Allen was now the first black bishop anywhere in America—and Jones surely thought back to a time when he and a pitifully young Allen (newly arrived in Philadelphia and full of fire from the revival circuit) would "commune" and talk of securing a place for blacks in the Methodist Church. When Jones died only a year after Allen assumed the role of AME bishop, Allen must have been sad that he would no longer see that eminent man on Philadelphia's streets.

But that was still years in the future. Back in 1794, Jones was showing Allen the virtues of a deferential touch when addressing white readers. We know that both Allen and Jones thought deeply about how white readers would respond to their writings because of several clues. First, they presented copies of their yellow-fever pamphlet to the Pennsylvania Abolition Society, a group composed of some of the nation's most sophisticated reformers (longtime president William Rawle was one of the nation's leading authorities on constitutional law). Second, Allen and Jones adopted key stylistic ploys to appeal to men in wigs. For example, they appended a testimonial from Philadelphia mayor Thomas Clarkson praising their civic engagement during the yellow fever. This little act shielded Allen and Jones from accusations that they had produced their polemic for selfish reasons (perhaps to get reimbursed from recalcitrant white citizens who benefited from blacks' labors). With Clarkson's letter, the black duo gained credibility among men in wigs.

Finally and most importantly, Allen and Jones utilized classical rhetorical flourishes to stylize the pamphlet's appearance. Consider the yellow-fever narrative's opening lines: "In consequence of a partial representation of the conduct of the people who we employed to nurse the sick, in the late calamitous state of the city of Philadelphia, we are solicited by a number of those who feel themselves injured thereby, and by several respectable citizens, to step forward and declare facts as they really were." This ornate introduction, filled with elegant locutions, mimicked high discourse to communicate something very simple: blacks had been publicly defamed and would seek to set the historical record straight. In classical politics, a refined style was substance.

By using an adamant though reasoned and deferential tone in his antislavery appeal, Allen similarly hoped to ingratiate himself to a skeptical public. Far from lecturing white readers, Allen presented himself as a mere messenger of unpleasant moral truths. God, he made clear, labeled slavery an evil, not a lone black author. The Lord, and not a band of black men, smoted "kings and princes" for not freeing slaves in the ancient world. He very nearly apologized for invoking the specter of divine vengeance for unrepentant American slaveholders. I do "not wish to make you angry," he stated, "but excite your attention to consider how hateful slavery is in the sight of . . . God."[51] Although critical of white masters, Allen never actually wrote, as would David Walker in 1829, that white slaveholders would rot in hell. He only implied that. It was a deft touch.

Many of Allen's contemporaries understood the imperative of a deferential discourse when addressing white readers. Too much anger or emotion from a black author, many African Americans knew, and white readers might simply stop reading. Not enough deference to alleged white superiority, and white readers might simply ignore black calls for freedom. Daniel Coker's 1810 pamphlet, "A Dialogue between a Master and Slave" (the only black-authored pamphlet printed below the Mason-Dixon line during the early national period) solved the dilemma of black expressiveness by having his African American character adopt a moderate tone when addressing a Virginia master. When the white character first hears the black abolitionist's plea for enslaved people's freedom, he appears dubious. But in Coker's morality play, the planter does indeed listen to the black preacher's abolitionist call. Why? "I am convinced by your tone," the master declares.[52]

It is striking how pervasive this deferential style was among African Americans addressing white figures in the early republic. Black authors knew that rhetorical deference carried their words farther and faster than outright hostility (even if anger boiled beneath the surface). "We wish not to offend," Allen and Jones stated in the yellow-fever narrative, "but when an unprovoked attempt is made to make us blacker than we are, it becomes less necessary to be overcautious on that account." Because they were slandered first, Allen and Jones were less hesitant to publicly critique white racial attitudes. Nevertheless, the black duo realized that they could make the most effective counteraccusations only after they had, in effect, doffed their caps to white readers' superior sensibilities.[53]

Even among nonelites, seeming deference paid dividends. In 1801, for example, a dirt-poor Philadelphia woman named Ann Childers adopted this high-Enlightenment style when addressing the Pennsylvania Abolition Society. Hoping to bind her son while away in Maryland (for unknown reasons but perhaps to carry out an indenture bargain made with her own master), she asked white abolitionists to watch out for her son's safety and send updates to her in Maryland. The heart-rending letter signaled Childers's ostensible regard for white authorities. "Sir," it reads,

> [I] take this opportunity of writing to you to let you [k]now that I am gone to M[arylan]d. Sir, I kindly thank you for taking care of my son. Sir pleas[e] to send one word by the bearer How my son comes on. Whether he be a good boy or wheather [*sic*] he is bound [indentured] or no.

Like a rhythm, or meter, Childers used the deferential "sir" over and over to build a bridge to white reformers. But, like Allen and Jones, she transcended her own deferential tone to make a none-too-subtle point. "I live to return," she forthrightly stated, and see "[my son] done well by, according to [your] promise." Childers expected white reformers to educate and apprentice her son. She closed by mimicking the standard closing line used by white statesmen, gentlemen, and friends in high politics: "Your humble servant, Ann/William Childers."

So, too, in their pamphlet of 1794 did Allen and Jones insert deferential headings to gain acceptance among men in wigs. "Sir," they began their public letter to Mayor Clarkson, "for the personal respect we bear you, and for the satisfaction of the Mayor, we declare that to the best of our remembrance we had care of the following beds and no more." As leaders of the black community, Jones and Allen went on, the mayor could trust that they did not sanction black pillaging or plundering.[54]

Yet, just as Childers had done, Allen and Jones mixed biting commentary with deferential discourse. "Sir, . . . Sir, . . . Sir," she wrote the PAS, before dropping the act and saying, in effect, "I hold you responsible for my son's condition!" Similarly, Allen and Jones took pot shots at whites who deigned to criticize blacks who risked life and limb to aid the sick and dying in yellow-fever Philadelphia. In one section of their document, after listing the nursing work performed by eight different black Philadelphians during the sick season (some of whom contracted the dreaded disease themselves), Allen and Jones crafted a baroque explanation to make a simple point: even when black nurses failed to offer the best help, they did *try* to do something in difficult and even dangerous times. Did whites do the same? "It may be said," they wrote in fancy tones, "in vindication of the conduct of those, who discovered ignorance or incapacity in nursing, that it is, in itself, a considerable part, derived from experience, as well as the exercise of the finer feelings of humanity."[55]

The duo dropped such innocuous verbiage in the very next paragraph, however, and pointed an accusatory finger at apathetic whites: "We do not recollect such acts of humanity from the poor white people." Lest anyone think this last remark was too uppity, Allen and Jones quickly returned to the protocol of deference by stating that "it is unpleasant for us to make these remarks." "But," they finished, "justice to our colour demands it." As they further explained (in yet another reversal), the time-tested ploy of posing as (black) gentlemen wronged allowed them to complain publicly.[56]

When Allen sat down to craft his antislavery appeal, he remembered all he had learned from reading in the republic letters, working with the more moderate and literate Jones on the yellow-fever narrative proper, and watching white abolitionists deal with judges, sheriffs, and statesmen. By using deference as a rhetorical weapon, and in a classical writer's manner reversing sensibilities at key moments to confront a disarmed audience, Allen hoped that he could gain white readers' attention. His literary strategizing made the seemingly simple antislavery appeal a classic of the genre.

4. *Silence Is Not Golden*

During the winters of 1796 and 1797, Richard Allen visited a home at Sixth and Market streets on business. Though Philadelphia financier Robert Morris had once owned the house, its most recent occupant was none other than the president of the United States, George Washington. Through his assistant Tobias Lear, the chief executive needed to hire chimney sweeps at what became known as the "President's House"— the first "White House" in American history (it housed Washington for two terms and John Adams for one). Allen ran one of the best chimney-sweeping operations in the City of Brotherly Love. He would be the president's man.

Of course, Washington did not have to worry about hiring free blacks at Mount Vernon, where a cadre of skilled slaves did all chores large and small. This was only one of the racial hurdles the president faced in Allen's Pennsylvania. Among other things, abolitionists had a public-directory listing in Philadelphia, slaves could mingle with a vibrant community of free blacks, and the citizenry at large frowned on Washington's use of enslaved coachmen to move about town (he had to hire a German indentured servant to mollify locals). On top of all this, the Quaker State refused to let federal officers ignore the abolition act.

No diehard defender of bondage by this stage of his life, Washington nevertheless believed that the best remedy for slavery was public "silence." Free of abolitionist meddling, masters could do the right thing and slowly embrace antislavery principles on their own clock. He was never completely comfortable as a master in emancipating Pennsylvania.

Allen vehemently disagreed with Washington's vow of silence. The founding generation, he argued, must publicly confront bondage for America to claim its rightful place as a redeemer nation. Allen hoped that a deferential essayist's touch would persuade gentlemen to agree. He cheered a few years later when the nation's deceased first president left intriguing evidence that he just may have read the former slave's antislavery appeal.

5

"We Participate in Common"
Allen's Role as a Black Mediator

After the turmoil of the previous few years, Richard Allen deserved a break. His walkout from St. George's had thrust him into a nasty confrontation with white clerics over black independence, and his yellow-fever work had thrust him into a nasty confrontation with racial stereotypes. On top of that, Allen was himself a weary survivor of the deadly yellow-fever epidemic. "In all this," as Job 1:22 states, he "sinned not, nor charged God foolishly." So why not just spend every day at his beloved Bethel—a converted blacksmith shop that sorely needed every repair Allen could muster—and otherwise tend to his flock of worshipers?

What makes Allen's middle years so intriguing is his refusal to retreat to the confines of his fledgling church. On the contrary, this seeming apostle of autonomy broadened his leadership activities during the late 1790s and early 1800s, consistently reaching out to white figures and institutions. True, Allen never forgot his Bethel base. He steadily built church membership, with over a thousand congregants at his formerly fledgling institution by the 1810s. Equally important—and somewhat contrary to Allen's iconic status as a promoter of black autonomy—he articulated a mantra of interracial harmony and black civic participation. A simple listing of Allen's activities reveals his broad-minded concerns. He published three important essays aimed largely at the white community, making these years his most prolific as a protest writer. He also joined the first fully executed black petition drive to Congress. Finally, he helped initiate a program of black moral uplift that appealed to white as well as black leadership sensibilities.

By consistently reaching beyond the black community, Allen helped redefine the meaning of early black leadership. More than a community activist (though always concerned with protecting the black community), black leaders like Allen envisioned African Americans as competent members of the broader body politic. For a brief but important period of time, they defined black patriotism as a formative part of American nationalism. Indeed, though opposed to slavery and racial inequality, and fully aware of the need to retain autonomous social and cultural institutions, black leaders in Philadelphia, New York, and other Northern locales emphasized their desire to participate in the rights and rituals of citizenship.

Once again, print culture served as the key vehicle for demonstrations of black civic inclusion—but it was not the only protest form that African Americans deployed. Through rallies, petitions, and print media, black leaders attempted to bring the concerns of the African American community as a whole before white legislators, community leaders, and religious elites. In doing so, black leaders like Allen became "mediators" of African American political life. Not so much the modern bargaining agent that contemporary readers may associate with the term, a "mediator" in early national culture used print to interface with a broad array of constituencies. The early republic saw a bevy of new men enter American political life through mediating activities, from the production of broadsides and newspaper articles to essays, reprinted sermons, and political addresses. These mediators functioned somewhat akin to publicists, and their strikingly modern understanding of politics helped secure the first peaceful transformation in American political history: the transition of power from Federalism to Jeffersonian Republicanism.

Although not formally involved in politics, Allen envisioned himself as a moral mediator—a black leader who mapped out a moral compass for his fellow Americans on the race issue. The American republic's very survival, he argued on several occasions, required virtuous white statesmen to act for the greater good of society—meaning black as well as white citizens—by adopting abolitionism as public policy. Discussions of virtuous leadership were not necessarily news to white founders, many of whom espoused the post-Revolutionary ideology of republicanism: that citizen virtue and self-sacrifice remained the foundation of the American republic. But Allen's inclusion of blacks in the American commonweal—not to mention his emphasis on antislavery—challenged many white leaders' understanding of just which voices mattered in republican culture. Did black voices matter? For the majority of white statesmen, the answer was a firm no—African Americans were neither citizens nor patriots. Black moral mediators vehemently but respectfully disagreed. As Allen put it in his eulogy of George Washington, African Americans "participate in common"—the common rights of citizenship, patriotism, and protest.[1]

1. A Bethel Base

Richard Allen would have understood well the famous dictum "all politics is local." His leadership stemmed from the most local place he knew of, Bethel Church. One of the first things Allen did was to create a Sunday school for black youth in 1794. Over the next decade and a half Allen continued to view himself as a community leader. Allen's church held revival meetings, housed protest rallies, and served as a key meeting place for the city's black elite.

Indeed, by the early nineteenth century, Bethel Church was black Philadelphia's largest and most important institution. Between 1794 and 1810, Allen saw church membership rise from the inaugural forty congregants to nearly four hundred.[2] Membership ranged from literate leaders like Allen to men who could not sign their own names on the church's first official document. Of the nine black trustees who authorized Bethel's incorporation in 1796, three signed with "their mark," the fabled letter X. Moreover, just as Allen hoped, Bethel continued to attract congregants from all socioeconomic stations, including artisans, mechanics, and day laborers. That Allen remained concerned with those struggling economically can be gauged by one crucial service his church provided: burial aid. When congregants lost a loved one and could not pay for funeral arrangements, Bethel offered loans, some of which were never repaid. By 1820, church leaders figured that Bethel had "lost from 12[00] to $1500 by crediting funerals."[3] Bethel Church mattered in both life and death.

Bethel also became a focal point of broader community action. In February 1798, for example, Allen led a series of revivals that converted white as well as black worshipers to the Methodist faith. For several days and chilly winter nights, as Allen excitedly informed Francis Asbury (now bishop of the Methodist Episcopal Church), large crowds gathered at Bethel Church for this "very great revival." Meetings stretched deep into the evening. "Many backsliders are reclaimed," he told Bishop Asbury, and the Lord would surely "bless the labors of his servants."[4]

Allen was soon synonymous with Bethel. In 1804, he helped start the African Society for the Education of Youth. White reformers and philanthropists were directed to send all communications simply to "Richard Allen at Bethel Church."[5] Despite his rising status, Allen realized that Bethel's importance transcended one man. It was sacred space for all of black Philadelphia. Over the following few decades, Bethel hosted some of the most important conventions of antebellum black history, including the inaugural gathering of the AME Church in 1816, America's first major anticolonization meeting in 1817, and the first national convention of black leaders in 1830. Within Bethel's protective walls, blacks could not only worship the Lord in peace and plot struggles for justice but also, as Allen put it, "build each other up."[6] No matter what he did to broaden the struggle for black justice, Allen remembered that Bethel's brothers and sisters were his foundation. "Upon this rock I will build my church," Jesus says in Matthew 16:18. For Allen, Bethel became that rock.

The price of forgetting black unity became clear when Allen crafted Bethel Church's articles of incorporation in 1796. Although he had departed a segregated white church a few years before, Allen had little choice but to remain within the confines of the Methodist conference of Philadelphia. That was the only way to claim a Methodist identity and secure preachers for the blessing of sacraments. As part of this process, Allen needed to produce a church constitution under the general heading of the Methodist conference. Ezekial Cooper, a Methodist elder and acquaintance, told him that this measure would also secure black church property. "He offered to draw the incorporation himself," Allen sighed, and "we cheerfully submitted."[7]

Allen sighed, according to the reigning historical interpretations, because Bethel's "Articles of Association" conceded too much authority to white Methodists. Article 2 gave the elder considerable control over Bethel itself (in "perpetuity," no less). Another important concession occurred in article 4, which declared that Bethel trustees could not "dispose of any part or parcel of the [church's real] estate . . . unless such grant . . . be made by and with the consent of the elder . . . appointed by Conference." As Allen himself later recalled, this section "consigned [our property] . . . to the Methodist conference." Article 10, which stipulated that "the Elder of the Methodist Episcopal Church . . . shall have the discretion and management of the spiritual concerns of the said Bethel Church," proved to be yet another sticking point. According to

Allen, naive black parishioners had been duped into agreeing to these power-reducing plans.[8]

The "Articles of Association" haunted Allen, setting the stage for a power struggle between white and black Methodists that lasted two decades. From that moment in 1796, Allen later recalled in his autobiography, "our warfare and troubles began afresh."[9] That war involved teams of lawyers, waves of Allen's parishioners, much of the good reverend's own hard-won financial resources, and Pennsylvania's supreme court. But the battle was much simpler than that. Allen always believed that white church officials simply refused to accept black independence. They tilted the Articles in the Methodist conference's favor and lorded it over black congregants every chance they got.[10]

White Methodists' efforts to control Allen's church were a bold reminder that the black community must remain vigilant. But Allen's claim of being duped is hard to fathom. As he put it, Bethelites, "being ignorant of corporations, cheerfully agreed" to the articles of incorporation.[11] Yet although Allen later insisted that Bethelites overlooked provisions that underscored white authority, he himself had that document published in 1799. Why would Allen trumpet a document that he had not read very carefully or that sacrificed black autonomy? Allen only published documents that illuminated black achievement. Although Allen later removed the 1796 act of incorporation from his autobiography (published posthumously in 1833), in 1799 he felt that it publicized a proud moment of free black accomplishment.

Allen was not a naive person. Recall that this was the man who paid his indenture agreement early and made sure that he had proper freedom documentation from his former master; this was the man who used his home as collateral for a business loan from scrupulous white abolitionists; this was the man who had already signed several property contracts with white men; and this was the man who, along with Absalom Jones, had kept detailed records of the money the two black leaders had lost during the yellow fever in 1793. Richard Allen naive? No way! He was a focused, confident, meticulous man. Allen portrayed himself in just this way. When Ezekial Cooper first approached him about the articles of incorporation, Allen recalled in his autobiography, black congregants registered immediate concern at the very idea. "Mr. C[ooper] proposed that we should make over our church to the Conference," Allen wrote. "This we objected to." So when Cooper later laid the articles before the black minister, how could Allen have overlooked article

10, which stated that white clerics "shall have the discretion and management of the spiritual concerns of the said Bethel Church"?[12]

Allen knew that incorporation would give Bethel Church the same standing as banks, libraries, and other state-sanctioned groups. As the "Articles of Association" declared, Bethelites could now "acquire and enjoy the powers and immunities of a corporation, or body politic in law."[13] In short, Allen knew the document would underscore black legitimacy in the eyes of the state. Pennsylvania's governor, who provided his official seal to the document, would see Bethel Church as no fleeting concern. The Pennsylvania Abolition Society had been incorporated in 1789 to legitimize the abolitionist movement. Allen wanted nothing less for Bethel Church. Perhaps this desire clouded his judgment.[14]

Or Allen may have been acting tactically, for securing incorporation of what was perceived as a radical black enterprise could be tricky. Allen's defiant exodus from St. George's Church did indeed upset key figures in Philadelphia society. Far from being naive, Allen shrewdly realized that the articles of incorporation might create an interdependent relationship with white Methodists (thereby gaining their support for incorporation) while maintaining black autonomy (thereby protecting Allen's black base of support).

Examining the Articles all these years later certainly supports this view, for, if read carefully, it is a document that does not simply subordinate black property rights to white Methodist wishes. Rather, it provides checks and balances between white authority and black power. In several articles, blacks are defined as "trustees" of the Bethel Corporation and given rights and appeal provisions. (According to the Articles, members and trustees could only be "of the African race,"[15] a provision eventually dropped after the Civil War.) Look again at article 10: while it gave white elders power over the "direction and management of the spiritual concerns of Bethel Church" (such as approving new members), it also added, "provided always that said Elder shall receive no person into the Society but such as one previously recommended by a trustee or trustees." In other words, Bethelites checked the power of white authorities through advise-and-consent provisions. Similarly, if the elder wanted to evict a Bethel member, article 10 gave him the power to do so, "provided always" that he get "the advice" of trustees. Article 4 warned Bethelites not to accrue debt on the church without consent of white elders but then added that two-thirds of trustees needed to be consulted as well.[16]

In this sense, the "Articles of Association" looked very much like the federal Constitution (with which Allen was familiar, having already successfully pursued a copyright for the yellow-fever narrative). There was much room for interpretation over just where ultimate power resided—with black trustees or white elders—and just what disaffected parties could do to seek final recourse (could whites take over black property, or did blacks have the right to self-determination through the election of black trustees?). Allen might well have believed that Bethelites retained ultimate power through the Articles; so too might white elders have believed in their sovereignty.

Allen might have viewed the Articles as a political compromise of sorts. As his other reform activities reveal, Allen hoped to build bridges between black and white citizens—to have an independent black church but also connections to white Methodists. This was God's true way, he believed; black and white Methodists' ability to reconcile racial differences boded well for American culture. Even though he did not draft the Articles, Allen would not have signed the document without assurances that it protected black power over church affairs and property. If things worked out, and white and black Methodists could coexist under the Articles, then that would be wonderful; if not, Allen could simply call on black trustees and votes to get out.

Which is precisely what happened. According to Allen, Methodist elders broke the covenant he had signed in 1796 and attempted to grab power from blacks. When this occurred in 1805, Bethel had grown bigger and stronger. So too had Allen's confidence as a leader grown. As Allen told the tale, the new disputes began when the Reverend James Smith arrived as elder. Brother Smith, Allen wrote, "waked us up by demanding the keys and books of the Church and forbid us from holding any meetings except by order from him."[17] The reference to handing over the keys was significant, and it must have shaken Allen to the core. In the Bible, St. Peter had the sacred charge of starting Jesus's church and holding the keys to the inaugural chapel. "I will give to you the keys of the Kingdom of Heaven," Jesus tells Peter, "and whatever you bind on earth will have been bound in heaven; and whatever you release on earth will have been released in heaven."[18] Perhaps thinking of these lines, Allen and his fellow trustees vigorously objected to Smith's demand of the keys. Smith held firm too, barking the word Bethelites had not heard since Allen walked out of St. George's a decade earlier: *"submit!"*[19]

After consulting with a lawyer, Allen discovered that the Methodist conference had a legal claim on Bethel. There was no black bargaining power within the Articles. Perhaps Allen portrayed himself as naive because he was embarrassed about assenting to the original document. But true to his resolute character, Allen would not be moved by legal niceties. In 1807, he put on a show of black community resolve that transcended the original articles of incorporation and reclaimed Bethel Church as a black-controlled institution.

The African Supplement was the result. A stunning document composed of seven articles—altogether half as long as the "Articles of Association"—the African Supplement unequivocally repealed white economic and clerical authority over Bethel Church. The brief preamble declared that the African Supplement aimed at "improving, amending, and altering the Articles of Association." Article 1 went even further, stating that the original requirement that blacks seek white approval before selling church property had been "repealed" and "altered." Bethelites, and not the Methodist elders, controlled the physical properties of the black church. Similarly, article 2 reversed white clerics' control of membership rolls. Bethelites, and not the elders, had the power to suspend recalcitrant members. Moreover, if white authorities wanted access to Bethel's pulpit, they must approach black trustees, not the other way around. On issue after issue, the African Supplement celebrated black autonomy.[20]

Black democracy abetted black autonomy. The preamble to the African Supplement invoked the "consent of two thirds of the male members of [Bethel] church." Historian Charles Wesley reports that forty-nine "male members of the Church" signed the document, twenty-nine of whom were illiterate. Allen himself claimed a "unanimous" vote in favor of the African Supplement (including female votes). Though Bethel remained within the organizational structure of the Methodist Episcopal Church, it did so as an equal member of the Methodist conference —or so Allen thought.[21]

In fact, a final legal showdown with white Methodists still loomed. The African Supplement "raised a considerable rumpus," Allen reported, with whites vowing revenge. But black parishioners remained steadfast.[22] The African Supplement symbolized their resolve to control Bethel Church. No wonder Allen did not reprint the "Articles of Association" again. The African Supplement, Allen felt, was the best testimony to free blacks' rising confidence as both a religious and political body.[23] It was, to borrow a phrase from another civil rights leader, a "stride toward freedom" itself.[24]

2. Two Eulogies

Clearly, Allen had his hands full as a community leader in the decade and a half following Bethel's breakaway from St. George's. That is what makes his turn-of-the-century leadership activities so intriguing, for amid the struggles over Bethel's future Allen attempted to broaden the struggle for racial justice by reaching beyond the black community. This black founder saw himself as a rising moral leader.

To see just how seriously Allen took his role as moral mediator, one need only look to a succession of outreach activities he undertook in a single year. In 1799, Allen printed a pair of eulogies of Southern white men who had come to support emancipation in one form or another, and he contributed to a congressional petition against slavery and the slave trade. Taken together, these protest activities further testified to Allen's still-strong belief in the possibility of nonviolent racial reform within American culture.

The first of Allen's eulogies saluted America's dearly departed inaugural president George Washington for liberating his slaves. On December 29, 1799, two weeks after Washington's death, Allen ended normal Sunday services at Bethel Church with solemn words on the great leader's passing. "At this time," he intoned, "it may not be improper to speak a little on the late mournful event." Black parishioners certainly knew about Washington's death, but they might well have wondered what the passing of a white president and Virginia slaveholder had to do with them. Allen quickly supplied answers. Washington's death, Allen proclaimed, is "an event in which we participate in common with the feelings of a grateful people—an event which causes 'the land to mourn' in a season of festivity."[25]

The rest of Allen's eulogy was short and pointed. In roughly five hundred words, he told his worshipers just why African Americans "have particular cause to bemoan our loss." "My friends," Allen explained, Washington had been a "sympathizing friend and tender father" to free blacks—doubtless an allusion to the fact that Washington had once provided a donation to the building of an "African church" in Philadel-

phia. There was more, Allen went on, for Washington "viewed our degraded and afflicted state with compassion and pity—his heart not in-
sensible to our sufferings." A famously reticent man, Washington did
not speak much publicly of his dislike for slavery. But he had emancipated his slaves in his final will. "Deeds like these are not common,"
Allen told people who did not need to be told that. More than liberation, Allen added, Washington provided for his former slaves' education and support.[26] In Allen's eyes, Washington's emancipatory will had
made him a true national hero, someone African Americans could
honor and respect.

Allen added a sly reference to black civic participation that made his
eulogy of Washington even more ramifying. For he labeled America a
color-blind nation. He told free blacks not just to honor Washington—
by being pious, respectful, and patriotic—but also to "love your country" as the great general did. This was no innocent reference.[27] The first
naturalization act of 1790 declared that only "white" Americans could
claim citizenship.[28] And although the Pennsylvania constitution did not
discriminate black from white rights, many white citizens assumed that
African Americans were not members of the body politic. In turning the
eulogy from an homage of Washington into a display of black citizenship, Allen thus confronted the very limited definitions of civic participation offered by white Americans.[29] "Your observance of these short
and comprehensive expressions will make you good citizens," he finished, making clear his own belief that blacks should be seen as members of the body politic.[30]

By focusing on race and black citizenship, Allen's abolitionist eulogy
veered away from every major address on Washington's death. General
Henry Lee's famous speech, given in Philadelphia on the day after
Christmas, was proper and fitting but pure hagiography. "What limit is
there to the extent of our loss?" he asked. "None within the reach of
my words to express," for Washington's death had shaken "the civilized
world . . . to its center."[31] This Virginian mentioned nothing about
Washington's emancipation edict. Indeed, very few white Americans
commented on it. Soon after Washington passed, notices about the former president's manumission of over one hundred slaves appeared in
Pennsylvania and Maryland newspapers. "General Washington has left
Mt. Vernon" forever, one Baltimore paper wrote, quoting a gentleman
from Alexandria, Virginia, who knew the patriarch. "His Negroes are

to be free after the death of Mrs. Washington." That, the paper commented, was virtue and leadership. But no public figure seemed to agree
—except Allen.[32]

The black founder's eulogy filled another void. While planning the
president's official burial procession through Philadelphia, no one
seemed to anticipate that African Americans would even want to participate in "the late mournful event" and claim this important civic occasion as their own. Although ultimately buried at Mt. Vernon, Washington was given a rousing funeral procession in Philadelphia on December
26.[33] The massive parade of citizen-mourners began at sunrise with a
sixteen-gun salute and continued with rifle shots every half hour until
sunset. The citizens' procession gathered at the old state house (where
Washington had presided at the Constitutional Convention in 1787)
and marched through the city on the way to Philadelphia's oldest and
most respected church, Christ Church. Papers reported that the procession formed into a massive, rolling crowd of mourners, well-wishers,
and others.[34]

Were African Americans part of this throng of citizens? Blacks were
normally a clear and visible presence on city streets, working, celebrating, protesting. When abolitionist Anthony Benezet died in 1784, blacks
filled city streets in his honor. But no paper reported black attendance at
Washington's funeral. In this sense, the processional matched the textual
record: Washington's death, like the nation itself, was for white citizens
only. The city's Episcopal churches issued a standard predrafted eulogy
of Washington that, while mentioning his "eminent virtues" and "illustrious actions," omitted any reference to emancipation. The only mention of blackness? Americans were told to wear black armbands for a
month.

Allen made clear that African Americans participated in this important national event. Indeed, even if he stayed away from the crowds,
Allen himself would have heard the guns, the dirgelike music, the steady
sound of feet marching through Philadelphia. Like other free blacks,
he might have watched the procession pass by Absalom Jones's St.
Thomas's Church. He may also have joined white abolitionists who
gathered to observe Washington's funeral march. In any event, Allen's
words indicate that he probably saw the processional. He wanted to
highlight the benevolent action of a man who had been "a sympathizing
friend" to the free black church in Philadelphia and, hopefully, an icon
of emancipation nationally.

Of course, Allen may have uttered harsher words within the confines of Bethel Church. Why did Washington delay liberation of his slaves? But because Allen envisioned addressing an interracial audience beyond his church, he would not make such thoughts known. Believing firmly that print media formed an important part of the struggle for racial justice, he arranged to have his eulogy published in the *Philadelphia Gazette*. It soon appeared in both New York City and Baltimore papers.[35]

The initial venue for Allen's printed eulogy is not surprising. Andrew Brown, coeditor of the *Philadelphia Gazette,* had known Allen since the yellow-fever epidemic of 1793. Brown praised Allen's address as a model of black patriotism, declaring that it "will show that the African race participate in the common events of our country—that they rejoice in our prosperity, mourn in our adversity, and feel with other citizens the propriety and necessity of wise and good rulers, of an effective government, and of submission to laws of the land."[36] If not an endorsement of abolitionism per se, these remarks did endorse at least hearing the words of a black abolitionist, something too rarely seen in the white press before 1800. And Brown did ratify Allen's vision of blacks as citizen-mourners. Still, that he needed to preface Allen's remarks illuminates Brown's concern with white readers' fears.

Allen allayed Brown's fears by mixing abolitionist commentary with patriotic and religious allusions. He noted blacks' sadness at Washington's death. He also artfully shrouded his eulogy in a series of biblical references. Layered and complex (favoring the Old Testament over the New and often pointing toward harsher biblical verses just before or after those he explicitly cited), these references consistently invoked a righteous God whom Washington honored but most Americans blasphemed by accepting slavery as the law of the land.[37] By citing 2 Samuel 15:30–31 (Washington's "head was covered"), Allen claimed that God sanctified the former president's abolitionism. But his use of Hosea 4:3–4 (Washington's death had caused "the land to mourn") raised the specter of American damnation for ignoring God's will. "Hear the word of the Lord ye children of Israel," Hosea 4:1 declares, "for the Lord hath a controversy with the inhabitants of the land because there is no truth, nor mercy, nor knowledge of God in the land." Similarly Allen praised Washington as an American prophet who had made an "acceptable fast to the Lord" (Isaiah 58:5), while also pointing out that "the wicked shall rot" (Psalm 112). Like a good preacher, Allen offered hope—but only to Americans who followed Washington's abolitionist lead.

His closing reference to the prophet Elijah offers the best example of Allen's coded use of biblical allusions for abolitionist ends. Returning to the theme of just why Americans should celebrate Washington, Allen asked that "a double portion" of Washington's abolitionist resolve be found in all Americans who now say "my father, my father—the chariots of Israel, and the horsemen thereof."[38] Taken from 2 Kings 2:9–12, this allusion conjured not just the hallowed image of the prophet Elijah but also that of his successor, Elisha. In the Bible, Elisha asks Elijah for "a double portion" of Elijah's power to perform miracles and hold off powerful foes. You shall have it, Elijah responds, only if you see me ascending to heaven. Elisha glimpses the prophet's rise, giving him Elijah's resolve, which steels him against doubters and enables him to secure the land of the ancient Jews. Allen's cagey use of Washington (Elijah) as a foil to "the whole of the American people" (Elisha's doubters) sharpened the eulogy's abolitionist meaning. Americans who celebrated Washington but did not eradicate slavery disavowed God himself. It also marked Allen as a modern-day Elisha: a prophet left to struggle against the evil of bondage on earth. Like a classically trained orator, Allen criticized American hypocrisy while ostensibly making Americans feel comfortable about their nation and its heroes. His eulogy was a masterful performance that prefigured the richly layered oratory of later black abolitionists like Frederick Douglass.[39]

Allen's inspiration for the eulogy is nearly as interesting as the speech itself. For the black preacher may have been the first African American leader to meet a sitting president. In 1796 and 1797, Allen's chimney-sweeping business cleaned the presidential chimneys at Sixth and Market streets. Though Allen almost certainly used apprentices to perform the physical labor, he collected monies from the President's House on at least two occasions. Did he see Washington? Protocol dictated that one of Washington's assistants pay Allen. But Washington was familiar with Allen's heroic yellow-fever work; he had also provided that donation to the African church in the early 1790s. Perhaps Washington wanted to meet Allen![40]

By going to the President's House to supervise chimney-sweeping work and collect money, Allen had a view into the very seat of American power that only foreign dignitaries, diplomats, and statesmen had. After visiting on Washington's birthday in February 1796 (perhaps around the same time that Allen's chimney sweepers worked there), Englishman Isaac Wells wrote a warm account of the President's House: "The society of the Cincinnati, the clergy, the officers of the militia, and several others, who formed a distinct body of citizens, came by [the house]. . . . The foreign ministers attended in their richest dresses and most splendid equipages. Two large parlours were open for the reception of gentlemen, the windows of one of which towards the street were crowded with spectators on the outside." Wells approvingly observed that "a public ball and supper" at the President's House "terminated the rejoicings of the day."[41]

The black founder and former slave also had a view into the paradox that was Washington's President's House: Virginia slaves in emancipating Pennsylvania. The gradual abolition act of 1780 stipulated that non-Pennsylvanians—eventually including federal officers—could bring slaves into the state for only six months before being subject to the law. To hold office in the nation's then capital, Washington rotated nine slaves (of the more than three hundred he had at Mount Vernon) between Philadelphia and Virginia. And when in the City of Brotherly Love, most of Washington's slaves lived in a converted smokehouse behind Richard Morris's former home.

This and other visual tricks—including a hidden passageway to allow slaves unseen movement through parts of the house—may have shielded white citizens' eyes from presidential bondage, but they did not keep blacks' eyes from Northern liberty.[42] In 1796, two of Washington's enslaved staff escaped: house servant Oney Judge and the celebrated chef Hercules. Washington actually had an indirect exchange with Judge, who made it to New Hampshire before being located by a Washington acquaintance. Why did you run, Judge was asked. "I wanted to be free—wanted to learn to read and write," she quickly replied. Washington pressed federal officers—including Secretary of the Treasury Oliver Wolcott, who hailed from Connecticut—to help recapture Judge. She refused to return unless the chief executive promised to liberate her. When the president angrily denounced such negotiations, Judge held her ground and kept her freedom. Hercules was never heard from again, though he probably made it out of Philadelphia safely too.[43]

Was Allen involved in either escape? Did he have contact with Washington's other slaves? Allen's eulogy of Washington left no commentary on these intriguing questions. On the one hand, he may have counseled against running away; Allen was no proponent of physical uprising. On the other hand, as a former slave, a black leader who served as an abolitionist go-between for slaves and kidnapped free blacks, and an

Underground Railroad operative, he also understood bondpeople's desperate struggle for freedom. The story gets more interesting. Allen collected money from the President's House in March 1796, two months before Judge's escape. In a fitting metaphor of her impending plans, she purchased a pair of shoes just before absconding. Perhaps more fittingly still, Allen's home doubled as a shoe shop around this time![44] These suggestive dots do not connect anymore than that. But Allen may have heard Judge tell tales of Virginia bondage and slaves' desire for freedom —and he may have helped set the stage for her departure from the President's House. As for Allen's congregation, it is not hard to imagine Bethelites facilitating Judge's (and Hercules's) flight. Judge ran errands in Philadelphia and met with members of the free black community. The existence of Philadelphia's free black community no less than an abolition law scared Southern masters like Washington. He was right to worry.

But we also know that Washington himself had increasing doubts about slavery toward the end of his life. Unlike any other Virginia founder, in fact, he determined to initiate his own gradual abolition act. Allen's eulogy hoped to illuminate the transformation of a well-known slaveholder into a nascent abolitionist and thereby make emancipation safe for the republic at large. Washington had apparently made his final abolitionist will a few years after Oney Judge escaped from Philadelphia. Did Judge's negotiations for freedom convince him to craft the emancipatory will?[45] Did Allen's 1794 antislavery appeal "to those who keep slaves," which Washington may have read while in Philadelphia, ring in his ears? These issues mattered less to Allen than the plain fact that the nation's first man had struck a powerful blow for black freedom. If the great Washington liberated slaves, then emancipation was not only safe but patriotic.

By printing his eulogy of Washington in one of Philadelphia's—and therefore the national capital's—leading newspapers, Allen also solidified his credentials as a moral leader on the slavery issue.[46] Allen's second published eulogy in 1799, celebrating the lesser-known antislavery activist Warner Mifflin, furthered the claim. The name Warner Mifflin raises few eyebrows today, but two hundred years ago, as Allen's eulogy attests, Mifflin made waves for attacking bondage in the heart of slave country. A Virginian by birth and Delawarean for much of his life, Mifflin hailed from a prosperous Eastern Shore family with over one hundred slaves. While still in his teens, the young man grew to hate slavery, allegedly discussing servitude with bondpeople themselves on his father's plantation. Marriage made Mifflin a slave owner. By the time he moved to Delaware, he held roughly three dozen slaves. It did not take long for the Quaker Mifflin to get out of this quandary. Just a few years before American independence, Mifflin liberated every single one of his slaves, and he had his father do the same in Virginia.

Influenced by both Pennsylvania Quakers and the PAS, Mifflin went even further than private manumission. He supported a gradual abolition act in the state of Delaware (which never passed), an end to the overseas slave trade nationally (which passed in 1807), and full rights for free blacks. His list of abolitionist accomplishments grew further still when Mifflin helped form the Dover Abolition Society in 1788. He died a decade later (at the age of fifty-three), fulminating to the end against bondage.[47]

Although born of radically different circumstances, both Mifflin and Allen worked as itinerants of a racial justice gospel. Mifflin not only knew Allen but also came to celebrate him. On his travels, Mifflin distributed Allen's 1794 abolitionist appeal. You must read Allen, he insisted to friend and foe alike. Allen returned the favor by memorializing Mifflin's insurgent spirit. Neither Washington nor Mifflin, Allen made clear, became trapped in Jefferson's guilty dilemma. They followed the word of the Lord, took practical steps to ban bondage, and treated blacks as equal Christians and potential citizens.

Indeed, Allen had known other Chesapeake slaveholders who straddled the line between slavery and freedom. For example, Benjamin Grover, whom Allen met on the Methodist circuit in the 1780s, had both slaves and free blacks on his Maryland property during the 1790s. Which way would he go? Allen pushed for full emancipation. In key urban areas—like Baltimore—emancipation made key gains during the 1790s largely because of increasing slave runaways. Frustrated masters struck freedom deals rather than waste more money tracking down escapees.[48]

Although no Southern state ever passed a gradual emancipation statute à la Pennsylvania, hundreds of masters followed Mifflin's and Washington's lead. According to one recent scholarly estimate, Virginia masters liberated nearly six thousand slaves between 1782 and the early 1800s.[49] If that paled when compared to Virginia's overall enslaved population (ballooning over three hundred thousand), then it still proved significant when compared to the number of slaves eventually released by Pennsylvania's gradual abolition scheme: roughly seven thousand. Despite these emancipatory trends, slavery still held sway in most Chesapeake locales. Allen's eulogies of both Mifflin and Washington thus sought to accelerate abolitionist policies in the new century. According to Allen, the true American patriot was a man of action and not merely conscience, and he was exemplified by the Southern masters who refused to sit idly by while Southern slavery grew.

As with Washington, Allen may have eulogized Mifflin first in Bethel Church. In 1799, he affixed a more formal ode to Mifflin to a pamphlet bearing Bethel's articles of incorporation. "We find many worthy characters who espouse the cause of the poor oppressed Africans," Allen observed, "men who, like Mifflin, devote their time and services freely to work out a deliverance for the poor African race." Allen "acknowledge[d] their kindness and friendly assistance," admitting that free blacks everywhere "hold ourselves indebted to them." "We cannot but regret the loss of that great and good man," he went on, "whose memory will not be forgotten for ages to come." According to Allen, Mifflin was the agent of freedom for "hundreds, if not thousands of the African race." Many slaveholders rejected his antislavery overtures, Allen somberly noted, but that only ennobled Mifflin in the eyes of blacks. "He died in that work he had been engaged in for many years," Allen concluded. "He will shine."[50]

Although Allen's twin eulogies of white men share a topical similarity, their differences are readily apparent. Allen's deferential but insightful words about Washington showed respect but hardly anything approaching warmth. For his fellow religious itinerant Mifflin, however, Allen's words are personable, amiable, and loving. Allen was after all an evangelical at heart, and he identified with Warner Mifflin and Francis Asbury, men who had traveled the countryside in the service of the Lord until their feet cracked with blisters. Allen knew their commitment to the gospel; he also knew their concern with interracial harmony. See, Allen's eulogy would essentially say, how Mifflin and I worked together for interracial understanding? Americans should go and do likewise.

Indeed, in shining the light on Mifflin in 1799, Allen may have been attempting to rekindle the interracial intimacies of itinerant life that had been so influential in his own passage to freedom in Delaware. Allen's memories of interracial class meetings and revivals—with black and white worshipers not only preaching the gospel together but rubbing elbows and even holding hands—were a model for bridging racial gaps. (It is worth noting that this experience may have been the basis for Allen's consternation at segregated seating arrangements at Philadelphia churches.) As Betty Wood and Sylvia Frey have reminded students of early evangelicalism, there was an "intense dialogue between black and white participants that formed the basis for the creation of a shared culture."[51] At the end of his life in the 1830s, nearly forty-five years away from his first itinerant work in the mid-Atlantic region, Allen vividly recalled the interracial intimacies of New Jersey preacher Benjamin Abbott, "that great and good apostle," as Allen called him, "one of the greatest men that I ever was acquainted with." Even more movingly, Allen highlighted the example of a New Jersey couple who reversed the roles normally assigned to blacks and whites, with his white hostess serving an exhausted Allen tea and biscuits after the black preacher's sermon. " 'A new commandment,' says He, 'I give unto you, that ye love one another,' " Allen said, quoting John 15:12.[52] Divisions between black and white dissolved when Allen revealed God's truth.

Allen was thinking in terms not only of the past but of the present and future as well. For even after his break from St. George's Church, he maintained ties with white reformers both in and beyond Philadelphia. One of Allen's prized possessions was the seventeenth-century Bible given to him by white abolitionist and Underground Railroad operative Thomas Garrett in 1802. In his famous post–Civil War book, *The Underground Railroad,* black abolitionist William Still relayed a story about the Garrett family that illuminates why Allen would have valued the well-worn text. As Thomas Garrett returned to the family home in Delaware County, Pennsylvania, he discovered that bandits had kidnapped a free black woman "in the [Garretts'] employ." As Quakers, the family disapproved of slavery. Thomas Garrett jumped on his horse, tracked down the kidnappers, and helped restore the woman to freedom. Philadelphia's black community saluted the family's long commitment to freedom by serving as pallbearers at Thomas Garrett's funeral.[53]

Allen's interracial intimacies extended further still. He hosted white Methodist minister George Cuthbert, who wrote glowingly of dining with his "good friend" Allen and his pious wife in 1797.[54] There could be no better example of Christian piety, Cuthbert commented, than Allen's wife. In 1804, Allen gave Frances Asbury a horse as a testament to nearly two decades of friendship. For Allen, interracial contact and fellowship was necessary if he was to be a true patriot and steward of the Lord.

Thus, although it is the lesser-known of the two eulogies, Allen's celebration of Warner Mifflin remains the black preacher's most moving expression of racial harmony. In Mifflin, Allen could see echoes of all the friendly white figures whom he had befriended through the years— reformers who supplied monetary pledges to his independent black church (Benjamin Rush), printers who did not shrink from publishing his pamphlets of protest (Andrew Brown), religious figures with whom he prayed (Warner Mifflin). "We cannot forget to acknowledge the tender care and kindness of a number of our friends, among the white people, in striving to break from off our necks the cruel bands of slavery," Allen proclaimed. Like Moses, Mifflin's "memory will not be forgotten for ages to come."[55] When he eulogized that good man, Allen thought there was hope for racial redemption after all.

3. "'We the People' Does Not Mean Them"

Allen needed cheering memories of interracial harmony as the eighteenth-century disappeared, for his involvement in a major black petition drive to Congress resulted in a stinging rejection of black civic participation. At the turn of the century, African American festive culture sharpened its claims on the republic. Parades and rallies in Northern urban centers now combined with newspaper essays and pamphlets of protest to underscore African Americans' desire to influence and enter the body politic. Richard Allen's twin eulogies of white emancipators were intellectual models for this emerging tradition, invoking both religious authority and patriotism to make the case for black civic integration. Far from outsiders, blacks displayed an understanding of law, democratic governance, and political rituals that, as Afro–New Yorker William Hamilton put it, "shall soon put our enemies to the blush, . . . and confounded, they shall quit the field and no longer urge their superiority of their souls."[56]

Although Allen and other African American leaders gained support from early abolitionists and a scattering of public figures, the majority of statesmen rebuked black founders' attempts to integrate American civic life. In New York City, free blacks were forced to hold an Independence Day rally on July 5, 1800, after white civic officials and merchants refused to yield streets on the nation's birthday (black New Yorkers wanted to celebrate the passage of the state's much-debated gradual abolition act, which liberated slaves born after July 4, 1799). The memory of that exclusion lasted all the way to Frederick Douglass's brilliant "Fourth of July" speech, given in Rochester on July 5, 1852, to protest continued racial exclusion in the American republic.[57]

Several months before black New Yorkers were excluded from July Fourth festivities, Afro-Philadelphians met a similar fate in the halls of the federal Congress. With Allen's help, Absalom Jones had circulated a black abolitionist petition through the city's African churches and reform groups. Seventy-three Afro-Philadelphians signed the memorial, which unlike an earlier petition was actually forwarded to the federal government and presented in mid-December 1799. St. Thomas's provided the majority of petitioners, and Bethel provided at least five signatories. Most of the petitioners (forty-nine) were illiterate, meaning black elites had to sign for them. By doing this, black leaders felt they had brought the protest voices of the masses to bear on the formal political process. As James Forten wrote to a white politician soon after the petition had been presented, the document reflected the interests of "700,000 of the African race," or roughly the number of African Americans in the United States according to the census in 1790.[58]

Like Allen's eulogies, Jones's petition focused on large goals—a congressional ban on the overseas slave trade, repeal of the federal fugitive-slave law, national consideration of gradual abolitionism. Though hopeful of some sort of congressional action relating to bondage (particularly abuses of the fugitive-slave law), neither Jones nor Allen could have hoped for immediate success on all of these matters. Indeed, the usually moderate Jones did not lecture white authorities about their duties.

Rather, the memorial sought to put abolitionism on the congressional map before the federal government moved south to Washington, D.C. In addition, Jones (and Allen) wanted to test African American claims to national citizenship. As Jones put it, white congressmen should not think black petitioners ungrateful for espousing abolitionism at the federal level, for free blacks merely considered themselves "equal objects of representation under the Constitution." In other words, "we the people" meant "us."[59]

To secure a congressional hearing, Jones exploited black elites' connections to sympathetic white figures. He probably enlisted former PAS member Nicholas Waln, who presented the memorial to the House of Representatives. Although the petition received a brief hearing, most congressmen found it subversive and unconstitutional. Some congressmen complained that the petition "was subscribed by a number of people who cannot even sign their name!" Others expressed anger at free blacks' claim to federal petition rights. " 'We the people' does not mean them," one Georgian sneered. Congress voted 84–1 to return the memorial to black leaders—the first "gagging" of an abolitionist petition in American history. Afro-Philadelphians gained a measure of redemption when Northern newspapers republished debates over whether or not to accept Jones's document, thus highlighting black founders' civic identities in the printed realm.[60] But that was a hollow victory, for Congress had not officially accepted the black abolitionist petition. African Americans had no standing in national political culture.

White rebukes of early black patriotism and civic engagement created powerful questions for African American leaders like Allen and Jones, and it pays to consider their deeper meaning. Just what was black patriotism and nationalism? Could African Americans ever hope to participate in the rites of American citizenship? Would free blacks be politically marginalized forever (making alternative protest ideologies more attractive)? In making moral claims on the republic and picturing black abolitionism as thoroughly patriotic, black founders tried to show that the dual projects of racial uplift and American nation-building were not incompatible. Forming a black church in response to white segregation, à la Allen's AME, and then shrewdly using that church to gather abolitionist petition signatures or to eulogize the nation's beloved slave-holding-cum-abolitionist president as a means of bolstering the freedom struggle were two sides of the same coin: perfecting liberty and justice for all. In this sense, black founders articulated a syncretic version of nationalism. Much like Afro-Christianity, early black nationalism took shape as a hybrid form. On the one hand, African Americans organized along the lines of black solidarity to protect community interests, establish autonomous institutions as bases of social support, and celebrate African heritage. On the other hand, black leaders sought to participate in the broader civic culture around them as a means of expanding the early civil rights struggle. Thus, Fourth of July parades, state and congressional petitions, newspaper debates, and pamphleteering campaigns offered black founders opportunities to exhibit black consciousness as well as an ostensible American patriotism. In short, early black nationalism was not interested in simple assimilation (or relinquishing a racial identity altogether); nor was it concerned merely with political and economic separation (a more familiar form of contemporary black nationalism). Rather, it was a skillful blending of American and African worldviews and traditions aimed at defending blacks as a nation within a nation.[61]

Needless to say, balancing black and American nationalisms was a tricky business. Many black founders, Allen included, eventually expressed sentiments that prefigured W. E. B. Du Bois's famous twentieth-century notion of double consciousness, or a warring of one's African and American selves. But for Allen and other leaders emerging during the early national period, there was still a window of opportunity to make the American republic a bulwark of black as well as white liberty.

It all came back to mediation in the public sphere, that artful projection of black views before white eyes. To achieve equality, defend black interests, and still not be accused of undermining American nationalism, black founders often presented themselves as the consummate representatives of republicanism. In particular, they posed as a loyal opposition to a morally corrupt American government. Borrowing ideas from early-eighteenth-century British Whigs, who argued that they were the standard bearers of English liberty, black leaders reemphasized the moral foundations of American freedom. Slavery violated both the Declaration of Independence and the deeper meaning of American nationhood by putting masters' interests above everyone else's. While Allen made such sentiments clear in his masterful eulogy of Washington, fellow Philadelphian James Forten, a freeborn sailmaker and wealthy businessman who offered loans to white as well black patrons, became perhaps the leading exponent of a black loyal opposition during the early 1800s. In fact, he was a key inspiration to the most radical of nineteenth-century abolitionists, William Lloyd Garrison. Forten's very life symbolized his complex sense of black nationalism and patriotism. After hearing the first public reading of the Declaration of Independence behind the Philadelphia state house in late July 1776 (at the tender age of nine), Forten envisioned himself as an American patriot. He later volunteered to serve in the navy, and, after being captured by a British ship, turned down an offer of freedom in exchange for becoming a British subject. America would remain, Forten declared, his mother country.[62]

Yet the American experiment in liberty, Forten knew, had a fatal flaw: racial injustice. Even the union's most liberal racial state of Pennsylvania could treat blacks as a lower caste devoid of rights and liberties. A fan of the British writer Addison, whose libertarian plays valorized liberty as the keystone of modern society, Forten resolved to pick up his pen and articulate black grievances. He authored perhaps the most soaring statement of a black loyal opposition in his 1813 pamphlet, "A Series of Letters by a Man of Color." Ostensibly an indictment of a proposed Pennsylvania law restricting black migration—including the threat of reenslavement for free blacks who did not register in towns they had moved to—Forten's essays were actually a meditation on black civic integration and allegiance. Testifying to Pennsylvania's unique status among American states (the first to adopt a gradual abolition law and one of the few polities offering theoretical equality to black citizens in its racially neutral constitution), Forten decried white statesmen's lack of racial sensitivity. Until African Americans could actually vote and hold office, he hoped to compel legislators to act as free blacks' protectors. In exchange for this temporary protection, he made clear, African Americans would ever remain loyal citizens.

Forten agreed with Allen, Jones, and a whole line of black thinkers who rested their claims to American identity on African Americans' nation-building efforts. As Richard Allen later put it in a famous letter to *Freedom's Journal,* America was a black homeland precisely because of slaves' and free black laborers' incessant toil for the country's prosperity and independence. "This land which we have watered with our tears and our blood," Allen proclaimed, "is now our mother country."[63] African Americans deserved the full fruits of citizenship. Black founders in New England, New York, and Pennsylvania echoed this same iconic phrase. As Peter Williams argued on July 4, 1830, recalling his enslaved father's struggles during the Revolutionary War, "we are natives of this country. . . . not a few of our fathers suffered and bled to purchase its independence. . . . we have toiled to cultivate it, and to raise it to its present prosperous condition; we ask only to share equal privileges with those who come from distant lands to enjoy the fruits of our labor."[64] Antebellum black activists uttered versions of this famous motto too. Citing James Forten, none other than Frederick Douglass argued in 1849 that the "Black people of this country are in fact the rightful owners of the soil of this country. . . . 'we are American-born citizens; we only asked to be treated as well as you treat your aliens.' "[65]

Douglass also hailed Richard Allen himself as the architect of a "new Declaration of Independence."[66] That the most important black abolitionist of the nineteenth century rested his activism on black founders' project of civic integration—the notion that black nationalism and American nationalism could thrive together—remains the best testimony to the significance and complexity of their thought.

4. Moral Mediation and the Black Underclass

Allen's civic leadership took an interesting turn in December 1807, when two free black men—John Joyce and Peter Matthias—murdered a white widow in her Philadelphia home. The woman, Sarah Cross, was about fifty years old and the owner of a small dry-goods shop. Joyce and Matthias entered her store one evening, shuttered the windows, and strangled Cross. After rummaging through her belongings, the two men fled. They were soon caught and incarcerated before being executed in March 1808.

Worried that stereotypes of marauding free blacks would resurface among white citizens, and compromise black claims to the fruits of American nationhood, Allen responded in two key ways. First, he ministered to Joyce and Matthias, helping to coax confessions and remorseful narratives from them both. He often came to the prison, prayed with each man, and made the long walk to the gallows with them. Allen even sang hymns with Joyce. "The tears that copiously flowed from his eyes," he recalled of his last meeting with the condemned man, "seemed now to be wiped away, while hope sprung up in his soul."[67]

Second, Allen published his thoughts on the matter for white as well as black readers. Entitled the "Confession of John Joyce" and "Confession of Peter Matthias," these twin works composed essentially one pamphlet dedicated to turning the headline news of black murder on its head. This was no "racial" crime, Allen argued, one borne of blacks' innate will to harm whites. Rather, Joyce and Matthias's heinous deeds flowed from their moral failures—moral failures, Allen emphasized, that afflicted white as well as black, rich as well as poor, powerful as well as powerless citizens.

Although among his least known works, the confession pamphlets figured rather prominently in Allen's evolving understanding of black leadership, racial politics, and moral mediation. Publicly demonstrating his moral authority within the black community, Allen lectured African Americans about the responsibilities of liberty. For free blacks, he asserted, the incident rang out like "a voice of thunder." "Many of you fear the living God and walk in his commandments," Allen intoned, "but, oh, how many are slaves of sin." Little transgressions—"dishonesty and lust," "drunkenness and stealing"—put people like Joyce and Matthias on a path toward major transgressions such as murder. Rather than leading a life dedicated to moral and racial uplift, according to Allen, they chose a life of frivolity, gambling, and drink. "See the tendency of midnight dances and frolics," he thundered, his accusatory finger wagging at his black brethren.[68]

Allen considered public stewardship of black morality part of his mediating role. Indeed, if Allen and Jones's yellow-fever pamphlet had warned the white community not to stereotype blacks, Allen's new pamphlet hoped to convince free blacks themselves to embrace moral uplift as a means of elevating the race in public eyes. Allen firmly believed in moral-uplift ideology. Piety, hard work, and prayer provided a moral grounding that kept bitterness from one's soul. As a former slave, Allen knew that despondency haunted bondpeople's thoughts. Yet, he continued, just when bondage appeared to be too powerful to overcome, "a hope arose" and the "love of God" opened the way to a "confidence" that faith would result in liberation. Joyce and Matthias's actions offered a preacher's perfect morality play, for, according to Allen, these men had let "darkness and perplexity" sink them into the "discouraging prospect" of theft and murder. Free blacks must vow as a community to be pious, sober, and virtuous. Only in that way would they avoid the misdeeds of Joyce and Matthias—and God's wrathful judgment.[69]

In writing so didactic a pamphlet, Allen hoped not only to lecture free blacks but also to mitigate white wrath. News reports verged on sensationalism, with allusions to Cross's "black" death at the hands of "black" men. "You have been convicted," Chief Justice William Tilghman told the accused in a statement that was printed in both newspapers and pamphlets, "of an offense of the blackest dye." If others committed murder in the name of passion or jealousy, he lectured, Joyce and Matthias had no such excuse. They killed "without pity or remorse!"

> But this was not all—you rifled her house of her money, clothing and bed; and proving yourself utterly destitute of human feeling, you went fresh from the scene, at the bare recital of which the heart recoils, to

partake of the amusements of a dance. You injured society in general, and the people of your own color in particular, by rendering them objects of public disgust and suspicion.[70]

The image of black plunderers revisited yellow-fever days. And so Allen also leaped into action to defend the black community. Rather than crafting a jeremiad about white racial sins, however, Allen now focused white readers' attention on the larger problem of lost virtue in American culture. Sin knew no color, Allen argued in an "Address to the Public" published with the confessions. "Murder is one of the most atrocious crimes of which depraved human nature is capable," he lectured white citizens. "Reader," he asked, "hast thou conceived murder in thy heart? Tremble, tremble, the eye of God is upon thee." All communities had people who drank, sang, and sinned in one way or another, he offered. God would judge sinners' transgressions, but white citizens should not judge African Americans—especially if they linked race exclusively to criminal behavior.[71]

Allen's attempt to broaden "the sin"—and lecture both black and white on morality—makes even more sense when one considers the state of early national reform. The dawn of the nineteenth century found reformers renewing their struggle against immorality, vice, and sin, which were linked to everything from crime to disease. Black no less than white leaders enshrined moral behavior as the cornerstone of the American republic, which was expanding in every direction (economically, demographically, geographically) and unleashing citizens' innermost desires. Political debates intensified leaders' focus on the behavior of common people. The election of 1800 saw Democratic-Republicans rout Federalists, bringing new men—artisans and mechanics—into the political process as never before. This democratic juggernaut raised questions about commoners' character and moral worth. Could they be trusted with political power? What would bind society together if virtue and deference faded?[72]

In Philadelphia, both black and white reformers created societies to suppress "vice and immorality" (everything from drinking to gambling). In 1809, black leaders formed the African Society for the Suppression of Vice and Immorality. "The object" of the group, Absalom Jones wrote to Judge Tilghman (he of the "blackest dye" lecture to Joyce and Matthias), "is highly commendable": to "produce reformations in the manners" of free blacks. Under the Society's leadership, black leaders would "visit the more dissipated parts of Philadelphia and offer advice, instruction and persuasive measures" about moral uplift. White leaders heartily approved.[73]

Indeed, the formation of black anti-vice organizations allowed African American leaders to participate in a broader moral-uplift discourse with white leaders. Anti-vice groups demonstrated black leaders' control of their own communities, a crucial component of white patronage of black clients like Allen and Jones. Needless to say, some African Americans found black leaders' moralizing hard to bear.[74] And Allen would soon face public challenges to his authority from inside the black community. Nevertheless, at this moment, black leaders believed that they were co-creator's of an American moral republic. As Chief Justice Tilghman had lectured Joyce and Matthias, "I am happy . . . to be informed that [black leaders] view your conduct with horror." Perhaps, he finished, the sad story of Joyce and Matthias would be a cautionary "example" to free blacks. Perhaps, Allen and other black leaders believed, moral policing was a bridge of understanding that would lead to interracial cooperation.[75]

In using the Joyce and Matthias pamphlets to link black moral uplift to the broader cause of interracial reform, Allen may have been thinking about his own leadership role in a key emancipation/uplift experiment. In July 1795, Bethel Church hosted a group of twenty-eight Jamaicans who had recently been liberated by famed English businessman David Barclay, who had inherited them as payment on a debt. Barclay commissioned the PAS to superintend the Jamaicans' manumission in the United States.[76] White abolitionists mobilized local reformers, seeking shelter, provisions, and apprenticing opportunities for former slaves. Richard Allen became abolitionists' main contact in the black community. In an abolitionist inventory of reimbursements related to the Barclay manumission, Allen received the largest single sum of any reformer: nineteen and a half Pennsylvania pounds for "sundries" purchased for the freemen.[77] With Allen's help, the PAS also sought suitable binding arrangements and "schooling provisions."[78]

Many of the Jamaican émigrés attended Bethel Church, allowing Allen to shine the spotlight on those black moral-uplift principles of religion and hard work. Barclay was pleased with Allen's work. As one of the banker's assistants happily wrote in 1797, the former slaves "had been properly attired and looked good, . . . [and] as far as I could see or learn [were] practicing [religious] precepts and commands." Allen beamed that his church became a trans-Atlantic link between emancipation and moral uplift.[79]

Allen's moral-uplift schemes prefigured moral-reform movements of the 1830s. Seeking to channel the explosive energies of a new revivalism then sweeping the nation, black moral reformers hoped to build an interracial coalition of activists that would revolutionize American racial sensibilities. They linked morally upright behaviors—temperance, say—to national abolitionism. Afro-Philadelphians James Forten and William Whipper led the antebellum moral-reform charge. At their first convention in Philadelphia in 1835, Whipper stressed four key points: "Education, temperance, economy, universal liberty." While many white reformers spoke about stopping Americans' excessive drinking, or their lack of piety, black moral reformers paired upright behavior with antislavery. Drunkenness, black moral reformers argued, led to poor treatment—even brutality—of slaves. So whites must shape up. When they did, they would see the black masses shaping up too. Indeed, by leading the moral-reform movement, black leaders showed an emerging white middle class that African Americans shared their moral values. As James and Lois Horton have pointed out, moral reformers saw "sober and successful black communities [as an] an argument for freedom."[80]

Although both moral-uplift and moral-reform movements shared a vision of moral rectitude as a defining part of American culture, they differed in critical ways. Uplifters like Richard Allen believed that black communities must police themselves. In addition, Allen spoke not to an emerging middle class but to a deferentially minded white leadership class—elite men of the young republic. Black founders' task was to convince white founders that African Americans were not bereft of virtuous leadership. And for this black leader, sin and crime were no less a part of white culture than they were of black culture. White Americans should therefore not use Joyce and Matthias's crime as an argument against emancipation.

This was an important message in 1808. The ending of the overseas slave trade on January 1, 1808, combined with the maturation of freedom certificates in Pennsylvania, prompted renewed public debates—and anxieties among whites—over free blacks' future in America. While white writers increasingly fretted about the prospect of interracial democracy—fearing, as Jefferson had, that people of color were an enemy in waiting[81]—black leaders reemphasized their sense of belonging to the American nation.[82] January 1, 1808, "immediately became an African-American holiday," Phillip Lapsansky has written, "and the first African American festival to generate its own printed literature." Between 1808 (when Congress, based in its new home of Washington, D.C., issued the ban of the slave trade) and the mid-1820s (when state emancipation festivals took root), blacks gathered on January 1 not only to "hail the end of the overseas slave trade" but to "consider their own role in American society."[83]

Black leaders met far in advance of the slave trade's closure. In May 1807, Bethel welcomed a "numerous meeting of Africans and the descendents in the city of Philadelphia" to plan commemorations of the event. Black founders discussed the "suitable manner of celebrating the day in which the importation of their brethren will terminate in the United States of America." A committee of five (led by Allen, Jones, and Forten, now the big three of black reform) issued a series of declarations that were to be read at the city's black churches at precisely 10:30 a.m., January 1, 1808. Far from a local celebration, this meeting resolved to export Afro-Philadelphians' ideas "throughout the union." The resolutions offered words of both defiance and deference, proclaiming that free blacks would mark the day annually and "endeavor to evince the gratitude we feel by acts of benevolence and brotherly regard one towards another by public praying and Thanksgiving." While thanking "the almighty father for having influenced the minds of men to condemn a trade which ought never to have commenced," the resolutions also praised the nation's white leaders. "We tender to the mild government under which we live, and to the friends of humanity in general, our grateful acknowledgments, for the services they have rendered . . . which has produced this happy event."[84]

Such language may have been tactical or heartfelt—or a mix of both. Like Allen's eulogies and Afro-Philadelphians' petition to the federal Congress, the slave-trade resolutions exemplified black founders' complex desire to integrate public discourse and civic institutions while simultaneously reminding white statesmen and citizens that domestic slavery undermined the moral authority of the American republic. Who would serve as the American conscience in the nineteenth century? According to Allen, free blacks would continue to be the prophets of a reformed and truly enlightened American racial republic—that is, if Americans themselves would listen to black founders' pleas for justice.

5. Ending the Trade

On January 1, 1808, Richard Allen stepped out of Bethel Church to watch the sun rise over a glorious new day. For the first time in his life, the international slave trade was illegal in the United States. The "infernal trade," as reformers called it, had shadowed Allen as an enslaved youth in colonial Philadelphia and haunted him as a rising free black reformer in the nation's capital city. And now it was gone! Despite setbacks—gradual abolitionism had stalled in Southern states and merchants of the domestic slave trade prospered—there was still reason to be optimistic about black freedom in America.

On that great day in January 1808, black leaders spoke at each of the city's African churches. Although Allen's speech is not extant, Jones's words have been preserved in pamphlet form. Choosing as his epigraph words from Exodus—"and the Lord said, I have surely seen the affliction of my people which are in Egypt, . . . and I am come down to deliver them out of the hand of the Egyptians"—Jones linked the abolition of the slave trade to divine prophecy. Indeed, testifying to his faith in the Fortunate Fall, Jones argued that the ending of the slave trade was actually part of a transcontinental wave of moral uplift that introduced Christianity to people of color. Now Afro-Christians would continue the battle against injustice in the Western world by pressing for national abolitionism and racial equality. In a tactical nod, Jones also urged blacks to salute white politicians and philanthropists who helped pass the national slave-trading ban.[85] As for Allen, he too hoped that 1808 marked the beginning of the end of racial injustice and the dawning of a new age of race relations.

Little did Richard Allen know what loomed on the horizon. Over the next decade and a half (as white church officials made another stab at Bethel, as racial prejudice intensified in the so-called free North, as slavery pushed westward into a host of new territories), the black founder would become so disillusioned with America that he considered turning his prophetic energies to racial redemption overseas.

6

A Liberating Theology
Establishing the AME Church

In October 1808, as the American slave-trading ban took effect, Richard Allen purchased a parcel of country property. Allen's rural home was in Darby, Pennsylvania, probably in a locale known as "Calcoon Hook," so named for the bend of a nearby creek. Located less than a dozen miles from Philadelphia, Hook's bucolic qualities had long attracted American gentlemen and naturalists (famed botanist John Bartram acquired tracts of land there). Allen purchased a second, contiguous property in 1812, giving the former slave just over thirteen acres of scenic land.[1]

Practicing the hard work he always preached, Allen cleared and improved the landscape. He built a barn big enough for a half-dozen horses (he owned at least five by the 1830s). And both he and his wife made sure the house was always well stocked for family and friends. It contained several beds, stacks of fresh linens, a stove, books, dried meats, "mantle ornaments, snuffers and a tray, lamps, crockery and glassware, framed portraits, [and] firewood." Even after the country home was later sold—Allen's will stipulated that half the property would be liquidated upon his death and the rest of the land sold later on—Pennsylvania's rural landscape beckoned Allen family members. As Kathryn Dockens, a lineal descendent of the black minister remembers, we "used to go out there to get away from the city in the summertime." Bad memories of the yellow-fever crisis of 1793 evidently cast a long shadow.[2]

Allen's country home may have ratified his belief in the American dream: work hard, pray, and see your life improve. With the international slave trade now closed, and abolitionism having taken root in every state north of Pennsylvania, Allen hoped for a better future for successive generations of African Americans.

However, the country home may also have been a psychological refuge for the black founder. Despite the passage of state and federal laws constricting slavery, American bondage thrived in the new century. New slave states entered the Union; sugar, rice, tobacco, and now cotton crops solidified the national economy; and the domestic slave trade transferred thousands of blacks from Northern to Southern locales. Richard Allen himself was very nearly a victim of the internal slave market when a slave catcher accused him of running away from a Southern plantation. Only Allen's public standing—and not the moral wrong of the domestic trade—saved his life. An acquaintance vouched for his free status, liberating Allen from a temporary stay in a Pennsylvania jail. The black minister showed Christian compassion by not pressing charges against the slave trader. But could he turn the other cheek when remembering that a similar fate doomed hundreds of free people of color annually, particularly on Pennsylvania's borderland, to the still fully legal domestic slave trade?

In fact, soon after purchasing his second country property, Allen's optimism about American race relations waned. The first signs of trouble appeared locally, with white Methodists' renewed attempts to take over Bethel Church. For Allen, the result was not only a life-and-death struggle over the independent black church in Philadelphia but also a reconsideration of blacks' struggle for justice. By the War of 1812, he began considering the necessity of a black safety valve beyond the United States. The African American dream of achieving equality within the new republic, he worried, may be a mirage.

1. The Path of the Righteous Is Beset on All Sides by the Wicked

Richard Allen's first legal confrontation with Methodist elders since the publication of the African Supplement (1807) occurred in Pennsylvania's supreme court. On January 7, 1815, justices sided against Allen in *Green v. The African Methodist Episcopal Society*. The case revolved around Bethel's expulsion of founding trustee Robert Green for bringing a lawsuit against other church members. Bethelites had violated the law, Green countered, by ejecting him without a fair hearing. The justices reinstated him, though the disgruntled Green never returned to Bethel Church.[3]

Historians know Green as a bit player in an escalating war over Bethel's autonomy. White clerics still seething over Allen's presumption of power backed Green's suit. Through this divide-and-conquer tactic, they hoped to put Allen in his place at last. Their gambit seemed to work, for the justices argued that Bethel could not expel a member through a select committee, especially if that committee was impaneled without the knowledge of the broader Methodist Episcopal Church hierarchy.

But a funny thing happened on the way to the state supreme court's decision. Far from a loser, Allen turned out to be a real winner. Why? For one thing, the court took Allen's church seriously. The justices held his "corporation" to the same standards as any other corporation in Pennsylvania. Citing precedent that had nothing to do with African Americans, the justices argued that Pennsylvania corporations must deal with a member's alleged indiscretions in a "legal and proper manner." In Philadelphia in 1815, that was a moral victory for Allen.[4]

The court decision also steeled Allen's nerves for a climactic year of battles with the Methodist conference in Philadelphia. Although short-term victory perhaps lulled white Methodists into thinking they could easily take over Bethel Church, Allen used the case to muster even more impressive defenses of his sacred ground. Not only did Allen gather some of the best legal minds as a defense team, but he also readied troops at Bethel itself. During the next year, no white cleric would pass Bethel pews in peace. When frustrated Methodist leaders returned to the Pennsylvania supreme court in January 1816, seeking yet again to rein in the recalcitrant black church, they received the greatest shock of all: justices now backed Allen's right to self-determination! A jubilant Allen soon gathered black leaders from Pennsylvania, New Jersey, Delaware, and Maryland to form the African Methodist Episcopal Church, one of America's first, and its most important, independent black religious denominations.[5]

Strangely, Allen's autobiography skipped over the riveting details of these final battles with Methodist elders, including both their attempt to sell Bethel Church out from under him during the summer of 1815 and his congregation's mass-action defenses later that same year. By not offering deeper insight on these matters, Allen may have undercut his own activist reputation. As a religious figure and stoic child of the eighteenth century, Allen was a naturally reticent man. Bragging did not suit his style. He also fervently believed that God was truly on the side of the oppressed, making deeper analysis of AME independence unnecessary.[6] But his limited retelling of Bethel's freedom struggle remains puzzling.

Of the supreme court ruling granting Bethel liberty, Allen stated rather undramatically that it "ended in our favor." "By Providence of God," he wrote, "we were delivered from a long, distressing and expensive suit." Allen said nothing more.[7]

Even members of Allen's church lamented his paltry recollections. AME bishop Daniel Payne, who never knew Allen, vented his frustrations at the black founder's silence. The very first writer to attempt a master narrative of the AME Church, Payne remembered sifting through reams of old documents and taking arduous cross-country journeys to interview AME old-timers gone gray. By grabbing "every pamphlet, every conference minute, quarterly, annual [report], . . . every scrap of paper that threw a ray of light upon the genesis and progress of the connection," he would bring AME history the respect it deserved. In the post–Civil War era, when history writing was being established as a professional discipline, the black church deserved nothing less. To Payne's dismay, his dogged research revealed little beyond Allen's autobiography—beyond mythology. The documentary record of AME liberation remained "both sparse and poor."[8]

Payne's desire to craft a master narrative was well-intentioned but perhaps missed the point. Allen self-consciously sought to build a founding mythology out of the many confrontations he had with church authorities. That founding myth, as he repeated in both *The Doctrines and Discipline of the AME Church* (1817), the first literary production of the new denomination under Allen's leadership, and his own autobiography (published posthumously in 1833), mirrored the struggles of the ancient Israelites under Moses, who wandered the desert after being liberated. Only after years of trials and tribulations did a suffering people (both the ancient Israelites and contemporary blacks) find a new Canaan thanks to just a just God.[9]

Bethel's founding mythology fit perfectly within the structures of early black history writing. For many black authors, religion contained "the truth of history": a providential vision of black life culminating in collective salvation at the hands of a just God.[10] In this sacred universe of meaning—of good and evil, right and wrong, justice and injustice—detail mattered less than morality. Thus, for Allen, black church-building transcended real-time events. Oppressed blacks were on the side of God and historical destiny. Although this rhetorical strategy dissipated by the twentieth century, it has echoed in modern civil rights movements. Martin Luther King's use of "Exodus typology," as Keith Miller observes, "invited listeners to . . . support his crusade [of good over evil] and thereby prevent the triumph of chaos." In King's universe, "racists temporarily upset cosmic justice with the disorder of racial injustice."[11] But, with faith in the Lord, African Americans would ultimately rout racial injustice. So too did Richard Allen cast Bethel's struggles as an epic battle between saints and sinners. For Allen, as for King, the details of oppressive events paled next to the fulfillment of biblical prophecies from Psalm 68: Africa "would stretch forth its wings," and "Princes would come out of Egypt."

Nevertheless, even Allen realized that Bethel's independence rested less on prophecy and myth and more on massive community resistance. Indeed, his autobiography consistently alludes to the significance of black collective action. "We" prevented white preachers from taking over the church, he wrote again and again. Allen was not using the hallowed "we" here; he referred to the reality of grassroots confrontation at Bethel—resistance that ultimately forced white Methodists to pursue a lawsuit against Allen in the winter of 1816. Prior to that, as both Allen and a host of AME history writers have recalled, the black congregation stood tall against virtually the entire Methodist establishment in Philadelphia.[12]

As far as white elders were concerned, black congregants must always defer to white clerics. For at least four years prior to the court case of 1816, a succession of Methodist leaders had attempted to preach at Bethel on their own terms and thereby claim sovereignty over Allen's congregation. The word "subjection" often rang out, as in Bethelites must always remain subject to white clerics' will. Although the War of 1812 disrupted plans for an outright takeover, Methodist leaders tried underhanded tactics to destroy Bethel Church. In July 1814, for example, elder John Emory published a circular that expelled Allen's congregation from the Methodist conference. Claiming to have the support of Allen's friend, Bishop Francis Asbury, Emory told black congregants that they would no longer be "served" for denying the pulpit to white preachers. With no one to administer the sacraments and perform baptisms, Bethel Church would fold. Methodist elders could then claim black church property. It was a great plan in theory, except that Allen's parishioners took no notice of it (compelling the Methodist conference to continue recognizing Bethel).[13]

Postwar peace found Methodist officials intensifying their efforts to "subject" Allen's church. These actions brought black parishioners out in force, even to the point of planning physical defenses of Bethel Church. The first sign of trouble came in April 1815, when a new elder, the Reverend Robert Roberts, attempted to take Bethel's pulpit without black trustees' approval. "Nothing but the aisles being stopped up by the congregation prevented him [from doing so]," Allen acolyte and early AME historian Noah Cannon wrote in the first formal history of the AME Church (1842). "And here," he continued, "a disturbance began."[14]

In fact, after this blockade, Methodist officials contacted lawyers to determine if African Americans could physically prevent white clerics from officiating at the black church. After studying the situation, Methodists' lawyers not only agreed that Allen had dubious claims to Bethel independence but also argued that the elders could even sell Bethel Church without Allen's approval.[15]

Cannon, a free black Methodist from Delaware who knew Allen around this time, later concluded that white Methodists had little choice but to resort to such shadowy tactics. Why? Black congregants simply refused to accept clerics' power. For example, after Methodist elder John Emory had posted a circular excommunicating black parishioners in July 1814 (as a prelude to claiming black church property), Allen "called the [Bethel] society together" for a mass meeting. "There were one thousand and fourteen [who] met," Allen declared in an unpublished letter (which Cannon had access to but has not survived). Black congregants "were unanimously of one mind": no one could take over Bethel Church without black trustees' approval. And even if white Methodists wanted to excommunicate recalcitrant congregants, Allen continued, they would have to use black church members on the jury, for Bethel Church was a sovereign entity within the Methodist conference. Every which way white authorities turned, they confronted the black masses.[16]

This frustration brought Methodist elders and their lawyers back to the merits of the African Supplement, the 1807 document crafted by Allen to guarantee black power at Bethel Church. Where Allen claimed that the African Supplement superseded the original charter, Methodist lawyers argued that it illegally seized power from white clerics. According to the elders, Allen had failed to inform St. George's about the African Supplement's claim to black sovereignty. "No notice was given to the Methodist Episcopal Church or to the Elder . . . of the design to alter the charter of Bethel Church," Pastor John Emory explained to lawyer Samuel Shoemaker in April 1815. Indeed, he claimed that as far back as 1807, when the Methodist conference had requested information "on the state of [Bethel] church," black trustees had blithely "mention[ed] having formed the Supplement to their charter but gave a false representation of the nature of it." Not until years later, Emory continued, did white authorities realize that black congregants had redefined their relationship to the church hierarchy.[17]

Methodist legal eagles seized on these claims, asserting that the African Supplement violated the original charter's dictate of black "subjection" to white authority. As Shoemaker commented, the African Supplement "breaks the union between the two churches . . . and withdraws and discharges the Bethel Church from its subjection to . . . the Bishops of the M.E. Church of Philadelphia." Bethelites' defiance, counsel Joseph Hopkinson warned, is therefore "liable to a prosecution at law," for they "have gone forward, unauthorized by any act of the [original] incorporation . . . and obtained a Supplement" that illegally enshrined black control. Far from a tweaking of the 1796 agreement, the African Supplement amounted to a "fundamental change" in power, shifting sovereignty to Bethel Church members. "This transaction," Hopkinson argued, "has been conducted with circumstances of misrepresentation, concealment and a want of good faith that seem to indicate a consciousness of wrong." The "pretended Supplement," he concluded, "is utterly void."[18]

Hopkinson then crafted a sentence that would ring in Methodist elders' ears. "In order to counteract this proceeding and bring its legality to the test of a judicial decision," he suggested, "I would recommend that the corporation go on exerting their powers as originally given, as if the Supplement had never been obtained." Translation: white Methodists were in control of Bethel Church, not black congregants. The result: an order to the sheriff to sell Bethel Church on June 22, 1815.[19]

Richard Allen must have been stunned when he saw the auction notice posted around town. "Sheriff's sale," broadsides proclaimed on June 12: Bethel Church had been "seized and taken" by Philadelphia officials and would be sold to the highest bidder.[20] Allen knew that any bidder for his church would have some connection to Methodist clerics. He also knew that he would have to dig deep financially to buy back the church. Then in its second incarnation—a brick building known as the "roughcast," which had replaced the old and converted blacksmith shop—the church sat on ground surrounded by black property owners.

Not only did Allen own a sliver of land on the church's northern edge, but a black waiter owned property south of Bethel and a black dry-goods dealer owned a lot behind it. Because the church included two contiguous rental properties once purchased by Allen, the auction would attract good bids. All Allen could do was pray—and bid high.

And this is precisely what the black preacher did. On that June day, Allen awoke early, prayed to the Lord for strength and wisdom, and then traveled roughly four blocks to bid on his church. Allen was actually well-prepared for this nearly tragic event. For years, he and the church had been accruing monies from rental properties around Philadelphia. In addition, Allen had given over church property to Bethel trustees in exchange for an annual stipend and bonds. Finally, Allen could count on the passing of the hat to raise extra money for his church. The man's diligence and foresight in acquiring rental property and making a deal with his own church would now be put to the best use of all: saving Bethel.

Here, Allen's self-conception as a black founder became central to the rescue of Bethel Church. Indeed, while white officials were concerned with gaining control of a renegade church, Allen viewed Bethel's sale as an affront to his dignity and achievement as a black leader. Allen's pride in building Bethel Church is illuminated in a remarkable but little-known pamphlet published in 1823. Although not about the sale of Allen's church itself, the pamphlet includes a deposition Allen gave before a local justice of the peace about his role as a church builder. If Allen's autobiography downplayed many of his efforts (public boasting did not befit a man of God, he believed), the deposition showed Allen's abiding sense of accomplishment at Bethel. Responding to the allegations of some disaffected Bethelites who claimed he had actually stolen money from the church, Allen stated adamantly that he had "been chiefly instrumental, under God, in building [Bethel] church." The pamphlet vigorously denied rumors of financial malfeasance and claimed that Bethel was, more than anyone else's, his creation. Allen was not going to let innuendo or gossip stain his image. And he was not going to let anyone buy his church.[21]

Both Allen and his congregation mustered that same sense of certitude when confronting white Methodists at the church sale. And perhaps in a similar sense of pride and accomplishment, Allen took no notice of this wicked attempt to destroy his beloved Bethel, refusing to dignify it in any way, shape, or form in his autobiography.

The sale and its aftermath ended up shocking white Methodists, who fumed as Allen walked away from the auction with Bethel Church. Making out his official report on the sale later that day, sheriff Jacob Fitler notified "the honorable judges" of Philadelphia who oversaw land transactions that he had put Allen's church up for sale. "When," Fitler continued, "Richard Allen of Philadelphia bought the same, . . . the brick meetinghouse and lot of ground" at Sixth and Lombard streets. The price Allen paid for his own church was the unbelievable sum of $9,600. Add on $525 for the rental lots near it, and Allen had paid to the city of Philadelphia a total of $10,125. It was no contest, Fitler reported: Richard Allen was simply "the highest and best bidder."[22] That was a princely sum in 1815, a fortune for people of any class or color. Allen used the money to buy back perhaps the most important free black institution in all of America.

2. Black Phalanx

Once again the owner of his church, Allen was still not free and clear of Methodist officials. If he was going to call Bethel a "Methodist church," officials lectured him yet again, then Allen must defer to the resident elder. In this ongoing narrative between Allen and white Methodists, only the names changed, never the result. Allen usually won. But Allen squared off against Methodist elders just one last time, for they took him all the way to the Pennsylvania supreme court and lost. Allen and his Bethel congregation faced down white clerics every step of the way. And they finally won.

This very last act of Bethel independence occurred in the months following Allen's repurchase of his church in June 1815. As the seasons turned, so too did the defeated and disgusted presiding elder—Robert Roberts—give way to the brash and apparently undeterred Robert Burch. This new elder sought to confront Allen once and for all. In December 1815, he announced at least twice that he would preach in Bethel Church, as was his prerogative as Methodist elder. Burch claimed an invitation from Allen's nemesis, former trustee Robert Green. But there can be little doubt that this was a ruse. Burch wanted to do what no one else had yet done: suppress Allen and his congregation.

As he quickly discovered, Bethelites were not beyond physical confrontation. When he first sought to preach at Bethel, Burch recalled, black congregants circulated rumors that they might violently challenge him. Burch even heard that "the people belonging to the congregation assembled at sundry times armed with deadly weapons to prevent me from officiating there." A concerned Burch visited Allen privately. Described later by Burch as "indisposed," Allen was hardly in a conciliatory mood. Surely you are joking, Burch pleaded with Allen—no one would act "contrary to the peace and happiness of society" by resorting to deadly force, would they? Allen, sitting comfortably in his longtime Spruce Street home, assured the fearful Burch that he had indeed heard those same rumors about black violence . . . and that they might be correct. As Burch told his lawyer, Allen merely "corroborated and confirmed the report" of possible black violence.[23]

Burch quoted Allen's final words very carefully, recalling that the black preacher had told him that if he "or anyone he should appoint would offer to officiate" (or preach) without Bethelites' approval, the congregation's angriest members would be "the hardest to fend off." Did this mean violence? Allen did not say yes, but he did not say no. The law, Bethelites believed, was behind them. But they were also ready to get in front of the church to physically repel white officials' intrusion.[24]

Allen was too shrewd and pious to condone violence. There can be little doubt that violence would actually have served white elders' purposes—illustrating that unruly black parishioners needed to be controlled from above—and that city officials would have entered the fray on their side. But Allen was clearly not afraid of using the image of unruly black congregants to make his point: the new elder could not simply waltz into Bethel Church and preach on his own terms. Indeed, Allen turned the tables on Burch, intimidating the would-be intimidator, for Burch departed the black preacher's home shaken and contrite. "I . . . did NOT attempt to preach to [Bethel]," he later explained.[25]

But apparently he did. According to Burch himself, on Thursday, December 28, just a few weeks after his audience with Allen, he marched down to Bethel, opened the church's doors, and shouted to an evening gathering of congregants that he would return to preach that Sunday. He then rushed away. This may have been a premeditated act. Burch was about to bring suit in court for the right to preach at, and thereby control, Bethel. He first needed a reason to go to court. Ironically, this strategy had been the advice of lawyer Joseph Hopkinson months before, albeit advice off-handedly given to blacks who might have been hurt by white Methodists' controlling moves. Just take control of Bethel, Hopkinson had told a previous elder, and do not back down. If Allen complains, let him go to court for redress. Now it was Burch who would go to the courts aggrieved and angry. To do this, he needed to have an offense—not a rumor—to report. He needed to have the pulpit denied him in deed.

Burch got this and more on December 31 at 3:00 p.m. in Bethel Church. In a riveting scene, the white cleric returned as promised to find Bethel overflowing with defenders. Allen's adherents filled every church pew, stood tall in the aisles, and occupied virtually every open space. To hinder Burch's attempt to get to the pulpit, Bethelites even stuffed benches and chairs into the aisles. Allen was strategically not present, so Bethelites had the pulpit occupied by Allen's eager and able assistant, the soap maker Joseph Tapsico. A stunned Burch simply looked on from afar and did not even attempt to get past these ample obstacles.

Burch waited for Tapsico to finish his sermon so that he might say a few words from the church's entryway. All the while, the congregation shouted. The white elder waited a bit more. When he tried to speak, the congregation responded with ear-splitting screams that Burch described as a "violent shout or ecstasy." Burch finally got a word in. Didn't Tapsico know that he "had made an appointment to preach" here? Tapsico "made no answer but continued to speak and took no notice of the deponent," Burch's lawyer scribbled matter-of-factly upon hearing the details later. "No man," Tapsico finally replied, his voice rising, "*has a right to speak in this congregation when I am speaking!*" Tapsico continued in more solemn terms: "*I* speak in the name of my God and in the name of the laws of my country." Much like Allen, he used the language of patriotism to bolster black nationalism within American culture. Without missing a beat, he returned to his homily. The congregation cheered. As Burch's lawyer dryly put it, "The deponent left the church."[26]

But Burch did not stop there. On January 1, 1816, Burch and the Methodist conference applied to the state supreme court for a writ of mandamus to be reinstated to Bethel's pulpit. As Allen recalled, Bethel's lawyers "repulsed his motion." The court did, however, grant Methodists a writ "to show cause why [black] trustees should restore him [to] the pulpit." Feeling confident, Allen's lawyers—including celebrated jurists Horace Binney, David Paul Brown, and Pennsylvania state attorney Israel Ingersoll—instead put the whole matter of black congregational control before the court. Allen was delighted at this turn of events, believing that no one would rule against congregational self-determination, whether black worshipers or white.[27]

Sitting in court on that January day, Allen watched his lawyers make elegant claims about Bethel's "right" to self-government, white Methodists' shaky claims to the black church, and (most importantly) white elders' lack of standing before the court. And he was positively elated when members of the court seemed sympathetic to Bethel's plight. Although Horace Binney "opened the case very copiously," Allen recalled, "the court [soon] appeared to be convinced" of Bethel's right to self-government. Leaving nothing to chance, Binney filled the rest of the day with Bethel's claims to power. No white minister, no elder, no person whosoever "had any right to the pulpit of Bethel," Binney argued, "contrary to the wish of the society." White Methodists were not voting members of the congregation. The African Supplement, and not the original "Articles of Association," governed Bethel's affairs. Even if black congregants granted the pulpit to a white cleric, he stated at one point, it "might be taken from him at [Bethelites'] pleasure," for they retained sovereignty. Allen must have smiled when one of the judges commented that white Methodists "held too high a hand over the colored people . . . and had no right to the church."[28]

The court then uttered words Allen long hoped to hear: Bethel church was free.

In a gushing letter to his friend Daniel Coker in Baltimore, Allen recounted the proceedings in court and out. His lawyers were great. But his congregation was simply marvelous, Allen told Coker, filling Bethel Church to prevent white preachers from taking the pulpit each and every time they tried. Bethelites' mass opposition to white rule became the state supreme court's salient image of the dispute. One judge had asked the Methodist elder pointedly "what profit he expected . . . by forcing himself upon [Bethel] contrary to their wishes?"[29] Relay this story as much as you can, Allen finished. If other black congregations employed mass action, they too could achieve independence.[30]

Perhaps this is why Allen refused to highlight the state supreme court ruling in his autobiography. For him, blacks' mass-action strategy, and not white jurists' decision, was the key to black freedom.[31] In this sense, Bethel's liberation took shape in a much wider context of black resistance, including both slave rebellions and self-emancipations. The years in which Allen and his congregants grappled with Methodist elders (from the 1790s through 1816) witnessed some of the most galvanizing black uprisings in the era of Atlantic slavery, from the Haitian Revolution to Gabriel's Rebellion. In addition, Bethel Church had a tradition of incorporating freed blacks and runaway slaves into its proceedings—it is not inconceivable that these men and women helped shape Bethelites' vigorous collective response to white bullying. With roughly fourteen hundred congregants by 1816, Bethel Church was a bastion of black power. And threatened blacks here no less than in the enslaved South deployed militant resistance to protect black freedom.

Of course, there is one big problem with such an interpretation. Allen had always thought that a nonviolent movement based on the principles of Christian love was the best means of liberating people of color. However, by 1816, he may just have come to the realization that white Methodists would take Bethel Church no matter how much love Allen offered. Think once again of Methodist elder Robert Burch's talk with Allen in December 1815. When asked if black congregants would physically challenge white clerics, the black preacher did not deny the prospect of violence. Rather, Allen let that threat hover above white officials' scheming heads. Although he opposed violence deep in his bones, Allen knew that white preachers would now think twice before taking Bethel Church. In this manner, Allen's congregation realized years before Northern militants like David Walker that mass action among free people of color—not merely slaves—could be an effective strategy of social dissent.

3. The Index

Why did Methodist elders attempt to legally gain control of Bethel Church precisely when they did in the 1810s? Allen's congregation was growing at a phenomenal rate. White officials hoped to rein it in before Bethel grew even larger. The details of Bethel's demographic explosion were there for all the public to see in a series of fascinating annual reports posted around Philadelphia. Known as "The Philadelphia Index," this annual broadside tallied births, deaths, and baptisms for every one of the city's churches. This gem of a resource allows historians a glimpse of the demographic factors shaping Bethelites' collective activism.[32]

Of course, the Index allowed Allen's contemporaries to see just which church was on the rise. During its first few years, Bethel grew slowly. In 1797–98, Allen's church recorded 14 baptisms out of a citywide total of 2,749 and 15 burials (out of 4,080). By 1801–2, Bethel had 114 baptisms (out of 1,838), and only 14 deaths (out of 2,159). Over the next decade, baptism numbers at Bethel hovered between 80 and 162 annually, while deaths never exceeded more than 47 per year.

Then Bethel grew even faster. After 1812, it averaged over 100 baptisms per year, and in some periods nearly 135 baptisms. By the War of 1812, Bethel routinely outpaced the city's leading Methodist church, St. George's. In 1812–13, Bethel nearly tripled the number of baptisms of its competitor (102 to 37). Two years later, Bethel quadrupled St. George's birthrate.

Bethel was now one of Philadelphia's fastest growing churches, not merely one of its fastest growing black churches. By the 1820s, Bethel reached upward of 200 baptisms annually. In 1821–22, Allen's church could claim that it contributed 8 percent of Philadelphia's total baptisms! Put another way, during the early 1800s, Bethel Church outpaced the aggregate growth rate of Philadelphia churches by a factor of two. If there was one birth recorded at the average white church, there were two at Bethel. Only a handful of churches were in this league: the German Lutheran Church (representing Pennsylvania's traditionally strong German population), St. Mary's Roman Catholic Church (representing the newfound demographic strength of Irish immigrants), and what became the United Methodists (St. George's plus three other Methodist congregations). Throughout the 1820s, Allen's church continued its impressive growth, providing between 4 and 8 percent of the city's baptisms annually.[33]

Two factors contributed to Bethel's remarkable growth. First, Philadelphia's status as a free black capital beckoned steady numbers of free blacks and former slaves to the City of Brotherly Love, many of whom arrived on Bethel's doorstep. One thinks immediately of David Barclay's flock of freed people, who arrived from a Jamaican plantation in 1795 and soon found themselves in the presence of Richard Allen. Sons and daughters of those émigrés later boosted Bethel's demographic power.

The second factor funneling blacks to Bethel was perhaps even more obvious: black citizens around the country viewed Richard Allen as a great leader. He cared deeply for his congregation and community, stopping at little to aid those who filled church pews each and every week. Take, for example, Allen's admission to the Philadelphia Dispensary. A medical-aid society formed during the 1780s, the institution offered members access to the group's doctors.[34] Allen paid annual dues for this privilege largely because it gave Bethel congregants—not just himself— medical care. A more personal example came from Jarena Lee, the first black female preacher in the AME Church and a single mother during the 1820s, who entrusted Allen with her young son when she traveled the revival circuit. For Lee and many others, Allen instilled a sense of confidence in free blacks' future. And that translated into long-term growth at Bethel Church.

Allen's own household offers a small window into Bethel's demographic burst. By the 1820s, Allen and his second wife, Sarah, had six children, four boys and two girls. They ranged in age from young kids to teenagers. Allen's eldest son, Richard Jr., by the end of the decade served as a recording secretary for annual AME conferences. But Allen's house was always filled with more than immediate family. Census records dating back to 1790 show that Allen consistently put up boarders (even when he was single and renting on Dock Street). By 1800, ten free persons were listed as part of the Allen household, which included Allen and his first wife, Flora (scholars do not know if they had any children); a decade later that number had climbed to fourteen people. The 1820 census, which first separated household members into age groups, found fifteen people residing with the Allens: three children under the age of fourteen (two boys and a girl), nine people between the ages of fourteen and twenty-six (eight men and a woman), one man between the ages of twenty-six and forty-five, and the heads of the household, Richard and Sarah Allen. Because twelve residents were younger than twenty-six years of age—and knowing that the Allens had only six children—we can assume that the household contained either apprentices or boarders or both. During the 1790s, Allen had several apprentices at his home, including Israel Tolman, a boy named "Paris," and Tilghman Fitzgerald (all of whom were probably chimney sweeps). We can also assume that some of Allen's apprentices and boarders attended Bethel Church.[35]

It is not at all surprising, then, that Methodist elders attempted to bring Bethel under control during the 1810s. The congregation was booming. Thankfully for Allen, church growth also sparked community defenses. And there was truly power in Bethel's growing numbers.

4. *A Chosen Generation*

No sooner had the Pennsylvania supreme court rendered its pro-Bethel decision than Allen joined with disgruntled black Methodists through-out the mid-Atlantic region to form the African Methodist Episcopal Church. This would be the first independent black denomination in Pennsylvania (Peter Spencer's African Union Church in Delaware actu-ally achieved independence a bit earlier). Over the next century, the AME Church became the single most important black-led group in North America and one of the largest religious denominations in the At-lantic world. The AME Church also had the honor of ordaining the first black bishop in Western history: Richard Allen.

The AME Church formed in April 1816. Regular communication among black leaders along the Atlantic seaboard illuminated the com-mon problem of race prejudice in the white church. As Allen remem-bered in his autobiography, "our colored friends in Baltimore were treated in a similar manner by the white preachers and trustees [of the Baltimore Methodist conference], and many of them driven away who were disposed to seek a place of worship rather than go to law." In other words, different city, same treatment: black Methodists in Baltimore were subjected to the whim and power of white leaders. This "induced us," Allen continued, "to call a general meeting" to discuss blacks' "grievances" and "promote union and harmony amongst ourselves."[36]

Allen's chief ally in this endeavor was Daniel Coker, a former slave and rising voice in free black circles. Allen and Coker may have dis-cussed some sort of regional or national church as early as 1810. At that time, Coker had just published "A Dialogue between a Virginian and an African Minister," the only black-authored pamphlet printed below the Mason-Dixon line in the early republic. A Socratic dialogue modeled on Caleb Bingham's 1795 essay of nearly the same name, Coker's pamphlet urged Southern masters to embrace gradual aboli-tionism. To make his case that emancipation gave rise to stable black communities, Coker listed prominent black preachers and their congre-gations along the Atlantic seaboard. Coker may also have printed this information to facilitate dialogue among black leaders. "Ye are a cho-sen generation, a royal priesthood and a holy nation," he quoted from 1 Peter 2, before providing readers "a list of the names of the African Ministers who are in holy orders of the author's acquaintance." At the top of that list (and not just because his last name began with an "A") was Richard Allen.[37]

Correspondence between Allen and Coker after Bethel's court victory further suggests that the two men were already thinking about a national church. On January 21, 1816, just ten days after Allen's court victory, Coker spoke before "a numerous concourse of people" at his own Baltimore church. Coker hoped that Afro-Philadelphians' uprising might become a model for his own congregation's freedom struggle. Comparing free African Americans' plight to that of Jews in the ancient world, Coker called Bethel's deliverance a divinely inspired event. "The Jews in Babylon were held against their will," he intoned, and "so were our brethren" in Philadelphia. But no longer.

Coker called for a new wave of free black organizing across state lines. "May the time speedily come," he proclaimed, "when we shall see our brethren come flocking to us like doves to their windows. And we, as a band of brethren, shall sit down under our own vine to worship and none to make us afraid."[38] Coker may have thought back to his pamphlet, which pictured the "several hundred members" of local black congregations as the potential backbone of a national black church. Philadelphia and Baltimore were clearly hot spots of black congregationalism, but Coker knew that African Americans in New York, New Jersey, Massachusetts, Delaware, and even South Carolina (places with vibrant African churches) would be interested in a national institution. Allen, who in a February 1816 note thanked Coker for such a rousing celebration of Bethel's freedom, agreed. A few months later, in April, the two men convened the founding convention of the African Methodist Episcopal Church.

That meeting assembled on April 9, 1816, at Bethel Church. Sixteen men from four different states (Pennsylvania, New Jersey, Maryland, and Delaware) attended, including Coker. For three consecutive days, delegates deliberated on matters ranging from ecclesiastical organization to just who would be the bishop of the new church. The fate of these deliberations went well beyond the few men meeting in Allen's church. Thousands of black congregants had already cast their lot with these AME representatives—perhaps as many as three thousand men and women, who had sent the delegates to Philadelphia in the first place. Just five years after the founding convention, the AME claimed over ten thousand adherents.[39]

Still, these numbers constituted a fraction of the number of blacks who remained within mainstream Methodist institutions dominated by white clerics and congregants. Daniel Payne estimated that by the 1830s, the AME contained only a quarter of black Methodists nationally. "The tendency of . . . this," Payne observed, "was to prove that the colored man was incapable of self-government and self-support." AME founders were very much aware that whatever they said or did during these three days in April would seek to "contradict . . . this slander." The AME's founding convention, in other words, transcended religious ideals and reflected on black self-determination.[40]

One shred of formality illuminated AME founders' political concerns. The official resolution under which the conference was organized declared that the people of "Philadelphia, Baltimore and other places who should unite with them shall become one body under the name and style of the African Methodist Episcopal Church." A simple declaration, perhaps, but one packed with meaning, for AME founders drew from two powerful organizing traditions: first, the religious dictum that the pious serve God as "one body"; and second, the American notion of a "more perfect union," dating to the Constitutional Convention of 1787. By organizing under their own official banner, AME founders depicted themselves as an orderly, respectable body of men. They declared, for instance, "that any minister coming from another denomination should be received in the same official standing . . . from whence he came." Although this little clause mirrored white religious practices, Allen and his colleagues hoped that it demonstrated black founders' understanding of institutional governance and proper organizational behavior.[41]

AME founders also used sacred secular language to place the new black church in a hallowed tradition of American freedom seekers. For example, the church's *Doctrines and Discipline* used phrases like "securing privileges" (a clear nod to the Constitution's phrase "securing to our posterity") and "promoting union" to describe the AME creed. Recall that Allen was familiar with the federal Constitution's copyright provisions, and it is not hard to imagine him using references to 1787 to secure the AME Church in Americans' consciousness.[42]

The delegates remained most concerned with the choice of bishop. Considering that his church had essentially set the stage for the AME's founding, there could be little doubt about Allen's ascension. But he was not a unanimous choice, at least during initial deliberations. Delegates divided over whether to go with the revered Allen or the seemingly more moderate Daniel Coker. Coker was a generation younger than Allen. Born in 1780 to a mixed-race couple (his mother was an indentured servant, his father a slave), he actually did something Allen would not do to gain his freedom: he ran away from his Maryland plantation to force his master's hand. Coker fled to New York, returning only when he could purchase himself out of bondage. Coker soon became a Methodist minister and leader of an African school in Baltimore. By the 1810s, he was a key black voice nationally.[43]

For delegates to the conference, Coker may have been viewed as a consensus-building choice over Allen, who could be unyielding, stern, and overbearing even when dealing with black congregants. Before the AME convention occurred, in fact, a dissenting group of Baltimore blacks accused Allen of high-handed behavior in handling Bethel's finances. Coker informed Allen about these scheming men, who evidently had plans for building their own church. After conducting a little research of his own, Allen labeled the dissenters a troublesome bunch unworthy of further attention. Nevertheless, these rumblings from black Baltimoreans confirm that Allen was not beloved by everyone.[44]

Although Coker was initially chosen as bishop, he did not last more than a few hours. According to some accounts, Coker was also viewed as a problematic leader of the nation's first black church. Coker may have refused the nomination because some of his brethren complained that he was too "light" complected. But Daniel Payne notes (and family sources confirm) that Allen was of mixed parentage too. Coker may also have elicited distrust for an alleged violation of black Methodist doctrine (speaking ill of other members). These explanations remain circumstantial. No documentation from the convention survives. Once again, all that exists is church legend. And this legend says that Allen was eventually viewed by delegates as the only person to lead the AME Church.[45]

And so, on the last day of the convention, Allen was named bishop. As tradition held, the laying on of five hands by other Philadelphia preachers established his ordination. We know one pair of hands belonged to Absalom Jones, who passed on soon after this incredible event. Just who were the other men? That too must remain part of an obscure AME past.

5. A Disciplined Body

Being ordained the first bishop of the African Methodist Episcopal Church in April 1816 was a crowning achievement for the former slave Richard Allen. But as the shrewd longtime leader of Bethel, he also realized that important details needed to be worked out. The most pressing of these matters was the ecclesiastical organization and theological grounding of the AME Church. Would it break free from all institutional forms associated with white Methodism? Yes and no. By 1817, Allen and his Bethel colleague Jacob Tapsico had coauthored the AME's founding text: *The Doctrines and Discipline of the African Methodist Episcopal Church.* Laying out everything from the ordination of ministers to the proper singing of hymns ("women shall sing their own parts"), the *Discipline,* as it became known, was the longest published document Allen had ever crafted. Nearly two hundred pages, the book stood as an enduring monument to black theology. By the 1830s, the AME had distributed thousands of copies, making it probably the second most popular—though not necessarily read—text in many black communities (behind the Bible itself).[46]

Much of the *Discipline* mimics the words and ideals of the mainstream Methodist Church. Indeed, the very title flowed from the founding books of Wesley's church. Richard Allen's AME congregation remained dedicated to the basic principles of Methodism which he had grown up with and staked his freedom on: all God's children were equal, the conversion experience remained the most important manifestation of one's saintliness, and outreach—or doing good works—was as significant as sanctification itself.

There were two important exceptions, however, to AME mimicry, and both of them flowed from the discriminatory experiences of black Methodists. As Albert Raboteau has pointed out, the AME Church "abolished the office of presiding elder" and maintained the original Methodist injunction on slaveholding.[47] Neither of these positions is hard to understand. After longtime battles with resident elders in both Philadelphia and Baltimore, AME officials did not favor local oversight of congregations. And after witnessing slavery's continuous growth in the South and Southwest—even among dissenting religionists like Methodists and Baptists—Allen was unlikely to equivocate on bondage. Indeed, he had already watched his old friend Francis Asbury waffle on

slavery in the revised *Doctrines and Discipline of the Methodist Episco-*
pal Church of 1798. That document, produced by Asbury and Thomas
Coke and published in Philadelphia, must have been a disappointing
read for Allen. "We declare that we are more than ever convinced of the
great evil of African slavery which still exists in these United States,"
Asbury and Coke hopefully proclaimed. But "what regulation shall be
made for the extirpation of the crying evil of African slavery?" they
asked in section 9 of the mainstream Methodist *Discipline.* The Methodist Church, they answered, could do nothing other than be "exceed-
ingly cautious what persons [i.e., slaveholders] they admit to official stations in our church." True, Asbury and Coke's *Discipline* did strongly
encourage local congregations to pursue abolitionist ends, as long as
they did not contravene state law or cause too much trouble to individual slaveholders. Still, only the act of slave trading could cause a member's expulsion. Otherwise, slavery required "deep attention" and not
much more. Slaveholders continued to operate within Methodist congregations.[48]

Contrast Asbury and Coke's document with Allen's *Discipline,* which
argued that slaveholding had no place in the AME Church and would
bring immediate expulsion. Of course, Allen's audience was in one sense
closed: only people of African descent could join the church (though
black slaveholders existed in the South). Yet, as with most documents
he produced, Allen was also thinking of white readers, in this case white
Methodists who might very well view his antislavery pronouncement as
a commentary on their own iniquitous position. Indeed, Allen remained
true to his 1794 antislavery appeal, "An Address to Those Who Keep
Slaves and Approve the Practice": slavery was hateful in the eyes of
God and would not be tolerated in any institution he headed. "We will
not receive any person into our society as a member who is a slaveholder," the AME *Discipline* commanded two decades later.[49] Even
slaveholders of African descent—black men and women who perhaps
bought relatives to secure their freedom—were excluded from membership until they manumitted bondpeople. Allen's admonition was a firm
ideological commitment to freedom.

Beyond bondage, the AME *Discipline* diverged from Methodist
founding texts in smaller ways. Take the very opening narrative. Like
the mainstream Methodist *Discipline,* Allen's text provided "a brief
account" of the church's creation. Unlike the narrative written by his
white counterparts, though, Allen emphasized the themes of Exodus

which were eternally relevant to people of color. Allen told the story of white Methodists' segregationist seating policies (which he dated to 1787), blacks' collective response, and the struggle to find a new Canaan. "From these, and various other acts of unchristian conduct," Allen (and Tapsico) wrote, "we considered it our duty to devise a plan in order to build a house of our own, to worship God under our own vine and fig tree."[50]

After these confrontations, Allen continued, black Methodists faced such "great opposition" from white preachers that they became "outcasts" among those who professed to be children of God. As black Methodists increased in number, they "experienced grievances too numerous to mention," including having their very own church nearly sold from under their feet. Blacks wandered in the wilderness of mistreatment but never wavered from their Christian faith. Finally, the Lord delivered them. This was the first time that Allen publicly told the story of white ecclesiastical oppression of blacks. He later had his son reprint virtually the same section in his autobiography. In both instances, he wished to show that by remaining pious and persevering black Methodists had received divine protection. As the Bible predicted, princes would indeed come out of Egypt and Ethiopia would rise again.[51]

This story also deeply informed AME theology. For, as Allen saw it, the AME was borne of, and must therefore remain, a church dedicated to social protest. The contrast with Methodist doctrine is striking. Whereas Asbury and Coke's *Discipline* stressed religious perfection and expansionism as the key aims of the Methodist Church (spreading "Scriptural holiness over these lands," as they put it in the 1798 edition, remained the church's goal), Allen stressed social justice as the unifying and driving force of his church. The court case that provided AME independence was thus not the key event in the church's history; once again, blacks' collective determination to struggle against injustice formed the ideological foundation of the church.

In this sense, although the AME *Discipline* ostensibly repeats language from its white Methodist counterpart, it is actually much more exciting and ramifying. In the AME *Discipline,* black congregants vote, organize, congregate, deliberate, and educate one another, all with an aim toward social uplift (not merely spiritual perfection), and all in a land that would, institutionally as well as socially, deny them even these liberties. Take "education of youth," a seemingly bland part of both the mainstream Methodist *Discipline* and Allen's AME *Discipline*. Methodists, both documents declare, must look to the education of youth as a key to institutional growth and success. When read in the context of the day-to-day discrimination that Allen described at the document's outset, however, this admonition seems revelatory for free people of color: black leaders *must* attend to the education of black youth "once a week," if possible, and at the very least "once every two weeks." Only in this way will black Methodists—and the community in which they live—rise to greatness.[52]

An even better example is church voting. Both *Disciplines* used the same language on this matter: bishops would be elected at the general conference, held every four years by constitutional order. Once again, to use the word "election" in the context of disfranchised black congregants made the AME *Discipline* different. If a bishop overextended his power, the AME *Discipline* declares, members of the general conference can, by a vote, "expel him for improper conduct."[53] Here, the AME *Discipline* enacted a spirit of black democracy that transcended Christian theology. As Asbury pointed out in the 1798 edition of his *Discipline,* the local episcopacy was the foundation of the Methodist Church, for there local citizens could pass judgment on preachers' status. By highlighting black peoples' voting power within congregational structures, Allen underscored self-determination as a core part of the AME mission.

The AME's achievement is even more impressive when put in the context of black religious struggles elsewhere. On the day he ascended to AME bishop, April 11, 1816, Allen was the acknowledged leader of the most influential black church in the Western world. A quick glance eastward at African American struggles within New York City's denominational landscape reveals Allen's unique status. Black New Yorkers formed one of the most fearsome reform communities in antebellum America. Yet New York's AME Zion Church, formed by disgruntled black Methodists in 1796 (and soon to be Allen's chief competition), was not even incorporated until 1820. Led by John Varick, a celebrated free black churchman and organizer, Zionites left behind the segregated world of a white Methodist church only to find that they had no standing in the New York conference. Not until Allen's bid for freedom did they gain a modicum of respect in New York circles. The group that Zionites had left behind, a band of black Methodists who remained at the John Street Church in New York City, had no choice but to remain under the control of white leaders throughout the early nineteenth century. Still another group of black congregants in New York founded St. Phillip's Episcopal Church in 1809—though they struggled for nearly forty years to achieve equal recognition in the church hierarchy.

St. Phillip's Church is best remembered for its leader, Peter Williams, Jr., a free black man and friend of Allen's whose enslaved father had risked his life during the American Revolution to save a white New Jersey patriot. St. Phillip's Church, like Absalom Jones's St. Thomas's Church in Philadelphia, achieved autonomy at the price of true freedom. Black Episcopalians could have their own churches in New York or Philadelphia, but they did not have voting rights at annual conferences or equal seating privileges at general meetings. As religious historian Craig Townsend has written, white officials in New York had been in contact with white officials in Philadelphia about how to deal with black congregants' push for freedom. The answer came in segregation: white Episcopalians, Philadelphia leaders told their New York counterparts, would deem blacks as separate and unequal within church hierarchies.[54]

That would never do for Richard Allen and the AME Church. And that is why they made their bold bid for freedom in 1816.

6. Another Portrait of Allen

In 1813, Richard Allen had his second portrait painted. This most famous likeness of the black preacher came amid Bethel Church's life-and-death struggles with Philadelphia's Methodist elders. The crisis may help explain another intriguing Allen mystery, for the portrait declares that he was "the founder of the African Methodist Episcopal Church in the United States of America, 1779." If that was true, Allen would have been nineteen years old at the time of the AME's founding—and still enslaved in Delaware. If it was a misprint, it does not fit with Allen's exacting personality, for he usually corrected misstatements relating to his church. So why did Allen let this seemingly problematic date stand in his signature portrait?[55]

Perhaps the date represented the first time that Allen thought about forming a black church. Even today Mother Bethel dates the church's unofficial beginnings to revival meetings Allen attended near Stokeley Sturgis's farm during the 1770s. Always a dreamer, Allen believed even then that he would form a great black church. Before he had a chance to craft an autobiography—Allen was fifty-three when he commissioned the portrait and still vigorous—the image and date alongside it served as an elegant form of testimony to a black founder's youthful vision about black uplift and achievement.

The 1779 date may also have been a radical political statement by the black preacher—the equivalent of a public-relations move to solidify the AME Church as a historic entity in the broader civic realm. No other date made this claim so well. For example, Allen could just as easily have chosen 1796, when Bethel secured official incorporation by the state of Pennsylvania. Of course, that date was compromised by its association with the disputed "Articles of Association," which had been crafted by a white cleric to keep Bethel Church under the thumb of Philadelphia Methodists. Allen could also have chosen his breakaway from St. George's Church (1787 or 1792, depending on various sources), though again this conjured disputation with white officials, who considered the breakaway illegal. Even 1807—the date of the African Supplement—was problematic because white officials rejected its legality. Moreover, the African Supplement had been crafted relatively recently; it did not signify hallowed black beginnings. But 1779 appeared historic and alluded to the American Revolutionary era. By selecting this date, Allen dared white officials to contradict his story of black church formation going back thirty years. In doing so, he turned the conservative nature of portraiture into a revolutionary act: a declaration of black independence from white authority.

The portrait posed one other irony. Allen proudly called himself the founder of a black church "in the United States." Over the next several years, Allen wondered if free blacks should remain in the United States. Perhaps, he came to believe after nearly losing his beloved church, emigration beyond American shores held the key to black redemption. Perhaps America was not a black homeland after all.

7

Stay or Go?
Allen and African Colonization

This land [of America] . . . is now our mother country.
—Allen in *Freedom's Journal*, 1827

Sometime in early March 1814, Richard Allen opened a letter from Paul Cuffee, the celebrated free black merchant and ship captain. "Esteemed friend Richard Allen," it began, "I hope by this time your [colonization] society has been all regular formed. I met with the people of color at New York. They appeared very zealous for the good cause of Africa and concluded to form themselves into society for the same purpose as that in Philadelphia." Soon to embark on another voyage to their shared homeland, Cuffee wanted Allen to have "all the information about obtaining liberty for Africa."[1] Cuffee also wanted to make sure that the black preacher still supported the growing cause of African colonization. Although no letter survives from Allen, he was indeed a proponent of Cuffee's plan. He held colonizationist meetings in his home, spread word of Cuffee's good work to white and black reformers alike, and expressed hope that African colonization would speed global black redemption.

Allen's embrace of African colonization—and his subsequent support of black-led emigration schemes—does not figure prominently in most biographical treatments.[2] More than any other issue, though, colonization/emigration illuminates Allen's constantly evolving activism—and his developing struggle over black identity and national allegiance. In joining Cuffee's crusade, Allen undertook one of the most radical experiments of his life: mass emigration of blacks beyond the United States. It was no mere flirtation. After African colonization faded from Allen's mind, Haitian emigration appeared on the reform horizon. After that

183

dream disappeared, Allen considered Canadian resettlement. As he put it in a September 1830 address, "the formation of a settlement in the British province of Upper Canada would be a great advantage to the people color . . . [where] we shall be entitled to all the rights, privileges and immunities of other citizens."[3] As his words reveal, the elder Allen doubted the ability of the United States to foster an environment of racial equality. And so, for the last fifteen years of his life, he meditated deeply on black exodus from, rather than black redemption within, the United States.

Why would a man synonymous with interracial democracy change course? By examining the prospect of racial justice overseas, Allen publicly testified to his increasingly divided soul. He was an American and not an American, a freeman and not a freeman, a man dedicated to saving America from racial sin and a man in search of a country free from racial sin. He was an African American and African trapped in America. To underscore Allen's alienation during these years, consider that he never embraced colonization/emigration plans during the late eighteenth century. He had plenty of opportunity to do so, for black as well as white reformers (both in Philadelphia and throughout the North Atlantic world) periodically proposed black resettlement schemes. Allen repudiated them all, believing instead that America could be reformed —that he could reshape American race relations. Yet Allen's confidence was shaken by the confluence of several events during the early nineteenth century: an intensification of antiblack feelings during the War of 1812, a stalled abolition movement, and white Methodists' vigorous attempts to grab Bethel Church. By the time Paul Cuffee contacted him, Allen wondered aloud about black destinies in America.

The shadow of the legendary St. George's exodus loomed large in the elder Allen's racial politics: if American oppression intensified, he began to think, then free blacks must seriously consider mass exodus as a means of achieving racial justice. To modern eyes, black separation appears to be a more familiar form of black nationalism. For Allen and black founders, Cuffee's colonization plan was only one of several possible responses to rigid racial oppression, and its seemingly orthodox black nationalist foundation did not reject Christianity or Western conceptions of rights and liberties as key parts of a future African republic. It was a very liberal form of black nationalism that Allen considered. And, as a black leader thinking about African Americans' limited freedoms in the United States, he thought it was a course of action that must be examined. Allen confided as much to a white colonizationist in 1817, who recalled that the bishop "spoke with warmth on some oppression which [blacks] suffer from the whites, and spoke warmly in favor of colonization in Africa." To secure their liberties, blacks might have to leave America. Fellow black founder James Forten agreed, arguing that African Americans would never truly become a people "until they came out from under the whites." Perhaps the time had come for a national version of the famous St. George's walkout.[4]

By supporting Paul Cuffee's plan to redeem Africa through religion and commerce, Allen also thought more seriously than ever about global African redemption. He did so at a propitious moment in black reform circles. Particularly in Northern urban locales, free black writers began examining the deeper meanings of African identity. The success of the Haitian Revolution raised African Americans' global consciousness, as did the struggle to end the international slave trade.[5] As James T. Campbell has written, early national black leaders "established the terms of debate for future generations of African-Americans struggling to make sense of their relationship to Africa." That struggle revolved around two simple questions: "what is Africa to me?" and, by implication, "what is America to me?" Although Allen had clearly thought about his "Africanness" before colonization (particularly in the formation of an "African" church and an "African" benevolent society), Cuffee's program prompted much deeper meditation on the matter.[6]

Finally, African colonization prompted Allen to think seriously about black political economy. Was the American republic dedicated merely to improving the lot of white men? he wondered. Could his free black brethren, particularly young African Americans streaming into Northern urban sectors, rise in America society as he did? For the first time in his life, Allen did not have easy answers to these questions. And so colonization/emigration looked better than ever.

1. *African Colonization*

Richard Allen was no stranger to African colonization schemes. The year after he arrived in Philadelphia in 1786, a Quaker philanthropist and physician by the name of William Thornton came to town with a proposal for a free black settlement on Africa's western coast. Thornton arrived with support from British and American reformers, not to mention political leaders like James Madison. Now he sought support from free black leaders in the City of Brotherly Love. That brought him to the doorstep of Allen's Free African Society. It also brought Thornton to a dead end. For despite the fact that Thornton promised to liberate his own slaves in the Caribbean, he did not believe in brotherly love across racial lines. White and black, he maintained, could not live together in harmony. An African colony of former slaves and free blacks, he believed, was providential, for it placed people of color on the other side of the Atlantic, far away from whites.

Both Allen and the FAS rebuffed Thornton's plan: interracial harmony, not intercontinental separation, must guide reformers' exertions. Thornton's plan gave up on American racial redemption far too soon, the FAS argued. Even when Thornton received support from Boston's black leaders, and even when free black leaders in Newport, Rhode Island, wrote that entrenched racial oppression made Thornton's plan enticing, black Philadelphians demurred. Time and "the shield of faith," the FAS observed, would redeem Africans in America.[7]

Because the Free African Society had sent an emissary to black communities in New England to gauge support for Thornton's plan, it is likely that black Philadelphians debated the efficacy of colonizationist schemes well after Thornton departed. As a matter of fact, the recent discovery of an emigrationist petition drafted by Philadelphia blacks shows that Allen and his brethren did reconsider the matter from time to time. Aimed at the Second Federal Congress, and bearing the signatures of over fifty Afro-Philadelphians, including Richard Allen, the memorial decried American racial animosity. Stating that "we have with other men . . . an unalienable right to life, liberty and the pursuit of happiness," the petitioners fervently hoped that Congress would do everything in its power to institute a national plan of gradual emancipation. Failing this, some Philadelphia blacks wanted Congress to start "preparing . . . an [African] asylum for such as . . . who are free." The model for such an asylum was Britain's colony of Sierra Leone, which had just been organized. Because free blacks were much "maligned" in American culture, the petition went on, African colonization would create economic opportunities for those men "who are now at a loss for a livelihood for ourselves and our families."[8]

The document is both revealing and perplexing. While supporting a federal plan of gradual abolition, the memorial also favored governmental support for voluntary African emigration. Moreover, although the memorial grounded black abolitionist claims in the Declaration of Independence—which emphasized universal freedom as America's founding creed—its authors felt that a black safety valve was vital for disgruntled African Americans. Most significantly, the petition, which may have been drafted in the wake of white opposition to black church-building efforts or fallout from the yellow-fever crisis, was never sent to Congress. This indicates disagreement among Afro-Philadelphians about African colonization itself. Indeed, because the signatures of Allen, Absalom Jones, and William Gray—black leaders vouching for the memorial—occupy a different column and are written in a different style from community members, it appears that the draft petition may have been the work of nonelite free blacks (who may have supported African asylum). The separate signatures of black leaders and community members may also indicate that men like Allen signed the emigrationist memorial only after the broader community had mobilized—and that black leaders tabled the document rather than present it to Congress. In short, Allen was not yet a true believer in African colonization.

Enter Paul Cuffee years later, when Allen's views of American racial reform soured and African colonization took on a completely different character. Just who was this man who commanded Allen's attention? Cuffee remains one of those figures fitted out in textbook clothing. A successful free black entrepreneur, ship captain, and Quaker reformer, Cuffee's renown reached all the way to the White House, where he successfully appealed to President Madison for state papers to continue trading through an embargo of British goods. By then, Cuffee had become interested in much more than voyaging to Africa. He dreamed of nothing less than full African redemption through the powers of Christianity and commerce. As Cuffee wrote in 1809, "I have for some years had it impressed on my mind to make a voyage to Sierra Leone . . . feeling a desire that the inhabitants of Africa might become an enlightened people." For Cuffee, enlightenment meant understanding democratic practice, the potential of international trade, and, most importantly, the Christian gospel. As he told white reformers, "I am of the African race; I feel myself interested for them." Cuffee especially hoped that black America's "first characters," as he put it, would back his plan. That meant black founders like Allen.[9]

Cuffee supported the African Institution, a British organization dedicated to maintaining the Sierra Leone colony of former slaves on Africa's western coast (created between 1789 and 1792). The African

Institution received support from all corners of the Atlantic reform world—Americans, Europeans, sons of Africa, native Africans. Cuffee made several voyages to the African colony between 1811 and his untimely death in 1817; he also met with Anglo-American reformers and published a pamphlet about his African travels.[10] In Sierra Leone, Cuffee helped organize the Friendly Society, a quasi-religious group dedicated to "promoting the good of any members, and colonists in general."[11] Based on both African traditions and New World benevolent societies, including Allen and Jones's Free African Society, the organization represented Cuffee's visionary scheme. Free blacks, Africa's proverbial prodigal sons, would return and revitalize native peoples and cultures through the wonders of Christianity, benevolence, moral uplift, and international trade.

Allen's support of Cuffee is not that hard to understand. Like Allen, Cuffee struggled from nothing to something. A child of a mixed-race family—an African father and Pequot mother—with seemingly no future in Revolutionary New England, Cuffee became an internationally renowned mariner and merchant. Also like Allen, Cuffee linked his sense of Christian mission to African redemption, though Allen had first envisioned such redemption occurring in the New World, not the old. Cuffee's life was one of constant striving, religious dedication, and educational improvement. His father, a native African, died when Paul was fourteen (in 1759). "Thus the care of supporting his mother and sisters devolved upon his brothers and himself," black minister Peter Williams observed in a pamphlet after Cuffee's death in 1817 (one of the first pieces of black founders' hagiography). Young Cuffee did not shrink from these filial duties. He "always brought the earning of his industry to his family," Williams added. After establishing his own successful shipping business, Cuffee became deeply concerned with community uplift. In 1797, he built a school and meeting house on his own property to facilitate black educational improvement. "How gratifying, to humanity is this anecdote!" Williams cheered.[12]

Cuffee's moral-uplift agenda certainly appealed to Allen, who later hailed Cuffee as a model black leader. Like Allen, Cuffee believed in the power of Christianity to lift oppressed people from the most degrading circumstances. Sobriety, industry, piety—these were the pillars of Cuffee's faith. As Cuffee told American congressmen in 1813, "being a descendant of Africa," he believed there was no greater global cause than "to promote the improvement and civilization of the Africans."[13]

Allen would have nodded his head in approval as Cuffee (on one of his visits to Philadelphia) regaled the black preacher with tales of his own hard upbringing and visions of African redemption. Pretty soon, Allen became a disciple of Cuffee's colonization plan itself.

2. *Allen and Cuffee*

Although the historical record remains silent on the first contact between Allen and Cuffee—it may have been as early as 1808—the two men probably met at a May 1812 conference between black activists and Philadelphia Quakers over the formation of a pro–Sierra Leone society.[14] The time was absolutely right for African colonization, Cuffee made clear to black as well as white leaders. Over the next couple years Cuffee pushed the black leadership triumvirate of Allen, Jones, and Forten to accelerate their support of the African cause.

He prodded Allen on several occasions. In March 1814, for example, Cuffee encouraged Allen to maintain his support of "your society" for African colonization. Black Philadelphians had by this time formed an auxiliary to the African Institution in London. Although James Forten and Russell Parrott (black elites based at St. Thomas's Church) seem to have been in closer contact with Cuffee, Allen hosted meetings of the group in his home and church. Because Allen often failed to return Cuffee's notes, the ship captain prodded him some more. In June 1814, Cuffee wrote Allen that he had not heard from the black preacher in some time but was nevertheless excited by James Forten's report that black Philadelphians supported African colonization. In March 1815, Cuffee again urged Allen to rally behind the African Institution, a particularly important moment to do so with the War of 1812 having ended. "I have to call thy attention to the African mission," Cuffee insisted. "I feel anxious that platform that has been in contemplation for so many years not be neglected but . . . advanced."[15]

Cuffee wanted money and bodies for his upcoming missions to Africa. He knew Allen could help. "Any information that thou can give," he pleaded in 1815, "will be kindly received." Allen answered by speaking positively about Cuffee's mission and remaining behind the African Institution right up until the ship captain's death in 1817. Even after the American Colonization Society had formed (tainting the very cause of African repatriation for many blacks), Allen told New Jersey colonizationist Robert Finley that he thought "highly of Paul Cuffee" and therefore highly of "the present plan of [African] colonization." Perhaps the only thing that prevented Allen from focusing more squarely on Cuffee's colonization plan was white Methodists' attempted takeover of Bethel Church between 1812 and 1816.[16] Nevertheless, the main point remains that black Philadelphians had formed an auxiliary to the African Institution by 1815 and that Richard Allen was among its members.

There are two equally powerful ways to conceptualize Allen's support of Cuffee-style African colonization: the "pull" of African redemption and the "push" of American racial oppression. On the one hand, Allen saw God's hand at work in Cuffee's plan. Africa would be "saved" by the intervention of African American reformers and the healing powers of Christianity. Moreover, Allen may very well have viewed the 1810s as "Africa's decade"—a new day for a troubled but still proud place. Now that free black communities had risen in America, and the international slave trade had been banned in both the United States and Great Britain, the sons of Africa could focus their reform energies on their ancestral land. For Allen in particular, African Methodism would be a redeemer religion once transplanted in Africa.[17]

Indeed, as intellectual historian Wilson Moses has argued, Cuffee and Allen were part of a generation of African American leaders that came to believe in the power of "Christianity, commerce, and [Western] civilization" to transform African societies into thoroughly modern Christian republics. African Redemptionism had many, sometimes contradictory, elements. Some black founders believed in the "Fortunate Fall": though horrible, the international slave trade had been a divine instrument to introduce Africans in the Americas to the redemptive power of Christianity, which they would now use to save African societies. African Redemptionism also drew on Africa's former glory, the birthplace of science, commerce, and learning. Finally, black founders relied on a powerful biblical discourse when envisioning African redemption. Like the ancient Israelites, African Americans were a chosen people charged with the task of redeeming a land from which they had been forcibly removed.[18] All of these notions combined to make African colonization appear to be a most noble idea by the early nineteenth century. Paul Cuffee let free black leaders know that it was also a feasible scheme. "My plan," he wrote in 1814, "is to take to Africa some sober steady habited people of colour in order to encourage sobriety and industry." Just hearing phrases like this could turn Allen into a Cuffee convert.[19]

Allen's support of Cuffee also flowed from his growing concerns about blacks' marginalized place in American culture. This forms "the push" side of the equation. The 1810s were a bruising decade for Allen. Of course, he nearly lost his church, having to actually buy back Bethel at public auction in 1815. Beyond that, there was a broader antiblack sentiment spreading through American culture, while at the same time blacks' economic opportunities decreased. Some of Allen's (and African Americans') most steadfast allies were aged or had already passed on— Francis Asbury, Benjamin Rush, Warner Mifflin. The 1810s, in short, was just the beginning of what James Stewart has called "racial modernity": a hardening of racial attitudes that undercut the post-Revolutionary idealism of white and black abolitionists alike.[20] For many white Americans, free blacks were a troublesome presence in the new republic. And that spelled real trouble for Allen.

3. Racism and the War of 1812

Cuffee caught Allen at a moment when the black preacher's doubts about forming an interracial society of God's children in America turned into a major concern. Indeed, Allen's interest in Cuffee-style colonization coincided with his own concerns about African American destinies in the Atlantic world. Were African peoples the only ones requiring redemption?

The War of 1812 with Great Britain intensified Allen's anxieties. Although African Americans had answered the call of duty from Philadelphia to New Orleans, there was no sign that their patriotism would bring full emancipation (in the South) and/or full equality (in the North). Black leaders had participated in the war fully expecting a new day of race relations. When called on to protect Philadelphia, they responded willingly. As British troops marched from the nation's newly built capital of Washington, D.C., which the Britons had sacked in the summer of 1814, Philadelphians feared their city would be the next major target. Many federal officials had already evacuated to the City of Brotherly Love, making the nation's former capital a capital in exile. Philadelphia newspapers were filled with patriotic declarations, fears of British dominion, and calls for civic defense. City fathers created a

Committee of Defense. This body met with an ever-growing number of militias, neighborhood associations, and well-known local leaders to coordinate anti-British activities. The committee eventually approached the black leadership triumvirate of Allen, Jones, and Forten to rally the black masses.

The trio responded by mobilizing twenty-five hundred African Americans for civil defense. In September 1814, Allen, Jones, and Forten marched the phalanx of men across the city to Grey's Ferry, on the city's western edge along the Schuylkill River, where they toiled for two arduous days building earthen barriers to repel any British forces moving on Philadelphia. The trio was subsequently cited by the defense committee for wonderfully responding to the call of duty. No one could deny blacks' heroism. Indeed, alongside a fabled black military engagement at New Orleans (called into being by future president Andrew Jackson), the Philadelphia rally became one of the iconic moments of nineteenth-century African American life. For their heroic defense of Philadelphia, Allen biographer Charles Wesley later proclaimed, "a vote of thanks was later given them by the committee [of defense]."[21]

The reality was more complex. For one thing, the defense committee initially rejected black troops, fearing that they would undercut the provisioning of whites. The word used by city officials was "improper"— as in, it would be "improper" to raise such a large group of African Americans for even nonmilitary uses. Unofficially, the committee's decision betrayed an old fear of blacks in wartime, who, once mobilized, might wreak havoc on white citizens, not just on invading British troops. The defense committee stated that black troops could only be used "as fatigue parties . . . detached from the white citizens who may be so employed." In short, black character and conduct were called into question before any black battalion had ever been raised.[22]

Some citizens wondered about free blacks' allegiance. In a leading Philadelphia paper, "A Citizen" asked why free blacks had not already mobilized for the city's defense. "At this critical juncture," the anonymous author observed, "when a great body of the male white inhabitants are engaged and preparing to meet the common enemy . . . it would be highly honorable if all the free people of color were to form themselves into parties and offer their services to the committee of defense." Mistakenly arguing that free blacks were exempt from taxes (and therefore not part of the body politic), the writer argued that African Americans could still prove their patriotism by "cheerfully giv[ing] their aid" to the American cause. The note raised fears about black allegiance to foreign powers, fears that dated back to early abolitionists like Ben Franklin and antiabolitionist slaveholders like Thomas Jefferson.[23] Although Richard Allen dutifully paid his taxes and could recall benevolent service dating to the yellow-fever crisis of 1793, many white citizens worried about his patriotism! Despite such fears, Afro-Philadelphians noted at the close of the war, "in the hour of danger, [free blacks] ceased to remember their wrongs, and rallied around the standard of their country."[24]

During the war, Allen, Jones, and Forten recruited a phenomenal number of would-be troops and workers. Even when it was clear that African American recruits would do scutwork to keep the broader military effort going, the black triumvirate made sure that black troops did their job. And when members of this battalion were later mobilized for military action (in segregated units under a white commander), black leaders once again supported the call. In their eyes, civic duty and patriotism did not stop at the color line.

Or did it? No sooner had the war ended than public debates reappeared over the success of Northern abolition and free blacks' future in a country that they had recently helped secure. Racial doom and gloom surrounded Allen in these years. Even abolitionists expressed concerns about black freedom after the War of 1812. Far from an age of black redemption, white abolitionists saw racial stalemate. The PAS apprenticing committee reported in 1815 that it could not find suitable indentures for many eligible blacks (free as well as enslaved), a key way for African Americans to transit from slavery and poverty to freedom and gain. Even for those blacks who had indentures, there was precious little opportunity to advance once the agreement ended. In other words, there was less opportunity for a Richard Allen to develop than ever.[25]

Prejudice explained a lot, the PAS believed, but so too did environment. Many African Americans, the apprenticing report continued, "are either brought up under the control of parents just emerged from slavery, whose weaknesses they entail upon them . . . or in menial stations of society, where they contract habits not less injurious to their future reputation." This dour, even pessimistic mood about a degraded black character pervaded the report. "Thus, generation succeeds to generation without that rise in the scale of human excellence which was hoped for." Because of this, "the cause of emancipation is weakening in our hands." And these were free blacks' most steadfast allies![26]

The PAS began favoring a domestic form of colonization. Abolitionists would move black children from their "degraded" parents to better situations. Of course, this would be done with the complete consent of black parents. Nevertheless, the PAS counseled its officers to rank domestic colonization as one of abolitionists' premier goals, perhaps equal to free black education and literacy.[27]

Pennsylvania abolitionists' concerns about the growing black underclass help us to understand Allen's world and mindset during the War of 1812 years. Both white abolitionists and black leaders like Allen confronted a rising tide of black indentures maturing with decreasing economic opportunities; they saw increasing immigration of European ethnic populations competing with black masses for skilled work; and they watched as white politicians—and even some philanthropists—began expressing concerns about the fruits of the first emancipation in Pennsylvania. With gloom setting in among white abolitionists, how could Allen not be pessimistic too?

In a later stab at Allen's pious and noble character, disgruntled AME members claimed that the good bishop had even taken to calling white people "evil" around this time.[28] Allen and his defenders vigorously disputed this assertion. But that such charges circulated at all says something about the mood of both Allen and black Philadelphia. It was all too easy to believe that whites had turned their backs on the cause of racial justice during the 1810s. It seemed that white Americans blamed free blacks for still being in America at all.

Allen had long since made his plea to white Americans that they held power over black destiny. His 1794 "Address to Those Who Hold Slaves and Approve the Practice" reminded Christians that God was just and would not forget the transgressions of slaveholders. In the here and now, Allen told his readers, white citizens must become the sponsors of black redemption by treating free blacks as part of their own family. That experiment, vaguely parallel to PAS initiatives at domestic colonization in the 1810s but with a totally different slant (blacks, in Allen's view, were not degraded, just ignored as would-be geniuses), would end slavery and bring blacks fully into the civic world. They would be not merely "useful persons"—a mild phrase sometimes applied to black laborers—but "good citizens" (as Allen himself noted in his "Eulogy of Washington"). Allen had already said all this in pamphlets, petitions, and speeches. But had anyone other than a deceased president listened?[29]

4. *Black Rentier*

Rather ironically, Allen doubted America when he became most economically grounded in American society. By the 1810s, Allen had long since retired from manual labor—the cutting, scheming, hauling, and dealing that had defined his early adulthood. Allen was making more in rental income alone (roughly four hundred dollars per year) than the average black worker in Philadelphia.[30] And by the time he spoke in favor of African resettlement to a white colonizationist in 1817, Bethel Church itself was completely free and independent of white Methodists' control. He was the world's first black bishop! On the personal front, Allen's family was large and prosperous. Allen was the embodiment of the black American dream.

So why consider trans-Atlantic redemption schemes?

Allen came to believe that African Americans would never be able to replicate his rise in the United States. He expressed such concerns many times. When James Forten told Presbyterian minister Robert Finley in 1817 that African Americans would never rise as a group until they had "come out from under the white people," Allen vigorously nodded his head in approval.[31] As Allen himself later put it, "our forlorn and deplorable situation earnestly and loudly demand of us to devise and pursue all legal means for the speedy elevation of ourselves and brethren to the scale and standing of men." Such elevation could no longer be achieved by remaining in the United States, he believed; rather, blacks needed an international outlet to speed the project of black redemption.[32]

How did Allen envision uplift? One interesting way of gauging his concern about free blacks' collective future is by revisiting his economic rise in Philadelphia—particularly his incredible collection of properties —and its impact on Allen's uplift ideology. If one did not remember that he was the pious founder of the country's leading black church, Allen's trajectory during the early national period mirrored that of virtually any up-and-coming American. Allen moved from day jobs to a single profession to a black rentier over a long and laborious period. But he had risen. Allen secured his elevated status not merely by becoming a minister but also by accumulating property. Allen secured land for Bethel Church, a private home, a country home, and several rental properties. Because property deals always spelled out a prospective buyer's profession, we can see Allen morph from "trader" and "grocer"

(1791–92) to master chimney sweep and dry-goods "Dealer" (1792–1805) to "Minister" and black property owner in the 1810s and 1820s.[33]

Over the course of his life, Allen purchased as many as ten pieces of property, some relating to Bethel Church, others to commercial gain or standing, and still others to his desire to live in the country away from urban life. Although a footnote in the already-bulging stacks of Philadelphia's land office, Allen's was one of the few black names to come up again and again during the 1790s and early 1800s. His property holdings around Bethel Church illustrate his strategic concern with property. Allen secured a foothold at Sixth and Lombard by purchasing land for Bethel Church and then steadily securing plots of land around it. Allen was not satisfied to simply buy the original lot where his church would one day stand. As Allen cast his eye around the lot's tenement homes and fields, he worried that someone could purchase them and topple his beloved church like a domino. Allen did not wait for such scenarios. He bid on property around Bethel as soon as it became available. After purchasing a large lot from lawyer and politician Mark Wilcox in 1791 for Bethel Church, Allen bought property alongside it from Joseph Lewis, a farmer.[34] And so it went: Allen scooped up property after property to fortify Bethel Church.

No purchase was too big or too small for Allen. In 1795, a few years removed from his loan from the PAS for fifty dollars (which he was still paying off), Allen bought a lot and "2 frame tenements" adjacent to Bethel Church from a carpenter named John Burk for three hundred pounds. The contract between the two men stipulated clearly that the money change hands "at or before" the sale—there would be no loan to secure the land. Allen promptly paid up, securing two rent-bearing dwellings just south of Bethel Church. In 1805, Allen and the AME purchased a slice of land "two inches and a half" wide (fronting Sixth Street) and sixty-four-feet deep, just big enough for a wall to enclose parts of Bethel property. Although the transaction was for only five shillings, it granted Bethel "sole use" of the precious space. No one could come along and chip away at Bethel's armor. In 1818, Allen bought still another lot on the north side of Bethel for $275. All told, Allen had secured four other pieces of property after purchasing the original land for Bethel.[35]

Allen had diligently saved money from his various day jobs (and from property rentals as he accumulated them) to buy new properties.

He bought his own house and Bethel Church land with cash (in the same year no less). And he never missed a payment on the few properties he secured through annual loans. Best of all, Allen made money back on his land deals. In 1805, he sold the former Burk property to Bethel trustees for 550 pounds, after originally purchasing it a decade earlier for 20 pounds a year. By the 1820s, Allen could count on hundreds of dollars per year from his several rental properties. That sum alone matched or exceeded the average income of many white Philadelphians.

It all had a purpose. Allen did not purchase property merely to claim economic superiority. Rather, he was trying to secure a solid, irrefutable black place in American society. Allen's persistent buying of property made an iron-clad claim on the city in which he lived, the country in which he was born, the very soil on which he daily stood. As he subsequently wrote, America was a land that he and thousands upon thousands of black laborers "have watered with our tears and our blood."[36] Securing a black place became intimately connected to his moral-uplift philosophy. Indeed, for much of his life, Allen believed that if African Americans worked hard, remained pious, and refrained from what he termed "midnight frolics," then they too would be in a position to buy property, rise, and claim an irrefutable place in American civic and social culture.[37]

"Place"—that word remained critical to Allen, and it helps explain why he worked so hard to accumulate property after property. Return once again to Allen's retelling of the AME's founding. Allen's narrative of Bethel's rise to independence takes the form of a biblical journey: black congregants moved from place to place before deciding that they needed their own church property. In other words, African Methodists were like the ancient Jews in Egypt—strangers in a strange land (Leviticus 19:33). "We had no place of worship," Allen wrote. Through Allen's agency, black Methodists secured church land. "We pitched upon a lot at the corner of Lombard and Sixth Streets," he said. After his black brethren found another lot, and decided to become Episcopalians, they asked Allen "to give . . . up" his property. Allen simply refused. "I told them [that] . . . I would sooner keep it for myself than to forfeit the agreement I had made. And so I did." That land became Bethel's forever home. Property equaled an independent identity for Allen.[38]

For confirmation of this vision, look to Allen's last will. In that document he proudly bequeathed property to every one of his six children and their families, an amazing feat for most nineteenth-century Americans but nothing short of remarkable for a free black man and former slave. "I give and bequeath to my son, John Allen, the house and lot on Spruce Street," he began his roll-call of property transactions, which continued for several paragraphs. "I give and bequeath to my daughter, Sarah Eddy, the east side of a three story brick tenement and lot . . . on Pine Street"; "I give and bequeath to my daughter Ann Adams the west side of the Pine Street property"; "I give and bequeath to my son Peter Allen, the south side of the lot with six frames" (or houses); "I give to my son, James Allen, lot and three houses south of Bethel Church."[39] Some of these properties had been in Allen's possession since the 1790s; others he had claimed later in life. But whenever he purchased these lots, he kept them in the family.

One gets a glimpse of Allen's uniqueness when comparing his will to that of his friend Absalom Jones. Roughly fifteen years his senior, Jones passed on in 1818, leaving a good deal of things to family and friends. Like Allen, Jones had also purchased a home in Philadelphia; unlike Allen, he bought his house before securing freedom. Jones was clearly an exceptional figure. Yet he did not accumulate and pass on the multiple properties that Allen did. Jones's will gave out some saved income, his beloved books and personal effects (a cane to Allen), and some china and silver. But, unlike Allen, he distributed no great amount of property. Allen was clearly an exceptional man among exceptional men. Only the great black businessman James Forten, said to be one of the richest Philadelphians of the early nineteenth century, was his equal.[40]

Perhaps Allen's focus on property had its roots in Delaware, where, he remembered, "slaves would toil in their little patches many a night until midnight to raise their little track and sell something to support them more than what their masters gave them."[41] Those "little patches" grew larger and larger in Allen's mind—and, just as in slavery, they would always be linked to black freedom and autonomy. Take Allen's purchase of a lot in the Northern Liberties in 1813. Though he had already acquired more than enough property for himself and for daily church operations, Allen struck a new deal for AME burial space. The property, located just north of Philadelphia proper, contained a one-story building and an undeveloped "piece of ground." The contract stipulated that the Bethel-owned property must be used for either religious worship or burials and "no other purpose whatever." It cost one hundred dollars, and it gave the church secure burial space for years to come.[42]

5. Allen and the Black Underclass

To return to Allen's pro-colonization stand, the question by the 1810s was whether or not free blacks could mimic his success. Could Afro-Philadelphians purchase property, move up the economic ladder, and gain an irrefutable place in society? On that critical question, Allen hedged for the first time in his life. He was just not convinced that future generations of free blacks could climb as he had. They were, in a very real sense, stuck.

Although not a serious political or economic thinker, Allen believed that there was something seriously wrong with African American political economy during the early nineteenth century. Through no fault of their own, free blacks faced a deplorable socioeconomic landscape, with menial labor and transient living conditions defining their lives. Few blacks could attain meaningful jobs; fewer still could attain significant amounts of property. Whichever way he defined wealth, status, and standing—the physiocratic way, which linked political economy to land, or the soon-to-be Marxian way, which defined one's labor as a productive tool—Allen found free black life in a grim state of affairs. There seemed to be no black future in a racist American landscape that refused to treat African Americans as equals, whether in the labor market or in politics. As he put it despairingly on one occasion later in his life, an ever-increasing number of free blacks "crowd into the Atlantic cities, dependent for their support on their daily labor." Sadly, these black masses "suffer for want of employment," with many people of color simply "becom[ing] domestics [to whites]." Allen called this "a precarious and degrading situation."[43]

Allen also worried about the fate of African American youth in the urban core. From his first extended meditations on the subject (that remarkable moral-uplift pamphlet in 1808) until his last public pronouncement (his pro-Canadian-emigration address to the first national black convention), Allen offered periodic commentary on the tough economic realities facing urban black youth. In an 1817 meeting with white minister and colonizationist Robert Finley, Allen registered specific concerns about the future of young black people in American society. "He considered the present plan of colonization," Finley recalled, "as holding out great advantages for the blacks who are now young." Perhaps in Africa, Allen came to believe, young black men (and women) could rise without the weight of racism holding them down.[44]

Allen's dire thoughts stemmed, in part, from his sobering meetings with Peter Matthias and John Joyce, the two young free black men executed in 1808 for the murder of a white widow storekeeper.[45] If one looks again at Allen's reconstruction of their lives, it is clear that he saw them as a sign of young free blacks' hard future. According to Allen, both Matthias and Joyce were enslaved not only to sin but to a broader discriminatory climate that framed their every move. This included how white Philadelphians would now look at their crime: blacks murdered not because they were sinners, or because they had few opportunities to surmount a meager existence, but because they were black.

Allen conceded that both men made poor choices. John Joyce, Allen discovered in his interviews, had come from Maryland, where he had been enslaved until the age of nine. Born in 1784, Joyce apparently gained quasi-freedom sometime in the late 1790s. He told Allen that, as a teenager, he went "into the service of the United States." He claimed to have sailed in the navy before returning to Washington, D.C., and marrying a servant in a doctor's home. After Joyce's wife had had an affair, he told Allen, "I left her." Stealing a horse and coming to Philadelphia, he quickly settled into the Cedar Ward area, working as stableboy, a servant, a coachman, and a waiter "in a tavern." He lived in one residence or another for only a brief time before moving on. To get by, he perpetrated small crimes, like stealing a watch. And he passed his time not by attending Allen's church but by sometimes "going out to dance late at night." Joyce told Allen that "I was depraved in morals and never belonged to any religious society," despite the fact that his own parents and relatives were Christians. For Allen, these lifestyle choices slowly led to Joyce's murder plot and the gallows. But the fact that Joyce had been born a slave and had few opportunities thereafter also weighed on Allen's mind.[46]

Peter Matthias had a similar life story, though Allen discovered that his role in the crime itself was murky and subject to dispute. Roughly the same age as his friend Joyce, Matthias had also been a Maryland slave. Unlike Joyce, Matthias had only recently been freed (sometime around 1805) and moved to Philadelphia. Like Allen, Matthias signed a deal with his owner to buy his freedom over a period of years. Also like Allen, Matthias moved to Dover for a while, doing day labor. When he finally did settle in Philadelphia, Matthias worked for none other than Benjamin Rush for "a few days." He did other small jobs, Matthias declared, and enjoyed "playing violin at dances." He claimed not to be religious and was no stranger to grog shops and midnight frolics. But he also claimed to have no knowledge of Joyce's murder plot. And so he went to the gallows a wronged man, guilty, in Allen's eyes, of bad luck or lack of piety—or both.[47]

Allen wrote down the confessions of both men and dictated each man's confession for correction (neither was literate). Both men, Allen stated, had "ample time for reflection on its contents." Neither opposed his rendering of their lives, or so Allen claimed. Nor did they mind his tending to their souls through prayer, or so Allen claimed. This allowed Allen to pronounce in the grandiloquent tones of a preacher holding fast against declension in the black community: "The path of sin is descending," Allen proclaimed, and "the feet of the wicked become swifter to do evil." Allen had been saved by God's grace. What about those below and around him who had not yet been saved? It seemed as though gambling, "midnight frolics," drinking, and dancing had increased in the black community. "Break off, O young man," he finished, "your impious companions . . . [for] they will drag you down to everlasting fire."[48]

Although Joyce and Matthias were of a completely different class and generation than Allen, he came to see them as typical examples. They represented promises gone unfulfilled in nineteenth-century Philadelphia. Not only had they turned their backs on religion, but society had turned its back on them. There was not enough educational support, economic opportunity, or true egalitarian feeling to give hope to younger generations of free blacks streaming into the city. Joyce and Matthias, Allen reported, had each arrived in Philadelphia just as opportunity and optimism for blacks began to narrow during the early nineteenth century.

So what did Allen want others to see? As a true moral uplifter, Allen challenged white readers to think of the crimes that they themselves had committed in word, thought, or deed. Did white citizens not usually get a second chance? Did they not usually receive forgiveness? Not Matthias and Joyce, he concluded—they received neither a second chance nor community sympathy. Whites saw them as young black men programmed to do wrong, which Matthias and Joyce internalized. They had limited opportunities at best and made the worst of them.

In 1808, Allen had hoped that his moral-uplift pamphlet would staunch wounds in the black community. But the problems associated with blacks' future, he came to see just a few years later, were larger than a sermon, or pamphlet, could rectify.

6. Cuffee Redux

Paul Cuffee's plan offered Allen another option: racial redemption in another land. Although Allen remained locked in a battle for Bethel's very survival during the War of 1812, the black preacher stepped up his support for the African cause soon after the war ended (1815) and his church achieved full independence (1816). African colonization meant many things to Allen. Now that he was bishop of his own church, the thought of a Methodist connection in Africa surely appealed to him. So too did the prospect of creating economic opportunities for the increasing numbers of black men and women he saw in the streets of Philadelphia. Finally, at an ideological level, Allen was increasingly frustrated with the limits of American democracy. He told a white colonizationist that "if he were younger, he himself would move to Africa."[49] For the good of both Africans and African Americans, he vowed to support Cuffee-style colonization.

With antiblack forces swirling around Philadelphia's black community during the 1810s, Allen's growing support of colonization should have been popular. It wasn't. In 1817, the grassroots black community rebuked Allen, Forten, John Gloucester, and other free black leaders for embracing colonization without consulting them.

The most famous confrontation occurred at a mass meeting at Bethel Church around January 15. Whatever the precise details leading up to the event—there is no official record of the proceedings—the mass meeting proved to be an electric affair. If black founders felt they could simply hold forth on colonization, they soon discovered otherwise. For as black elites held court near Allen's pulpit, carefully outlining the advantages of African colonization, the black masses in the pews and hallways shouted their position: no colonization! James Forten recalled that Allen's church reverberated with an ear-piercing "no" when he and other leaders asked black Philadelphians to cast an affirmative vote for colonization. Hearing the collective "no" of over three thousand people crammed into Bethel Church must have been a jarring experience for Allen. What must have been most surprising, however, was the public rebuke offered to black founders' claim to speak for the masses. Men like Allen and Forten had cultivated leadership positions based not simply on economic or social standing but on their status as community spokesmen. Now these icons discovered that their political judgment had little support among those they ostensibly represented. The black masses were eager to speak back to, and even disagree with, black elites. For Richard Allen, this was only the beginning of such challenges.[50]

Black Philadelphians' denunciation reflected key changes in the colonization movement in the few short years since Cuffee had promulgated his African plan. Perhaps the most notable change occurred in the leadership of the cause. Where previously white reformers and free black leaders had dominated it, by 1817 American slaveholders infiltrated colonization as a means of both spurring private manumission (in the South) and ridding the nation of free blacks. The formation of the American Colonization Society (ACS) in Washington, D.C., at the end of 1816 illustrated this new leadership dynamic, for prominent slaveholders including both Henry Clay and James Madison served in many key positions. Colonization soon took on a more ominous antiblack tone, as white Northerners flocked to the cause. Massachusetts politician Edward Everett spoke for many Northern colonizationists when he supported colonizing free blacks, whom he described as vagabonds, criminals, and a drain on Northern society. Kentuckian Henry Clay labeled free blacks as useless. By the 1830s, colonization became the fastest growing racial-reform movement and the first one that brought Northerners and Southerners together on a plan of removing blacks from American shores.[51]

African Americans responded with a spate of anticolonization meetings, led by that massive gathering of Afro-Philadelphians at Mother Bethel Church. Subsequent generations of black activists cited "the spirit of 1817" as exemplifying black abolitionism. It is somewhat ironic, then, that free black leaders like Allen did not initially oppose colonization. Frustrated by racial stalemate in the United States, and interested in learning more about ACS plans, Allen met with both black and white colonizationists. In Allen's eyes, black elites had to consider the merits of every plan aimed at racial justice, including ACS schemes for African repatriation. Allen's grassroots brethren believed that colonization entailed forcible removals of African-descended people, something reminiscent of the slave trade. They also worried that colonization would not work so well for the less fortunate and less well-off members of the black community. Indeed, as wealthy and respected men, Allen, Forten, and Cuffee could go back and forth among continents. Could others do the same, the black masses wondered, or would they be trapped on one side of the Atlantic or the other without powerful patrons nearby? There was, in short, a real divide between black elites and black masses over colonization.

The passion with which Philadelphia's black masses articulated their grievances in Bethel Church startled Allen, Forten, and other leaders. But it is also a credit to these same black elites that they quickly rallied to the anticolonizationist standard, giving it a political and ideological gloss that transcended the moment. Black founders created a series of official resolutions that took the form of a protest pamphlet against colonization. Drawing on decades of black protest both in and beyond Philadelphia, and simultaneously giving voice to the black masses around them, African American leaders issued a stirring proclamation: "Whereas our ancestors (not of choice) were the first successful cultivators of the wilds of America," the preamble to the resolutions began, "we their descendents feel ourselves entitled to participate in the blessings of her luxuriant soil, which their blood and sweat manured." Black Philadelphians condemned "the unmerited stigma . . . cast upon the reputation of the free people of color" by the American Colonization Society and opposed the very idea of African colonization. In one of the most famous parts of the Philadelphians' protest, the free black community solemnly pledged "that we never will separate ourselves voluntarily from the slave population in this country." Quite simply, the document declared, slaves are "our brethren." Because neither of the document's two authors—James Forten and Russell Parrott—had been enslaved, Allen must have played some role in the articulation of such thoughts. He had made a similar pledge of support to enslaved people in 1794. He would not turn his back on the enslaved.[52]

The significance of black elites' anticolonizationist conversion echoed decades later. The details of the 1817 meeting forgotten, a rising generation of black and white reformers embraced the banner of anticolonization first issued at Allen's church. Indeed, the "immediatist" abolition movement of William Lloyd Garrison and Frederick Douglass took as its founding faith sentiments from 1817: colonization was a chimera, America was a black homeland, and Americans must confront the evils of slavery and racism if they would claim the heritage of both Christianity and revolutionary republicanism. Both Garrison and Douglass quoted directly from Afro-Philadelphians' anticolonization meeting. So too would Allen reprise its sentiments in his famous letter to *Freedom's Journal* in 1827. Thus, although the black masses had issued the initial colonizationist rebuttal, black leaders quickly rushed to their side and gave it political visibility.[53]

Allen's role in the colonization debate has not been examined very closely. Although he corresponded with liberal colonizationists into the 1820s, he believed that the masses—including many of his own parishioners—had spoken. His job as a black leader was now to stand tall against the American Colonization Society. James Forten said something similar to Paul Cuffee: because black community members were so "decided against the measure," he wrote, black leaders "have agreed to remain silent" on the ACS. But black leaders actually helped nonelites carry the anticolonization crusade forward with memorable words and deeds. As Allen later put it, "this land which we have watered with our tears and our blood, is now our mother country and we are well satisfy to stay where wisdom abounds, and the Gospel is free."[54]

In this vein, the 1817 meeting at Bethel Church reified Allen's position as a leader. The black masses did not completely reject elite leadership; rather, they may have been asking for a more forceful exertion of black leaders' presumed powers to speak for the race. The language of the Philadelphia protest bears a strong resemblance to Allen and Jones's yellow-fever pamphlet of 1794: both called for black unity in the face of public assault. And both documents relied on the acknowledged status of black leaders to protect black masses in the public realm. Those who could speak publicly, Allen and Jones agreed, had a duty to do so. Put another way, the colonization meeting of 1817 was not yet a revolution from below; instead, it served as a wake-up call for Allen's leadership group. Black elites had to remain grounded in the affairs of the community.

This realization became even clearer later that summer when a second anticolonization meeting was convened in Philadelphia. Held this time at a black schoolhouse, the August 1817 meeting addressed the formation of a local auxiliary to the American Colonization Society. Worried that forcible deportations of free blacks might very well ensue, black leaders assembled the community to plan a new response. Once again, black elites turned to print to express the broader black community's feelings. Although the pamphlet addressed white Philadelphians in general, black leaders eventually presented it to the American Convention of Abolition Societies, a national consortium of gradual abolitionists that met biennially through the 1830s (usually in Philadelphia). Pitched in the gentlemanly terms that black elites had learned to use when addressing white statesmen and citizens, the document reasoned through black opposition to the ACS. Far from a bombastic appeal, the pamphlet "humbly and respectfully" expressed African Americans' "apprehensions." After stating that free blacks had through their own industry, piety, and perseverance created an irrefutable place in American society, the memorialists respectfully "renounce and disclaim every connection with" the ACS. Better that Americans focus on abolishing slavery and acting as true Christians, the document continued, than exile free blacks to the distant shores of Africa. And, once again, Afro-Philadelphians took an oath of allegiance to their enslaved brethren in the South, promising never to voluntarily leave them in bondage.[55]

Intriguingly, the document made clear that free blacks did not oppose "all plans of colonization." Did this reflect Allen's input? Probably, although other black leaders also remained intrigued by the redemptionist potential of colonization plans (James Forten continued to express his support of the African plan, as did John Gloucester, a former slave and a founding minister of the first African Presbyterian Church). In fact, at a private meeting held between the January event at Allen's church and the August event at the black schoolhouse, Allen and ten other African American leaders met with a distinguished white colonizationist and preacher from New Jersey, Robert Finley. Scholars once thought this stealth meeting had occurred prior to the Bethel Church gathering, for it seemed as if Finley was attempting to rally black leaders to the colonizationist cause. Whatever the date, the closed-door session shows how seriously white as well as black colonizationists took Afro-Philadelphians' grassroots rejection of the plan.[56]

Nevertheless, Finley wrote of black leaders' continued support of some form of colonization, especially one unconnected to the slaveholder-dominated ACS. The white preacher quoted Allen by name, noting that he was a vociferous proponent of the great Cuffee's plan. As Finley put it, Richard Allen "spoke with warmth on some oppression which [blacks] suffer from the whites, and warmly in favor of colonization in Africa."[57]

For the normally cool and composed Allen to flash red hot on this matter was certainly revealing. If he flirted with colonization, but did not reject *in toto* his claims to American identity, Allen was expressing his divided soul: no matter how far he traveled in American society, he would always be stigmatized by race. Perhaps, then, the time had come to truly embrace his African roots. He would return home, even if only in his colonizationist dreams.

7. *Psalm 49*

In the spring of 1820, a small band of African American colonizationists set sail for the Sherbo colony on the West African coast. Linked to Sierra Leone, the struggling colony hoped to attract an idealistic cadre of settlers. Among those who departed on this voyage was the man who had initially been selected as bishop of the African Methodist Episcopal Church, Allen's friend Daniel Coker. Although his very brief stint as the leader of the AME had ended ignominiously, Coker now bid for glory by taking a group of acolytes not much bigger than Christ's original group of disciples to their African homeland. "He shall go to the generation of his fathers," they hummed in unison from Psalm 49. The group arrived in Sherbo weeks later, exhausted but enthused. Coker stayed in Africa the rest of his life, leaving sons and daughters, and grandsons and granddaughters, to greet subsequent generations of African American travelers. In 1891, AME bishop Henry McNeal Turner marveled that Coker's family had established an African lineage dating back over sixty years. Who said African colonization could not possibly work?[58]

Certainly not Richard Allen, at least not in the decade preceding Daniel Coker's departure. Indeed, although Allen was not with Coker's committed colonizationist troops, he had helped pave the way for Coker's journey by keeping the vision of colonization alive and well in the mid-Atlantic black community. Allen was so optimistic about black-led African colonization that he prepared his own son for missionary work across the Atlantic. Word spread all the way to New England, where, as the Boston *Christian Disciple* informed its readers in August 1816, Richard Allen Jr. had recently begun studies at the first seminary for black youth in America, with the express purpose of spreading the Afro-Christian gospel to the shores of Africa. Meeting in Philadelphia's Augustine Hall—named after Augustine of Hippo, an early African bishop—five black seminarians undertook a "classical and scientific education preparatory to theology." In a moving tribute to the seminary's broader meaning to black uplift, even Afro-Philadelphians without children paid "liberally" into the institution's subscription fund, according to a circular written by black Presbyterian minister John Gloucester (whose own son Jeremiah studied next to Richard Jr.). Proud parents of color and their sponsors then gathered to watch the young pupils' first examinations in June of that year. "Let youth instructed in a knowledge of the scriptures," the circular announced, "be raised up, to display the Cross, from the Mouth of the Nile to the Cape of Good Hope."

Like so many other black founders (Coker, Forten, Peter Williams, William Watkins, Prince Hall), Allen took the African plan seriously because he believed he had to—American society gave him little choice but to think about trans-Atlantic black redemption. The antiblack musings of new generations of white colonizationists, combined with Paul Cuffee's death in September 1817, undid black elites' support for African colonization. These events also forced Allen to think more deeply about his and Africans' claims on the United States. There was a voice inside him that sang deeply of America as his "motherland."

But there was another voice that hummed Allen's faith in international black redemption plans. Tellingly, Allen interpreted the anticolonizationist outburst at his church in January 1817 as yet a further proof of blacks' degraded condition in America. Now more than ever black people needed a safety valve, he believed, for the black masses rising uncomfortably below black leaders would not sit quietly much longer. Allen had once viewed Cuffee-style African colonization as a remedy for free black frustrations. With that dream gone, Allen became an even more vociferous proponent of a new cause: emigration to the world's first black republic of Haiti.

8

Allen Challenged
Shadow Politics and Community Conflict in the 1820s

In the basement of Mother Bethel Church, the Richard Allen Museum displays a small but important piece of black political history: a voting machine. The polished, medium-sized wooden box once featured images of Bethel trustees—woodcuts, most likely—placed above a series of holes slightly bigger than a marble. These slots allowed all Bethel voters (unlettered as well as literate congregants) a chance to be heard during church elections. Although the machine probably dates from after Allen's time, it is a reminder that free black Northerners created a vibrant world of politics where they could, in autonomous churches, benevolent societies, and reform organizations.

Scholars will never know if Richard Allen (or most black founders) voted in local, state, or federal elections. Although he claimed to be an equal citizen of both the Commonwealth of Pennsylvania and the American republic, Allen never mentioned suffrage in any letter, pamphlet, or autobiographical recollection. Evidence suggests that Pennsylvania blacks voted only sporadically before the Civil War, largely in locales with fewer concentrations of African Americans. In Allen's Philadelphia, free blacks faced customary prejudice at the polls, meaning that few urban dwellers (even black elites like Allen and James Forten) voted during the early republic. In 1838, Pennsylvanians crafted a new state constitution that explicitly forbade black voting rights. Not until the postbellum era would black Northerners enjoy wider access to the polls.[1]

Nevertheless, as Bethel's voting machine illustrates, free blacks vigorously practiced "shadow politics": the mimicry of formal political activity in black-controlled institutions. By staging annual elections for trustees or holding referenda on church policy, Bethel inculcated knowledge of, and respect for, the principles of democratic citizenship. For people who did not have much power in the civic realm, shadow politics gave black voters sovereignty over community policies. As early as 1807, Richard Allen used shadow politics to secure passage of the African Supplement, which eliminated white clerics' constitutional power over Bethel Church. As Allen recalled, the African Supplement was passed "by and with consent of two thirds of the male members of [Bethel] church."[2]

Although the style of shadow politics—voting, campaigning, electioneering—illustrated free blacks' deeper understanding of their "deliberative rights" as American citizens, the location (within black cultural groups and communities) suggests a more complex sense of allegiances and identity.[3] Indeed, the intensification of political activity within antebellum free black society generally, and at Bethel Church in particular, exemplified the evolution of a more militant black consciousness. Internalizing and maximizing black political power may have become more important to many African Americans than attempting to integrate civic institutions. And this may have been one of the wellsprings of modern black-power movements.

Of course, democracy challenges its practitioners to balance majority and minority interests—and it is notoriously antideferential. Allen discovered this during the 1820s, when antideference movements threatened the black founder's long-held leadership position. The story of Allen's biggest internal challenge began on June 6, 1820, when a small group of disaffected parishioners "detached themselves from Bethel Church and organized themselves into a distinct society." The breakaway group soon elected a dozen trustees, rented a schoolhouse for Sunday services, and took the name "Wesley Church." According to Wesley records, "these members left for reasonable causes," though dissidents never fully explained them. Allen believed that the breakaway attempt flowed from base men and base motives. Yet whatever Allen may have thought, he could not ignore the reality of this secession movement, for the upstart Wesleyites quickly settled on a piece of property just ninety feet behind Bethel Church![4]

Wesley no longer stands in Bethel's shadow, having long since moved to a new location. But the genesis of Wesley Church formed an important part of Allen's biography during the tumultuous 1820s. The key members of the Wesley breakaway were not only disaffected Bethelites; they also charged the respected Allen with financial impropriety and moral high-handedness. The Wesley breakaway thus marked the black underclass's most sustained response to Allen's brand of leadership and leadership class. It was part of a democratic revolution within the black community. For the first time in his life, in other words, Allen confronted members of his own church who wanted complete freedom from the black founder.

Allen's confrontation with black democracy included another divisive issue: African American women's right to preach. Just as the black underclass challenged elite black leaders' status as community spokesmen, so too did a Methodist itinerant named Jarena Lee challenge black men's status as church patriarchs. Though both developments were rooted in local black politics, they stemmed from a much broader antideferential wind sweeping over American culture at the beginning of the nineteenth century. Like Thomas Jefferson and James Madison, white founding figures who lived to see Jacksonian democracy challenge their deferential notions of politics, Richard Allen lived to see black community divisions threaten his leadership position. The black founder's vigorous response indicated his unwillingness to pass gently into retirement. As long as the Lord allowed him to remain in the secular world, Allen would attempt to shape black politics locally, nationally, and even internationally.

1. Detaching from Bethel Church

Wesley Church enjoyed a most interesting organizational existence during the 1820s and 1830s. After seceding from Bethel, Wesleyites affiliated with the black-led AME Zion Church in New York City before becoming an affiliate of the white-controlled Methodist conference in Philadelphia—the very one Richard Allen had fled years earlier. Wesley briefly became "St. Phillip's Church" around 1826, before reorganizing under its original name. Always struggling to pay monthly and quarterly accounts—from candles to rent—Wesley officials ingratiated themselves to black philanthropists and church leaders who helped them survive. The Benezet Philanthropic Society, a black benevolent group formed in 1812, offered Wesleyites a substantial start-up loan in 1820, and individual lenders floated bonds to trustees for the building of the church. Even then Wesley barely survived.[5]

The precise details of the breakaway that brought the church into being remain less than clear, but it all evidently began during the late spring of 1820 when a man named Jonathan Tudas was accused of violating Bethel Church rules. The offense? Tudas allegedly exposed himself to a woman in a basement and fathered a child (with a white woman) out of wedlock.[6] More scandalously, Bethel officials found that Tudas had offered to help the woman abort the pregnancy. As with other moral offenses of this kind, Bethelites like Tudas were judged by church trustees. The judgment was usually firm and final. If found guilty, a congregant was tossed "out of society," meaning the congregation. This policy mirrored almost exactly white Methodist rules, and historian Carol George has rightly argued that one reason Allen insisted on Bethel's independence in the first place was that white Methodist clerics often levied harsher judgments against black offenders.[7] Allen even called some Methodist elders "tyrants . . . to the colored people." "They would turn them [black congregants] out of society, giving them no trial, for the smallest offense, perhaps only hearsay."[8] In Bethel Church, Allen believed that his judgments would be fair and impartial.

But Tudas did not think so—and he did not go quietly to his Bethel banishment. First, he persuaded a small band of Bethelites that they were next on Allen's radar. These fearful men (perhaps a half dozen) followed Tudas out of Bethel Church and formed Wesley Church in June 1820. Next, Tudas wrote an anti-Allen pamphlet at the beginning of 1823, which he circulated among (and read to) his followers. Entitled variously "Richard Allen's Journal" and "Facts Relative to the Government of the African Methodist Episcopal Church, Called Bethel," the manuscript covered Allen's career as patriarch of Bethel Church from 1794 to 1820, especially alleged financial misdealings.[9] Finally, he convinced many of his Wesley adherents that the time had come to challenge Allen's role as a community spokesman. One of Tudas's main allies was William Perkins. In another time, both Tudas and Perkins might have emulated Allen. Just as Allen had once been a dealer in the 1790s, so too did Tudas and Perkins work as dealers (of used clothes) in the 1810s. But whereas Allen moved up from dealer to property owner to preacher, reverend, bishop, and most respected community leader, Tudas and Perkins remained stuck in a laborer's life. And they did not like lectures from Allen on moral uplift.

They were eventually joined by others who disliked Allen's leadership style. Used-clothes dealer and preacher Simon Murray came into the fold after arriving from New York's AME Zion Church (a separate denomination that competed with Allen's AME for black acolytes in mid-Atlantic communities). Recognition from the New York congregation,

Wesley dissidents hoped, would legitimate their own church. Robert Green, Allen's arch enemy who had once squared off against the black founder in Pennsylvania's supreme court and attempted to buy Bethel Church for white Methodists in 1815, joined Wesley too.

Then Wesley Church underwent its own membership disputes. Although the congregation slowly added members, most of the initial seceders (including Murray, Perkins, and Tudas) disappeared by 1826 when Wesley received official incorporation from the state of Pennsylvania. By the 1830s, the church was growing again, with a congregation of roughly one hundred worshipers. With the seceding members gone, Allen even visited the church before his death.[10]

Yet what makes the Wesleyites' story so compelling is not simply that they broke away from Bethel Church and endured internal dissension but that they forced Allen to fight back publicly with all the vigor he could muster. Allen's initial struggle against Tudas and his disaffected brethren was reminiscent of the yellow-fever epidemic of 1793. On that occasion, however, Allen focused his attention on the white community's misperceptions of free blacks. Here, Allen confronted members of his own community. And both sides struggled mightily to win.

2. Allen as Lightning Rod

How did the black founder become a lightning rod in his own church and community? Begin with Allen's banishment of Jonathan Tudas for immoral conduct: not merely an act of individual castigation, it was part and parcel of Allen's moral-uplift ideology. Allen fervently believed that free blacks must work hard to lift themselves from economic hardship, remain pious in the face of life's many struggles, and refrain from any behavior (dances, frolics, drinking) that he thought stigmatized the broader black community. Indeed, interested though he might have been in an international black safety valve, Allen remained convinced that uplift principles must guide free black communities wherever they took root. According to Allen, black moral uplift furthered the antislavery cause. "I entreat you to consider the obligations we lie under," he had told free blacks as early as 1794, for "lazy" and "idle conduct" "only strengthen[ed] the bands of oppression."[11] Allen's sermonizing agitated some free blacks beneath him, particularly during the 1810s and 1820s, when abolition sagged nationally and antiblack racism swelled in Northern locales like Philadelphia. Work hard, pray, and try to rise, Allen always preached to his brethren. Follow the bishop's moralistic rules to the letter or get sacked, men like Tudas and Perkins increasingly replied.

Allen turned uplift ideas into policy at the newly independent Bethel Church. By the early 1820s, church records show that moral-conduct issues were perhaps the key daily matters on which black trustees ruled. In fact, the most important action taken at many quarterly meetings was the penalizing or banishment of Bethelites for various moral offenses: public drunkenness, gambling, domestic abuse, sexual affairs. Allen accepted no falls from grace in his church, and he was not afraid to levy harsh judgments on profligate parishioners.[12]

From this moral-uplift context, move next to Allen's leadership before, during, and after the Wesley breakaway crisis. Although aged and sometimes ill, Allen remained the unquestioned patriarch of his church. Not only did he make clear that immoral conduct would not be tolerated, but he also steadfastly backed trustees' harsh judgments against virtually all backsliders. There was no appeal, no mitigating circumstances that could save Tudas from his fate. The only thing Allen wanted was piety and truth. Well after Tudas had been banished, Allen challenged him to face up to the charges of immoral behavior, though such an admission would not bring Tudas back into Bethel's fold. An *éminence grise* for many African Americans in Philadelphia and beyond, Allen was in no way ready to relinquish control of his church. As he wrote in the middle of the Wesley breakaway dispute, he had been "chiefly responsible for building Bethel Church" over the past three decades.[13] He would not fade out of the limelight now that it had achieved independence from whites and he had settled into his golden years.

In fact, Allen used the Tudas dispute to demonstrate his continued authority within the black community. This became clear during the summer of 1822 when a group of contrite Wesleyites approached him about a reunion. The activities of Murray, Perkins, and Tudas evidently began to chafe Wesley moderates, so much so that none of these men were included in the church's first official history (a brief pamphlet from 1842 outlining its two decades of existence).[14] Allen dominated reunion talks, serving as the lead negotiator between moderate Wesleyites and their Bethel brethren. Of course, when negotiations failed, Allen became an even bigger target of those who disliked his firm leadership style and principles.

Reunion talks centered on a "special meeting" held at Allen's home on August 5, 1822. The bishop hosted two sets of black representatives, remorseful Wesleyites and hopeful Bethelites, minus the Tudas/Perkins band of seceders. The gathering's stated purpose was to consider "uniting the two churches" in such a way that left Wesley somewhat independent though under the ultimate control of Bethel Church. Because both groups of trustees approved of the reunion, the meeting resolved that "the Rev. Richard Allen [would] preach" the following Sunday at Wesley "and take spiritual charge" of the institution thereafter. Reunion would officially occur on two further conditions: first, that a supermajority of the male members of both Wesley and Bethel Church assented to the plan; and second, that Allen would "wait upon Samson Levy, Esq., and the council of the trustees of Wesley Church" regarding "the amicable way and proper way of uniting the two churches." Allen planned to do this the very next day—August 6—before reporting back to the two groups of trustees.[15]

The next evening found Wesley and Bethel trustees back at Allen's home. Allen told them that he "had waited upon the counsel, . . . and [Samson Levy] appeared to be well pleased with the uniting."[16] Levy agreed to draw up a deed that put Bethel and Wesley back together. Although Bethel would have financial control of Wesley's facilities, Wesleyites would remain autonomous in certain key ways—including the choice of ministers. The arrangement appeared eerily similar to white Methodists' plans to oversee Bethel Church years before. Nevertheless, according to plans formulated at Allen's home, "the male members of Bethel and Wesley Church[es]" would be "called together at Bethel Church," and "a statement of union should be given to them." A vote would then take place, first by Wesleyites and then by Bethelites, with two-thirds of congregants from each church in favor of the motion needed for it to pass.[17]

A few days later, Allen prepared to close the deal. Confident that he had acted honorably and with appropriate discretion, he put the "reunion" issue to a vote. The proceedings were reported to be "conducted with great solemnity." Allen addressed the male members of both churches in the confines of Bethel. Rising after "singing and prayer," he gave a brief but pointed "exhortation" stressing "the utility of living in love and union one with the other." As agreed on at his house several days before, the male trustees of both churches were then asked to vote. The question was put forward, "Who would be in favor of the union?"

An overwhelming majority of Wesley officials responded in the affirmative. After "the question was recessed," Bethelites voted, with only three persons opposed to the motion. Allen spoke again. He was, he said, "glad to see [you] so unanimous in favor of uniting one with the other." Only then did he declare, in the manner of a minister officiating at a wedding, that "Bethel and Wesley was one."[18]

Allen closed by telling congregants that both churches would remain physically intact. Those wanting to worship at Wesley were free to do so. Bethel trustees would take spiritual charge of the church (providing preachers for baptisms and the administering of sacraments and also providing financial support to the financially strapped institution).[19] With official business seemingly done, Allen announced that he was "now going a-round to the Wesley Church" to speak to the entire congregation there about reunion.

And then a near brawl broke out.

What happened? Allen would have said that a democratic vote had just placed Wesley Church under Bethel's charge, and he was merely going to Wesley Church as an emissary of good will. Dissidents Tudas and Perkins would have replied that they wanted to keep Wesley Church beyond the control of Bishop Allen. Both sides concurred that Allen's address to Wesleyites was accompanied by pushing, shoving, and a memorable personal confrontation between the black bishop and one of his unconquerable critics. According to Bethel officials, Allenites were physically prevented from entering Wesley Church by William Perkins and a few other ruffians. "As Rev. Richard Allen was near the Church," they reported, "William Perkins, James Bird, [Rev.] Simon Murray and Tobias Sipple came a-running across [the street] to oppose the people [from] going into the Church." Perkins stood "at the gates" and literally "push[ed] . . . people off the steps." But Allen was "conveyed in by some of the Trustees of the Wesley Church." Amid all the pushing, pulling, and screaming, Allen took the pulpit. The doors were closed. Standing silent for a moment at the front of the church, he looked over the congregation. "Silence," he called out. "In the name of the commonwealth . . . *SILENCE!*"[20]

Citing his status as the founder of an officially incorporated church, Allen craftily used his American identity to quell community discord. State authority (in the form of Pennsylvania's act of incorporation for Bethel Church) flowed through him, he made clear. After the crowd quieted, he explained the nature of the vote just completed at Bethel and offered "a short sermon." All the while, Perkins "behaved very badly indeed," again according to Bethel records. "He ran up into the gallery and jumped out . . . into the pulpit," before sidling up to a still-cool Allen. Perkins next tried to harass the bishop and interrupt prayers. He "disturbed the congregation very much." Finally, in an attempt to break Allen's concentration, he "spit several times" on America's first black bishop! Allen did not flinch. Perkins was escorted out. After prayers, the meeting ended.[21]

But Allen left without achieving his hoped-for result. The fracas had shaken congregants of both churches. In short, there was no reunion. Tudas (and presumably Perkins) soon took Wesley's case to the public, publishing a harsh and unauthorized biography of Allen. Then they took him to Mayor's Court in Philadelphia. Allen and Bethel trustees met on October 3 about the pending lawsuit, which charged them with assaulting certain Wesleyites (Tudas, Sipple, Perkins) and attempting to take over Wesley property. Taking the matter very seriously, Bethel trustees mandated that the church should "procure $300 to defray the expenses" of the case. They would do so by charging congregants a quarter a week. In an important step, a committee of three without Allen was appointed to raise the funds. Had Allen finally become too hot to handle? Or was it merely other people's turn to help out? Church records do not say. In any event, by January 1824 the court rendered a judgment against Bethel. Tudas and Perkins were themselves soon banished from Wesley, but the church never again considered reunion with Bethel. As Carol George has observed, "Allen's missionary activity only 90 feet from his front door was a dismal failure."[22]

3. Black Paper War, Black Class Politics

Though judged in the wrong by the Mayor's Court, Allen clearly felt that he had been the injured party. In March 1823, he and Bethel trustees published a pamphlet vindicating the black founder's leadership position. On the surface, this production merely replied to Tudas's work, the no-longer-extant "Facts Relative to the Government of the African Methodist Episcopal Church Called Bethel." Although the Tudas pamphlet had a minuscule readership at best (the print run was tiny), its contents circulated through the black community through word-of-mouth. In fact, reports of Tudas's oral rendition of the manuscript reached Allen, who discovered from two different sources that he was accused of embezzling money from Bethel and eliminating supposed truth-telling whistle-blowers (like Tudas).[23] If Tudas himself remained an unreliable narrator (he had already been ejected from Absalom Jones's church for being a troublemaker), these were still serious charges.[24] Worried that the dissident Tudas would shape the battle of public perception—and possibly history's view of the black founder too—Allen issued a comprehensive assault on the man and his movement.

The pamphlet Allen and his supporters published in 1823 bore a striking title: "The Sword of Truth." Never one to be trifled with, Allen vigorously responded to Tudas's allegations. Allen had not been profligate as Bethel treasurer, the pamphlet declared, nor autocratic when counseling reunion between Bethel and Wesley churches, nor meanspirited when evicting the sinning Tudas from Bethel Church. On issue after issue, Allen and his allies attempted to quash Tudas's allegations of bad "government of the African Methodist Episcopal Church called Bethel."[25]

Although not the work of Allen alone, the document doubtless took shape at the bishop's behest. At the very front of the document, Allen's words appeared in a short but sharply worded testimonial. Under the subheading "Remarks by Richard Allen," it took aim at his accusers. "Having been connected with Bethel Church ever since it was built," Allen testified, "and having been chiefly instrumental, under God, in building it, I feel it a duty I owe to the public and myself to precede the following pamphlet with some introductory remarks." The charges against him were utterly "false," Allen claimed (he never misappropriated funds, nor had he served as treasurer for as long as Tudas alleged). The accuser was "some wicked, mischievous person," he added (who had been expelled from Bethel for inappropriate behavior). And, Allen alleged, Tudas's means of attacking him were underhanded and base (a scurrilous pamphlet circulated underground).[26]

Allen's moralistic voice came through in the reverberating tones of a sermon. If this was not a personal vendetta by Tudas, Allen asked, why did his opponent not "come forward and declare himself to be innocent"? Allen referred to the charges that Tudas had impregnated a white woman out of wedlock. Standing up to these allegations would earn Tudas respect, for he "would have come out like the pure gold from the refiner, more pure after the fiery trial." But that was the key, Allen slashed on, for his accuser could not face the truth. "His innocence is out of question," Allen huffed.[27]

As for charges of financial impropriety, Allen claimed to have the support of "several respectable gentlemen" who, having gone over Bethel's books, would testify to the black preacher's integrity. He also submitted two affidavits for the public's perusal about Tudas's base intentions. Given before Philadelphia alderman Abraham Shoemaker, the documents illuminated Tudas's "malicious" conduct. A gesture of both gentlemanly conduct (having the decency to bring his case to the public in this "proper manner") and legalistic acumen (utilizing the legal system, not innuendo), Allen hoped that the depositions painted a picture of a dirty man (Tudas) looking for dirt in the wrong places.[28]

Allen presented the testimony of James Derrickson, an illiterate dry-goods dealer formerly associated with both Tudas and Perkins. A member of Bethel Church when the Wesley dissidents bolted, Derrickson may already have been sympathetic to Allen. But he also claimed to have evidence of Tudas's premeditated anti-Allen behavior. Derrickson reported coming into "Tobias Sipple's cellar" one day in February 1823 when Tudas was talking about his pamphlet on "Richard Allen's life." Tudas had been working on it for several days and needed "some more [slanderous] information" on the black bishop. Tudas admitted that the pamphlet was so hot that "he was going to leave out some sections, or else the law would take hold of him" for libel. According to Derrickson, Tudas also begged for money to print the document—further evidence, Allenites claimed, of his base intentions. So few people had subscribed for Tudas's book that he could not pay the printer. Derrickson left, refusing to accept Tudas's book as truth. "I observed that I was wearied of hearing so much blackguard stuff," he told the Philadelphia alderman in an interesting wordplay ("blackguard" was an old English term referring to ungentlemanly innuendo).[29]

Allen submitted another deposition from the literate James Ennis, who reported that he too had encountered Tudas skulking around in February 1823 for nasty notes on Allen. He was "down at William Perkins' cellar," Ennis stated under oath, and "heard Jonathan Tudas say that he thought [his pamphlet] was a very good piece of composition for him, as a coloured man, to put out respecting Richard Allen's proceedings from the year 1794 to the year 1820." According to Ennis, Tudas "carried around" his mendacious manuscript for several days, looking for anti-Allen acolytes. Like Derrickson, Ennis claimed that Tudas told his allies that he had to gut parts of the manuscript because of their slanderous nature. Nevertheless, Ennis finished, a few copies of the pamphlet were "now in circulation."[30]

"It will be seen," Allen stated confidently, "that these [depositions] are duly attested by a magistrate, in a proper manner, which will show that I have not given assertion without proof." In sum, Allen declared, Tudas's so-called "facts . . . [were] no facts at all, but a tissue of base and unfounded lies." "I need not weary the patience of the reader by extending these remarks further," he finished. Allen's words offered a stark reminder of his formidable presence in Philadelphia's free black community.[31]

Beyond denying Tudas's allegations, Allen's pamphlet sought to dispel any notion that he acted inappropriately with Wesley Church. Unlike Bethel's confrontation with the Methodist conference years before —in which white clerics sought to direct Bethel without black congregants' consent—Allen attempted to negotiate a middle way for Wesleyites. Indeed, although Bethel records do not fully illuminate hard-core Wesley dissidents' views, there is no disputing Allen's remarkable attempt to bridge the divide between the two churches.[32] Allen said that he would meet with Wesley's lawyers (to understand their concerns), and he did. Allen said that he would report the results of this meeting back to Wesley's trustees (to illustrate his openness), and he did. Allen pledged to abide by congregational votes (to convey his respect for democratic process), and he did. Allen believed that Tudas had scared certain Bethel members into forming Wesley Church. When many of those same parishioners expressed an interest in reunion, he acted prudently.

In another life, Allen might have been a first-rate attorney. In 1823, he was trying to keep a lid on community divisions by painting Tudas and his allies as a small and wicked band of dissenters determined to derail a black founder. But in printing such a vigorous counterattack on members of the free black community, Allen actually exposed class tensions and social divisions cleaving Afro-Philadelphia. This was a remarkable shift for Allen. Recall that his very first pamphlet had spoken *for* the black underclass. When printer Mathew Carey accused "the vilest of the blacks" of pilfering white homes during the yellow-fever epidemic, Allen vigorously defended marginalized members of his community. "We are solicited," Allen (and Jones) noted in 1794, "by a number of [black] people who feel themselves injured [by Carey's claim] . . . to step forward and declare facts as they really were."[33]

By contrast, in the "Sword of Truth" pamphlet Allen defended himself against slanders levied by members of the black community—and he did so in front of a much broader community of readers in nineteenth-century Northern culture. Never had Allen aimed so squarely at free blacks (his 1808 pamphlets on John Joyce and Peter Matthias condemned sin, not black sinners); never had he registered such anger at those who challenged his black founding status. He did so now with a vengeance. And in doing so, he made visible the social divisions threatening the community he presided over.

Allen clearly represented the black elite. His very outmaneuvering of Tudas in the printed sphere demonstrated mastery of what gentlemen then called "the art of the paper war."[34] Allen's contacts and long experience in the world of print allowed an expeditious publication and distribution of his pamphlet. Tudas, on the other hand, could barely get his document printed and paid for, and when he did get a small number of copies published, they only circulated in black Philadelphia's underground (which Allen read as unrespectable) locales. Tudas's originals cannot be located today, even with the most sophisticated digital archiving techniques. The pamphlet is listed as "not extant." Allen's document had an officious tone and appearance (which he deemed respectable), including as it did formal depositions buttressing his case.

Because Tudas's pamphlet has not survived, it is hard to provide his (and Perkins's and Murray's) case a full hearing. But we can still use the pamphleteering battle as a way to examine black Philadelphia's class divisions. In one important sense, Tudas's document attempted to give public expression to simmering class politics during the 1820s. The economic backdrop is certainly important in this regard, for both Tudas and Allen battled in a deteriorating economic environment for many urban blacks, albeit from diametrically opposed positions. The problem in examining these divisions, of course, is that the 1820s also marked the rise of new and more virulent forms of antiblack racism in Northern cities.

But black class divisions were real and often important in Allen's Philadelphia. Emma Lapsansky-Werner has noted that black Philadelphia was a study in economic contrasts by the 1820s and 1830s. Standing tall at the top 5 percent were economic elites: Bishop Allen,

Merchant Prince James Forten, the elegant Cassey family (who styled hair and sold perfumes to "people of colour"). Below them sat a much larger group of black citizens, many of whom owned "no real property and only negligible personal property." Stated in bald statistical terms, there were roughly one thousand black worthies and roughly fourteen thousand "poor people" of color in Philadelphia by the time of the first major abolitionist census in the 1830s.[35]

Although slightly better off than many Northern black communities, Afro-Philadelphia's income disparities could not be stuffed under the rug. In fact, the 1820s marked their emergence in new forms. For instance, black elites began a rhetorical campaign that used the language of "respectability" to appeal to an emerging white middle class's sense of refinement. With an interracial alliance based on common appeals to morality, achievement, and respectability, black leaders hoped to vanquish racism. Black elites' message might be paraphrased as, "We have achieved, and we are not like either black or white rabble, so treat us equally." More specific evidence came in the form of the AME hymnal, which Richard Allen and Daniel Coker refined by reducing the number of camp (or field) songs. Whereas in 1801 Allen had mixed spirituals and camp songs with traditional Methodists hymns, by 1818 only a fraction of these gritty camp tunes remained.[36] And only a few years after this, Allen made an interesting linguistic alteration to his own yellow-fever pamphlet: "A Narrative of the Proceedings of the Black People" became "A Narrative of the Proceedings of the Coloured People," a more refined reference to men and women of African descent as defined by the leading men (and women) of African descent.[37]

By the mid-1820s, after the Wesley imbroglio settled down, Allen and Bethel trustees even began referring to themselves as "gentlemen." In a Bethel election for three trustees (who were elected on a rotating basis, much like congressmen) held on April 6, 1825, three "gentlemen" stood as candidates, including Allen. The point? Black "gentlemen" viewed themselves as legitimate community leaders.[38]

Such language reified class tensions by seeking to differentiate black leaders from their marginalized brethren. If white racism overshadowed these class divisions, it did not destroy them. Surely Allen was not turning his back on black Philadelphians from below. But he was in each act and deed shaping a vision of black society that was imbued with principles of moral uplift—work hard, pray, be humble, and, when called on, defer to black founders. And make no mistake, Allen wrote as a black founder. His tone in "The Sword of Truth" pamphlet might be described not merely as defensive but as peevish. How dare this vile man challenge me on such base grounds!, Allen effectively declared. A white New England Federalist could hardly have been more dismissive.

On the other hand, both Tudas and Perkins occupied the lower rungs of black society (though not the bottom-most ones) as dry-goods/used-clothes dealers who had not moved very far up the economic ladder. The free-born Tudas hailed from New Jersey and had known Allen for several years. Going back to the War of 1812, he had joined in the Allen-Jones-Forten crusade to fortify Philadelphia against a British invasion, taking the honorary title of "Captain" after volunteering to run a regiment of black laborers constructing an earthworks dam along the Schuylkill River. After that, Tudas became a rather well-known malcontent. He was kicked out of St. Thomas's Church for "sowing the seeds of discord." And he had a reputation for perpetually plotting and scheming, what his wary Wesleyite colleagues eventually described as "getting uneasy." All the same, Tudas joined Bethel Church in the late 1810s, supposedly even attending the famous inaugural AME meeting of April 1816 as an unelected observer of events.[39]

Like Tudas, William Perkins had been around Philadelphia for a few years prior to the Bethel blowout. Before his most memorable confrontation with Allen in 1822—spitting in the bishop's face—he ran a dry-goods business and hired himself out as a general laborer. In 1820 and 1821, Wesley trustees paid Perkins to dig out the basement of their new church edifice, the one located right behind Bethel. Here was a man used to eking out a menial existence. In a rather touching move that perhaps testified to his sensitivity about remaining on the fringe of proper black society, Perkins never signed his name the way it should have been spelled. Whereas others designated him "Perkins," he stubbornly signed church documents as "Purkins." He was literate on his own terms.

However he chose to sign his name, Perkins could often be found at a below-the-street business location, usually a cellar located in an alley. In their pamphlet defending Allen, Bethelites offered none-to-subtle class jabs at Perkins, Tudas, and their followers, men who had circulated a scandalous anti-Allen publication in the basements and "cellars" of black Philadelphia, locales Perkins was all too familiar with. What kind of constituency were cellar dwellers and alley cats? Bethelites wondered aloud.[40]

But educational and social hurdles be damned, Tudas and Perkins dreamed of becoming key players in a new church beyond Allen's reach. This becomes abundantly clear when reading through the earliest accounts from Wesley's receipt book. Because there had been some debate about financial openness at Bethel, Wesley's constitution specifically called on trustees to keep open books. The church's receipt book is thus a prize possession, showing just who paid what to precisely whom to build and maintain Wesley Church. It is the kind of record that does not exist for Bethel Church. In fact, one might venture further down this interpretive lane: Though Allen proved that he never misused Bethel funds, he made clear that he was the leader in charge of them. All people had to do was ask him for the account books, a gesture that underscored both Allen's hallowed leadership position and the age in which he had matured—the late-eighteenth-century world of founders who took care of things for those beneath them. Wesley Church's receipt book, on the other hand, came from a more democratic time, when no one person was thought to be the essence of an institution. And, in the absence of testimony from Perkins and Tudas, the receipt book reveals their mindset.[41]

Perkins took seriously his role as lay church builder. The new church would bear the imprint of his own sturdy hands, as church officials paid him on several occasions for laboring there. Wesley's account book reveals that Perkins was also part of a money-raising trio that secured several hundred dollars to defray church-building expenses (how reminiscent of Allen's fund-raising efforts!). As one of the moneymen, he had to sign his name every few months to a receipt book keeping track of interest paid on those bonds. The money he had helped raise was used to hire a carpenter, lay shingles, and glaze windows. In short, Perkins's ledgers in the account book were a symbol of his newfound standing at Wesley Church: he assumed a status that he simply did not have at Bethel. Put another way, Perkins was no longer a rag dealer dreaming of ascending but a church founder. In 1821, Perkins even went to New York for a "ministre" there, his own reference to a meeting at Christopher Rush's AME Zion Church. He proudly signed the receipt book, noting that Wesley trustees had repaid him for "expenses" relating to this official church business.[42]

Tudas also hoped to receive a preaching post at Wesley. As his former Wesleyite friends noted, Tudas believed that Bethel had been corrupted by Allen's leadership and that Wesley Church now needed Tudas's own clerical guidance to survive. Indeed, perhaps even more than Perkins, Tudas hoped for some sort of elevated rank in the new church. When he did not receive it, Tudas rather bizarrely urged fellow dissidents to reaffiliate with Bethel. The key to this curious move? Tudas thought Bethel might bestow on the newfound peacemaker a leadership position. According to Wesley officials, Tudas became so desperate that he (and Perkins) began calling meetings on the matter sometime in 1822. The two men "rejected the old Methodist discipline" (the white-controlled Methodist conference) and rather tellingly "refused to be governed by the New York Discipline" of AME Zion. Tudas and Perkins wished to rejoin Allen's "African" discipline (probably as an autonomous church under the guidance of the AME). "They had done what they had done," Wesleyites recalled Tudas and Perkins as saying, "and they did not mean to retract." But when Wesley officials sanctioned the idea and met with Allen (sans Tudas or Perkins), the two men got "uneasy" again. They eventually refused to agree to a reunion between Wesley and Bethel churches. Finally, seeing that they would play no greater role in either church, Perkins and Tudas were forced to resign from both institutions.[43]

But it is too simple to focus merely on Tudas and Perkins as the essence of the Wesley breakaway. More than a dozen people left Bethel Church in the summer of 1820 for what they deemed "reasonable causes."[44] There were deeper divisions in Bethel Church than those created by just a few men. These divisions reveal the desire of some rank-and-file Bethelites for a power base beyond Allen and his "gentlemanly" trustees. Indeed, when one recalls that many Wesleyites joined Tudas for fear that the revered Allen would throw them out of the AME without recourse to an appeal, it is clear that more than a few former Bethelites believed the time had come to find their own wings and fly.

Absent a document explaining these Wesleyites' innermost thoughts, we must again play detective. Looking at the Wesley-Bethel dispute from a socioeconomic angle provides another glimpse into the conditions shaping the battle. There were really three levels of black society involved in the breakaway imbroglio. First, the original dissenters (Tudas, Perkins, Murray, Sipple) formed the lowest economic tier. Both Tudas and Perkins, the ringleaders of the anti-Allen crusade, were laborers, journeymen, and dry-goods dealers. Robert Green was a coachman and dealer, and Simon Murray was a lay preacher and clothes dealer. Only James Bird had a skilled trade, that of shoemaker.

The second, or broader, Wesleyite group—those who left Bethel but were not hard-core dissidents—contained laborers and dealers but also a few skilled tradesmen: sailmaker Edward Johnson and mastersweep Robert Brown. Many Wesleyites were also literate: over two-thirds of the thirty-six men who created the church's official charter in 1826 could sign their own name. They were not transient figures who faded in and out of community institutions.[45]

Finally, Bethel trustees appeared to be a notch up economically from even Wesley's leaders. Beyond Allen, four of the eight Bethel trustees were mastersweeps (businessmen who employed apprentices): Joseph Coxe, Jonathan Trusty, William Brown, and James Greene. Bethel trustees also featured a cartman (Clayton Durham), an oysterman (James Wilson), and a waiter. Several of these men had moved slightly up the economic ladder over the years. James Greene was a sawyer and waiter before becoming a "sweepmaster." Similarly, William Brown had worked for just such a man as Greene, but by 1823 he called himself a "mastersweep" too. Joseph Cox, Bethel's recording secretary, had been a ticket porter before becoming a mastersweep.[46]

So most African Americans occupied lower-class occupations, and there were small degrees of difference among Bethelites, Wesley trustees, and hard-core dissidents. Nevertheless, the slight graduations separating Bethel trustees from Wesley trustees, and Wesley rebels from both sets of trustees, translated into ideological divergences. Bethel figureheads, men of the most settled economic and social position, felt themselves to be leaders within black society. The men underneath them who formed and maintained Wesley Church had a middling status in the black community. They needed to get out from under the thumb of established elites like Allen, even though they continued to respect his revered status. And below these middling men were figures like Perkins, a day laborer who hoped against hope to become a leading light at Wesley but was seemingly too gruff for many of his colleagues. Perkins had the most to overcome and the least to lose—and when things turned sour, he (and Tudas) turned with a vengeance on the most established of figures in black society, Richard Allen.

Still, Tudas's and Perkins's rigid opposition to Allen's leadership may have been a function not simply of class anger but the slightly more nebulous label of social status. Allen was identified as the leading figure in black Philadelphia. By the 1820s, some of those men under Allen's thumb came to resent him. They wanted institutional space of their own. This might help to explain why even Wesley trustees eventually decided to remain independent from Bethel: they wanted to retain social power at their own church.

For Allen, black society's social and economic divisions foretold an ominous future. In fact, class or status battles within the black community may have bolstered his increasing interest in Haiti (and later, Canada) as a safety valve. Perhaps such emigration outlets, he mused, might prevent younger blacks from getting caught up in a vicious cycle of despair . . . and striking out at their leaders. For Allen, the narrowing of economic opportunities, not to mention whites' increasing hostility to free blacks in the North, meant making such an outlet available. And black class politics made the safety-valve option even more appealing. It is little wonder, then, that after Allen put the Wesleyite dispute behind him in the mid-1820s, he focused intensely on Haitian emigration, becoming this time no silent supporter of that cause but one of its leading lights.

4. *Allen's Church in the 1820s: Class, Literacy, and Politics*

The establishment of Wesley Church right behind Bethel was not the only sign that black community politics had become fractious by the 1820s. Other institutions experienced similar undercurrents of discontent, with lay congregants less inclined than ever to defer to black leaders' wishes. A decade before Allen's showdown with his own former congregants, Absalom Jones's church experienced what the Reverend William Douglass later referred to as "an angry tumult" and "temporary division" within the supposedly cozy confines of St. Thomas's. After a band of worshipers had secretly initiated talks with a Jamaican man of color to minister at Jones's church, a "party spirit" manifested itself among congregants. Those favoring the new minister "seceded" but returned within a year.[47]

A more serious secession movement occurred at First African Presbyterian Church. Founded in 1807 by legendary black preacher Stephen Gloucester, African Presbyterian quickly became a fixture in the black community before splitting apart. Gloucester was a former slave from Tennessee who had so impressed white Presbyterians that they helped to liberate him. Black Philadelphia's growth convinced white Presbyterians to bring Gloucester to the City of Brotherly Love, where his preaching prowess built First African Presbyterian Church (dedicated on May 31, 1811). Blessed with what one white preacher called "a vigorous mind and strong common sense," he was "a gentleman in all his manners."[48]

But gentleman Gloucester's death in 1822 (at the age of forty-six) created a battle of succession at his beloved church. Would the new leader be the founder's son, a talented lad named Jeremiah? Or the more established figure of Samuel Cornish, who was affiliated with New York Presbyterians (and was soon to be the cofounder of *Freedom's Journal*)? While black Presbyterians resolved these disputes through a series of peaceful meetings and referenda, they could not transcend what a white historian writing in the 1880s called "irreconcilable differences." Those who favored Gloucester's son—nearly seventy-five people in a congregation of several hundred—left the church that his own father founded and created Second African Presbyterian in 1824. It seemed that founders—black or white—lived long at their own peril. Stephen Gloucester died before he had to witness the breakup of his beloved church, but Allen lived on. And he saw less deference to rulers than ever before.[49]

This change raises a key question about Allen's church during the 1820s: what was the relationship between laity and leaders? Despite the fact that Allen and several of his trustees had moved up the economic ladder, the majority of Bethel's rank-and-file members occupied the same menial status as Tudas, Perkins, and most black Philadelphians. Evidence to support such a claim has been traditionally hard to come by, partly because some Allen church records have not survived and partly because they never existed. So how can historians examine Bethel's rank and file? One aftereffect of the Bethel-Wesley dispute—and a great example of shadow politics—provides perspective. For just a few years after the anti-Allen lawsuit of 1823 (and partly in response to the monetary demands of it), Bethel trustees staged a congregational referendum on the sale of church property (excluding Bethel itself and church burial grounds). According to Bethel rules, at least two-thirds of the male members over twenty-one and in good standing had to vote yes for such a motion to pass. And so, on October 25, 1828, Bethelites went to the polls. That vote saw eighty-four men cast a yea ballot by signing their name to a sheet of paper. Best of all for scholars, results of this vote have survived.[50]

The vote demonstrates that a majority of the eighty-four yes voters worked in laboring or nonskilled positions. Amid a scattering of skilled tradesmen, the bulk of Allen's church appears to have been composed of laborers and unskilled workers of various types. Frustratingly, scholars can get only a glimpse of the individual lives of these eighty-four petition signers, for only twenty-seven people on the list can be traced definitively in a city directory. Of these men, twenty worked in some sort of unskilled profession. Benjamin Jackson worked as a laborer, as did Caesar Laws, Isaac Sutton, Andrew Till, and Joseph Lacount. John Parker and George Menokan were porters, James Riley and Jonathan Lacount worked as oystermen, and Christopher Stratton struggled as a waiter. A majority of these men (twenty of twenty-seven) were also illiterate. On the other hand, literate Bethel signatories are a bit easier to track, and, not surprisingly, they were often (though not always) skilled tradesmen. Peter Jones was a mariner; James Johnson, a painter; George Miller, a carpenter; and David Pederson, a businessman (a "dealer of clothes," significantly, not a used-clothes dealer).[51]

The high percentage of illiterate congregants and unskilled laborers suggests that church elders may have believed it was their role to speak on behalf of those underneath them. When voting in early church elections or referenda, illiterate rank-and-file Bethelites placed their mark ("X") next to a signature provided by literate churchmen—leaders who literally took hold of a quill and spelled out that congregant's name. This policy mirrored those used by illiterate free blacks who signed contracts with white figures or, later, who voted in local, state, and federal elections in the post–Civil War South. In those instances, white registrars or lawyers asked for a free black person's name, spelled it out, and then called for his "mark." The process could be humiliating and humbling. Was it any less so when free black church members had to sign an "X" in front of literate black leaders?

Yet illiteracy did not completely undercut shadow politics in the black community. No one challenged the right of illiterate men to vote on such key matters as the disposal of church property. Although Allen lamented in 1816 that free black communities remained largely "unlettered," he himself had long worked with illiterate church members to build Bethel into the powerful autonomous institution it had become.[52]

And he had done so since Bethel's inception, when three of eight signatories to the 1796 "Articles of Association" used the "X" of illiteracy. The State of Pennsylvania raised no objections either. In 1799, at least five Bethelites signed Absalom Jones's abolitionist petition to Congress, including two men who were illiterate (interestingly, forty-five of the seventy men to sign that petition were illiterate as well). Similarly, the majority of signers to the 1807 African Supplement—claiming black congregants' sovereignty over white Methodist elders—were illiterate. In short, a relatively high level of illiteracy among Bethelites before 1830—ranging from a third of original trustees in the 1790s to over half of the adult males voting in the congregation referendum of 1828 —did not stop black politics from functioning at any time.[53]

If Allen's church is any sort of guide, then, neither black leaders nor rank-and-file church members deemed illiteracy a hurdle to political activism and expression during the early republic. And Allen's church, like black churches around the country, was a place where a robust form of politics occurred. W. E. B. Du Bois later famously found that the majority of early-nineteenth-century Afro-Philadelphians were illiterate, though younger generations of free blacks (those maturing between the 1810s and the Civil War) did receive progressively better schooling. And yet this fact of illiteracy, Du Bois knew, did not stop the first generation of "freedmen" from publicly protesting for equality and building the many autonomous free black institutions that grounded African American Northerners over the next several decades. Nor did high illiteracy rates among adults forestall the staging of democratic rituals— referenda, electioneering for church trustees—in black communities.[54]

In this sense, one could read Allen's political showdown with rebels as a barometer of the black community's health. But Allen did not read it that way.

5. Jerena Lee

Although black shadow politics uncovers key information about non-elite Bethelites, it says little about rank-and-file women. Church voting through the 1820s adhered to a tradition that crossed racial boundaries: most women did not vote. They may have, as free black women later did in Reconstruction Southern locales, advised black men who could cast church ballots.[55] But we do not know for sure.

We do know that some black women began challenging notions of patriarchy. And Allen was on the front lines of this development as well. The key figure was Jarena Lee, a free black woman from New Jersey who, after an initial dispute with Allen over black female preaching in Bethel Church, compelled the bishop to expand African American women's roles beyond the black republican mother and helpmate.[56] Lee was drawn to Allen from the moment she heard him preach in 1811. The details of that encounter illuminate Allen's appeal among many marginalized voices in Philadelphia's black community, particularly women. A free black female cook who attended Bethel encouraged Lee to attend services with her one day. Lee was adrift personally as well as spiritually. Her first marriage ended tragically when her husband (a local black minister) died young and left her as a single mother. No religious denomination appealed to this former minister's wife, but a sermon from Allen changed that. "This was the people for me," she declared instantly.[57]

Allen and Lee's first meeting did not go well. Allen's initially stark stand against female preaching hit Jarena Lee square in the face. Allen told Lee that "our discipline knew little of women preachers."[58] Allen was evidently referring to Methodist discipline, not AME discipline specifically (their initial encounter occurred before Allen had official sanction as AME bishop). Lee withdrew, though with what can only be called an Allenite sense of determination, she remained in the Philadelphia area, preached on her own, and soon returned to Bethel Church ready to dedicate herself to Allen's brand of black Methodism. When a preacher fell silent at Bethel services one day, Lee jumped up and held forth. Duly impressed, Allen became an active supporter of Lee's preaching (if not of her formal investiture as a female minister), intervening on her behalf before recalcitrant ministers and congregations in and beyond Philadelphia. On one occasion in Washington, D.C., in the late 1820s or early 1830s (Lee did not specify the date), a black minister "strove to stop my ministerial mission." As Lee recalled, "Bishop Allen, being a man of renown, and hav[ing] grace abounding in his heart, sent a letter . . . to intercede for me."[59] She got her wish and was soon preaching in the nation's capital.

With Allen's sanction, Lee traveled to a host of other locales as an official representative of the AME Church. This is quite important, for although Lee is often viewed as the progenitor of women's rights within the AME Church, her missionary work also validated Bethel's expansion efforts during the 1820s. Perhaps this is why Allen encouraged Lee to preach with him at some of the biggest revivals on the mid-Atlantic circuit. Allen and Lee appeared together at a large camp meeting in Delaware during the summer of 1824. As Lee remembered, "the ministry were all for me," and she even spoke before the governor. A "greater display of God's power I never saw."[60]

If her mere presence antagonized some AME ministers, it also emboldened women and their families at the grassroots level to become sure-footed Methodists. This certainly endeared her to Allen. In many local communities, including Philadelphia, church membership was as much filial as individual, with husbands and wives joining places of worship together. Women remained the cornerstone of these churches. Bethel's founding in the 1790s was predicated on wives following husbands out of St. George's Church. Then Lee came along and, for the first time, publicly spoke to the challenges facing pious women of color. "I send by whom I will, for all are one in Christ Jesus," she later wrote, referring to Paul's famous Epistle (Galatians 3:28).[61] By bringing black women into the fold, Lee encouraged families to join and strengthen the AME Church.

Although building on a tradition of black women's itinerancy, Lee published the first spiritual autobiography by a black female Methodist. Appropriately, the very day she collected the printed copies of the book in 1836, Lee sold the first edition to none other than Allen's second wife, Sarah. "At 4 o'clock, P.M.," Lee recalled, "my mind was directed to a Presbyterian sister [to purvey copies of the book], and on my way, I met Bishop Allen's widow who bought one, and that afternoon I sold one dollar and fifty cents' worth."[62]

No mere delightful encounter, Jarena Lee and Sarah Allen's meeting represented a potentially transitional moment for black Methodist women in nineteenth-century America. Indeed, for many subsequent AME commentators, Lee and Sarah Allen represented the bookends of free black women's identity: Lee as the insurgent female preacher and Sarah Allen as the archetypal black republican mother or helpmeet. This is ironic, partly because both women contributed much to the AME's growth in the early nineteenth century and partly because neither of their positions was mutually exclusive of the other. Lee recognized Sarah Allen as a revered figure in Bethel Church, and Sarah Allen sympathized with Lee's struggle to speak and preach unfettered. And in both instances, Richard Allen was an enabling figure. He encouraged his own wife to be not only a helpmate but also a charitable worker beyond the home (with her husband's aid, Sarah Allen started a free black female benevolent society, the Daughters of Conference, during the 1820s). Allen also entrusted his wife with part of his estate after his death, including the collection of rental dues on various properties.

Despite her exertions outside the home, "Mother Allen" became the icon of an AME cult of domesticity. Daniel Payne celebrated her domestic-sphere work as the epitome of black female identity. "Her house was the resort of the brethren who labored in the ministry," he stated. "Long will her motherly counsel be remembered."[63] James Handy, a free black Baltimorean who knew both Bishop Allen and his wife, included Sarah Allen in his own list of AME pioneers. "She was a remarkable woman," said Handy, "and a valuable help to the Bishop in his early work in the Church." For Handy, Mother Allen was the quintessential helpmate. As he put it, she frequently "helped the bishop out of many straights in which he found himself."[64]

In this vein, Handy made famous the story of Sarah Allen's heroic effort to garb AME ministers in respectable clothing after many of them arrived at an annual meeting in the most disrespectable rags. As was the custom for church leaders in the early nineteenth century, the Allens housed black ministers traveling to the AME annual conferences in Philadelphia. Although he realized the socioeconomic challenges facing his charges, Richard Allen was nonetheless distressed to discover how many ministers appeared in "seedy" clothing. So distressed was the bishop that he refused "to adjourn them to dinner." When told of the ministers' appearance, Mother Allen led an all-night sewing brigade that produced a line of brand-new pants and jackets from the barest homespun.[65] The ministers departed the Allen home the following day looking positively sparkling. Little wonder that, as Hallie Brown (the head of the National Association of Colored Women) later wrote, "the name of 'Mother Allen' is a household word in the homes of African Methodism."[66]

As Mother Allen's patronage of Jarena Lee illustrates, she was also not afraid to think of black womanhood in even broader terms than either Payne or Handy accorded her. In this sense, envisioning Sarah Allen and Jarena Lee as opposites obscures their mutual commitment to community uplift. Nascent nineteenth-century female reformers charted new directions by becoming, as one scholar has put it, "community caretakers and sources of social stability" outside their own private homes.[67] This was particularly important in dynamic urban environments, where the very idea of black community encountered an array of social and economic challenges. By becoming social reformers outside the home, women created enduring bonds of community. In free black Philadelphia, both Mother Allen and Jarena Lee embraced the concept of community activist/caretaker, carving out new identities for black women. Whether as a rising preacher, a benevolent worker, or a fundraiser for the AME Church, black women would be viewed as central to the cause of black redemption.

As Richard Allen's support of Lee testifies, the great bishop probably believed that black women could be a powerful presence both in the church and on the preaching circuit, not merely in the home. Not everyone agreed. In the decades following Allen's death, debate over black women's public role escalated in AME circles. Whereas Richard and Sarah Allen had both been supporters of Lee's itinerant preaching during the 1820s and early 1830s, subsequent AME leaders refused to condone her ministerial activities. In an attempt to make black community life appear more respectable, church leaders urged black women to tend exclusively to the domestic sphere. Bishop Daniel Payne published several treatises on free black women's domestic roles. His ideas resonated in broader debates over women's place in American culture. Black women, the powerful Payne declared, must become guardians of the home, domestic educators of black youth, and matriarchs of respectability. This would not only help uplift the race on its own merits but appeal to respectable whites as well.

Debates about black women's role in and beyond the domestic sphere continued during the nineteenth century, as a handful of AME women stepped prominently outside the home. In 1857, Philadelphia educator and missionary Mary Still used the AME newspaper, *The Christian Recorder*, to publicize black women's roles as church builders and literary agents—even as she herself argued that women were primarily responsible for creating nurturing environments for black youth. In 1885, Amanda Smith Berry became the first female minister officially ordained by the AME, though that ordination was rescinded two years later.[68] And what happened to Jarena Lee? She persevered until 1849, when she passed on, the same year that Mother Allen died in Philadelphia.

6. *Allen's Community: Unity in Diversity*

At the beginning of 1828, *Freedom's Journal* hailed Richard Allen as an icon of black society. "Though aged," the paper stated, Allen remained "zealous in the cause of his depressed and injured race." Who would disagree?[69]

Certainly not a young black man named Mifflin Wistar Gibbs. The son of a minister at Wesley Church (he was born in the middle of the Bethel-Wesley dispute in 1823), Gibbs nevertheless grew up in awe of Allen. His father had taken him to Bethel Church to observe greatness in the black community. As a teenager, Gibbs apprenticed to a black contractor who rebuilt Bethel. Over sixty years later, Gibbs still vividly remembered having "heard the founder, Bishop Allen, preaching in the wooden building. He was much reverenced."[70]

For a man who eventually earned a law degree, worked as a judge in the Reconstruction South, and counted both Frederick Douglass and Booker T. Washington as friends, Gibbs was not one to offer platitudes. His reverence for the black bishop notwithstanding, Gibbs recalled Allen as appearing "feeble" by the late 1820s, with a "shambling gait as he approached the close of an illustrious life."[71] Perhaps the Wesley imbroglio signaled that Allen's—and black founders'—influence neared an end.

Allen did not think so. In 1823 he commissioned another portrait (the last of three painted during his lifetime) to reestablish his image as a black founder. Entitled "The Revd. Richard Allen, Bishop of the First African Methodist Episcopal Church in the U. States," the painting was done by none other than Rembrandt Peale, scion of the nation's first artistic family (which included father Charles Wilson Peale) and image maker of President George Washington.[72] Though the least known of Allen's images in our own time, Peale's portrait briefly became the iconic image of the black founder during the 1820s. The painting captured a distinguished and intense but visibly older Allen leaning on a Bible, the graying sixty-three-year-old bishop's shoulders noticeably slouching. If not the vigorous image of his previous portraits, this one still displayed Allen's confidence—he commanded people to look his way.

The portrait also became the model for a stippled engraving by Joseph How executed on "the 10th day of December, 1823." Part of a fascinating series of engravings of Philadelphia's black elite that challenged the racist imagery of "'bobalition" (or antiblack) broadsides, the engraving probably made its way to the best black homes in Pennsylvania. Every time someone looked at it, they knew instantly that Allen remained a formidable presence in African American reform circles. He was, in short, not relinquishing the reins of black leadership to anyone.

Founders who live long sometimes see too much. Allen lived long enough to see the nearly unthinkable: a secession movement within his own church. But Allen was no granite icon, unable to respond. He re-

"The Revd. Richard Allen," Rembrandt Peale (painter), Joseph How (printer), 1823. Allen's last portrait, done by the celebrated painter Rembrandt Peale (son of the legendary Charles Wilson Peale) when the black founder was sixty-three years old. Famous for his depictions of white statesmen, including George Washington, Peale captured Allen's image as an *éminence grise* in the black community. Joseph How created a stipple engraving of the portrait, which became part of a small series of prints of black religious figures during the 1820s. (Courtesy of the Library Company of Philadelphia)

Left: "The Revd. John Gloucester," J. Robinson (painter), Benjamin Tanner and W. R. Jones (engravers), Joseph How (printer), 1823. Included in How's series of prints was this image of John Gloucester of the African Presbyterian Church. (Courtesy of the Library Company of Philadelphia). *Right*: "The Revd. Jeremiah Gloucester," Robert Tiller (engraver), 1828. This portrait of John Gloucester's son, Jeremiah, who began his preaching duties at the African Presbyterian Church, further battled against antiabolition caricatures in the Philadelphia press. (Courtesy of the Library Company of Philadelphia)

plied with a vigor that would have impressed almost any American founder—Madison, Jefferson, Washington. The only surprising thing is Allen's target: members of the black underclass.

For Allen, community discord initially seemed to be the work of a few malcontents who had not followed his moral-uplift agenda. The more he thought about it, though, the more he saw the Wesley secession movement as a symptom of socioeconomic distress within the black community. Largely the result of intensified Northern racism and lack of economic opportunity in the urban core, the problem would not disappear. Younger generations, who grew up not as Allen had in the glow of Revolutionary-era slogans about building the world anew but in a more competitive and shrill environment, expressed much less optimism about the racial future in America. And they no longer deferred automatically to founding figures like Allen. He had to respond in new and creative ways to lead African Americans to glory. In Allen's eyes, that was what black founders would always do.

9

A Black Founder's
Expanding Visions

In August 1824, Richard Allen penned a letter unlike any he had ever written. "Sir," the note solemnly began, "it is with the most sincere feelings of respect and gratitude that I address these lines to you. My heart is warmed with gratitude toward you for the kind and affectionate offers that you have extended to a poor and oppressed people in the United States and in opening them a refuge where they will enjoy the blessings of freedom and equality." His words were imbued with a deep sense of propriety on the occasion because Allen addressed a head of state: Jean-Pierre Boyer, president of Haiti, the first black republic in the Western Hemisphere. Hoping to boost his country's sagging economy, Boyer beckoned disaffected free black Americans by offering land, economic opportunity, and political freedom. In Richard Allen, Boyer found a hearty advocate of Haitian emigration. After Haitian envoys visited Philadelphia, Allen began taking names of potential émigrés. In just a few months, he gathered five hundred names and sent roughly fifty people on their way to the Caribbean island. "I daily receive correspondence from many persons of color in varied cities and towns requesting information on the requirements of emigration," he confidently told Boyer. "I have no doubt that in little time there will be thousands more."[1]

Allen addressed Boyer as perhaps *the* leading free black advocate of Haitian emigration in the United States. Now in his seventh decade, bowed by age and arthritis, Allen was in no way scared of such a challenge. Recall that only a few years before, Allen and other black leaders had been flatly rebuked by Afro-Philadelphia's masses—in the confines of Allen's own Bethel Church no less—for even considering African colonization. Other black founders had backed away, but Allen remained intrigued by emigrationism. Boyer's offer refocused his attention on the matter. Allen told the Haitian president that the idea of a black homeland beyond American shores sounded increasingly seductive to his ears. As he put it, many African Americans eagerly anticipated journeying to Haiti and "establish[ing] a happy bond with the [new] land in which they dwell."[2]

Historical wisdom holds that Allen's emigrationism was part and parcel of AME expansionism.[3] With the AME Church officially free from white control, and African colonization repudiated by the black masses, Allen dreamed of national and international church growth. This narrative contains much truth, for Allen's Haitian musings came amid a remarkable period of AME outreach. By 1830, Allen's no-longer-fledgling church encompassed branches from Brooklyn to Buffalo and the Chesapeake Bay to the Allegheny Mountains. As the Western Hemisphere's only black republic, Haiti made sense as a future AME destination. When dealing with Haitian officials, Allen probed the issue of religious liberties, no doubt thinking of his own disciples' ability to preach where the great revolutionary Toussaint L'Ouverture had once lived.

But there was much more to Allen's Haitian dream than religion. The black founder viewed Haiti as part of a *political* project he began in the 1810s: finding a safety valve for oppressed African Americans. Indeed, Allen believed that Haitian emigration offered African Americans something white citizens increasingly enjoyed: a frontier outlet. The western frontier, Allen realized, would not be suitable for African American migrations precisely because it replicated Northern- and Southern-style racial domination. To find a black safety valve required international visions. Allen focused on Haiti as the best hope for African American redemption.

1. An AME Empire

Growing the AME Church nationally, not expanding globally, was Allen's first concern during the 1820s. Yet church growth brought Allen into contact with a series of younger reformers who, in turn, compelled him to think about his role as a black founder in a dynamic new era—an epoch increasingly defined by modern transportation technologies, mass migrations, and the fluidity of national and even international identities.

In its first decade of formal independence, the AME grew at nothing less than a remarkable rate. In 1816, the church represented less than a thousand adherents scattered among just a few regional branches. A decade later, that number stretched to ten thousand people throughout the American union. Soon after establishing the AME *Discipline* (1817), Allen formed the AME Connection, an interstate religious society that provided organizational coherence to Bethel's build out. Earliest expansion occurred along the Atlantic seaboard. Within the mid-Atlantic region, for example, the AME spread beyond black Methodists' Philadelphia and Baltimore strongholds to many other parts of Maryland. By the early 1820s, the Baltimore Annual Conference, with Bishop Allen presiding, welcomed 331 black Methodists from Maryland's eastern shore, by then home to a very young enslaved lad named Frederick (who later married a free black Methodist woman from Baltimore, escaped to Northern freedom, and took the name Frederick Douglass). AME branches also appeared in Allen's boyhood home of Kent County, Delaware; in Brooklyn, New York; and New Bedford, Massachusetts. Allen's church reached into the heart of slave country too, where he himself had once refused to travel for fear of being reenslaved. By 1822, in fact, Charleston, South Carolina, contained the second-largest AME branch in the country—nearly fifteen hundred black congregants.

During the 1820s, AME branches also took root further west: Pittsburgh, Pennsylvania; Mt. Pleasant, Ohio; and Buffalo, New York. From the five original locales represented at the AME's founding conference in 1816, there were over forty congregations by 1822. By 1828, AME churches had leaped over international borders, sprouting in Upper Canada. By the 1830s, Bethel's banner was flying in Indiana. Although some churches remained relatively small, their overall meaning was anything but minimal. Allen's church was not only growing but meeting the needs of an ever-increasing number of free African Americans, particularly in newly settled areas of the United States. If Steubenville and Mt. Pleasant, Ohio, reported fewer numbers than Allen preached to during an average week in Philadelphia (forty-five in Steubenville, twelve in Mt. Pleasant), the plain fact was that free black congregants *were* now in Ohio and they organized a church whose very name symbolized black autonomy, uplift, and pride. In short, Allen's church was becoming identified with black freedom nationally.[4]

Indeed, AME outreach efforts expanded political as well as religious opportunities to free black communities everywhere. The Buffalo congregation offers a wonderful case in point. Counting only a dozen members in 1828, it nevertheless grew into a vital spot for American blacks over the following several decades. Buffalo's AME membership became key participants in both the Underground Railroad and the black convention movement. Buffalo, soon dubbed the Queen City (for its shipping dominance on the Great Lakes), even hosted the 1843 national black convention, the first ever held outside the Atlantic-seaboard communities of Philadelphia and New York City.

No bystander to church growth, Allen reveled in AME missionaries' exertions. He could be found, stooped and slow of foot but energetic as ever, at "lovefeasts" in Delaware and Maryland, at annual conferences in Baltimore and New York, at revivals in New Jersey and rural Pennsylvania. He made a palpable impression on an entire generation of black preachers emerging in the nineteenth century. Just as Henry Highland Garnet recalled his youthful encounters with "Papa Allen" in New York City, so too did future AME minister James Handy write glowingly of his audience with the famed black bishop in Maryland. "At a Conference held in Baltimore, in 1829," Handy remembered in 1902, "Bishop Allen put his hand on my head and said [to my mother,] 'Maria take good care of this boy; he will be one of my successors.'"[5] Handy was only three years old at the time, and he was never sure if the story was apocryphal. But he chose to believe it all the same, and the story became a firm and everlasting part of his memory. As Handy bragged, he could claim to have met every single AME bishop of the nineteenth century, going all the way back to the church's estimable founder, Richard Allen.

If black Methodism's remarkable rise during the 1820s relied on an itinerant tradition, it also required the tools of modernity. Allen's church gets little attention for its rather sophisticated use of new transportation networks and printing techniques (which Allen had long used). But Allen's preachers used modern means of travel, modern means of communication, and even modern means of organization. Allen himself used the steamboat to make strategic stops in New York City and Baltimore, and members of his ever-expanding flock pushed into the New York–Ohio hinterland by using both the Erie Canal and Great Lakes steamers. One itinerant of Allen's gospel remembered hopping on a railroad car "for some part of the route" between Washington and Baltimore around 1830—probably one of the earliest rail lines in America.[6]

To bind the AME network, Allen turned to print. He ordered batches of mass-produced preaching certificates, each of which was signed by

Allen to systematize itinerancy.[7] The certificate's professional look was certainly impressive—featuring the motto "Given under my hand" near the blank space where Allen signed—and it let anyone know that the AME had a serious organizational grounding. Allen's church also distributed thousands of copies of the AME *Discipline,* making it one of the most widely owned black books of the nineteenth century. At a Philadelphia annual conference in 1833, as Bishop Daniel Payne wrote with near astonishment, "one thousand copies of the Discipline [were] printed at a cost of $70, and five hundred bound at a cost of $40."[8]

Through print and rail, canal boat and standardized notes, Allen's AME constantly grew. But before Allen expanded the AME globally, he met with a talented array of black activists who made him look beyond religion to the politics of black movement.

2. *Visitors*

Church expansion furthered Allen's reputation nationally, prompting a bevy of young men and women to visit him during the 1820s. Allen became so busy that he created a self-styled "conference room" in his Spruce Street home.[9] Jarena Lee, the talented female preacher and exhorter who got her start under Allen, recalled the simultaneous mix of apprehension and calm that she felt walking toward the private home of so famous a black man. "As I drew near the street in which his house was," she remembered, "my courage began to fail me." Almost turning away several times, she suddenly felt a sense of peace. "As soon as I came to [Allen's] door, my fears subsided, the cross was removed, all things appeared pleasant—I was tranquil."[10]

Celebrated black pamphleteer and organizer David Walker was perhaps the most prominent of those who imbibed Allen's insurgent sensibility, hoping to redeploy it for a new age of struggle. Born free in North Carolina in 1786, Walker steadily moved up the Atlantic coast before eventually settling in Boston during the 1820s. Before he published his famous "Appeal" in 1829, Walker had contact with either Allen himself (Walker's magnificent biographer, Peter Hinks, cannot determine for certain) or AME preachers then spreading the Word. Walker was inspired by Allen's outreach programs, that impressive phalanx of black itinerants moving about in seemingly free fashion even as white citizens everywhere restricted black voting rights, black job opportunities, and black migration itself. "See his ministers in the states of New York, New Jersey, Pennsylvania, Delaware, and Maryland," Walker proclaimed, "carrying the gladsome tidings of free and full salvation to the colored people."[11] Mass political organizing à la Allen's AME, Walker argued, would speed black redemption.

As Walker's example suggests, Allen drew black leaders from hundreds of miles away. Take the case of Morris Brown, a free black South Carolinian who hurriedly moved to Philadelphia in the fall of 1822 when white authorities attacked his AME branch in Charleston hoping to uncover Denmark Vesey's slave rebellion.[12] The church was soon obliterated by raging white citizens who assumed that black Methodism (and not merely a small band of enslaved plotters) had sponsored black insurrection. To Allen, news of a foiled slave rebellion would not have been surprising. But that the AME Church was the center of a post-rebellion investigation—well, that disturbed him. One can only wonder at Allen's innermost thoughts, for he never left any explicit commentary on Vesey's plot. But Allen offered eloquent testimony of another sort when Mother Bethel welcomed hundreds of Charleston AME refugees heading north.[13]

Morris Brown quickly became Allen's confidant. No sooner had Brown arrived in Philadelphia than Allen made sure that he had both a spiritual and a literal home. At an October 2, 1822, meeting of Bethel trustees at Allen's Spruce Street house (roughly two months removed from the foiled South Carolina rebellion), AME Church fathers guaranteed to pay "the board of Reverend Morris Brown and such ministers and preachers as shall board with him thereafter."[14] By October 15, Brown appeared on the AME's board of trustees alongside Allen. He may have told Allen tales of Vesey's international designs. Like Allen, Vesey had once been a slave before hitting the numbers in a local lottery. The bounty bought Vesey's freedom but no sense of justice. Inspired by the glowing example of Haitian rebels and disgusted by recent political compromises that allowed Missouri to enter the American union as a slave state, Vesey planned a massive slave rebellion that would lead liberated bondpeople to Haiti. Before he could set his plan in motion, though, Vesey was betrayed by an enslaved man who parlayed that betrayal into freedom. Vesey and his followers went to the gallows for their vision of liberty or death. Brown fled north to Allen's AME.

Brown and Allen were far from strangers. They first met at an AME annual conference in May 1818 (held in Philadelphia).[15] They met again

"Bishops of the AME Church," John H. W. Burley, 1876. This Reconstruction poster placed Allen at the center of the AME Church and among a constellation of distinguished black bishops, including Morris Brown. After fleeing South Carolina in the wake of Denmark Vesey's aborted slave rebellion, Brown found a home at Bethel Church. Note as well the AME's proud link to Haiti at the right. (Courtesy of the Library Company of Philadelphia)

the following year at another annual conference (this time in Baltimore). Then, in June 1818, Brown's congregation welcomed a half-dozen AME representatives to Charleston, where they met in violation of the city's ordinance that black Christians gather only when "a majority of the congregation shall be white." The meeting ended with a night in jail for South Carolina blacks and their Northern guests.[16]

Allen clearly took to Brown, a man who harbored such stout beliefs in black Methodism that he went to jail to protest Charleston's crackdown on the free black church. But the two men shared more than denominational commitment. Though born free in 1770 in Charleston (his mother was black and his father white), Brown (like Allen) was self-educated, pious, and dedicated to racial uplift. He fought for black freedom, taught slaves to read, and stood up to white clerics who discriminated against blacks' burial rights. By 1816, when he and Charleston's black Methodists broke free from whites and joined Allen's AME, Brown was the recognized leader of nearly as many disciples as Allen was, roughly fourteen hundred. Though Brown towered over Allen physically, he had a similarly determined, resolute personality.[17]

Cut to 1822, when Vesey's plot threatened Brown's life. Did Rev. Brown know of Vesey's plans? Perhaps. Probably. How could he not? When black bodies started swinging from ropes and the AME Church was razed, Brown did not stick around for violent interrogations. Allen certainly took a courageous stand in publicly opening his church and home to Brown. A bounty on his head notwithstanding, Brown was for Allen a true brother in God's army. And the fact that he represented a significant number of black refugees who might tangle with white workers in Northern cities like Philadelphia scared Allen not at all. It says much about Allen's character that he so quickly accepted Brown.

Over the next few years, the two ministers could be found traveling and preaching together at revivals in Delaware, New York, and Maryland.[18] Allen saw in Brown a man who could further propel church leadership nationally, taking the AME west and even south. (Brown in fact did this after Allen's death in the 1830s, presiding over AME branches in Indiana). Perhaps Allen also saw himself serving the mentor's role to Brown that Francis Asbury once provided to him in the 1780s. Allen testified to this sentiment by supporting Brown's ascension to bishop in 1828, after Allen himself went into semiretirement.

Brown was an Allen apostle, and he clearly bolstered Allen's vision of AME growth nationally. But how far could the AME spread in America? And how far could African Americans stretch claims to equality in the United States? These questions haunted Allen even as his church grew domestically.

Another visitor compelled him to think seriously again about blacks' future abroad. The man had a regal-sounding name: Prince Saunders. And he arrived in Philadelphia touting the grand potential of Haitian emigration. Born free in New Hampshire and educated at schools throughout New England—he was himself a teacher for a spell—Saunders traveled around the Atlantic basin in the early nineteenth century to take the pulse of black life. After visiting Britain and the Caribbean, he believed that Haiti would be the site where African redemption would most gloriously occur. He returned to America to spread the word.[19]

Saunders first spoke in Allen's Bethel Church on September 30, 1818.[20] For several weeks prior to that, he had been making his way through Philadelphia's reform community, giving copies of his recently published book, *Haytian Papers,* to worthy white men like William Rawle, the noted abolitionist lawyer, and Dr. James Logan, the celebrated physician.[21] Saunders stayed in town for several months, getting involved in black educational and protest initiatives (he presented an educational essay to the American Convention of Abolition Societies, which met in Philadelphia in December 1818). Though he spoke in Allen's church, Saunders briefly joined Absalom Jones's St. Thomas's congregation, before departing in a dispute that still baffles historians. Saunders then went back to where he thought he belonged, Haiti.

Saunders's Haitian scheme impressed many free black Philadelphians, for over the next several years Haiti remained on the mind of not only Allen but also James Forten, Belfast Burton (the well-known healer and physician), and hundreds of black businessmen, laborers, and artisans. Black leaders, Saunders had written, must acknowledge Haiti as the site of a black "enlightenment" that would equal those of Europe and the United States. In Haiti, slaves and free blacks had already waged a revolution for political freedom. Moreover, Haitian leaders manifested a "high sense of the social, moral and practical obligations" under which they operated as emissaries of the only black republic in the world. Finally, Haiti was a thoroughly "black" country. Blacks governed, administered laws, and wrote all the "official documents." "I upon my honor declare," Saunders stated, "that there is not a single white European at present employed in writing at any of the public offices." Everyone in power was "a man of colour."[22]

In an America that denigrated free black achievement, and denied most people of color the right to vote, Saunders's glowing Haitian reports certainly appealed to Richard Allen. The black preacher was also won over by Saunders's ability to fuse notions of Christian brotherhood to racial redemption. Borrowing from the language of revivalism that was so meaningful to Allen, and adhering to a moral-uplift philosophy that was shared by Allen's entire generation of black founders, Saunders challenged African Americans to consider themselves free agents in an ever-expanding world. The Lord Almighty gave black reformers a choice: they could act to change their destiny or remain apathetic. "My brethren," Saunders called out, "the friends of humanity have asserted that we are susceptible of improvement like the whites."[23] Black leaders should now prove it, he challenged, by striking for Haiti.

As his words illustrate, Saunders had an intense belief not only in Haiti but also in the power of black leaders to transform the Atlantic world, something Allen felt ever more strongly about now that he headed a burgeoning church. Saunders was also a Christian moralist who believed in the power of the divine spirit to alter human events. He was a worthy successor to the esteemed Paul Cuffee, a person whom Allen had once singled out as perhaps the model free black leader. One believer to another, Saunders helped Allen truly believe in the possibility of African redemption in Haiti.

3. Allen and Haiti in the 1820s: Now Is the Time

Although Allen had shown interest in black-run emigration plans, from Cuffee-style African colonization to Saunders-style Haitian migrations, the exigency of church building had usually diverted his attention. By the mid-1820s, though, with his church growing nationally, Allen began to explore Haitian emigration with a verve and focus that made him a point man on black exodus from the United States. Certainly, Allen's international visions were sparked by the remarkable migrations already occurring around him, from his own AME's blossoming to Americans' westward expansion to the flood of European immigrants daily arriving in port cities like Philadelphia. Black mass movement, he came to see from his own domestic missionaries (who reported to him from boats, canal ships, and trains), was more than possible. Just as clearly, Allen hoped to expand his church beyond American shores. Moreover, Allen's experiences as a free black leader in a racist country also led him to reconsider African American destinies beyond the confines of the United States. Haiti thus became both a political and a religious refuge for Allen—a safety-valve option for both black missionaries and black masses. He embraced emigration firmly and convincingly.

Allen conveyed these sentiments to Haitian president Jean-Pierre Boyer in that remarkable letter from August 1824. Calling America a land of "oppression" for even liberated African Americans, Allen thanked Boyer for having "extended to a poor and oppressed people in the United States . . . an asylum where they will enjoy the blessings of freedom and equality."[24] And this is what Boyer had recently done: encouraged free blacks to leave their land of oppression and go to the Haitian republic, where land, opportunity, and equality awaited. Allen did not just listen to such overtures—he acted. He wrote Boyer a gushing letter of support; he hosted Boyer's hand-picked representatives at his church and home; he filled a ship with black émigrés bound for Haiti; he headed Haitian emigration efforts in Philadelphia; he kept a file of pro-Haiti letters for distribution to both black and white allies. Freedom had always been sweet to Allen, but the prospect of Haitian equality and justice for all had a particularly resonant sound now. Too old to go himself, Allen hoped to steer as many of his brethren as possible to the only black republic in the Western Hemisphere.

The time had never been better to embrace Haitian emigration.[25] Since Allen first hosted Prince Saunders in 1818, Haitian emigration had become a hot topic in reform circles. While abolitionism and white-led colonization movements sagged, Haitian emigration took off. "Everything relating to the Republic of Haiti at the present period is interesting," white reformer Benjamin Lundy offered in the *Genius of Universal Emancipation* in March 1825. "The eyes of the colored people are directed thither, as . . . an asylum for the unfortunate of their race, at whom the shafts of prejudice and bitter persecution are pointed."[26] In a major article in the *North American Review*, the nation's leading intellectual journal, Alexander Everett (brother of famed orator and Massachusetts governor Edward Everett) argued that Haiti, and not Africa, would solve America's racial ills. For white Americans eager to resettle "troublesome" blacks, Everett wrote, Haiti was at a "congenial" distance from former masters. For free blacks, Haiti offered a potentially "flourishing and prosperous community" that African settlements did not.[27]

News that mighty France had officially recognized its former colony as an independent nation in August 1825—the first major Western power to do so—inspired African Americans all along the Atlantic seaboard to consider emigrating to the revolutionary island. "The joy which swells our bosoms," Baltimore's William Watkins proclaimed on August 15, 1825, "is incommunicable." "Of all that has hitherto been done in favor of the descendants of Africa," he went on, "I recollect nothing so fraught with momentous importance." Haitian independence, he gushed, was surely an event "that tends to the exultation of our color and character." And, Watkins finished, Haitian independence offered a clear sign of divine intervention. "That the arm of the Lord is stretched for the deliverance of the sons of Africa, in different parts of the habitable globe, is no longer in doubt with me."[28]

By the time Watkins spoke, Allen had already embraced Haitian emigration. In June 1824, he welcomed Haitian envoy Jonathas Granville to Philadelphia. Allen knew that "Citizen Granville," who had the bearing of a well-educated, well-heeled francophone Haitian, had arrived with the express purpose of attracting black émigrés to Haiti. The *Philadelphia National Gazette* reported that Granville had stepped foot in America that summer "with sufficient means to aid the immediate emigration of at least 6000 of the people of color." The paper's correspondent noted that he "had the pleasure of conversing with [Granville] and formed a very favorable opinion of his understanding and feelings." Indeed, "though a person of color," Granville's "information, diction, sentiment and manners place him upon the level of the good society of any country." And so, the white reporter concluded, Granville's visit and ideas deserve "respectful consideration [from] every quarter."[29]

Allen gave him more than a respectful reception. He held several special meetings between Granville and his Bethel congregation. On June 29, 1824, for example, Allen asked Granville to come to his home for the first of several question-and-answer sessions with AME ministers, exhorters, and would-be missionaries. Allen's congregants, already wary of anything that hinted of colonization, queried the graceful and cool Granville about the Haitian scheme. Was there really economic opportunity? Was there really political freedom? Was there truly religious liberty? Allen conceded to Boyer that there was initially "much opposition" among free blacks to Granville's emigrationist overtures. But, Allen stated, "I extended my help to [Granville] in everything within my powers" and "invited the people to gather in my church and explained your propositions to them." Bethelites were then "well-disposed to accept [Granville's] propositions." With Allen's help, Afro-Philadelphians' sights were set on Haiti. By the late summer of 1824, Allen started filling a registry with the names of prospective émigrés, a number (he himself said) that quickly topped five hundred people.[30]

As Granville told Allen's congregation, and as Boyer himself explained in written appeals, Haitian officials offered several levels of support to free black émigrés. First, the Haitian government would defray the cost of travel for roughly six thousand people. Second, it would provide free land and four months of provisions to settlers who built their own quarters and improved the land.[31] Finally, the Haitian government offered immediate political and constitutional equality to African Americans entering the country. These last words filled Allen's head with much hope: full equality and *citizenship* upon merely setting foot in the black republic of Haiti! Although Allen and Bethelites interrogated Granville on the deeper realities of religious *liberty* in Haiti, Allen expressed particular joy at the prospect of free black citizenship and equality.[32]

Black émigrés were not the only ones who held out high hopes. For Haitian leaders like Boyer and Granville, the prospect of an industrious and determined free black labor force was also the stuff of dreams. A young country reeling from embargoes, economic dislocation, and perpetual debt, Haiti needed an infusion of black settlers and strivers. Who else should Haitian officials attempt to lure than the black men and women who had built American plantations into the engines of empire? To "build out" their own country—to encourage settlement of productive land, increase market activity, and create prosperous towns—Haiti would now do what America had traditionally done: bring the world to its shores. In a pamphlet published in 1824 by white New York reformer Mahlon Day, and reprinted in Philadelphia, Haitian officials guaranteed black settlers land, liberty, and unfettered pursuit of happiness as masters of their own Haitian domain. Haiti, meanwhile, would get African American "cultivators" whose "industriousness would "improve uncultivated or neglected land."[33]

As Day's pamphlet illustrates, Haitian officials shrewdly exploited black leaders' anxieties about American society while also picturing African Americans as a typically American group. Black settlers exhibited the skillfulness, industry, sobriety, and thriftiness that would revolutionize Haiti. Many years after the glorious Haitian Revolution had ended, Day's pamphlet declared, there were still places that "have been deserted, and are running up in bushes." Yet these plots of land showed marvelous potential, being "intermingled with coffee plants, cotton," and other staple crops that black settlers could turn to gold. Who better than African Americans to spin such an economic transformation? The need for skilled tradesmen—"carpenters, blacksmiths, Taylors"—meant that Haiti could also spawn a prosperous group of middling artisans and mechanics, black men (and women) who had little opportunity to fully express their talents in the ever-oppressive United States. Emigrants might also become self-sufficient farmers or savvy producers of marketable goods. Haiti already contained much cultivated land—"coffee, sugar canes, fruits, vegetable, etc."—which could be made immediately available to black émigrés.[34] In sum, Haitian emigration appeared to be a boon for an island nation struggling to recapture economic glory, as well as a saving grace for free black Americans desperate for new opportunities.

Allen certainly believed in the redemptive powers of Haiti. Beyond hosting Boyer's man in the City of Brotherly Love, and putting émigrés on ships to the Caribbean nation, Allen trumpeted Haitian emigration in other visible ways. He became the leader of the Philadelphia Emigration Society. He also shared a steady stream of correspondence from Haiti with abolitionist Benjamin Lundy, who often reprinted these glowing letters in the *Genius of Universal Emancipation*. From "Dr. Belfast Burton," Allen's friend and now a visitor to Haiti, *Genius* readers learned that the Haitian government would indeed provide suitable land to African American settlers; Boyer's promise was no illusion. Thus, Burton told Allen, even black mechanics and laborers could get a freehold in Haiti. The government offered land rentals (for those who would not build their own place or who preferred a preexisting one) and pledged to support settlers "until they can support themselves." "Preparations for schools are [in the] making," Burton went on, and blacks' "religious freedom is most perfect."[35] "I will remark," Burton giddily told Allen, "that no man can have any just conception of the country without seeing it, as I had no idea of there being any such place on earth." Most of the 270 emigrants Burton talked to in the Haitian city of Samanah "say it surpasses their most sanguine expectations, and that they would not return to the United States again, if lands were given to them there for nothing."[36] Allen nodded his head in agreement and passed the letter to Lundy.

Allen also forwarded a note by a former white colonizationist, the Reverend Loring D. Dewey, who marveled at Haiti's opportunities. An evangelical preacher and Allen acquaintance, Dewey visited Haiti to cut through the Haitian hype. He also told Allen that Haiti was no illusion. By simply following his list of "Hints and Recommendations"—settlers should be industrious, pious, and persistent, he charged—the average emigrant's "situation [would be] better here in five years than that of white emigrants to the new countries of the [American] West in ten."[37] Allen nodded again and forwarded Dewey's note to the *Genius*. As Dewey told Allen, Haiti was indeed a black West, though better. The land was productive, the climate magnificent (no harsh winters!), and the political/social environment—black settlers, he called out, would be "on your own land"—conducive to black uplift. Merely "decent industry," he ventured, would produce double the results of what white settlers would get in the West.[38] In this and other ways, Dewey highlighted the omnipresent differences between an enlightened Haiti (where all were citizens regardless of race) and the despotic United States.[39]

Dewey was a true believer, touting Haiti to Allen and anyone else who would listen. Let African American emigrants come to the island of Haiti, he wrote Baltimore lawyer and emigration advocate Daniel Raymond on February 3, 1825, "with the intention of being good and industrious citizens, . . . and they will soon feel themselves in the enjoyment of their rational privileges in the midst of people like themselves, who tread the soil they own in the dignified manliness which a conscious equality, alone, imparts to human deportment." For Dewey, as for Allen, there was much to be said about a scheme that allowed blacks to "leave the land of their degradation" and rise elsewhere. In Haiti, they could finally forget the United States, "where they must always be seen by a race of superiors . . . [as] necessarily subject."[40]

What Allen's correspondents alluded to—what Allen himself believed he was participating in—was a complete transformation of the politics of race in the Atlantic world of the 1820s. With black and white activists coadjudicating the cause, Haitian emigration was perhaps the first interracial reform movement in America. Recall that the nation's leading abolitionist organizations, like the Pennsylvania Abolition Society, remained segregated throughout the early national period. Moreover, African Americans (apart from Paul Cuffee) did not form a significant part of the American Colonization Society's leadership cadre, North or South, locally or nationally. Haitian emigration flowed from, and was largely controlled by, African-descended people themselves. Prince Saunders, a neo–Paul Cuffee, not only advocated the scheme at a very early stage but also vouched for it before black communities along the Atlantic seaboard. Jonathas Granville, a mixed-race Haitian figure of great bearing and respect among free black Americans, worked his way through New York City's, Philadelphia's, and Baltimore's black communities, visiting churches, reform groups, and black leaders to make his case personally for the Haitian scheme. Then there was Boyer, a black head of state who made a public offer of land and political rights to his oppressed brothers and sisters in the United States. These were all model men of color in the Haitian cause.

Finally, American blacks often had control of local emigration groups —and thus decision-making power on a day-to-day basis. In Philadelphia, Richard Allen himself headed the local Haitian Emigration Society, and he helped place people on ships destined for the Caribbean. White figures were often the go-betweens in the Philadelphia-Haitian plan, while blacks were the leaders. In New York and Baltimore, when white figures did join and support Haitian-emigration groups, they did not overwhelm African Americans. In New York City, the esteemed Peter Williams was a leading emigration advocate; in Baltimore, William Watkins served that role. Like Allen, both of these men worked *within* their own communities to support emigration. In no way did emigration seem like a slaveholder's plot to rid America of free blacks.

Rather, for Allen, Haitian emigration became the functional equivalent of something white citizens had: a western safety valve. White citizens down on their luck or hoping for a new start could journey to frontier locales—the Ohio country, Kentucky, Tennessee, Alabama, Mississippi, and Louisiana. Although African Americans also migrated to these frontier areas during the 1820s (recall that Allen's AME had already spread to western New York and Ohio), black leaders feared that resettlement *within* the American polity would replicate patterns of racial discrimination found along the eastern seaboard. Allen emphasized these ideological dimensions of Haitian asylum, telling Boyer that "the voice of freedom is sweet to our ears." Haitian officials, he predicted, should expect "thousands" of African American exiles.[41]

The Haitian safety-valve option also had important class dimensions for black leaders like Allen. Haitian officials and their American advocates consistently emphasized the desirability of "industrious," "sober," and "economical" emigrants. This did not preclude black laborers at all. Indeed, as one of the leading emigrationists put it, "all classes and descriptions of free people of color . . . are included in the invitation of President Boyer." On the other hand, Boyer, his representatives, and even Allen emphasized that all emigrants should be of "good character."[42] In his own letter to Boyer, Allen remarked that most of the roughly fifty emigrants he had dispatched to Haiti in August 1824 "are respectable and industrious people." Belfast Burton's letter to Allen had appealed to respectable "mechanics" to emigrate to Haiti, for they were much in need and would find good prospects. In Allen's and Burton's eyes, Haiti offered great potential for those in the lower and middling ranks who wished to better themselves by embracing moral-uplift principles: work hard, remain pious, and watch yourself rise in society. If America was not hospitable to black uplift, then perhaps Haiti would be. Allen told Boyer that demand for Haitian-emigration options was strong, for he received many notes from free blacks in "cities and towns"—presumably those who desperately wanted to escape the squalid conditions of Northern urban life—eager to learn of Haitian prospects.

Allen's support of Haitian emigration may have been framed by class conflicts emerging in Philadelphia—not to mention his own church—during the 1810s and 1820s. Concerned that black youth and black laborers were both in danger of succumbing to the ills of racism as well as a sagging economy (the Panic of 1819 hit urban locales like Philadelphia particularly hard), Allen saw Haitian emigration as "open[ing] a refuge where [blacks] will enjoy the blessings of freedom and equality."[43]

Perceptive white reformers recognized emigration's multifaceted appeal to leaders like Allen. Haiti was *not* a quasi-colonization plot hatched by slaveholders but a direct response to continued racial injustice in the United States. If this language sounded ominously like that of the early colonizationist pleadings of the Reverend Robert Finley (who had visited Allen and noted that blacks faced a prejudice that *created* degradation), it ultimately veered away by blaming whites for not truly confronting their racist minds. "O that there were magnanimity in my country—a genuine Love of true freedom," Loring Dewey wailed at one point from Haiti. Americans "boasted" of liberty but failed to deliver it to people of African descent. And even now, Dewey went on, they failed to support Haitian emigration. "I believe in the promise of Ethiopia," he declared, even though he doubted white Americans' ability to reform the American nation. Haiti would bring Ethiopian freedom dreams to reality.

The yelps of African colonizationists and Southern masters against Haitian emigration further fueled black support for it. At roughly the same time that Allen and Dewey touted the revolutionary nation's potential, a Virginia paper starkly warned American masters of the consequences of a vibrant Haiti, one stocked with Ethiopia's vengeful sons and daughters. Taking issue with claims that Haiti was far enough away from American masters to pose any problems, the *Petersburg Intelli-*

gencer commented in July 1825 that "we confess there is something in the geographical position of Haiti which we do not like." "We should not wish to see a powerful nation of blacks rise up so near us," the paper finished. Like other critics, the author of this piece tried to couch his opposition to Haiti in loftier terms—the "perfidy" of Haitian officials who duped free blacks into leaving America—but readers soon saw Southern masters' true concern: Haitian emigration siphoned off support for African colonization. And African colonization, having no direct bearing on slavery and having the further virtue of settling emancipated blacks much further away from restless Southern slaves, was quite simply preferable to most Virginia masters.[44]

Haiti, then, offered a fearful model for many slaveholders. Southerners who publicly challenged Haitian proponents made this all too clear. If free blacks "colonized" Haiti, they would build that nation into a thriving enterprise. This would mean full diplomatic recognition of a black revolutionary republic. This could mean the end of the Southern states as they were then configured—white masters controlling black slaves. Indeed, as one Maryland paper put it, "the naked example of a *flourishing* black empire established through a bloody but successful revolt of slaves on the very confines of our union is in itself of terrible import to those whose misfortune it is to be slaveholders." Any fool could see the "danger" of a vibrant Haiti. Maryland masters betrayed another fear: that Haiti would become a refuge for fugitive slaves. The formation of an Emigration Society in Baltimore, and the ensuing departure of free blacks for Haiti, scared masters into pressuring the Maryland General Assembly for a new law "to prohibit the transportation of absconding slaves to Hayti." The law stipulated that "no officer of a vessel shall hereafter receive on board . . . any negro or mulatto 'til such negro or mulatto shall produce a regularly authenticated certificate of freedom from some clerk of this state." The penalty for violating this edict was one thousand dollars for ship captains, with the money being split between the state and a fugitive slave's master.[45]

Haitian emigration offered Allen and other free blacks a mirror image of African colonization. Many things appeared the same: blacks' departure from the United States, whites' subtle antislavery motives, racial redemption in another land. In reality, though, the image of Haitian emigration was the complete opposite of African colonization. Whereas the racial discourse of African colonization depicted free blacks as burdensome figures, Haitian-emigrationist discourse often pictured them as strong (if disaffected) people. Whereas African resettlement was a new errand into the wilderness—far from American slaveholders—Haitian emigration put blacks in the Western Hemisphere's republican order. Whereas African colonization was quickly dominated by whites, Haitian emigration had interracial leadership groups, with black leaders maintaining much power.

Haitian dreams thus created a marvelously ironic discourse in early national life. Just as Haitian officials themselves celebrated free African Americans as saviors, so too did many slaveholders fear that emigrating free blacks would turn Haiti into an economic, demographic, and political powerhouse—one that might be powerful enough to threaten the American slaveholding republic! On the other hand, many African colonizationists and antiabolitionists continued to picture Africans in America (free and slave alike) as shiftless, lazy, criminal, corrupt, inferior in mind and intellect, a drain on society, and a people best removed or enslaved. There is, indeed, a powerful paradox in the anti-Haitian-emigration stand of certain white figures who, all the same, favored African colonization. How could African Americans be simultaneously pictured as powerful and pathetic? Allen and his allies believed that Haitian emigration laid bare white colonizationists' contradictory sensibilities. For their part, Haitian officials gleefully extracted white masters' concerns over Haitian emigration from American papers and kept them in a clipping file.

In fact, Citizen Granville served not merely as a Haitian representative in America but as a window onto racial debates intensifying in the United States in the mid-1820s. He copied dozens of articles and letters from American papers and then translated them into French for all Haitian officials to see. One magnificent example of the contorted nature of slaveholders' and colonizationists' opposition to Haiti appeared in the *Philadelphia National Gazette* on June 19, 1824. Printed just as Granville had arrived in the city, the article featured a none-too-subtle swipe at pro-ACS figures in New York City who registered "alarms" at Haitian emigration. The mere mention of the word Haiti, it seemed, sent the ACS into a tizzy. The New York colonizationist stated that

> if the question was a merely abstract one of whether it be better that our coloured population should be colonized on the inhospitable shores of Africa, amidst savage tribes and at a distance from civilization, or on

the fruitful and teeming soil of Saint Domingo, . . . it would not require
. . . a moment of hesitation.[46]

In that case, Haiti would win. But, of course, the Haitian question did
not involve abstractions. As the article proclaimed, Haitian emigration
added up to the very real probability that free blacks would rise and
then threaten American masters. They would encourage fugitive slaves
to settle there; they would compel Americans to recognize the black republic diplomatically; and they would always symbolize the power of
racial revolution. It would be much better, then, to move African Americans as far away as possible from American shores. For that reason,
both Northern and Southern African colonizationists needed to vigorously oppose Haitian emigration.

If the debate did not involve such serious consequences, Allen would
have laughed at African colonizationists' and slaveholders' fears of free
blacks' potential power in Haiti. There was, however, one issue that
Allen did not joke about. He remained vitally concerned with the religious dimensions of Haitian emigration. In his letter to Haitian president Boyer, Allen actually reported that the "first obstacle that presented itself" to the Haitian scheme has been "the issue of freedom of
conscience in the worship of the Supreme Being." Citizen Granville's
initial meetings with Bethel congregants, Allen continued, had "dissipated this concern." Haitian officials, Granville had stated, respected all
manner of Christian practice, including non-Catholic denominations
like African Methodism. A relieved Allen found such comments so satis-
fying that he assented to the passage of fifty Bethelites in the summer of
1824, including "two among them to serve as preachers until such time
that I shall be able to send a regularly ordained minister."[47]

But Allen's concern did not vanish with one simple meeting. The
bishop, his church, and Citizen Granville revisited the issue of Methodist missionaries in Haiti several times in the space of one month. On
November 3, 1824, Allen called a special meeting of "the ministers,
preachers, exhorters, trustees and Leaders" so that they might collectively think about a minister's duties and rights overseas. Although the
imminent departure of Bethel member Thomas Roberson for Haiti
prompted Allen's concerns—a group of nearly fifteen Bethelites voted to
officially "set apart" Roberson as an AME minister with full standing
in Haiti—Allen was also gearing up for AME missionary work in Haiti.

A few weeks later, Allen's church formed "a Committee of 20 . . . to have an interview with Granville, the Haytian agent, in order to ascertain the best place to send missionaries." As November wore on, Allen convened still another meeting, at which a committee of seven was appointed "to draw up an instrument stating certain requests" for Haitian officials, namely, the specific rights and liberties accorded "a Methodist Minister" in Haiti. "What is the privilege of a Methodist Minister in the Republic of Hayti?" the group (which included not only Allen but also Morris Brown) wanted to know. At a fourth meeting on November 29, Granville met with his Bethel questioners one last time to discuss religious issues.[48]

For Granville and some Haitian officials, Allen's continued concerns about religious liberty in Haiti was somewhat surprising and even irritating. With racial oppression confronting African Americans in the United States, and supposed social and economic refuge awaiting them in Haiti, why would black leaders like Allen worry so much about their religious liberty? Granville even made some snide remarks privately to Boyer about what he viewed as American blacks' misguided concerns. Nevertheless, Granville assured black Methodists that all would be well in Haiti. He and Allen then prepared for a busy season of black migration.

4. International Dreams to Remember

In November 1827, Richard Allen wrote another letter. Like his note three years earlier to Haitian president Boyer, this one concerned the potential Atlantic crossings of free people of color. Unlike that earlier letter, however, Allen now made his thoughts known to the public at large. In a short, pointed essay published in *Freedom's Journal*, the nation's inaugural black newspaper based in New York City (it ran from 1827 to 1929), he lashed out at the plan of African colonization, by then firmly associated with the American Colonization Society. It became his most famous pronouncement on the subject of colonization and one of his better-known pieces of writing. "Dear Sir," Allen addressed the editors, "I have for several years been striving to reconcile my mind to the colonization of Africa in Liberia, but there have always been, and there still remain great and insurmountable objections against the scheme." In 550 words—vintage Allen—he offered a cogent, biting

commentary on the subject that became both a keynote for his generation of black founders and a template for ascending reformers. African
colonization, he commented, threatened the lives of free blacks North
as well as South, secured Southern bondage, and failed to consider the
views of most African Americans themselves, who by and large rejected
white-led colonization schemes. "Can we not discern the project of
sending the free people of color away from this country?" Allen wondered. "Is it not for the interest of the slaveholder, to select the free people of color out of the different states and send them to Liberia? Will it
not make their slaves uneasy to see free men of color enjoying liberty?"
Perhaps more importantly, Allen argued that African colonization denied African American claims to American citizenship. In a memorable
and much-copied statement, one that echoed in the words and ideology of Frederick Douglass years later, Allen proclaimed, "Africans have
made fortunes for thousands, who are yet unwilling to part with their
services. . . . [T]his land which we have watered with our tears and our
blood, is now our mother country and we are well satisfied to stay
where wisdom abounds, and the Gospel is free."[49]

It did not take long for other black leaders to praise Allen's anti-ACS
stand. After reprinting Allen's letter verbatim in his famous "Appeal,"
David Walker observed simply, "the name of this very man will stand in
the pages of history among the greatest divines who have lived."[50] Peter
Williams used Allen's language in 1830 when he informed black New
Yorkers that America was indeed African Americans' "mother country"
and that they should not shrink from claiming equal rights in either the
North or the South.[51]

Most historians have saluted Allen's clarion call as a milestone in
black protest—America is a black motherland, Allen said loudly, and
colonization a fraud—but they have paid less attention to the document's meaning in Allen's life. After taking such a strong stand on behalf of Haitian emigration (and before that having expressed strong
support for African colonizationists like Paul Cuffee), was Allen now an
opponent of all emigration schemes? The answer is no. Allen was attempting to differentiate African colonization from Haitian emigration.
As a matter of fact, his continuing support of Haitian emigration and
communications with former African colonizationists like white New
Yorker Loring Dewey (who roamed Haiti even as he dismissed African
settlement as impractical) raised concerns among some black reformers
that Allen was also friendly with the American Colonization Society.

His visibility on the Haitian emigration issue may have blurred the lines between the two causes. The *Freedom's Journal* essay, so tightly focused as it was on African colonization, explicated Allen's opposition to the ACS but also cagily left room for other emigrationist schemes.

Put another way, Allen took up his pen not merely to condemn the ACS but, indirectly, to explain his support of Haitian emigration. If one reads between the lines, in fact, Allen insinuates that he could very well support black-led emigrationism because of its explicit concern for African Americans' voices and ideas. African colonizationists, he noted, "have not duly considered the subject" of African repatriation in light of black opposition. And in any event, he added, most members of the ACS "are not men of color." Conversely, Haitian emigrationism grew out of African Americans' hopes and dreams and had many (and prominent) black supporters, from Haitian dignitaries to working-class men of color in the United States. Black agency made all the difference to Allen.

But Allen's denunciation of the ACS raises other interesting questions. Was the idea of "Africa" still relevant in constructing trans-Atlantic black identity? In his essay, Allen repudiated African colonization in part by critiquing the current state of African culture. Native Africans, he observed, were "heathens." Allen's belief in the "Fortunate Fall"—the notion that African society had been corrupted by the international slave trade but would also be redeemed by former slaves carrying out a divinely inspired plan of Christian conversion—led him to criticize Africans as unchristian and premodern. Yet Allen also played an ingenious game of rhetorical reversal on colonizationists. Whereas supporters of African colonization had castigated the "Sons of Africa" —that is, free blacks—as a troublesome presence in the Western world who could rise only in their native land of Africa, Haitian emigrationists like Allen argued that African-descended people were a powerful and rising group no matter where they lived, except perhaps on African soil. Why? At least rhetorically, Haitian emigrationists like Allen pointed out that fixing the problems wrought by the international slave trade required good-faith exertions from all Christian peoples and nations. Merely dumping a couple thousand liberated slaves on the western coast of Africa would not begin to restore a continent plagued by centuries of European and then American invasion. As it stood in the 1820s, according to Allen, the American Colonization Society was still a front for Southern masters who merely wanted to rid themselves of free blacks and shore up bondage. African redemption, he argued, mattered little to them.

Thus, Allen's rather harsh-sounding language about African "heathens" was not a repudiation of his African heritage but, rather, a reenvisioning of just where African redemption would occur. For Allen, as for other black leaders of the 1820s, African redemption would not— could not yet—occur on African soil. Rather, it was destined to happen in the Western Hemisphere, where since the American Revolutionary era African Americans had built free communities that could stand tall in the modern world. American society's racial ills prevented a full flowering of African glory. Perhaps, Allen hoped, Haiti would be the site of global African redemption.

5. The Idea of Emigration in the Black Mind

Richard Allen's dream that African American migrations would alter the racial politics of the Atlantic world did not materialize. Most of the several thousand emigrants to Haiti returned home over the next several years, frustrated by the arduous struggles they faced in a supposed land of riches. African Americans in Haiti confronted linguistic, cultural, and religious hurdles.[52] Ironically, Haitian emigration's failure compelled African Americans to rediscover (or reembrace) their American identity. Haiti was not a black paradise and asylum after all. Information remains scant on these returning migrants—seeming lack of religious liberty (as well as the persistence of Vodou) and economic hardship loomed large—but the point is that many returned to America poised for a new era of struggle for black liberty *within* the United States. That is certainly one reason why antebellum abolitionism became so fiery and intense: most black leaders and communities realized they could not export the struggle for racial justice. They had to build an abolition movement inside American culture capable of routing racial injustice. Still, for many black leaders like Allen, the tension between black patriotism and more militant versions of black nationalism (including emigration) remained unresolved into the antebellum years.

Indeed, both Haitian emigration and the idea of Haiti remained a strong part of African American intellectual life and protest for the rest of the nineteenth century. The AME Church retained branches in Samanah and Port-au-Prince, Haiti (with a total of nearly two hundred congregants).[53] One of these AME acolytes might have been Allen's own son, Richard, who not only visited Haiti but lived there for several years (it was perhaps Richard Jr., a scrivener and multilingual translator of French and Spanish, who wrote Richard Allen's original note to the francophone Boyer in 1824). Subsequent black abolitionists used Haiti as a foil for American racial prejudice. William Wells Brown, Frederick Douglass, and James Theodore Holly, among others, located in Haiti a revolutionary past eternally relevant for a new African American destiny. As Holly, a pioneering black nationalist, put it after the Civil War, "Providence seems to have made our peculiar task by the eligibility of our situation in this country, as a point for gaining easy access to that island."[54] With Haiti so close, many nineteenth-century African Americans had an ideological and even geographical escape hatch.

In this sense, Allen's vision of Haitian emigration fits squarely within the main currents of black political protest during the nineteenth and twentieth centuries. As Robin Kelley has convincingly put it, "few scholars or activists today take proposals to leave America and return to Africa or some other homeland seriously." But whether or not such emigrationist plans have been "impractical" or "escapist," he continues, they have served historically as a measure of how "black people imagine real freedom." "The desire to leave Babylon, if you will, and search for a new land tells us a great deal about what people dream about, what they want, how they might want to reconstruct their lives."[55] Richard Allen's Haitian dream was not simply to create an outpost of the AME Church but to establish a political asylum for disaffected citizens of color. Mass migration, he believed, might not only bolster the security of the only black republic in the Western Hemisphere but also make a profound political statement to American slaveholders, intellectuals, and religious men. Redress racial inequality or see a powerful people depart the country that they helped to build, he seemed to say. A preacher easily accustomed to thinking in biblical terms, Allen's Haitian dream was clearly indebted to the story of Exodus. The only problem was that the revolutionary island did not ultimately seem to be the Promised Land.

Yet even in failure black migration to Haiti and back was striking. In an age of mass movement, Haitian emigration was notable as evidence of the economic and logistical power of people of color. The six thousand to twelve thousand emigrants to Haiti easily outpaced freed blacks sent by the American Colonization Society to Africa (numbering roughly twenty-five hundred between 1820 and 1830). These numbers also matched the numbers of workers assembled to build the Erie Canal and the number of troops deployed to subdue Native Americans in the southeastern borderlands. And when they did return home, black immigrants from Haiti must have been a sight too. No longer arriving in slave shackles on ships from either Africa or the Caribbean, black people, as Richard Allen put it in 1827, were coming back to claim America as "our mother country."[56]

With the great experiment of Haitian emigration clearly untenable for the majority of African Americans in the foreseeable future, and African colonization stigmatized by the great black founder, Allen believed the stage was set for a new and more vigorous collision with racial injustice inside the United States than ever before. He was eager and ready for this last challenge of his life. Even then, however, he wanted a black safety valve somewhere beyond America.

10

Last Rights

> But oh! Dear Sinners, that's not all that's dreadful,
>   You must before your God appear,
> To give an account of your transactions,
>   And how you spent your time when here.
>   —Richard Allen, *Life, Experience, and Gospel Labours*

Richard Allen cherished the image of the journey. In both poetry and prose, he pictured his life as a great series of journeys converging at one transcendent point: eternal redemption. As a young free man of color, he had traveled hundreds of miles on the mid-Atlantic revival circuit saving souls for the Lord. As a spokesman for the black community in early national Philadelphia, he had read African American experience and identity through the prism of Exodus—perhaps the greatest journey in recorded history. As an elder statesman in an ever-changing Atlantic world of reform, he supported black emigration as his chosen people's next possible stride toward freedom.

By the 1830s, Allen focused on the journey to the next world. A faithful Christian obsessed with "qualifying" for heaven—nothing was predestined to this generation of religious itinerants—he continually sought to do "good" work in the eyes of the Lord. Do good and ask for nothing in return, he was fond of saying.[1] Allen was busy on some reform cause or another until the very day he died. Indeed, though seemingly frail, he remained a perfect example of Newton's first law of physics: bodies in motion tend to stay in motion. Only death would slow the great preacher down.

What did he do? After he turned seventy, Allen helped organize the first National Convention of Colored Persons to systematize the struggle for racial justice among black leaders. He also served as a key advocate of the Philadelphia Free Produce Society, which supported free over slave labor. Finally, he began assembling his autobiography, which, as the first narrative of a black founder, instructed rising generations on the importance of moral and racial uplift.

But the central tension in Allen's later years—whether American society would become the black promised land—remained unresolved until the last months of his life. By the 1830s, both slavery and racial injustice had grown so considerably that Allen urged African Americans to consider the virtues of the newest emigration destination, Canada. Conversely, Allen's autobiography once again emphasized the possibility of black redemption within the United States.

Rather ironically, Allen passed away just as a more radical abolitionist movement emerged, declaring holy war on racial injustice and giving hope to a whole new generation of reformers. Not so ironically, Allen's autobiography reminded rising reformers of the giant shoulders on which they stood: those of black founders.

1. A Birthday Moment: Allen as Black Celebrity

On February 14, 1828, Richard Allen hosted an elegant but understated birthday party at his Spruce Street home. Now sixty-eight, Allen and a merry band of well-wishers rejoiced by singing the black bishop's favorite hymns. Despite Allen's desire to keep things quiet and dignified, the birthday party became national news. *Freedom's Journal* let black communities from Boston to Virginia know the importance of February 14. In fact, partly because of such coverage, Allen's birthday soon was celebrated as an African American festive day.

But the *Freedom's Journal* article offered more than birthday salutations. It highlighted Allen's status as a touchstone of the black founding generation. "Bishop Allen was the first person that formed a religious society among the people of color in the United States of America," the paper declared, while repeating what would become a familiar litany of Allen's accomplishments. He founded the Free African Society, which became a model for "upwards of 40 African benevolent societies" in Philadelphia alone, not to mention the AME Church, "whereby we were enabled to worship Almighty God, under our own vine and fig tree, with none to harm, nor yet make us afraid." "We are thankful that Almighty God still spares him for the good of the African race," the paper cheered.[2]

Hagiography of black founders fit perfectly with the spirit of the times. The United States had recently celebrated its fiftieth anniversary, causing a wave of nostalgia for the founders. The twin deaths of John Adams and Thomas Jefferson on July 4, 1826—half a century after they had collaborated on the Declaration of Independence—served as a stunning emblem of America's jubilee. (Unlike Washington's death, Jefferson's passing prompted no eulogy from Allen). Now that the American nation had survived past infancy, these old statesmen could elegantly fade from the spotlight.[3]

Richard Allen was a black founder still going strong. And the graying preacher still moved gracefully to meet demands on his time. On many days, Allen could be found walking near Bethel Church, his trusty gold-capped cane (bequeathed to him by Absalom Jones) firmly in hand. More importantly, he stayed involved in the struggle for justice, refusing to live on the accomplishments of the past.

Evidence came in 1827, when he became interested in a new racial-reform group: the Free Produce Society of Pennsylvania. Years before Abraham Lincoln's Republican Party rallied around the motto "free soil, free men, free labor," the Free Produce movement emphasized the value of both free labor and non-slave-derived goods. Paying attention to trans-Atlantic debates in Britain and the Caribbean (which calculated the cost of white sugar in terms of black blood), Free Produce advocates sought to change the terms of debate over American slavery. Rather than aim only at the heart or the head—by using emotional and intellectual rationales to compel masters to emancipate enslaved people —abolitionists would shoot for the pocketbook as well. Of course, Quaker involvement guaranteed that the Free Produce movement also made a strong moral case against bondage. But the scheme was a big step past the days of genteel gradual abolitionism. By defining slavery as immoral and unprofitable, Free Produce advocates hoped to eliminate the market for slave-produced goods. It was a form of moral and economic boycott.

Free Produce was perfectly pitched to a man like Allen. The plan melded moral and economic arguments into a coherent antislavery design. As a member of the Colored Free Produce Society put it in 1830, following a meeting at Mother Bethel, "every individual who uses the produce of slave labor encourages the slaveholder, becom[ing] also a participator in his wickedness."[4] By investing Northerners with a sense of moral control over bondage, Free Produce advocates like Allen thought they could magnify the ramifications of Southern slavery. In short, Free Produce made Northern consumers feel responsible for the life and death of enslaved people, for with every purchase of a slave-derived good, they might hear the groans of the oppressed.

Allen believed that the Free Produce movement would reenergize American abolitionism. Although both the Pennsylvania Abolition Society and the American Convention of Abolition Societies remained operational, neither group wished to declare all-out moral war on slavery. Indeed, Pennsylvania abolitionists had rescinded anti-Missouri petitions during the early 1820s because they believed hard-core abolitionism would imperil the union.[5] Particularly during the opening decades of the nineteenth century, white abolitionists portrayed themselves as corporatist reformers concerned equally with gradual emancipation (usually at the state level) and the American union. On the other hand, the fast-growing American Colonization Society pictured free blacks as a problematic presence in the United States—it was a quasi-abolitionist group at best. In this reform landscape, just who was willing to take on slavery's essential immorality?

Recognizing organized abolitionism's troubled state of affairs, Allen welcomed the Colored Free Produce Society to Bethel Church in December 1830. The meeting attracted five hundred people, including white reformers. Although little detail of the event remains, Allen's Free Produce gathering was clearly part of a growing movement in the City of Brotherly Love. A female Free Produce Society had just formed, the *Genius of Universal Emancipation* happily announced in September 1829, attracting over one hundred people. Future stars of immediate abolitionism—such as Lucretia Mott of Philadelphia—gained invaluable organizational experience within the Free Produce movement. They also learned of the antislavery movement's growing trans-Atlantic links, as many American Free Produce advocates remained in contact with British reformers. Each cup of tea sweetened with West India sugar, British and American abolitionists proclaimed, represented another enslaved person's death.[6]

Thus, Allen's support of the Free Produce movement again placed him in the vanguard of American abolitionism. Just as in 1794, when his antislavery appeal heralded the advent of black abolitionism in the public sphere, so too did Free Produce signal the beginning of a public-relations battle over bondage. Free Produce might be envisioned as a kinder and gentler version of Garrisonian and Walkerite immediate abolitionism, which appeared on the horizon. In both cases, abolitionists decided that Southern slaveholders needed a significant push from Northern citizens—no longer would reformers defer to the sensitivities of Southern masters and Northern politicians concerned about union. Now abolitionists would dedicate themselves to the cause of black freedom, not to sustaining a morally corrupt but united American nation. Both Garrisonian and Walkerite activists also mobilized Northern public opinion against Southern slaveholders and their allies—just as Free Produce activists had before them. Abolitionism was being conceived as a mass movement, and Free Produce paved the way by beckoning ordinary people to get involved in a great moral and economic debate over slavery.[7]

Allen noted one other virtue: Free Produce rekindled the flames of interracial reform. For the first time in years, white antislavery reformers visited Bethel Church and saw in its leader a dedicated abolitionist worthy of emulation. For a man who could still not officially join the Pennsylvania Abolition Society this was cheering news indeed. Perhaps racial justice was possible in America after all.

2. Black National Convention

Allen's faith in Free Produce as a vehicle for racial justice was challenged by some disturbing events that occurred at roughly the same time. In 1829, Ohio passed the most severe anti-free-black laws of any Northern state, leading to a black exodus from the Western Reserve. Then in May 1830, Allen read about similar laws passed in Louisiana. In a *Genius of Universal Emancipation* article entitled "Free Colored People," editor Benjamin Lundy exposed a new law that ejected "all free blacks" who had entered the state since 1825. The law also warned whites from circulating any antislavery material that threatened "to disturb the peace," which of course meant anything critical of bondage. There were other disturbing provisions too: the law required free blacks to register with local authorities and prohibited them from gaining literacy skills and formal education. "The blow has been struck!" Lundy thundered in tones similar to those of his brash assistant, William Lloyd Garrison, then on trial for libeling a New England slave trader. "And the free colored people, or a considerable portion of them, must leave the state. Where, it may be asked, will they go?" Lundy, who had previously printed pro-Haitian-emigration notices, answered, the Caribbean.[8] Other black leaders, having cooled on that prospect, looked instead to Canada. Allen did more than look—he produced a major pro-Canadian-emigration statement in the fall of 1830.

Allen presented his Canadian prospectus at the first national meeting of black activists ever assembled in America. As free people of color around the country confronted the passage of "black codes"—a precursor to the more famous Reconstruction-era black laws disfranchising former Southern slaves—black leaders from Boston to Baltimore called for a new wave of organizing and protest. Bostonian David Walker issued one of the most stirring calls for continent-wide black protest at a meeting of the Boston General Colored Association in December 1828. If black activists North and South organized the masses, he asked, "what mighty deeds would be done by them for the good of our cause?"[9] The time had come for a national meeting of black abolitionists.

Indeed, as Allen discovered, Walker was far from a lone voice. Black activists in both New York City and Baltimore soon called for a national meeting of black leaders. But no one was going to upstage the great black preacher. In April 1830, he summoned Hezekiah Grice, originator of the convention idea, from Baltimore. Knowing that black New Yorkers desperately wanted to claim the mantle of hosting the first convention of African American reformers, Allen proposed Philadelphia as a better site. (By the 1830s, black Philadelphia's population surged to near fifteen thousand people.) Why, he exclaimed, Bethel Church, ever identified with black autonomy, could be the convention's headquarters! Grice seemed to agree. "My dear boy," Allen then told the young man, "we should do something before these New Yorkers beat us to it."[10] After Grice departed, Allen formed a steering committee to bring the Philadelphia convention to fruition. A few weeks later, between September 20 and 24, 1830, delegates to the American Society of Free Persons of Color met at Bethel Church.[11]

The Philadelphia convention was the first of a dozen national meetings held before the Civil War. Black conventions witnessed the rise of such luminaries as Frederick Douglass, Henry Highland Garnet, William Wells Brown, and Martin Delany. They also became the equivalent of a black Congress, with activists convening to discuss a range of critical issues, from emigration and colonization to black political economy and the formation of a national black newspaper (Frederick Douglass's

Rochester-based publication, the *North Star,* resulted from one such discussion in the 1840s). During the 1830s, black conventions assembled five times, three times in Philadelphia and two in New York City. These meetings became, in essence, a coda for the black founding generation; after the last convention was held in New York City in 1835, black activists did not meet again until 1843 in Buffalo. The latter date and locale marked a transition among black leaders, for no black founder survived to attend the Buffalo meeting, the first not convened along the Atlantic seaboard. By then, with a vigorous interracial antislavery movement fighting a holy war against slavery in United States, black emigration was no longer a major concern.[12]

The inaugural convention convened by Allen predated the advent of radical abolitionism (which emphasized racial justice inside America) by several months.[13] Many black leaders, including Allen, still considered emigration a crucial part of the struggle for racial justice. "Our forlorn and deplorable situation," Allen called out, "earnestly and loudly demand of us to devise and pursue all legal means for the speedy elevation of ourselves and brethren to the scale and standing of men." And so, when they gathered at Bethel, the forty delegates representing black communities from Ohio, Pennsylvania, Maryland, and Delaware debated the potential advantages of Canadian migration. With rising racism in the North and slavery's expansion in the South and West, the delegates wondered if they could ignore Canada as a future site of black redemption.[14]

For Allen, this was a bittersweet recommendation. In "An Address to Free Persons of Color in the United States," signed by Allen and distributed in pamphlet form, the man who now went by the title "senior bishop of the AME church" once again testified to his divided allegiances. Calling African Americans the "sons" and "daughters" of the United States—men and women "who have been born and nurtured on this soil" and "whose habits, manners, and customs are the same in common with other Americans"—he nevertheless claimed that people of African descent were made "to bleed" and "drink of the cup of affliction" at the pleasure of white citizens. Noting that he and other black abolitionists maintained "a firm and settled conviction" in the Declaration of Independence as the guarantor of "life, liberty and the pursuits of happiness," Allen nevertheless expressed excitement at "the formation of a settlement in the British province of upper Canada, [which] would be a great advantage to the people of color" in America. Sorrow and anger at blacks' degraded social and civic standing in the United States framed Allen's every word. America was both a "great Republic" and, he bitterly implied, a land of "barbarians."[15]

Black freedom in Canada appeared to be unfettered. Although slavery had long existed in the British-controlled province of Upper Canada (present-day Ontario), it was on the verge of extinction when Allen pitched his plan. As early as 1793, royal authorities had approved a prohibition on the importation of slaves and provisions for a gradual abolition of Canadian slavery. At the beginning of the nineteenth century, a Canadian judge issued a ringing denunciation of slavery by declaring that bondage violated British law. "This combination of administrative policy, legislation, and judicial rulings so discouraged slaveholding that few slaves remained in the Canadas by the time the Emancipation Act of 1833 formally abolished slavery," one authoritative historical account states.[16] Continuing a reexamination of imperial slavery that dated to the 1770s, America's great enemy Great Britain appeared to be in the abolitionist vanguard at the end of Allen's life.

Fugitive slaves already recognized Canada as a refuge. Newspaper reports of runaways to Canada had circulated during the War of 1812. By the 1820s, with outposts of the AME Church firmly established there, Upper Canada looked like a northern Haitian Republic—it was an antislavery borderland. Worried American slaveholders even pressed Congress to meet with royal officials about guaranteeing the rendition of fugitive slaves. For black leaders like Allen, Britain's refusal to yield on this point further underscored the desirability of Canadian resettlement. By August 1830, black reformers had established the Wilberforce Colony—a nod to British abolitionist William Wilberforce—as the first expatriate settlement in Upper Canada. And three more settlements were planned during the 1830s.

Although Allen may not have been the sole author of the essay on Canadian emigration—ex-slave and political activist Junius C. Morel, who served as the convention's recording secretary, probably helped draft it—he was more deeply invested in the cause than nearly every other delegate.[17] Allen had examined the prospect of black migration to various locales for over fifteen years, and he had already sent AME missionaries to Canada.[18] Allen was also on record as opposing African colonization because of the difficulty black missionaries would have practicing their faith "in a foreign land" so far from family and friends. Canada, on the other hand, mimicked many American social, geographic, and religious trends—except sanctions of slavery. It really appealed to the elder Allen.[19]

In fact, "An Address to Free Persons of Colour in the United States" bears much resemblance to Allen's moral-uplift essays. Like those works, the convention pamphlet lectured free blacks on the efficacy of moral-uplift principles. "Before we close," it declared, "we would just remark that it has been a subject of deep regret . . . that we as a people have not availingly appreciated every opportunity placed within our power by the . . . friends of humanity in elevating our condition to the rank of freemen." What did Allen mean? With so many urban blacks working as "domestics," postwork leisure activities dominated black culture. "Our mental and physical qualities have not been more actively engaged in pursuits more lasting," Allen commented. White racism explained part of the problem, though Allen asserted that black degradation could be linked "in a great measure to a want of unity among ourselves." By going to Canada as a unified body, embracing moral-uplift principles of piety, thriftiness, and hard work, and assuming political and economic control of the black community, Allen believed that racial uplift would occur on a scale not yet seen in the Western Hemisphere (including in Haiti).[20]

Allen's emphasis on Canadian migration, like his preceding interest in Haitian emigration, flowed from his broader belief in black self-determination. To be successful in any transnational venture, Allen thought, African Americans needed to remain in control of both the means of travel and the ultimate destination. And the relative ease of travel among countries in the Western Hemisphere made both Canada and Haiti popular among black emigrationists. For many die-hard white colonizationists, on the other hand, African repatriation promised to put great distance between free people of color and slaves, not to mention whites and blacks.

Although he remained in contact with a few well-meaning colonizationists, Allen's convention address reiterated his firm opposition to African repatriation. "Not doubting the sincerity of many friends who are engaged in that cause," he observed, "yet we beg leave to say, that it does not meet with our approbation." Considering his vocal support of Canadian emigration, Allen added a seemingly curious statement: "However great the debt which these United States may owe to injured Africa . . . still we who have been born and nurtured on this soil, we whose habits, manners, and customs are the same in common with other Americans can never consent to take our lives in our hands and be the bearers of the redress offered by that society to that much afflicted country." By linking African American identity to the "habits, manners, and customs" of the United States, while at the same time picturing America as a rigid land of oppression, Allen appeared to be contradicting himself. But he was actually addressing the dynamism of modern black identity. The overseas slave trade had brought people of African descent to the Western Hemisphere, from which they imbibed both Christianity and revolutionary republicanism. Finding a country that protected these traditions, and at the same time allowed African-descended people to realize their full potential as statesmen, scientists, and businessman—as a nation of equal citizens—was Allen's primary goal. That led him to Haiti and subsequently Canada as the new promised land.[21]

As with Haitian emigration, the prospect of Canadian resettlement led Allen back to his American self. Even as he made clear that people of color had little choice but to consider locating "a place of refuge" beyond the United States, Allen believed that the "inestimable and invaluable" principles of the Declaration of Independence—liberty and justice for all—must remain the basis of any new black nation. Put another way, Canadian emigration would be based on the principles of the American Revolution and the great African American addendum to it: racial equality. "Under [Afro-Canadian] government," he claimed, "no invidious distinction of color is recognized, . . . [and] we shall be entitled to all the rights, privileges, and immunities of other citizens."[22] Here, Allen envisioned what might be called a third way of black reform, or a liberal black nationalism. Like Frederick Douglass and Martin Luther King, Jr., after him, Allen believed deeply in the principles undergirding American society (particularly freedom of religion, property rights, and representative governance); unlike those reformers, and somewhat like Martin Delany and Malcolm X, he felt that transnational migration gave blacks the best chance to achieve racial justice, even though any new black nation would be based on the principles of Christianity and Western democracy. His later politics on black nation-building and racial redemption were quite complex and, to our eyes, riddled with contradictions. Allen did not attempt to work out these difficulties until he sat down to compose his autobiography just a few months after the convention. And then he did so by essentially eliminating Canadian emigration from his official life story. Clearly, he was ambivalent about the emigrationist project itself. Just as clearly, he felt he had no option but to pursue the possibilities of Canadian resettlement.

As president of the black convention, Allen remained concerned with matters beyond emigration as well. This might well be his last public performance, he thought (in December 1830, he met with a lawyer to finalize his will). He therefore wanted to reiterate black activists' respectability as well as their respect for the principles of democratic governance. As the convention pamphlet illustrated for all the world to see, black leaders held open meetings, voted on a range of issues, kept official minutes, and worked through various subcommittees—all hallmarks of democratic practice. Allen made sure not to appear as a mere figurehead. As the minutes show, he was elected convention president and served on two committees—the corresponding and soliciting committees.

He also displayed years of leadership savvy in dealing with problems large and small. When, for instance, Allen's old comrade Belfast Burton stormed into Bethel Church wondering "by what right" the initially small gathering of black conventioneers had organized, Allen "hinted" to a colleague that Burton might "be elected an honorary member." As other delegates arrived, and similar imbroglios developed, Allen helped smooth them over. Reading reports of the convention's activities, one pictures Allen as a combination of the steely George Washington and the crafty Ben Franklin at the Constitutional Convention of 1787. He focused delegates' attention on the key issue—Canadian emigration—and brought a sober, dignified bearing to daily proceedings. As a minister officiating in his own church, he even served as convention chaplain, calling meetings to order promptly at 10:00 a.m. with "chaste and appropriate prayer."[23]

Did it matter? Beyond reformers, few white citizens took note of the black convention. True to form, none of the major Philadelphia newspapers covered the event (just as they had not reported on the initial breakaway of black parishioners from St. George's Church during the 1790s and the mass anticolonization meeting held at Bethel Church in 1817). Thankfully for Allen and other black reformers, gradual abolitionist Benjamin Lundy's *Genius of Universal Emancipation* did take notice (*Freedom's Journal* had ceased operations in 1829, leaving a void in the black press). Lundy wrote that Allen's convention had been an "important undertaking." Not only had some of the "most intelligent colored people in the country" assembled in Bethel Church, but they followed the lead of the "venerable Bishop Allen," who "presided over the convention" with grace and authority. And, Lundy continued, the meeting adopted resolutions on Canadian emigration with "vigor."[24] In October 1830, Lundy printed Allen's convention "Address" under the headline "Colony in Canada." Allen's pamphlet, Lundy noted, "is an important document and deserves the perusal of every friend of the colored race." To make sure that black commoners had a proper understanding of Canadian emigration, Lundy wrote that black leaders had also printed a relatively cheap map ("25 cents") of Upper Canada.[25]

As Lundy's reportage suggested, Canadian emigration remained the salient issue of the first national black convention. That would not be the case in succeeding years. After Allen's death in 1831, and the rise of an immediate-abolition movement dedicated to racial justice in America, future black conventions let the issue die a gentle death. Both black-led emigration and white-led colonization movements appeared to be the antithesis of what reformers now referred to as "modern" abolitionism: an interracial struggle against racial subjugation North and South.[26]

Perhaps it was not so strange, then, that Richard Allen's own autobiography elided the black founder's longtime support of emigration.

3. Autobiography

On December 9, 1830, Richard Allen signed his last official document: a will and testament distributing his considerable real-estate holdings and personal effects among family members. He bequeathed property to nearly a dozen kinfolk. Allen's longtime home at 150 Spruce Street went to his son John Allen; a multiple-rent-bearing three-story "brick tenement" building and series of lots on Pine Street was divided among his two married daughters, Sarah Eddy and Ann Adams, and his son Peter; and two houses and lots on Lombard Street near Bethel Church were bequeathed to his granddaughter and grandson, Sarah Eddy and Richard Nathaniel Adams, respectively. Allen asked the executors of his estate to sell his country home in Hook, Pennsylvania, after he died, thus defraying any remaining debts.[27] Allen's will also provided rental income and personal property to his "beloved wife," Sarah, and it allowed the Bethel Church Corp. for a period of ten years to pay only the annual interest on a bond it owed the black bishop. Even Allen's most cherished personal effects found new homes. To friend Joseph Cox, he gave a "silver head cane and Burkitt's commentaries on the New Testament"; to black preacher Joseph Corr, he bequeathed his "six vols. of Josephus works."[28]

With the will formalized—signed by Allen, his lawyer, and two witnesses—Allen signaled that his secular journey was nearing an end. Bouts of illness had already prevented his travels to AME meetings in Baltimore and New York. Ailing and confined to Philadelphia, he made sure his earthly affairs were in order. Should the Lord call him to the next world, Allen would go in peace.

One matter still weighed on his mind, however: the production of an autobiography. At some point in the 1820s, he began keeping a journal; he also dictated autobiographical vignettes to his son, Richard Jr. Clearly, Allen knew that his life made for a captivating and instructive tale. All that remained was the task of collating his recollections into a coherent narrative, which Allen and his son undertook just before the black preacher's death. The haunting images of death that pervade the latter section of the autobiography suggest that Allen may have been working on his life story in his final weeks. "My God," he wrote, "I entered into life without acknowledging thee, let me therefore finish it in loving thee."[29]

In crafting his autobiography, Allen had three main goals. First, he wanted to illuminate the sacred beginnings of the AME Church. He also hoped to highlight the rise of free people of color, the group that Allen had so gloriously represented for much of his adult life. Finally, Allen desperately wanted the broader public to view his story as every American's story—a humble person's rise from nothing to something through hard work, piety, and a firm belief in the American ideals of freedom and justice for all. "I have been earnestly solicited by many of my friends," Allen wrote in a brief preface, "to leave a small detail of my life and proceedings." The result was a posthumously printed book entitled *The Life, Experience, and Gospel Labours of the Rt. Rev. Richard Allen . . . Written by Himself and Published by His Request.*[30]

First published in 1833, the book became an iconic text in AME circles, forming the basis of nearly every history dealing with Allen and the black church. The epigraph fronting the document conveyed Allen's innermost sense of himself: "Mark the perfect man, and behold the upright: for the end of that man is peace."[31] Taken from Psalm 37, these lines picture a black founding figure who believed that his job in death

THE

LIFE, EXPERIENCE,

AND

GOSPEL LABOURS

OF THE

Rt. Rev. RICHARD ALLEN.

TO WHICH IS ANNEXED

THE RISE AND PROGRESS OF THE AFRICAN
METHODIST EPISCOPAL CHURCH IN THE
UNITED STATES OF AMERICA.

CONTAINING A NARRATIVE OF THE YELLOW FEVER IN THE
YEAR OF OUR LORD 1793:

WITH AN ADDRESS TO THE
PEOPLE OF COLOUR IN THE UNITED STATES.

WRITTEN BY HIMSELF,
AND PUBLISHED BY HIS REQUEST.

Mark the perfect man, and behold the upright: for the end of
that man is peace.—Ps. xxxvii. 37.

PHILADELPHIA:
Martin & Boden, Printers.

1833.

Title page of Allen's autobiography, *Life, Experience
and Gospel Labours of the Rt. Rev. Richard
Allen . . .* , 1833. The first autobiography of a black
founder, this book reprinted some of Allen's most
forceful political writings, including his yellow-fever
pamphlet, his antislavery appeal, and the African Supplement. By doing this, Allen hoped to keep his activism eternally relevant to black abolitionists. (Courtesy
of the Library Company of Philadelphia)

was to pass on the wisdom he had accumulated in life. According to
biblical scholars, Psalm 37 is best characterized as a "wisdom Psalm."
"In this category . . . the priests were teachers of the religious traditions
of which they were custodians and guardians." More particularly, wisdom Psalms taught that "faithful obedience to the revealed will of God
brings material and spiritual prosperity."[32] As a version of the wisdom

Psalm, Allen's autobiography underscores not just the importance of piety but the necessity of collective black struggle in Western culture.

Of course, autobiography already had a long tradition by the time Allen wrote his, and Allen had many other literary models from which to draw: spiritual autobiographies (including works by Methodist founder John Wesley), Afro-British autobiographies (including multiple editions of Olaudah Equiano's life story, which had circulated in Philadelphia during the 1780s and 1790s), and American autobiographies (including Benjamin Franklin's iconic uplift narrative of his life).[33] Indeed, if he just missed the explosion of the slave-narrative genre in the decades leading up to the Civil War, Allen still worked at a propitious moment in American letters. Beginning in the 1820s, Americans sought to collect their memories of growing up, and helping to build, the new republic. The fiftieth anniversary of the American Revolution marked an obvious point of reflection for statesmen and cultural elites. But the movement to remember the republic's early history took root among an incredible array of people—laborers, lawyers, obscure politicians, businessmen, farmers, soldiers.[34] Throughout his life, Allen had wanted to get African American history down on paper and away from the margins. Now his narrative gave a historical face to black founders.

Still, Allen produced no conventional text. This "small detail" of his long and extraordinary life amounted to just seventy pages, only a third of which recounted Allen's upbringing and spiritual strivings. The rest of the document mixed previously published political protest with narratives of religious witness (what Allen termed "Acts of Faith," "Acts of Hope," and "Acts of Love"). Of the autobiographical musings, Allen created only fourteen pages of new material; the remaining ten pages, dealing with the formation of Allen's church, came directly from *The Doctrines and Discipline of the AME Church* that Allen had originally co-written in 1817 with Joseph Tapsico. In fact, the autobiography stopped with the formation of the AME Church in 1816 and included no recollections of the 1820s and 1830s. This was far from a master narrative of the great man's life—something akin to Frederick Douglass's constantly updated autobiographies. Rather, Allen's last book was a relatively short and varied collection of scenes covering significant parts of his life and protest.

This is not so surprising. Because African American writers have routinely been defined outside mainstream history and culture from Allen's time to our own, many of them experiment with hybrid autobiographical genres, picking and choosing among styles.[35] Allen did not wish, for example, to render his life in the form of the eighteenth-century slave narrative, which highlighted Afro-Christian conversion but also ended with an enslaved person's freedom (a trait that also characterized ante-bellum American slave narratives). Allen spent just a few pages on his life in bondage, famously noting that "slavery is a bitter pill." The rest of his story dealt with black freedom. Allen also did not wish to write merely a spiritual narrative that emphasized his Christian conversion and search for moral perfection—that would leave out the key elements of racial reform.

Allen wanted to tell a story that had not yet been told: black found-ers' rise in early national America. It is easy to forget that Allen's was the first autobiography written by a free black leader in nineteenth-century culture. No other black founder left a personal narrative—not Prince Hall, not Paul Cuffee, not even Allen's great friend Absalom Jones. (Even the last two black founders, Peter Williams, Jr., and James Forten, did not leave autobiographies after they died in 1840 and 1842, respectively.) With no models available, Allen probably struggled to find his form.

So he mixed and matched genres. As a way of conveying his wide-ranging activism, for example, Allen reprinted some of his classic politi-cal tracts: the African Supplement, "A Narrative of the . . . Coloured People" during the yellow-fever epidemic, the 1794 antislavery appeal ("To Those Who Keep Slaves and Approve the Practice"), and the 1794 "Address to the People of Colour." By publishing these documents, Allen gave his historical endeavors a palpable "present tense" feeling. Like the story of Exodus, they were not merely about a storied past; rather, their eternal truths allowed contemporary black activists a way of understanding the modern world of race relations and their place in it. God was indeed just, Allen's documents argued—but that was not enough. According to the Gospel of Richard Allen, racial justice would occur only through collective black struggle.

Significantly, Allen placed the African Supplement first among his re-printed works, even though it was not chronologically the first docu-ment he had produced. In doing this, Allen underscored the document's ideological saliency, both to him and to free people of color throughout the United States. Originally crafted in 1807 to reclaim Bethel Church from white authorities, the African Supplement highlighted black self-determination. The document's ringing endorsement of black collective action in the face of white hostility pictured the black masses as a potential political force. As the leader of this black phalanx, Allen appeared relevant to younger reformers who might never meet him. The last line of the Supplement recalled black congregants' declaration of sovereignty at Bethel Church: "And it is hereby agreed, provided, and declared," article 7 stated, "that any article or provision . . . heretofore made and agreed on, inconsistent with, or altered by these present articles [such as white claims to church control], shall be deemed and taken to be repealed and absolutely *void,* so far as they may be inconsistent or altered." In other words, free blacks built the church, and now they would maintain control of it.[36] That was a historic move, Allen made clear, that current generations of black reformers should follow.

He also reprinted the famous yellow-fever pamphlet, though with a revised title. Instead of "A Narrative of the Proceedings of the Black People," Allen now called it "A Narrative of the Proceedings of the Coloured People." This seemingly subtle change made an important distinction in the intellectual life of nineteenth-century black leaders. Whereas "black" connoted evil in Christian theology, "coloured" represented a more refined image. The message? Free people of color had risen above a degraded status.[37] Despite this linguistic alteration, the reprinted yellow-fever narrative made another strong statement about black self-determination. In fact, because he did not cover the yellow-fever episode in his personal narrative, the pamphlet told two historic tales—the first recalling black founders' revisions of Mathew Carey's wrongheaded history of the yellow fever and the second recalling Allen's seminal involvement in the secular struggle for racial justice. Here was a black church leader who expanded his activism beyond the ecclesiastical sphere! Faith and the struggle for justice went hand in hand. The original narrative's last lines assumed a telling guise when reprinted in Allen's autobiography years later: "God and a soldier, all men do adore, in time of war, and not before; When the war is over, and all things righted, God is forgotten, and the soldier slighted."[38] Do not forget the soldierly struggles of black founders, Allen counseled those around him.

Perhaps the most interesting part of the autobiography was Allen's "Address to the People of Colour." Originally appended to the yellow-fever narrative, the essay counseled piety and perseverance among both free and enslaved people. To the free people of color, for example, Allen repeated his moral-uplift plea: "Let your conduct manifest your grati-

tude toward the compassionate masters who have set you free; and let
no rancor or ill-will lodge in your breast for any treatment you may
have received from any [person]." Considering that he had originally
written the yellow-fever document in a more optimistic age—roughly
a decade after the passage of Pennsylvania's gradual abolition act of
1780—this statement to antebellum African Americans might appear to
be out of step with the times. After all, David Walker, who worshiped
Richard Allen, had recently reprinted his own "Appeal to the Colored
Citizens of the World," in which he called for massive black uprising
against racial injustice. With slavery and racial inequality rising, Walker
believed that black leaders could not counsel anything less than a militant response.[39]

So why did Allen republish this rather moderate document and not
his most recent address to the people of color, a rousing pro-emigration
essay presented just a few months prior to his death? The problem tran-
scends document choice, for emigrationism received absolutely no coverage in Allen's life story. (Nor did the Wesley secession crisis, and its
corollary theme of black class conflict, rate mention). If the autobiography had examined his emigrationist musings, Allen may well have become a hero to late-nineteenth- and twentieth-century black nationalists, from Martin Delany to Malcolm X. But he chose not to emphasize
this side of his life. Why?

Scholars can again play the game of "perhaps" here: perhaps Allen's
son removed any references to African, Haitian, or Canadian emigrationism from his father's recollections. This would certainly make sense
in the activist world of the early 1830s, when radical abolitionists vigorously battled not just Southern slavery and Southern masters but the
American Colonization Society. When Allen passed away in 1831, that
struggle had only just begun. But when Allen's son finally published the
document in 1833, radical abolitionism had assumed a more definite
shape and achieved considerable notoriety, not least of all for excoriat-
ing colonizationists. Perhaps Richard Jr. wanted to reshape his father's
image, casting him not as an ambivalent race leader but as an undying
American freedom fighter who set the stage for radical abolitionism.

Just as likely is the possibility that Allen himself wanted a clean slate
at the end of his life. Looking backward to a seemingly simpler time remains a common feature of American autobiography. By reprinting his
1794 address to the people of color, for example, he revisited a more
deferential era when black leaders could speak both to and on behalf

of the masses. Allen may also have hoped to relegate his emigrationist musings (and class/status conflicts within the black community) to
the historical back burner. Although he truly believed that emigration
would open new opportunities for free people of color (and stem internal black discord), Allen did not want to highlight the issue at the end
of his life. With even respected black emigrationists (like former *Freedom's Journal* editor John Russworm) facing ridicule, the topic was too
hot to examine now. By returning to moral-uplift initiatives from early
on, Allen thought he could build a renewed sense of hope among white
as well as black reformers.

Thus did Allen's autobiography instruct free blacks to follow in his
footsteps by working hard, remaining pious, and, in the end, claiming
American society as their own. The subtitle of Allen's autobiography offered an interesting testament to black claims on the American republic:
it was the story of "the rise and progress of the African Methodist Episcopal Church *in the United States of America*" (emphasis added). Similarly, Allen's reprinted "Address to the People of Colour" contained a
cautionary tale for antebellum blacks. Recalling the bitterness that almost consumed him as a young Delaware slave, especially when "the
prospect of liberty almost vanished away and I was in darkness and perplexity," Allen admits that he very nearly chose death over life. "I mention [this] experience to you," he continued, "that your hearts may not
sink at the discouraging prospects you may have and that you may put
your trust in God." Faith in a just God brought salvation to the young
Allen. A similar faith among antebellum slaves, the black preacher argued, would produce miracles.[40]

Ideologically, Allen's autobiography claimed the American nation as
a black homeland at the same moment that support for the American
Colonization Society peaked North as well as South. Would African
Americans ever become part of the nation's civic fabric? Even in Allen's
longtime home of Pennsylvania, the capital of early American abolitionism and the site of the world's first gradual abolition law, white citizens'
doubts about black equality abounded. Evidence came from the black
founder's old nemesis Mathew Carey. Born only a few weeks before
Allen in 1760, the Irishman-turned-American-patriot lived just a few
years longer than the black bishop (he died in 1839). By the 1820s, the
great printer had retired from a prosperous (if contentious) reign as the
prince of American publishers. Nevertheless, Carey remained one of the

early republic's most important public men. And in his later years, Carey embraced African colonization as the republic's saving grace.

Carey became convinced that African Americans had no place in America. Southern slavery would die, he believed, as it should. But he also believed that free blacks must be colonized. Although Carey ardently took up this cause in 1832, he probably became interested in it years earlier. Carey found colonization a convincing way to solve America's race problem. His first pamphlet contained pro-colonizationist information from as far back as 1815—the very time when Allen himself began thinking about African colonization as a way to solve black dilemmas. Indeed, Carey cast an incredulous glance at the 1820s. Americans—black and white—should have totally embraced colonization as soon as the first ship of ex-slaves sailed for Liberia in 1821, he declared. "This publication has been produced," he stated in 1832, "by a conviction that even among those enlightened and opulent citizens who have expressed the warmest approbation of the system of colonization, it has not met with a degree of support in any degree commensurate with the beneficial consequences which . . . it cannot fail to produce." Slave rebellions proved the folly of having "two heterogeneous casts in the same country [slave and master, white and black], without the least probability . . . of an amalgamation." New World abolition, unlike that of the "Greeks and Romans," had to surmount racial obstacles. And this was just not possible.[41]

Carey alarmingly explained that the black population was growing at a faster rate than whites. "It appears," he stated, "that while the slaves nearly tripled their numbers" in a place like South Carolina since 1790, "the whites were only doubled."[42] This only increased the possibilities of successful black rebellion, as slaves gathered strength over time. And, he added, there was the problem of free blacks. They seemed out of place—not citizens, not slaves—while their numbers grew too. Think ahead, Carey continued: if there were 760,000 blacks altogether in 1790 and 2 million in 1830, there might be over 5.5 million by, say, 1860 and 7.4 million in 1870. What should whites do? The answer, Carey claimed, was to embrace colonization. America must become a white man's country.

Life, Experience, and Gospel Labours challenged Carey's logic by depicting African Americans as exemplars of the American dream of attaining uplift and equality. Like the Pilgrim fathers, oppressed blacks had sought religious liberty; like the Revolutionary founders, black founders struggled mightily for political liberty. As Allen's antislavery appeal argued, black abolitionism's seemingly radical call for universal emancipation and equality drew from nothing less than the Bible and the Declaration of Independence. In the person of black founder Richard Allen, African Americans had as legitimate claims on the nation as anyone. In this sense, it is not hard to see Allen worrying once again that the Careys of the world would have the last, misleading word on black struggles for justice unless he published his own narrative.

In replying to age-old fears of black emancipation and equality, Allen's autobiography also revisited the theme of interracial activism. While his reprinted antislavery appeal—"To Those Who Keep Slaves and Approve the Practice"—strongly condemned bondage, it also pictured religion as a bridge of understanding between the races. In addition, Allen republished "A Short Address to the Friends of Him Who Hath No Helper," a brief salute to early white abolitionists like Benjamin Rush and Warner Mifflin. Both of these documents looked forward as well as backward, emphasizing the absolute necessity of white aid in the struggle against American bondage. Indeed, Allen may have been challenging younger generations of white reformers to check their claims to originality. For antebellum abolitionists who often pictured themselves as antislavery innovators—such as William Lloyd Garrison—Allen's text offered a history lesson: he was there first. In fact, Allen's words from 1794 could have been plucked from Garrison's *Liberator* in the 1830s: "You feel our afflictions," he had commented about early white abolitionists.

> you sympathize with us in the heart-rending distress, when the husband is separated from the wife, and the parents from the children, who are never more to meet in this world. . . . Your righteous indignation is roused at the means taken to supply the place of the murdered babe. . . . you blow the trumpet against the mighty evil; you make the tyrants tremble. . . . You ask for this, nothing for yourselves, nothing but what is worthy the cause you are engaged in."[43]

Considering that early abolition societies remained segregated, refusing to accept the likes of Allen, Jones, and Forten, the black preacher's words may appear prescriptive too: great things are expected from white allies in the 1830s. Immediate abolitionists who promised to treat black activists as "co-adjutors" of the new movement must not betray African Americans.[44]

Allen's religious commentary further underscored his belief in the biblical ideal that "the Lord has made of one blood all nations" (Acts 17:26). He placed three short religious testimonials—"Acts of Faith," "Acts of Hope," and "Acts of Love"—before the 1794 "Address to the People of Colour." These articles of faith not only testified to Allen's belief in an all-powerful and redeeming God but also conveyed his continuing conviction in the evangelical awakening of his youth—an awakening whose interracial precepts were now being repeated in the massive revivals of the 1820s and 1830s. Though he preached at camp meetings into his late sixties, Allen cherished decades-old memories of interracial revivals in Maryland, Delaware, Pennsylvania, and New Jersey. The autobiography celebrated the many white figures with whom the young black man had preached, dined, prayed, and even lived, making those hopeful days among the most significant in Allen's life.[45]

With the Second Great Awakening in full swing by the time Allen constructed his autobiography, he reminded readers that he was a powerful moralist who could speak to white as well as black audiences. Whether rich or poor, black or white, male or female, Americans were moral free agents who could embrace God's commandments or ignore them at their peril. For the first time in his literary career, in fact, Allen wrote as a moral perfectionist. Demonstrating a keen understanding of the religious rhetoric circulating on the antebellum revivalist circuit, Allen lectured anyone who would listen on the perils of covetousness, pride, and irreligiosity. "How can my hopes of everlasting life be well grounded," he wondered at one point, "if I do not [constantly] strive and labor for that eternal inheritance [of Heaven]?"[46] The answer came in working selflessly to uphold the Lord's prayer. "With [what] great reason did our Saviour so solemnly charge his disciples to beware of covetousness, since we see it borders so nearly upon infidelity?" he asked in another portion of the autobiography. The answer came in understanding Christian charity, which eschewed selfish accumulation of worldly goods. "How strangely inconsistent is the narrow-hearted man with himself, with his own settled principles!"[47] As Allen observed in still another passage on perfection, "Our blessed Lord has not committed his goods to us as a dead stock, to be hoarded up, or to lie profitably in our own hands. He expects that we should put them out to proper and beneficial uses."[48]

As a Christian moralist nearing the end of his life, Allen wanted to make sure that the fundamental elements of his faith remained visible to everyone. As Allen concluded, "the love of this world is a heavy weight upon the soul, which chains her down and prevents her flight towards heaven." Charitable work compelled a "disengagement" with the secular realm, allowing the soul to "mount upwards." In the end, this was the only way to "qualify" for heaven.[49] Even when speaking of moral perfection, Allen did not fail to appeal to interracial harmony. Christ's greatest commandment, Allen said, was "that ye love one another. By this shall all men know that ye are my disciples, if ye have love for one another. This is my command, that ye love one another as I have loved you" (John 13:34). For white as well as black citizens, Allen's autobiography issued a last great call for empathy and equality.[50]

Although not as expansive or emotionally charged as subsequent black autobiographies, Allen's narrative remains an inspiring tale. He conjured many memorable images. Recalling his difficult conversion experience, Allen stated that when he accepted the Lord as his savior, "all of a sudden my dungeon shook, my chains flew off, and glory to God, I cried." His soul now "filled," Allen felt compelled to go "from house to house, exhorting my old companions, and telling to all around what a dear Savior I had found." Similarly, Allen's memory of his freedom moment has become iconic: Allen's second master agreed to let the young slave buy his freedom after hearing a soul-searching sermon that concluded with these fateful words: "thou art weighed in the balance and found wanting." With that phrase, Allen neatly summarized black abolitionists' most stunning reminder to masters, that the Lord would wreak divine vengeance for the sin of slaveholding.[51] This line of thinking alone made Allen's autobiography relevant to the next generation of black reformers, for it established in print the founding principles of liberation theology: God was on the side of the oppressed.[52] Allen certainly wanted to remind black reformers about their moral obligations to love their enemies. But that message could be easily drowned out in an increasingly polarized antebellum political culture. Still shining, however, was the inspirational story of a black leader who had overcome great odds to achieve much. Just as Ben Franklin's autobiography sanctified the American work ethic, so too did Allen's autobiography sanctify black struggle and protest.

If Allen's autobiography had no immediate predecessors among black founders, it foreshadowed at least one major black leader's personal narrative: Frederick Douglass. Indeed, Allen's constant shifting of genres anticipated Frederick Douglass's second major work, *My Bondage and My Freedom*. Written a decade after his first autobiography (*Narrative of the Life of Frederick Douglass, a Slave*, 1845), this new rendition sealed Douglass's status as the premier antebellum black activist. As John Stauffer has observed, Douglass radically "altered his narrative framework" in *My Bondage and My Freedom*, particularly by shifting personas. Whereas the first part of the book recounted Douglass's "life as a slave" through a relatively seamless narrative of events (artfully rendered, as always, by Douglass), the second part detailed his "life as a freeman" by reprinting an appendix of speeches. Stauffer comments that Douglass was "struggling to create a new genre and find an appropriate style for representing himself as a freeman." Just as for Allen, the traditional slave-narrative genre was confining to a black person seeking to unleash his or her inner self and detail the triumphs and tragedies of freedom in America.[53]

In Douglass's case, the narrative section of *My Bondage and My Freedom* stopped when he broke from white reformer William Lloyd Garrison's camp, several years after he had attained liberty. To highlight his activist career beyond Garrison, Douglass republished his political speeches chronologically, taking the reader right up to the moment he authored the second autobiography in 1855. "Douglass [now] presents himself as a performer," Stauffer wonderfully concludes, "a successful black orator—unadorned, as it were, unmediated by a narrator." This was the only way that Douglass could capture "the fragmented evolution of [his contemporary] public persona": a black man whose life could not be reduced to a past in slavery and who now struggled for equality as a free person of color in antebellum America.[54]

Allen faced a similar conundrum in constructing his autobiography. His life was multifaceted and complex—and it could not be reduced to a single label: church builder, political activist, Christian moralist, freed slave. In death, as in life, Allen wanted to remain a vibrant presence in the many communities to which he belonged. He was an African, an American, a former slave, a Christian, a prophet, an institutional founder, an abolitionist. *Life, Experience, and Gospel Labours* attempted to capture all these personas while emphasizing the two bedrock themes of his life: faith in God and collective black struggle.

"Whoever hopes for great things in this world," Allen wrote, "takes pains to attain them."[55] The black preacher had hoped for much and paid a price for his many exertions. He now gave his life story to the ages.

4. *Death*

When Richard Allen passed away at the age of seventy-one on March 26, 1831, black Philadelphia stopped in its tracks. The bishop was known to have been ailing, but this measure of finality caught even his brethren by surprise. Bishop Morris Brown, who owed his career to Allen after the celebrated preacher opened his house and church to the South Carolinian following the Denmark Vesey slave rebellion, took three days to convene a special meeting about how best to honor the black founder. This delay spoke volumes about Allen's missing presence. Allen had always been there, it seemed, to smarten people up. What would Afro-Philadelphians do now that he was gone?

The immediate question revolved around honoring Allen. A deeply religious man who forswore religious adornments and fussy birthday celebrations, Allen did not want a massive funeral. Morris Brown certainly knew Allen's beliefs on the matter. Brown headed the Union Benevolent Sons of Mother Bethel Church, a charitable organization that oversaw church burials, aided those who could not afford funerals, and served as caretakers of Bethel Cemetery plots. The Benevolent Sons had started in 1826 with Bishop Allen's encouragement and support. When Allen's funeral came, there was to be nothing fancy, nothing extraordinary. Nevertheless, as Brown well knew, the black founder's death must be marked in some proper way!

The Benevolent Sons finally convened a special meeting on March 29. The group asked the Union Church Society, another Bethel charitable organization, to attend. This august group of leaders assembled down the street from Bethel Church (at another hall owned by the AME) to debate all the options. One person suggested that AME members "wear crapes on their badges" as a sign of respect. That motion was defeated as too elaborate. After more deliberation, church leaders agreed on a simple declaration. They would "meet . . . and form a processional to the funeral of the late Bishop." No pomp, no circumstance. Allen well-wishers could follow the processional as they saw fit. Morris

Brown made another announcement: the Benevolent Sons would not have to expend one penny for Allen's burial, "the charitableness of the bishop" having filled funeral coffers in advance. Even in death, Richard Allen's determination and will were too strong to ignore.[56]

Needless to say, word of the processional spread quickly throughout the black community. Allen's funeral turned out to be a grand affair. "The immense concourse of colored people who attended the funeral of this pious patriarch exceeded perhaps anything of the kind witnessed in this country," one observer recalled. "No other African corpse . . . was ever attended to the place of internment in America by so great a number of more sincere mourners."[57]

Allen's death was reported in several papers, though no Philadelphia daily did more than state facts. *Poulson's Daily Advertiser,* which had reported on the death of Allen's first wife thirty years before, carried a short notice on March 31, 1831, five days after his passing. "Died, the Reverend Richard Allen, first bishop of the AME church, departed this life on Saturday . . . about 20 minutes before six o'clock in the afternoon, aged 71 years." *Poulson's* also noted that Allen's "friends and relatives are respectfully invited to attend his funeral this morning at nine o'clock, from his late dwelling, 150 Spruce St." The *Philadelphia Gazette and Daily Advertiser* had a similar notice the day before. Several other mainstream Philadelphia papers reported nothing.[58]

Among reform papers, both the *Genius of Universal Emancipation* and the recently inaugurated radical abolitionist journal the *Liberator* offered more extended treatments of Allen's death—but not much. So busy was Garrison with the new antislavery struggle that the *Liberator* actually apologized for not having spent more time on this great man's death. "Perhaps some of our Philadelphia friends will favor us with a notice," he suggested.[59]

For those who read significance into dates, Allen died only a few days before Easter. If people were too busy to take notice at precisely that moment, then Allen's spirit would surely be resurrected in the future, as countless black abolitionists, AME ministers, and civil rights reformers would call on his memory to validate the struggle for racial justice. As one black Ohioan said with little fanfare but great cogency at the close of the Civil War, it was none other than "Richard Allen, the great pioneer of the A.M.E. Church, with the spirit of inspiration, diffused through every part of his physical organization, [who] felt that God had made of one blood all men to dwell on the face of the earth and that all men are created free and equal that they are endowed by their Creator with certain inalienable rights, that among these, are life, liberty and the pursuit of happiness." "Liberty was his object," the Ohioan finished. Long since gone, Allen would never be forgotten, taking his freedom-loving views to the very "shores of the heavenly world."[60]

Conclusion
Richard Allen and the Soul of Black Reform

In the summer of 1853, the *Pennsylvania Freemen* reported a miraculous occurrence: the great Richard Allen was haunting the slave South. The abolitionist paper based its report on a Southern correspondent who worriedly watched as blacks in New Orleans founded educational groups and autonomous churches "in direct violation of the laws of the state." "Bishop Allen, of Philadelphia, occasionally visits [here]," the Southern observer continued, "to look after the fortunes of his black flock, and no doubt infuses into them a spirit of hostility to the whites, and counsels them against holding any intercourse with the hated and despised race that has so long tyrannized over the descendants of Ham." When understood in the context of radical abolition, the publication of *Uncle Tom's Cabin,* and rising slave restiveness, Allen's haunting could only be considered part of a broader "evil" that hovered over slavery and the American republic—the "evil" of black abolitionism and equality.

After letting the white writer's image of a resurrected Allen briefly take hold of readers' imagination, the abolitionist editor commented on the black preacher's earthly mission and legacy:

Now, sir, it is well known in this and other communities, that Bishop Allen, of Philadelphia, has been deceased over twenty-two years. He never while living visited Louisiana, his business never calling him there, nor in the vicinity of this foul-mouthed slanderer of the dead. He was a man respected in all parts of the world, by all creeds and denominations—even by the slaveholder. When attending annually to his spiritual concerns in the South, he was, as I have frequently seen, and heard him say, respected as much as any man he met with. It appears that since the publication of Poor Tom's Cabin, that the agents of the devil don't know whether to begin on earth or in heaven to get subjects for direction.[1]

The *Pennsylvania Freeman* then republished Allen's 1794 antislavery appeal in its entirety, highlighting slavery—and not abolitionism—as the true evil haunting American society. Once again, Allen's words rang out for their cogency and eloquence. "If you love your children, if you love your country, if you love the God of love," he had originally intoned in the Age of Jefferson, and now again in the Age of Lincoln, "clear your hands from slaves, burthen not your children or your country with them."[2] For Allen and radical abolitionists alike, emancipation was saintly and utterly American. And embodied in a black founder like Allen, emancipation was as old as the nation itself.

As this pre–Civil War exchange illustrates, Allen's image could easily be called on at significant moments in the nation's struggle with racial injustice. Nineteenth-century black abolitionists knew this better than anyone. In 1855, James McCune Smith, perhaps the leading black intellectual and scientist of the age—fluent in several languages, he was also the first African American physician (graduating from the University of Glasgow in Scotland)—hailed Allen as the very soul of black reform. Writing in *Frederick Douglass's Paper,* a Rochester-based monthly magazine that supplanted the *North Star,* McCune Smith recognized the black founder as a representative figure of an ever-expanding spirit of "human freedom" in the Atlantic world. For anyone who doubted this notion, McCune Smith invited readers to visit "the corner of Lombard and sixth streets" in Philadelphia, where Bethel Church still stood. "It is," he wrote, "on the site of a revolution or reform, which happened 70 years ago, a reform which, in grasp of free thought, determined energy, spiritual Majesty, holy zeal, and gospel of truthfulness, equaled, if it did not excel, any kindred event in the history of humankind." "Like some Iona in the midst of the brutal barbarism of American Christianity," he grandly concluded, referring to the tiny Scottish island that became the cornerstone of Catholicism during the Dark Ages, Allen and his church forged new directions for both African American and American liberty.[3]

Famed black abolitionist and congressman John Mercer Langston made a similar claim at the end of Reconstruction. Asked to speak at an Allen memorial ceremony in 1876, the year that Philadelphia proudly hosted an exhibition celebrating the centennial of American independence, Langston hailed Allen as among America's original "abolition worthies"—and a man whose equalitarian spirit and moral courage was needed more than ever. "All nations, all races of men delight to honor their mighty dead," he observed, as a bust of Allen was placed at Bethel Church. This occasion, Langston declared, marked the first time that African Americans from around the country had produced a public statue of a black hero. Allen was a most fitting figure with which to begin publicly memorializing black history. Not so ironically, the very struggle to bring the Allen monument to Philadelphia during the nation's hundredth birthday revisited the black founder's own attempts to transcend the marginalization of African American protest culture. The head of the Philadelphia exposition demanded that the magnificent bust of Allen—produced by the mixed-race sculptor Edmonia Lewis—must be moved a month after the event ended. Mother Bethel, and not a public park, became the statue's forever home.[4]

Nevertheless, Allen's apotheosis as an African American patriot took root well after his death, as black reformers searched for icons who could bolster their claims to full citizenship. Indeed, for black abolitionists both before and after the Civil War, Allen was the representative African American: the consummate race man whose rise from slavery to freedom contained the ultimate expression of American genius. Following themes established in Allen's autobiography, they saw the black founder not as a divided soul but as a perfect foil to the American Colonization Society's argument that free black and white citizens could never live together peaceably—that African Americans were a degraded and dangerous people who must remain subjugated or be exported well beyond the United States. Not only did Allen claim an American identity during the Revolutionary era—in other words, at the nation's birth —he espoused interracial brotherhood throughout much of his life.

As usual, Frederick Douglass offered the most commanding black abolitionist salute to Allen during the late nineteenth century. Becoming increasingly accustomed to memorializing heroic racial reformers after the Civil War—Lincoln, Garrison, Henry Highland Garnet—the aged Douglass gave one of his last memorable literary performances in a February 1894 celebration of Allen. Though born in 1818 on an Eastern Shore Maryland plantation, Douglass never actually met Allen. But he knew of the black founder's fame even before reaching Northern freedom (his first wife was an AME adherent). Over time, he grew to respect Allen's ideas, particularly the black preacher's claim that America was a black homeland. For Douglass, who long battled the coloniza-tionist menace, Allen provided a weighty rebuttal to the notion that America was a white man's country. In his tribute, Douglass called Allen nothing less than the author of a "new Declaration of Indepen-dence" and racial equality.[5]

Douglass had apparently been thinking about Allen's significance for some time. In September 1893, he memorialized the black founder at the Chicago World's Fair. "Among the remarkable men whose names have found deserved place in American annals," he commented, "there is not one who will be longer remembered or whose memory will be more sacredly cherished by coming generations of colored Americans than will the name and character of Richard Allen." Douglass had care-fully prepared his speech by revising several typewritten drafts. At one point, he forgot to note that Allen considered himself to be a "citizen" of the then-still-slaveholding American republic—a mistake he quickly corrected with a scratch of the pen. At a time when Douglass meditated on the post–Civil War "lesson of the hour" for black and white Ameri-cans, the great reformer thought that Allen's example remained eter-nally relevant. The black founder believed that African Americans were entitled to full citizenship and equality in American society and that, contrary to the fears of white founders like Jefferson, emancipation would work if only white citizens followed the dictates of both Christi-anity and the Declaration of Independence. "There is therefore reason to believe," Douglass concluded, "that were Richard Allen alive today surrounded by the improved conditions which now surround the col-ored people in this country, he would be the leader of his people now precisely as he was in his day and generation." From the post-Revolu-tionary reconstruction of race relations to postbellum Reconstruction itself, Douglass made clear, Allen's dream of interracial harmony still resonated.[6]

If nineteenth-century reformers hailed Allen as a founding represen-tative of black abolitionism—the notion that full equality must follow emancipation—then many twentieth-century writers viewed him as per-haps the original black liberationist. As times changed, and a succession of new issues arose (the fate of black labor, international anticolonial-ism, the meaning of black art in modernist circles), Allen remained rele-vant to new generations of activists. At the turn of the century, W. E. B. Du Bois celebrated Allen's liberationist Christian ethics as a model for rising black reformers. Prior to the advent of the African Methodist

Episcopal Church, Du Bois famously wrote in *The Souls of Black Folk,* Christianity was a religion of masters and a pacifying faith for slaves. In the hands of Allen (and other black founders), Afro-Christianity became a liberationist creed, brimming with confidence about racial justice in an age when most white leaders doubted black equality. If his contemporaries (read: Booker T. Washington) channeled the black founder's insurgent mentality, Du Bois implied, then they might well achieve Allen's dream of universal equality.[7]

James Baldwin, writing on the centennial of Lincoln's Emancipation Proclamation, called Allen one of the great "poets" of black aspiration. Using Allen's liberationist phraseology as the keynote to his own life in letters—"my dungeon shook, my chains flew off," he mimed in *The Fire Next Time*—Baldwin alluded to Allen's significance as a lyricist of the black experience. Not simply a church builder or religious man, Allen was the first in a long line of black leaders who attempted to liberate black identity from the shackles of white perception and make the black experience itself revolutionary and transformative for the nation as a whole. "Great men have done great things here," Baldwin wrote to his young nephew (and symbolically to the rising generation of civil rights protesters in 1963) in the preface to his searing book, "and will again, and we can make America what America must become."[8]

Baldwin, like a growing roster of black leaders during the modern civil rights era, saw black suffering as redemptive. In this view, he borrowed not simply from the towering figures around him but from the black founder. Allen, like Baldwin (and Martin Luther King, Jr.) argued that blacks' will to overcome oppression had profound consequences for American destiny. Like Baldwin (and even King in his later years), Allen had grave doubts about his ability to truly liberate white citizens from centuries of antiblack racism. But Baldwin revered Allen precisely because the black founder refused to yield blacks' moral authority. Perhaps that is why Baldwin, who grew up in the black church but then left it behind as he matured as both a writer and intellectual, so cherished Allen's image. For Baldwin, Allen's redemptive prophecies and iron will steeled all those who came after him, secular reformers no less than the faithful.

Without even mentioning his name, other modern commentators followed Allen's lead: African Americans served as America's moral conscience. "If a label must be attached in my leadership," the Reverend Jesse Jackson declared in 1976, "as a minister of the Gospel I prefer 'moral leader.' Moral leadership, which essentially deals with ideas and values, is a universal category."[9] Ralph Ellison, author of *The Invisible Man* as well as some of the most insightful (and still underappreciated) essays on the many meanings of black identity, offers perhaps the best example of someone who modified Allen's thought for a new age. For Ellison, as for Allen, African Americans were destined to be the country's—the world's—moral doppelganger. "When the white American . . . says, 'this is American reality,' the Negro tends to answer . . . 'perhaps, but you've left out this, and this, and this. And most of all, what you'd have the world accept as *me* isn't even human,' " Ellison (reared in an AME home) wrote in 1953.[10] Allen said almost exactly the same thing in 1794 when he pointed out that whites "stigmatize us as men, whose baseness is incurable, and may therefore he held in a state of servitude, that a merciful man would not deem a beast to." Yet, Allen finished, "you try what you can to prevent our rising from the state of barbarism you represent us to be in."[11] But, Allen shot back, black humanity would always shine through racial oppression. Years before Ellison's amazing book, Allen sought to raise African Americans—and blackness itself—from invisibility to triumph.

Allen would be quite comfortable with these multiple (and not mutually exclusive) visions of his founding fame: black abolitionist and patriot, liberationist, redemptive visionary. Indeed, though always a pious Methodist, he never doubted that his leadership had secular consequences. In this sense, Allen can be labeled a founding figure of many black "isms" aimed at emancipating, redeeming, and uplifting the race: black liberalism (for his emphasis on civil rights and socioeconomic equity as the keys to African American redemption), black communalism (for his continued emphasis on group autonomy and uplift), black nationalism (for his early focus on race pride and his later emphasis on black emigration), and even black conservatism (for his long-standing emphasis on the principles of moral uplift and achievement). At the base of each of these beliefs is the notion that the modern black condition required visionary leadership. As Michael Dawson, one of the leading interpreters of African American political ideology, has argued, virtually "all black ideological visions" converge at a similar notion: the American nation was not (is not yet) a land of universal freedom, a "Shining City Upon a Hill."[12]

Nevertheless, Dawson (like other theorists of black ideology) does not spend much time on Allen or black founders as the progenitors of many of the ideologies he examines. This is perhaps understandable, for Allen was not an intellectual given to extended meditations on the black condition. In addition, in our post-civil-rights age of identity politics, Allen appears to be the representative figure not of a broad-based political ideology but of black autonomy and African communalism.

And so how in the end should we understand Allen? I think he is best remembered as the nation's first black prophetic leader. Generally, prophetic leadership emphasizes a people's or a nation's destiny. Prophetic leaders have crowded the American past. Both colonial and Revolutionary-era founders foretold America's redeeming role in world culture. Puritan John Winthrop's famous 1630 shipboard sermon ("Modell of Christian Charity") outlined perhaps the first vision of the American Promised Land. Ever since, statesmen, writers, and reformers have been reimagining the nation's grand destiny.[13]

Black prophetic leadership has historically critiqued American glorification in favor of a broader vision of national salvation.[14] Black prophetic leaders have been integrationists and nationalists, religious visionaries and secular prophets. Moreover, although black prophetic leaders like Allen coveted biblical understandings of blacks as agents of divine history, their protest thought flowed very much from modernity. Allen's activism depended on technology (print culture), democratic political theory (group mobilization and allegiance), and ideological sophistication (from liberal black nationalist beliefs to variations of black power). Like nearly every black prophetic leader who followed him, Allen used these tools of modernity to engage in a searching examination of the American racial state. He highlighted race as America's original sin and African Americans as the nation's redemptive conscience.

Seeing Allen as a black prophetic leader, rather than an ideologically limited reformer, allows us to respect his evolving activism as well as his foundational concern with achieving black freedom and justice.[15] Allen's rather elliptical journey, moving back and forth between positions of nationalism and civic integration, prefigured the struggles of Frederick Douglass, W. E. B. Du Bois, Martin Luther King, Jr., and others. When young, each of these men prophesied a black future predicated on liberal notions of postemancipation race relations. And they all believed that black consciousness-raising activities would change white views of African Americans. The failure of liberal idealism led all these figures to more complex views of the black condition, including flirtations with black emigration, black nationalism, and socialism.

Although it may seem like a superficial way to end a biography of Allen, it is not too much to say that he was a forerunner of the most famous black prophetic leader in American history, Martin Luther King, Jr. Like Allen, King matured within the Christian Church before becoming a spokesperson for civil rights. Also like King, Allen's early activism—establishing the AME Church—overwhelms his more radical later years (King's socialist phase versus Allen's embrace of black emigrationism). And both leaders were accused at some point in their careers of being disconnected from the grassroots.

Yet both men defined the era of black protest in which they matured. And they both helped define the broader black freedom struggle as a vital part of the American experiment. Neither Allen nor King retreated to the confines of his church. Rather, they utilized their increasingly prominent positions to levy broader moral critiques on the American nation. King called black suffering redemptive for the American soul in the same way that Allen argued that black freedom was the true barometer of the success (or failure) of American democracy. In the hands of both Allen and King, African American history was both progressive and inspirational. "The problem of race and color prejudice remains America's greatest moral dilemma," Martin Luther King declared in a 1962 speech. "When one considers the impact it has upon our nation, internally and externally, its resolution might well determine our destiny."[16] Over a century and a half before that, Allen told white Americans that resolving the dilemma of liberty and slavery, of racial iniquity in the land of supposed freedom, would tell the tale of the nation's destiny. "It is in our posterity enjoying the same privileges with your own," he observed in tones that prefigured King's "I Have a Dream" speech, "that you should look for better things."[17]

In his famous study of slavery in the age of democratic revolution, David Brion Davis ended by referring to the racial ramifications of the early-nineteenth-century German philosopher G. W. F. Hegel's *Phenomenology of Mind*. Davis writes, "it was Hegel's genius to endow lordship and bondage with such a rich resonance of meanings that the model could be applied to every form of physical and psychological domination." In doing so, according to Davis, "Hegel bequeathed the message that would have a profound impact on future thought," particularly the notion that "man's true emancipation, whether physical or spiritual, must always depend on those who have endured and overcome some form of slavery."[18] Davis's thrilling insights are only half right, for Americans did not really need the philosophical observations of European thinkers to confront the paradox of slavery and freedom, mastery and liberty in a nation dedicated to equality. Indeed, black founders like Richard Allen had already linked black struggles for justice to American and global liberation. The nation we inhabit today—multiracial but far from beyond the conundrum of race as a defining feature of national consciousness—is as much a product of Allen's prophetic soul as Hegel's, or Jefferson's.

Notes

NOTES TO THE INTRODUCTION

1. Gary B. Nash, "New Light on Richard Allen: The Early Years of Freedom," *William and Mary Quarterly*, 3rd series, vol. 46, no. 2 (April 1989): 332–40; Charles Wesley, *Richard Allen: Apostle of Freedom* (Washington, D.C., 1935).

2. Mother Bethel Church pastor Jeffrey N. Leath, monthly letter, October 1993, in Bethel Archives, misc. archives.

3. David Walker, "Appeal to the Colored Citizens of the World" (Boston, 1830), reprinted in Richard Newman, Patrick Rael, and Phillip Lapsansky, eds., *Pamphlets of Protest* (New York, 2000), 97–99; Rev. John M. Palmer, "Was Richard Allen Great?" (Philadelphia, 1898), 1–10.

4. "Rev. Richard Allen, Founder of the African Methodist Episcopal Church," engraving published by "J. Dainty," Philadelphia, 1813, with words inscribed anonymously afterward.

5. Stokeley Sturgis wrote a quasi-pass on behalf of Allen on August 27, 1783, vouching for his character for those who might meet the young preacher on his travels. A copy of this little-known document is held in the Richard Allen Museum, Bethel Archives.

6. Wyman speech, reprinted in the *Christian Recorder*, February 8, 1865.

7. Turpin speech, reprinted in the *Christian Recorder*, November 25, 1865.

8. See report of "Allen Day" in the *Christian Recorder*, February 18, 1865.

9. In addition to Wesley's work on Allen, see Carol V. R. George, *Segregated Sabbaths: Richard Allen and the Rise of Independent Black Churches, 1760–1840* (New York, 1973); Gary B. Nash, *Forging Freedom: The Formation of Philadelphia's Black Community, 1720–1840* (Cambridge, Mass., 1988), which contains a wealth of great information on Allen's rise to prominence; Albert J. Raboteau, *A Fire in the Bones: Reflections on African American Religious History* (New York, 1999), which features a wonderful section on Allen as a church builder; and Dee E. Andrews, *The Methodists and Revolutionary America, 1760–1800* (Princeton, N.J., 2000), which provides many terrific insights on Allen and African Methodism.

10. For the best books on eighteenth-century African-American figures, see

Douglas Egerton, *Gabriel's Rebellion* (Chapel Hill, N.C., 1996); John Saillant, *Black Puritan, Black Republican: The Life and Thought of Lemuel Haynes, 1753–1833* (New York, 2002); and Julie Winch, *A Gentleman of Color: The Life of James Forten* (New York, 2002). For terrific black Atlantic world biographies, see Madison Smart Bell, *Toussaint L'Ouverture: A Biography* (New York, 2007); Vincent Carretta, *Equiano, the African* (Athens, Ga., 2006); and Jon F. Sensbach, *Rebecca's Revival: Creating Black Christianity in the Atlantic World* (Cambridge, Mass., 2005).

11. David Levering Lewis, *W. E. B. Du Bois: Biography of a Race, 1867–1919* (New York, 1993).

12. The classic study remains Arthur Zilversmit, *The First Emancipation: The Abolition of Slavery in the North* (Chicago, 1967).

13. See Benjamin Quarles's great book, *The Negro in the American Revolution* (Chapel Hill, N.C., 1996); and Sylvia R. Frey, *Water from the Rock: Black Resistance in a Revolutionary Age* (Princeton, N.J., 1993).

14. As notes in succeeding chapters illustrate, there is an increasingly rich literature on early national emancipation. A great place to start is Joanne P. Melish, *Disowning Slavery: Gradual Emancipation and "Race" in New England, 1780–1860* (Ithaca, N.Y., 1998).

15. See Daniel A. Payne, *A History of the African Methodist Episcopal Church* (Nashville, Tenn., 1893), 85. Henry Highland Garnet recalled Allen in the *Christian Recorder,* February 20, 1869. I am indebted to John Stauffer of Harvard University for showing me this wonderful description of Allen.

16. Garnet, *Christian Recorder.*

17. Ibid.

18. Richard Allen, *The Life, Experience, and Gospel Labours of the Rt. Rev. Richard Allen. To Which Is Annexed the Rise and Progress of the African Methodist Episcopal Church in the United States of America. Containing a Narrative of the Yellow Fever in the Year of Our Lord 1793: With an Address to the People of Colour in the United States* (Philadelphia: Martin & Boden, 1833) (hereafter cited as LEGL), 16.

19. *Freedom's Journal,* February 22, 1828.

20. LEGL, 50.

21. On the history of liberation theology among slaves and free people of color, see James H. Cone, *Black Theology and Black Power* (New York, 1969). See also Dwight N. Hopkins and George Cummings, eds., *Cut Loose Your Stammering Tongue: Black Theology in the Slave Narratives* (Maryknoll, N.Y., 1991).

22. Richard Allen, "An Address to Those Who Keep Slaves and Approve the Practice" (originally published in 1794 in Absalom Jones and Richard Allen, "A Narrative of the Proceedings of the Black People during the Late Awful Calam-

ity in Philadelphia, in the Year 1793"), reprinted in Newman, Rael, and Lap-sansky, *Pamphlets of Protest*, 41–42.

23. See, especially, Raboteau, *A Fire in the Bones*, 26–38.

24. Ira Berlin's critical and beautifully written book, *Generations of Captivity: A History of African-American Slaves* (New York, 2003), especially the pro-logue, makes a powerful case for reading free blacks as essentially maroons.

25. On the significance of Caribbean slave rebels in the creation of a demo-cratic society, see especially Laurent Dubois, *Avengers of the New World: The Story of the Haitian Revolution* (Cambridge, Mass., 2004), prologue.

26. For a magnificent analysis of slaveholders' pre–Civil War fears, see Wil-liam W. Freehling, Preface to *Road to Disunion*, vol. 2, *Secessionists Trium-phant* (New York, 2007).

27. Psalm 37:37 is printed on the title page of LEGL; emphasis in original.

28. See Payne, *History of the AME Church*, 85–86.

29. See "Some Letters of Richard Allen and Absalom Jones to Dorothy Rip-ley," *Journal of Negro History* 1, no. 4 (1916): 436–43.

30. John Edgar Wideman, *The Cattle Killing* (New York, 1996), 157.

31. Paula J. Giddings, "Lives of the Poets," a review of *Lyrics of Sunshine and Shadow: The Tragic Courtship and Marriage of Paul Laurence Dunbar and Alice Ruth Moore*, by Eleanor Alexander, *New York Times Book Review*, Au-gust 18, 2002.

32. LEGL, 7.

33. See Andrew Burstein's two fine books, *The Inner Jefferson: Portrait of a Grieving Optimist* (Charlottesville, Va., 1995) and *Jefferson's Secrets: Death and Desire at Monticello* (New York, 2005).

34. See, especially, David McCulloch, *John Adams* (New York, 2001), intro-duction.

35. *Freedom's Journal*, February 22, 1828.

36. *Freedom's Journal*, June 22, 1828.

37. The 1817 Philadelphia petition was reprinted in William Lloyd Garri-son, *Thoughts on African Colonization* (Boston, 1832), 9.

38. David Brion Davis of Yale University, email to author, May 23, 2003. See also David Brion Davis, *Inhuman Bondage: The Rise and Fall of Slavery in the New World* (New York, 2006), esp. 180–81.

39. William Banks, *Black Intellectuals* (New York, 1999), 3–4. See also John S. Mbiti, *African Religions and Philosophy*, 2nd ed. (New York, 1992).

40. On the definition and meaning of black founders, see also Richard S. Newman and Roy E. Finkenbine, eds., "Black Founders in the New Republic," introduction to a forum in the *William and Mary Quarterly*, 3rd series, vol. 64, no. 1 (January 2007): 83–94.

41. On Dexter, see Richard S. Newman, Roy Finkenbine, and Douglass

Mooney, eds., "Philadelphia Emigrationist Petition: An Introduction," *William and Mary Quarterly*, 3rd series, vol. 64, no. 1 (January 2007): 161–66, which contains a brief biography.

42. Daniel Coker, "Dialogue between a Virginian and an African Minister" (Baltimore, 1810), reprinted in Newman, Rael, and Lapsansky, *Pamphlets of Protest*, 52–65.

43. Allen to Boyer, August 22, 1824, reprinted in Jonathas Henri Granville, *Biographie de Jonathas Granville, par son fils* (Paris, 1880).

44. Du Bois's *Souls of Black Folk* (1903) is available in dozens of reprints, including the Oxford World's Classics edition (New York, 1997), edited by Brent Hayes Edwards.

45. Joseph J. Ellis, *Founding Brothers: The Revolutionary Generation* (New York, 1997), chap. 3.

46. Allen's "Eulogy of Washington" was reprinted in the *Philadelphia Gazette*, December 31, 1799.

47. On black republicanism, see Saillant, *Black Puritan, Black Republican*, particularly the discussion at 73. On the religious dimensions of republicanism, see Jonathan D. Sassi, *A Righteous Republic* (New York, 2001).

48. See Gordon S. Wood, *The Radicalism of the American Revolution* (New York, 1991).

49. For a great summary of deliberative versus persuasive politics in early American history, see John L. Brooke, "Consent, Civil Society, and the Public Sphere in the Age of Revolution and the Early American Republic," in Jeffrey L. Pasley, Andrew W. Robertson, and David Waldstreicher, eds., *Beyond the Founders: New Approaches to the Political History of the Early American Republic* (Chapel Hill, N.C., 2004), 207–50, esp. 231–34.

50. Black founders do not garner much attention as religious visionaries in early America. This is particularly striking when one examines recent popular books on religion and the founders. In otherwise excellent studies, neither Jon Meacham's *American Gospel: God, the Founding Fathers and the Making of a Nation* (New York, 2006) nor David L. Holmes's *The Faiths of the Founding Fathers* (New York, 2006) deals with black religious figures during the founding era. For quotation, see Meacham, *American Gospel*, 27.

51. I treat this theme more intensively in " 'We Participate in Common': Richard Allen's Eulogy of Washington and the Challenge of Inter-Racial Appeals," *William and Mary Quarterly*, 3rd series, vol. 64, no. 1 (January 2007): 117–28.

52. See Thomas Jefferson, *Notes on the State of Virginia* (1781–1782, published 1785), usefully digitized at the University of Virginia Library's Electronic Text Center: http://etext.virginia.edu; quotation at 264.

53. See Pasley, Robertson, and Waldstreicher, introduction to *Beyond the Founders*.

54. See Dainty's 1813 engraving, "Rev. Richard Allen, Founder of the African Methodist Episcopal Church."

55. Bernard Bailyn, *To Begin the World Anew: The Genius and Ambiguities of the American Founders* (New York, 2005).

56. Benjamin Franklin and the Pennsylvania Abolition Society, "Address to the Public" (Philadelphia, November 1789) and "A Plan for Improving the Condition of the Free Blacks" (Philadelphia, October 1789).

57. Allen, "An Address to Those Who Keep Slaves."

NOTES TO CHAPTER 1

1. *Pennsylvania Gazette,* February 14, 1760.

2. Ibid.

3. Egerton quoted the novelist James Baldwin. See Egerton, *Gabriel's Rebellion,* 3.

4. LEGL, 5.

5. "To the People of Colour" (originally published in 1794 in Jones and Allen, "Narrative of the . . . Black People"), in Dorothy Porter, ed., *Negro Protest Pamphlets* (New York, 1969), 21–22.

6. Ibid., 7.

7. The standard biography of Benjamin Chew remains Burton A. Konckle, *Benjamin Chew, 1722–1810* (Philadelphia, 1832). The Historical Society of Pennsylvania houses the Chew Papers, including new collections generously donated by Cliveden, Chew's wonderfully restored Germantown home, now restored as a historic site.

8. Nash, *Forging Freedom* 15–16.

9. I am grateful to Philip Seitz, curator of history at Cliveden, for providing me access to his amazing database, "Chew Family Slaves."

10. Information on Chew slaves born in 1760 from ibid.

11. Certificate from Stokeley Sturgis to Richard Allen, circa 1783, about Allen's freedom. Copy obtained from Bethel Archives.

12. Gary B. Nash, *The Urban Crucible* (Cambridge, Mass., 1982).

13. Nash, *Forging Freedom,* 1–11.

14. On Pennsylvania slavery, see Gary B. Nash and Jean R. Soderlund, *Freedom by Degrees: Emancipation in Pennsylvania and Its Aftermath* (New York, 1990).

15. For expert examinations of Northern bondage, see especially David N. Gellman, *Emancipating New York: The Politics of Slavery and Freedom, 1777–1827* (Baton Rouge, La., 2007); Graham Russell Hodges, *Slavery and Freedom in the Rural North, African Americans in Monmouth County, New Jersey, 1665–1865* (Madison, Wis., 1997); and Melish, *Disowning Slavery.*

16. See Sidney Kaplan, *The Black Presence in the Era of the American Revolution* (Washington, D.C., 1973), 81–89.

17. Jean R. Soderlund, *Quakers and Slavery: A Divided Spirit* (Princeton, N.J., 1982).

18. "Venture Smith, Narrative of a Slave's Capture" (Middletown, Conn., 1798). On Smith generally, see John Wood Sweet, *Bodies Politic* (Baltimore, 2004).

19. Before Gary Nash's careful research showed that Stokeley Sturgis was Allen's second master, scholars had little clue about "Mr. Stokeley's" identity. See Nash's groundbreaking article, "New Light on Richard Allen," cited in the introduction, n. 1. D. W. Meinig, ed., *The Shaping of America: Eight Geographical Perspective on 500 Years of History*, vol. 1, *Atlantic America, 1492–1800* (New Haven, Conn., 1986).

20. William H. Williams, *Slavery and Freedom in Delaware* (Independence, Ky., 1999), 110–11.

21. LEGL, 6.

22. Ibid.

23. Williams, *Slavery and Freedom in Delaware*, 110–11.

24. LEGL, 6.

25. See Roger D. Abrahams, *Singing the Master: The Emergence of African-American Culture in the Plantation South* (New York, 1992), chap. 1, appendix 1.

26. *Pennsylvania Gazette*, September 5, 1765.

27. LEGL, 17.

28. Williams, *Slavery and Freedom in Delaware*, 110–11.

29. LEGL, 11.

30. Frederick Douglass, *Life and Times of Frederick Douglass* (Boston, 1892), 141.

31. LEGL, 7.

32. Mother Bethel website, www.motherbethel.org.

33. LEGL, 7–8.

34. See Payne, *History of the AME Church*, 83.

35. See James Oliver Horton and Lois E. Horton, *In Hope of Liberty: Culture, Community, and Protest among Northern Free Blacks, 1700–1860* (New York, 1997); Nash, *Forging Freedom*; Shane White, *Somewhat More Independent: The End of Slavery In New York City, 1770–1810* (Athens, Ga., 1991).

36. On the PAS, see Richard S. Newman, *The Transformation of American Abolitionism: Fighting Slavery in the Early Republic* (Chapel Hill, N.C., 2002).

37. On Methodism, see Andrews, *The Methodists*, chaps. 1–2. See also Betty Wood and Sylvia Frey, *Come Shouting to Zion: African American Protestantism in the American South and British Caribbean to 1830* (Chapel Hill, N.C., 1998).

38. Asbury to his parents, January 24, 1773, in Elmer T. Clark, ed., *The Journal and Letters of Francis Asbury,* 3 vols. (London, 1958), 3:260–65.

39. LEGL, 17.

40. Andrews, *The Methodists,* 123–24.

41. Wesley, "Thoughts upon Slavery" (London, 1774), available online at http://gbgm-umc.org/UMW/wesley/thoughtsuponslavery.stm.

42. See Adam Hochschild, "British Abolition: The Movie," *New York Review of Books* 54, no. 10 (June 14, 2007): 73–75.

43. LEGL, 5–7.

44. Nash, *Forging Freedom,* 95–96.

45. LEGL, 6.

46. Ibid., 5.

47. Quotations come from little-used sections of Allen's autobiography, "Acts of Faith," "Acts of Hope," "Acts of Love," LEGL, 25–28.

48. Ibid.; see also Richard Allen, "To the People of Colour," in LEGL, 47–48.

49. Graham Russell Hodges, *Black Itinerants of the Gospel: The Narratives of John Jea and George White* (Madison, Wis., 1993), introduction, esp. 1–19.

50. On the international dimensions of black activists, including religious itinerants like John Marrant, see Cassandra Pybus, *Epic Journeys of Freedom* (Boston, 2006).

51. LEGL, 6.

52. See, for instance, Frederick Douglass, *Three Addresses on the Relations Subsisting between the White and Colored People of the United States* (Washington, D.C., 1886), 3–23.

53. LEGL, 6–7.

54. Ibid.

55. Ibid.

56. Ibid.

57. For a wonderful reprint of Allen's manumission deed, see Nash, "New Light on Richard Allen."

58. LEGL, 7–8. See also Andrews, *The Methodists,* 89–90, 140–41, 147.

59. LEGL, 8. Because Pennsylvania currency was notoriously unstable during the early 1780s, this is only an approximation. My thanks to Cathy Matson and Bob Wright for advice here, though the calculation is mine alone.

60. Nash, "New Light on Richard Allen."

61. On masters' deviousness in New York City, see White, *Somewhat More Independent.*

62. Nash, "New Light on Richard Allen."

63. Certificate from Stokeley Sturgis to Richard Allen, circa 1783, about Allen's freedom. Copy obtained from Bethel Archives.

64. As mentioned in note 5 to the introduction, Sturgis had written a quasi-pass on behalf of Allen on August 27, 1783.

65. LEGL, 10.

66. Ibid, 8.

67. Both the PAS and the Philadelphia Yearly Meeting prepared such testimonials for use in Britain. See, for example, the Philadelphia Yearly Meeting, "Meeting of Sufferings, Minute Book, 1785–1802," October 18, 1787, in Haverford College's Quaker Special Collections. I remain indebted to Douglass Mooney of URS Corporation in Philadelphia, a wonderful historical researcher, for showing me a copy of this pamphlet.

68. LEGL, 9.

69. See Allen's antislavery appeal, "An Address to Those Who Keep Slaves."

70. LEGL, 11–12.

71. Ibid.

72. Asbury to his parents, January 24, 1773, in Clark, *Journal and Letters of Francis Asbury*, 3:260–65.

73. Ibid.

74. LEGL, 9–10.

75. Ibid.

76. Donald G. Mathews, *Slavery and Methodism: A Chapter in American Morality, 1780–1845* (Princeton, N.J., 1965), 10.

77. Allen's first portrait appears in Kaplan, *Black Presence*, chap. 3, plate 4.

NOTES TO CHAPTER 2

1. LEGL, 31.

2. Ibid., 11.

3. Ibid., 12.

4. See PAS report on visiting people of color from December 1, 1795, in "Committee for Improving the Condition of Free Blacks: Minutes, 1790–1803," PAS Papers, Reel 6.

5. On the rise of black Philadelphia, see Nash, *Forging Freedom*; Julie Winch, *Philadelphia's Black Elite* (Philadelphia, 1993); and Winch, *A Gentleman of Color*. On slave runaways and abolitionist aid in Pennsylvania, see also Newman, *Transformation of American Abolitionism*.

6. Newman, *Transformation of American Abolitionism*, chap. 3.

7. James Forten, "Series of Letters by a Man of Colour" (Philadelphia, 1813), reprinted in Newman, Rael, and Lapsansky, *Pamphlets of Protest*.

8. See Nash and Soderlund, *Freedom by Degrees*, 127.

9. Newman, *Transformation of American Abolitionism*, chap. 3.

10. Paul A. Gilje and Howard B. Rock, *Keepers of the Revolution: New Yorkers at Work during the Early Republic* (Ithaca, N.Y., 1992), 221–23.

11. On black mariners, see Horton and Horton, *In Hope of Liberty,* 69–70; and W. Jeffrey Bolster, *Black Jacks: African Americans Seamen in the Age of Sail* (Cambridge, Mass., 1997).

12. On the Allen apprentice case, see the PAS's "Committee of Guardians Report," September 17, 1790, PAS Papers, Reel 6, 47–57.

13. *Pennsylvania Gazette,* August 13, 1788, and September 14, 1791; quotation from the second ad.

14. "Committee of Guardians Report," February 16, 1793, PAS Papers, Reel 6, 55.

15. Nash and Soderlund, *Freedom by Degrees,* 192–93.

16. Allen, "To the People of Colour," in Porter, *Negro Protest Pamphlets,* 22. See also Hodges, *Black Itinerants of the Gospel,* introduction.

17. LEGL, 12–13.

18. Ibid.

19. Ibid.

20. Ibid. Andrews, *The Methodists,* 144–50, is particularly good at recounting the meaning of Allen's initial vision of a black church within Methodist religious circles.

21. See Nash, *Forging Freedom,* 98–99.

22. "Preamble and Articles of Association of the Free African Society, April 12, 1787," reprinted in Wesley, *Richard Allen,* 269–71, quotations at 269, 270.

23. See William Douglass, "Annals of the First African Church in United States of America, Now Styled the African Episcopal Church of St. Thomas, Philadelphia" (Philadelphia, 1862). For a terrific treatment of the broader meaning of the FAS and black autonomy, see Craig Steven Wilder, *In the Company of Black Men: The African Influence on African American Culture in New York City* (New York, 2001).

24. "Preamble and Articles of the Free African Society," 269.

25. Horton and Horton, *In Hope of Liberty,* 126–30.

26. Michael C. Dawson, *Black Visions: The Roots of Contemporary African-American Political Ideologies* (Chicago, 2001), 86.

27. The story is told in many places, beginning with Wesley, *Richard Allen,* 66–68.

28. The charges against Allen, brought June 20, 1789, are usefully recounted in Wesley, *Richard Allen,* 66.

29. Ibid, 65.

30. LEGL, 15.

31. On Washington's donation to an African church, see Nash, *Forging Freedom,* 164.

32. Finding precise dates for these activities remains problematic, for documentation is scarce. Allen bought land for the church in 1791, claiming in his autobiography that he had been authorized to do so by the FAS (see LEGL, 15).

FAS records note that Allen was no longer a member by this time. But there is no other authoritative documentation on the matter.

33. LEGL, 21.

34. Raboteau, *A Fire in the Bones,* 79.

35. James T. Campbell, *Songs of Zion: The African Methodist Episcopal Church in the United States and South Africa* (New York, 1995), vii–viii.

36. Raboteau, *A Fire in the Bones,* 79.

37. Carol George used the phrase in her book's title, *Segregated Sabbaths.*

38. LEGL, 14.

39. See Richard Allen and Jacob Tapsico, *The Doctrines and Discipline of the African Methodist Episcopal Church* (Philadelphia, 1817). For quotations, see LEGL, 13–14.

40. LEGL, 13–14.

41. Ibid.

42. See Milton Sernett, *Black Religion and American Evangelicalism: White Protestants, Plantation Missions, and the Flowering of Negro Christianity, 1787–1865* (Metuchen, N.J., 1975), 117–18, 219–20. See also Nash, *Forging Freedom,* 118–19.

43. Phillip Lapsansky, interview with the author, January 21, 2003.

44. Douglass, "Annals of the First African Church," 1–5.

45. Nash, *Forging Freedom,* 118–19.

46. *Colored American* (published in New York), October 14, 1837.

47. Ibid.

48. Ibid.

49. LEGL, 15.

50. Ibid., 13.

51. Ibid.

52. Rush, quoted in Nash, *Forging Freedom,* 116; emphasis in original. On Nicholson, see Cynthia Shelton, *The Mills of Manayunk* (Baltimore, 1986).

53. Ibid., 119.

54. *Colored American,* October 14, 1837.

55. LEGL, 14–15.

56. Nash, *Forging Freedom,* 115.

57. LEGL, 14–16.

58. Ibid.

59. Ibid.

60. Ibid., 16. See also Andrews, *The Methodists,* 139–50; and Nash, *Forging Freedom,* 119.

61. LEGL, 16–17.

62. See Andrews, *The Methodists,* 139–40.

63. Asbury, quoted in Wesley, *Richard Allen,* 79.

64. Dickins was a familiar figure during the yellow-fever crisis, working

with black as well as white leaders to save the city. He knew Allen, Jones, and James Forten.

65. Charles M. Laymon, ed., *The Interpreter's One-Volume Commentary on the Bible* (Nashville, Tenn., 1971), 21–22.

66. Ibid., 23.

67. For the AME's original charter, see "Articles of Association of the African Methodist Episcopal Church" (Philadelphia, 1799).

68. "A List of the Members of the African Methodist Episcopal Church in the City of Philadelphia," c. 1794, originally in the St. George's Church archives, and now (as a photocopy) in Bethel Archives, Richard Allen Museum. Dee Andrews first publicized the list in *The Methodists*, 147–50. The list, which is only partially legible and may not have correct spellings for all members, includes such names as Esther Freeman, Lucy White, Jane Anderson, Cynthia Bill (Bull?), Esther Claypoole, and Jane Given.

69. Two dates exist for Allen's marriage to Flora: October 19, 1790 (Bethel Church), and October 19, 1796 (documented at St. George's Church). The earlier date seems more probable, for Flora Allen signed property deeds prior to 1796. Still, the latter date may signify an official sanction of the marriage.

70. Quotation from William Culbert's journal, courtesy of Richard Allen Museum display, Bethel Church.

71. Flora Allen was listed as a cosigner of a lot that Richard Allen purchased in 1792 at Sixth and Lombard (adjacent to land he already owned), which would become part of Bethel Church property. See contract between Joseph Lewis and "Richard Allen and his Wife, Flora," August 10, 1792, in Bethel Archives.

72. On Flora Allen's death, see *Poulson's American Daily Advertiser,* March 12, 1801.

73. Hallie Brown, *Homespun Heroines and Other Women of Distinction* (1926; repr., New York, 1988), 12.

74. See Absalom Jones and Richard Allen, "A Narrative of the Proceedings of the Coloured People during the Late Awful Calamity in Philadelphia, in the Year 1793," in LEGL, 35.

75. Brown, *Homespun Heroines,* 12.

76. See Payne, *History of the AME Church,* 87.

77. For the classic definition of "republican motherhood," see Linda Kerber, *Women of the Republic* (Chapel Hill, N.C., 1980).

78. Though it focuses on a later era, Julius H. Bailey's *Around the Family Altar: Domesticity in the African Methodist Episcopal Church, 1865–1900* (Gainesville, Fla., 2005) provides insightful treatment of women's public and private roles in the church.

79. Payne, *History of the AME Church,* 84.

80. LEGL, 24.

1. See Allen and Jones, "Narrative of the . . . Black People" (Philadelphia, 1794), reprinted in Newman, Rael, and Lapsansky, *Pamphlets of Protest,* 27–41; see also Wesley, *Richard Allen.*

2. LEGL, 1–2.

3. On Philadelphia's growth, see Gary B. Nash, *First City: Philadelphia and the Forging of Historical Memory* (Philadelphia, 2002).

4. Billy G. Smith, *The Lower Sort: Philadelphia's Laboring People, 1750–1880* (Cambridge, Mass., 1993), 9.

5. Ibid., 28, 29.

6. Allen used the address in two runaway-apprentice ads in the *Pennsylvania Gazette.* See the paper for August 13, 1788, and September 14, 1791.

7. See land deed between Richard Allen and John Willson, January 22, 1791, in Bethel Archives.

8. For information on Allen's Spruce Street neighbors, see the 1795 Philadelphia directory, "Hogan's Prospect," 144–47.

9. Ibid., 52.

10. Ibid., 164.

11. See the minutes of the PAS "Committee of Employ," special meeting on the prospective loan to Allen and Jones, July 6, 10, and 30, 1793, in PAS Papers, Reel 6.

12. Payne, *History of the AME Church,* 84.

13. See PAS "Committee of Inspection," March 26, 1793, PAS Papers, Reel 6.

14. See PAS "Committee of Education," November 20, 1793, Reel 6, for a report on paying black schoolteacher Eleanor Harris thirty dollars to teach at the PAS school.

15. PAS "Committee of Employ," special meeting on the prospective loan to Allen and Jones, July 6, 10, and 30, 1793, in PAS Papers, Reel 6.

16. The Committee of Guardians' report on "Jones & Co." in September 1793 was buried amid yellow-fever exertions and not unearthed until a meeting of March 25, 1794 (PAS Papers, Reel 6), when white reformers considered Allen and Jones's request for loan forbearance.

17. See the anonymous letter to the *Pennsylvania Gazette,* September 30, 1794.

18. Ibid. Baltimore had an outbreak of the fever and blamed its northern neighbor.

19. See Mathew Carey, "A Desultory Account of the Yellow Fever" (Philadelphia, October 16, 1793), 2; Richard Varick of New York to Matthew Clarkson of Philadelphia, fall 1793, reprinted in "Minutes of the Proceedings of the

Committee Appointed September 14th, 1793" (Philadelphia, 1794), 64; J. H. Powell, *Bring Out Your Dead,* edited by J. Kenneth Foster, Mary F. Jenkins, and Anna Coxe Toogood (Philadelphia, 1949; repr., 1993).

20. Powell, *Bring Out Your Dead,* 67–68, 107.

21. For reports on and from Bush Hill Hospital, including Allen's admission, see "Minutes of the Proceedings of the Committee Appointed on the 14th September 1793" (Philadelphia, 1794), 11.

22. See the appendix entitled "Numbers of Houses, Deaths, etc., in the Respective Streets, Alleys and Courts in the City of Philadelphia," in ibid.

23. On yellow fever in American history, see Molly Caldwell Crosby, *The American Plague: The Untold Story of Yellow Fever, the Epidemic That Shaped Our History* (New York, 2006).

24. Allen and Jones, "Narrative of the . . . Black People," 37.

25. One of the best treatments of yellow fever in Philadelphia comes from Ron Chernow's biography of Alexander Hamilton, a member of George Washington's cabinet who came down with the sickness in Philadelphia. See Chernow, *Alexander Hamilton* (New York, 2004), 448–53.

26. *Pennsylvania Gazette,* October 8, 1794.

27. On yellow fever's toll in Philadelphia, see Foster, Jenkins, and Coxe Toogood's fine introduction to Powell, *Bring Out Your Dead.*

28. *Federal Gazette,* October 1, 1793.

29. *Federal Gazette,* October 2, 1793. See the same paper on September 15 and 23, 1793.

30. *Federal Gazette,* September 15 and 23, 1793.

31. *Federal Gazette,* September 11, 1793.

32. MSS. correspondence of Dr. Benjamin Rush, Historical Society of Pennsylvania, Part IV (Vol. 38): 1793. I am indebted to Clint Roderick, a gifted young historian, for this citation and for many fruitful conversations about Rush and Allen.

33. Allen and Jones, "Narrative of the . . . Black People," 33.

34. Ibid.

35. *Federal Gazette,* September 7, 1793.

36. On John Allen, see Andrews, *The Methodists,* 319n. 122; Nash, *Forging Freedom,* 130.

37. From the *Massachusetts Magazine,* December 1793, reprinted in Kaplan, *Black Presence,* 87.

38. Allen and Jones, "Narrative of the . . . Black People."

39. Ibid., 34.

40. Ibid., 40.

41. Ibid., 34, 39.

42. On the percentage of blacks in various Southern locales, see in particular

William Freehling's magisterial books, *Road to Disunion,* vol. 1, *Secessionists at Bay, 1776–1854* (New York, 1989) and *Road to Disunion,* vol. 2, *Secessionists Triumphant* (New York, 2007).

43. *Federal Gazette,* October 2, 1793.

44. Historian Jacqueline Miller has called this saga "the wages of whiteness"—the belief that equal pay applied only to whites. In one striking example, Miller discusses the experiences of a Quaker widow named Margaret Morris. In mid-September, after her son, John, and his wife, Abigail, contracted the fever, Morris obtained the services of "a black man and [a white] woman who were but just nursing at another place." Again, in early October when two other members of her household became ill, Morris hired another black man and a white woman each at the rate of three dollars a day. After both of these individuals came down with the fever, Morris quickly found a replacement—another white woman. In short, Morris hired both black men and white women as nurses during these trying times, apparently paying them comparable wages. When Morris complained to family members about the cost of care, however, she disparaged only black nurses, noting that "many of them [blacks] became extortionate in their demands, exacting the sum of three, four, and five dollars a day for their attendance." I am indebted to Professor Miller of Seattle University for sharing her incredible research with me. See Margaret Morris to Richard Hill Morris, September 19, 1793, Margaret Morris Papers, Quaker Collection, Haverford College (hereafter cited as QCHC); Morris to Milcah M. Moore, September 25, October 10, and October 24, 1793, Edward Wanton Smith Collection, QCHC; Morris to Richard Hill Morris, October 10, 1793, Margaret Morris Papers, QCHC; Morris to [Sarah and George Dillwyn], October 24, 1793, Edward Wanton Smith Collection, QCHC; and Benjamin Smith to Margaret Morris, September 7, [1793], Gulielma M. Howland Collection.

45. *Federal Gazette,* September 23, 1793.

46. *Pennsylvania Gazette,* September 10, 1794.

47. See Mathew Carey's updated treatments, including "A Short Account of the Yellow Fever" (Philadelphia, 1793), 1–10.

48. References condensed from Allen and Jones, "Narrative of the . . . Black People."

49. Phillip Lapsansky, interview with the author, February 17, 2004.

50. Allen and Jones, "Narrative of the . . . Black People," 33–34, 37.

51. Ibid., 38.

52. On American print culture generally, see, for example, Michael Warner, *The Letters of the Republic* (Boston, 1990). On black literacies, see, for example, Joanna Brooks, *American Lazarus: Religion and the Rise of African-American and Native American Literatures* (New York, 2003); and Elizabeth McHenry, *Forgotten Readers: Recovering the Lost History of African American*

Literary Societies (Durham, N.C., 2002). On black modernity, see Paul Gilroy, *The Black Atlantic: Modernity and the Double Consciousness* (Cambridge, Mass., 1993). On black history writing, see John Ernest, *Liberation Historiography: African-American Writers and the Challenge of History, 1794–1861* (Chapel Hill, N.C., 2004). For a different reading of the meaning of black letters—black literature as a counterpublic—see Joanna Brooks, "The Early American Public Sphere and the Emergence of a Black Print Counterpublic," *William and Mary Quarterly* 62, no. 1 (January 2005): 67–92. For a reply, see Newman and Finkenbine, "Black Founders in the New Republic."

53. Allen and Jones, "Narrative of the . . . Black People," 34–38.

54. Ibid., 37–40.

55. Ibid., 34–35.

56. See Bruce H. Mann, *Republic of Debtors: Bankruptcy in the Age of American Independence* (Cambridge, Mass., 2003).

57. See the PAS "Committee of Inspection" report, March 25, 1794, in "Committee for Improving the Condition of Free Blacks," PAS Papers, Reel 6. More than the financial consequences, according to the remarkable research of independent scholar Karl E. Johnson of Philadelphia, the lingering debt and failed nail factory almost drove a nail into the heart of black leadership: Allen and Jones later confronted each other in court over responsibilities for payments, financial obligations, and damages relating to the aborted business. Details of the court case remain obscure. But Allen and Jones's friendship endured these strains.

58. See PAS "Committee of Inspection" reports on Allen and Jones on the following dates: March 25, April 29, May 27, and June 24, 1794, in "Committee for Improving the Condition of Free Blacks," PAS Papers, Reel 6.

59. Ibid.

60. See Franklin and the Pennsylvania Abolition Society, "Address to the Public" and "A Plan for Improving the Condition of the Free Blacks."

61. Report from the PAS "Committee of Inspection," June 24, 1794, in PAS Papers, Reel 6.

62. See PAS "Committee of Education" report, February 25, 1794, in "Committee for Improving the Condition of Free Blacks," PAS Papers, Reel 6.

63. See Nash and Soderlund, *Freedom by Degrees,* 97. The anonymous pamphlet in question was entitled "Sermon on the Present Situation of the Affairs of America and Great Britain, Written by a Black and Printed at the Request of Several Persons of Distinguished Characters" (Philadelphia, 1782).

64. On Hammon, see introduction to Newman, Rael, and Lapsansky, *Pamphlets of Protest,* esp. notes on 27–28.

65. On Woodward's print shop in early national Philadelphia, see especially Rosalind R. Remer, *Printers and Men of Capital* (Philadelphia, 1996).

66. Allen and Jones secured copyright for the "Narrative of the . . . Black

People" on January 23, 1794, in Philadelphia (number 55 within the Pennsylvania district between 1790 and 1800). See James Gilreath and Elizabeth Carter Wills, eds., *Federal Copyright Records* (Washington, D.C., 1987), 16.

NOTES TO CHAPTER 4

1. "Address of M. Carey to the Public" (Philadelphia, April 4, 1794), 5. At first, Carey sought to reply to a writer named "Argus," who accused Carey of cowardly departing Philadelphia from mid-September through much of October. Carey claimed that he went to Baltimore (as planned prior to the fever) on a business trip from September 16 through early October. But he used a portion of his address to reply to Allen and Jones. Interestingly, when Carey republished his pamphlets and essays in the 1820s, he listed his reply to Allen and Jones *first*. See "Address to the Public Respecting the Conduct of the Coloured People during the Late Fever . . . ," in M. Carey, *Pamphlets and Papers*, 7 vols. (Philadelphia, 1826), 3:197–204.

2. Allen, "An Address to Those Who Keep Slaves." Because Allen and Jones cosigned other sections of the yellow-fever pamphlet but not this one, scholars know that Allen was the single author of the antislavery address. In addition to this evidence is the fact that Allen claimed authorship of the address at the end of his life. See LEGL, which reprinted the antislavery address as his own production.

3. Ibid.

4. See Newman, *Transformation of American Abolitionism*, chap. 3. See also Henry Wiencek's fine study, *An Imperfect God: George Washington, His Slaves and the Creation of America* (New York, 2003).

5. On Haitian émigrés to Pennsylvania, see Winch, *A Gentleman of Color*, 135. On black revolutionaries in the Caribbean, and their trans-Atlantic import, see in particular Dubois, *Avengers of the New World*. On the Philadelphia manumission of Haitian slaves, see Nash, *First City*, 126.

6. For a very good recent study of emancipation in New York, see Gellman, *Emancipating New York*.

7. Allen, "An Address to Those Who Keep Slaves," 42.

8. Jefferson, *Notes on the State of Virginia* (1781–1782), 264.

9. See Freehling, *Road to Disunion*, vol. 1, sec. 3, esp. chap. 7.

10. *Banneker's Almanack and Ephemeris for the Year of Our Lord 1793* (Philadelphia, 1792), section entitled "Extract from Jefferson's Notes on Virginia."

11. Allen, "An Address to Those Who Keep Slaves."

12. Ibid.

13. See Jefferson, *Notes on the State of Virginia*, 264.

14. Allen, "An Address to Those Who Keep Slaves."

15. See also Franklin and the Pennsylvania Abolition Society, "Address to the Public" and "A Plan for Improving the Condition of the Free Blacks."

16. Allen, "An Address to Those Who Keep Slaves"; see also Forten, "Series of Letters by a Man of Colour," in Newman, Rael, and Lapsansky, *Pamphlets of Protest,* 69.

17. Allen, "An Address to Those Who Keep Slaves."

18. On PAS petitioning strategies in the 1790s, see Newman, *Transformation of American Abolitionism,* introduction and chaps. 1–2.

19. For the Africanus-Rusticus newspaper debate, see the (New York) *United States Gazette,* March 3, 1790.

20. See George F. Tyson, Jr., ed., *Toussaint L'Ouverture,* Great Lives Observed Series (Englewood Cliffs, N.J., 1973), Washington and Jefferson quotations at 93, Gallatin quotation at 94.

21. Prince Hall, "A Charge" (Boston, 1792, 1797), reprinted in Newman, Rael, and Lapsansky, *Pamphlets of Protest,* 45–50.

22. Allen, "An Address to Those Who Keep Slaves."

23. Allen, "To the People of Colour," in Porter, *Negro Protest Pamphlets,* 21–23.

24. See Allen, "An Address to Those Who Keep Slaves" and "To the People of Colour."

25. LEGL, 5.

26. On black early national black letters, see Ernest, *Liberation Historiography.*

27. The Allen Bible is pictured online at http://www.motherbethel.org/museum/exhibit/digitalrepository.html.

28. Allen Dwight Callahan, *The Talking Book: African-Americans in the Bible* (New Haven, Conn., 2006), xiii.

29. On the importance of this theme in black ideology, see also Saillant, *Black Puritan, Black Republican,* 64.

30. *Expository notes, with practical observations upon the New Testament of our Lord and Saviour Jesus Christ. Wherein the whole of the sacred text is recited, the sense explained, and the instructive example of the blessed Jesus, and his apostles, to our imitation recommended. By William Burkitt, M.A. late Vicar and lecturer of Dedham, in Essex,* printed first in New Haven by Abel Morse, for the Reverend David Austin of Elizabeth-town in 1794; a second printing occurred in New York by T. Dunning and W. W. Hyer in 1796 and was the first American edition, corrected from the twentieth European edition. My thanks to Kathryn Ostrofsky of the University of Pennsylvania, a budding scholar, for these citations.

31. Burkitt's preface is reprinted in the Dunham Family Bible in America Museum, available online at http://www.hbu.edu/hbu/Address_to_Family_Governors_from_William_Burkitts_.asp?SnID=508094954.

32. Thomas Scott, *A Commentary on the Whole Bible* (Boston, 1804). Scott's preface is reprinted in the Dunham Family Bible in America Museum, available online at http://www.hbu.edu/hbu/Thomas_Scotts_Commentary_on_the_Bible_1804.asp?SnID=508094954.

33. *The Whole, Genuine and Complete Works of Flavius Josephus, the Learned and Authentic Jewish Historian*, ed. Archibald Woodruff and John Turner (Philadelphia, 1795).

34. *Josephus: The Complete Works* (Philadelphia, 1960), ix.

35. See, for example, the *Pennsylvania Gazette*, March 5, 1745.

36. See the Woodruff and Turner edition of *Whole, Genuine and Complete Works of Flavius Josephus*. Allen's name appears on the "List of Subscribers' Names" at the end of the book.

37. See Allen and Jones, "Narrative of the . . . Black People," 33–41; and Josephus, *The Antiquities of the Jews*, in *Whole, Genuine and Complete Works*, 23.

38. See Richard S. Newman, "'We Participate in Common': Richard Allen's Eulogy of Washington and the Challenge of Interracial Appeals," *William and Mary Quarterly*, 3rd series, vol. 64, no. 1 (January 2007): 117–28, citing Washington's "Farewell Address" at 127.

39. See Prince Hall's first pamphlet, "A Charge" (Boston, 1792).

40. See, especially, Joanna Brooks and John Saillant, eds., *"Face Zion Forward": First Writers of the Black Atlantic, 1785–1798* (Boston, 2002).

41. The classic treatment of this subject remains Warner, *Letters of the Republic*.

42. Allen, "An Address to Those Who Keep Slaves."

43. The penmanship exercise and other documents by black pupils in abolitionist schools can be found at the Historical Society of Pennsylvania's wonderful website, http://www.hsp.org, under the heading of "Education."

44. Anonymous, reprinted in Kaplan, *Black Presence*, 87.

45. A good summation of Allen and Jones's friendship, through documentary excerpts, can be found in ibid., 81–94.

46. Wesley, *Richard Allen*, 93–94.

47. On the broader significance of black Masonry, see Peter P. Hinks, "John Marrant and the Meaning of Early Black Freemasonry," *William and Mary Quarterly*, 3rd series, vol. 64, no. 1 (January 2007): 105–16.

48. Kaplan, *Black Presence*, 81–94.

49. See ibid., 83.

50. Jones and Allen collaborated on the yellow-fever narrative in 1794, a black petition drive to Congress in 1799, and an earlier, though undated, unofficial congressional petition drive on emancipation and emigration. On this last issue, see in particular Newman, Finkenbine, and Mooney, "Philadelphia Emigrationist Petition."

51. Allen, "An Address to Those Who Keep Slaves."

52. See Coker, "Dialogue between a Virginian and an African Minister," 63.

53. Allen and Jones, "Narrative of the . . . Black People," 36.

54. Allen and Jones's Clarkson testimonial appears in Porter, *Negro Protest Pamphlets*, 17–19.

55. See Allen and Jones, "Narrative of the . . . Black People," 34–41.

56. Ibid.

NOTES TO CHAPTER 5

1. Allen's eulogy first appeared in the *Philadelphia Gazette*, December 31, 1799, and was then reprinted in the *New York Spectator*, January 2, 1800, and the *Baltimore Federal Gazette*, January 3, 1800. On "mediation" in early politics, see especially David Waldstreicher and Stephan R. Grossbart, "Abraham Bishop's Vocation; or, The Mediation of Jeffersonian Politics," *Journal of the Early Republic* 18, no. 4 (winter 1998): 617–57.

2. For a good summation of Bethel's growth, see in particular Andrews, *The Methodists*, 148–50.

3. See Richard Allen et al., "The Sword of Truth" (Philadelphia, 1823), 6–7.

4. See Wesley, *Richard Allen*, 89–90.

5. Ibid., 79–80; Allen et al., "Sword of Truth," 1–2.

6. Wesley, *Richard Allen*, 79–80; Benjamin Tucker Tanner, *An Outline of Our History and Government for African Methodist Churchmen, Ministerial and Lay, in Catechetical Form* (Philadelphia, 1884), 145–49.

7. Allen is actually unclear on just who advised him to incorporate with the aid of white officials. In *Doctrines and Discipline of the AME Church*, 4–5, he refers to John McClasky; in LEGL, 18, he refers to his friend Ezekial Cooper. See Andrews, *The Methodists*, 148–49.

8. The original act of incorporation was signed by Pennsylvania officials on September 12, 1796. Allen himself reprinted the document just a few years later as "The Articles of Association of the African Methodist Episcopal Church of the City of Philadelphia in the Commonwealth of Pennsylvania" (Philadelphia, 1799). Quotations at 5, 8–9. See also Andrews, *The Methodists*, 149.

9. LEGL, 18.

10. Wesley, *Richard Allen*, 144.

11. See Allen and Tapsico, *Doctrines and Discipline of the AME Church*, 4–5, and LEGL, 18–19.

12. LEGL, 18; "Articles of Association," 8–9.

13. "Articles of Association," 14.

14. As with all corporations, Pennsylvania's governing elite signed documents attesting to official incorporation, including Governor Thomas Mifflin,

"Master of the Rolls" Matthew Irwin, and Attorney General Jerad Ingersoll. For their inscriptions, see "Articles of Association," 12–16.

15. See ibid., 6, 9.

16. Ibid., 5, 8–9.

17. LEGL, 18.

18. Matthew 16:19

19. LEGL, 18.

20. Allen placed the African Supplement at the end of his narrative of Bethel Church's creation. See LEGL, 22–24; quotations from 22–23.

21. African Supplement, 22; Wesley, *Richard Allen,* 144.

22. LEGL, 19

23. Ibid., 21.

24. See Martin Luther King, Jr., *Stride toward Freedom* (New York, 1958).

25. In addition to appearing in the *Philadelphia Gazette,* December 31, 1799, Allen's eulogy is also conveniently reprinted in Philip Foner and Robert James Barnham, eds., *Lift Every Voice* (Tuscaloosa, Ala., 2000), 53–56.

26. Ibid.

27. Ibid.

28. See Evelyn Nakano Glenn, *Unequal Freedom: How Race and Gender Shaped American Citizenship and Labor* (Cambridge, Mass., 2002), 24.

29. On black civic participation in the early republic, see in particular Patrick Rael, *Black Identity and Black Protest in the Antebellum North* (Chapel Hill, N.C., 2002). See also Saillant, *Black Puritan, Black Republican*; David Waldstreicher, *In the Midst of Perpetual Fetes* (Chapel Hill, N.C., 1997). For an interesting view on black attempts to reach a "public" during the colonial and Revolutionary eras, see Sweet, *Bodies Politic.*

30. Allen, "Eulogy of Washington."

31. Lee's eulogy is reprinted in *Eulogies of George Washington* (Boston, 1800).

32. See Joseph Ellis's insightful biography, *His Excellency, George Washington* (New York, 2004), 455–57, 468.

33. On Washington's death more broadly, see Francois Furstenberg, *In the Name of the Father: Washington's Legacy, Slavery, and the Making of a Nation* (New York, 2006), 86–87.

34. *Carlisle Gazette,* December 26 and December 27, 1799.

35. Once again, Allen's eulogy was reprinted within a week: first in the *Philadelphia Gazette* on December 31, 1799, then in the *New York Spectator* on January 2, 1800, and finally in the *Baltimore Federal Gazette* on January 3, 1800.

36. The editor's remarks are reprinted in Foner and Barnham, *Lift Every Voice,* 54.

37. I am indebted to Jim Hooper of the Baylor School in Chattanooga, Tennessee, for insight on Allen's biblical references.

38. Interestingly, other writers use this biblical reference when referring to Washington, though they did not see his death in millennial terms. See, for example, an item from the *New York Commercial Advertiser,* reprinted in the *Philadelphia Gazette,* December 30, 1799 (a day after Allen's church eulogy).

39. On Douglass's Fourth of July speech, see James A. Colaiaco, *Frederick Douglass and the Fourth of July* (New York, 2006). On both religious oratory and print in the early national period, see especially Christopher Grasso, *A Speaking Aristocracy: Transforming Public Discourse in Eighteenth-Century Connecticut* (Chapel Hill, N.C., 1999). On black religious oratory in general, see Keith D. Miller, *Voice of Deliverance: The Language of Martin Luther King, Jr. and Its Sources* (New York, 1992); Nick Salvatore, *Singing in a Strange Land: C. L. Franklin and the Transformation of America* (New York, 2005); and Sassi, *A Righteous Republic.*

40. Allen collected monies on March 14, 1796 ($16.60) and March 25, 1797 ($7.80). I am indebted to Anna Coxe Toogood and Joe Becton of the National Park Service at Independence National Historical Park for information on this matter. See "Washington's Household Account Book, 1793–1797," entries for March 14, 1796, and March 4, 1797, in *Pennsylvania Magazine of History and Biography (PMHB)* 31 (1907): 177, 344.

41. Isaac Weld, Jr., *Travels through the States of North America during the Years 1795, 1796, and 1797* (London, 1799), excerpt reprinted in "The President's House in Philadelphia," part of the Independence Hall Association's ushistory.org website, http://www.ushistory.org/presidentshouse/history/quotes.htm.

42. On the secret passageway unearthed during excavation by the National Parks Service, see the *Philadelphia Inquirer,* June 7, 2007.

43. The work of independent scholar Edward Lawler, Jr., and *Philadelphia Inquirer* reporters (led by Stephen Salisbury) has been seminal in public reexaminations of the President's House, which is now being commemorated under the stewardship of the National Park Service and the City of Philadelphia. See "The President's House in Philadelphia: The Rediscovery of a Lost Landmark," *PMHB* 126, no. 1 (January 2002): 5–96; see also *Philadelphia Inquirer,* March 24 and October 31, 2002, and June 3, 2007 (for a recapitulation of the issues at the site). See also Wiencek, *An Imperfect God,* esp. chap. 9, 322–23, for a fine retelling of Judge's escape.

44. By 1798, Allen was listed on the Philadelphia tax rolls as running a shoe shop out of his Spruce Street home. As with his other business endeavors, he may have been operating the shoe-repair shop earlier. On money given to Judge to buy shoes, see "Washington's Household Account Book, 1793–1797," in

PMHB, entry for May 10, 1796, 182. Thanks once again to Anna Coxe Toogood for this reference.

45. Wiencek, *An Imperfect God*, 333–34.

46. On Allen's moral-uplift ideology, see Clarence Walker's fine book, *Rock in a Weary Land: The African Methodist Episcopal Church during the Civil War and Reconstruction*, introduction.

47. Mifflin speech reprinted in the *Coloured American*, January 20, 1838.

48. According to the federal census of 1790, Benjamin Grover's Maryland property, "Mine Run 100," had one slave and one free person of color. Of Baltimore County's 1,725 families, 391 contained slaves, 115 contained free blacks —and 34 families had both! On Washington's meditations on slavery, see Ellis, *His Excellency, George Washington*, 278–88, 447–52. On Maryland's decreasing slave population and black runaways' impact on abolitionist trends, see T. Stephen Whitman, *The Price of Freedom: Slavery and Manumission in Baltimore and Early National Maryland* (Lexington, Ky., 1997), esp. chaps. 1, 3, 5.

49. See Eva Sheppard Wolf, *Race and Liberty in the New Nation: Emancipation in Virginia from the Revolution to Nat Turner's Rebellion* (Baton Rouge, La., 2006).

50. See the untitled address at the end of the "Articles of Association," 17–19.

51. Wood and Frey, *Come Shouting to Zion*, 122.

52. LEGL, 58.

53. William Still, *The Underground Railroad* (Philadelphia, 1871), 648–49.

54. See Newman, "'We Participate in Common,'" 124.

55. Allen, "Articles of Association," 17.

56. William Hamilton, "An Address to the New York African Society for Mutual Relief" (New York, 1809), reprinted in Dorothy Porter, ed., *Early Negro Writing* (Boston, 1971), 33–41.

57. See Waldstreicher, *In the Midst of Perpetual Fetes*, 328–29.

58. Forten wrote to Massachusetts representative George Thacher. See Winch, *A Gentleman of Color*, 154–56.

59. The Jones petition is reprinted in Kaplan, *Black Presence*, 237–39.

60. Ibid.

61. Scholarship on black nationalism has expanded markedly. Among the most insightful treatments include Sterling Stuckey's seminal book, *Slave Culture: Nationalist Theory and the Foundations of Black America* (New York, 1987), which places Southern slaves and African culture at the center of black nationalist ideologies; Patrick Rael's excellent revisionist study, *Black Identity and Black Protest in the Antebellum North*, esp. chap. 6, which, like my work here, focuses on black Northerners' contributions to the definitions of black nationalism; and Wilson Moses's pathbreaking study, *The Golden Age of Black Nationalism* (Hampden, Conn., 1978), which similarly views black nationalism

as wide-ranging and influenced by Western as well as Africanist ideologies. See also Waldstreicher's *In the Midst of Perpetual Fetes*, chap. 6, for a fine examination of early black Northerners' double consciousness on race and nation.

62. On Forten, see Winch's masterful biography, *A Gentleman of Color.*

63. *Freedom's Journal*, November 2, 1827.

64. Williams quoted in Albert J. Raboteau, *Canaan Land: A Religious History of African Americans* (New York, 2001), 27.

65. See Douglass's speech in the *National Anti-Slavery Standard*, May 3, 1849. See also Bostonian Maria Stewart's allusion to this phrase in her 1835 collection of speeches, "Productions," reprinted in Newman, Rael, and Lapsansky, *Pamphlets of Protest*, 125.

66. See Wesley, *Richard Allen*, 265.

67. Richard Allen, "Confession of John Joyce" (Philadelphia, 1808), and Richard Allen, "Confession of Peter Matthias" (Philadelphia, 1808).

68. Allen, "Confession of John Joyce," 1–5. Because both pamphlets repeat substantial amounts of information, I cite page numbers only from the Joyce pamphlet.

69. "To the People of Colour," in the "Narrative of the . . . Black People," originally published in 1794 and republished by Allen's son in his autobiography (LEGL) in 1833. In the LEGL version, Allen changed the pronoun from "we" to "I," so that the section read, "I was a slave once." The original version is reprinted in Porter, *Negro Protest Pamphlets*, 21–22.

70. Tilghman's speech was also reprinted in Allen's pamphlet. See Allen, "Confession of John Joyce," 5.

71. Ibid., 14.

72. See documents relating to this theme in Gordon S. Wood, *The Rising Glory of America* (Boston, 2006).

73. Material relating to the African Society for Suppression of Vice and Immorality is reprinted in Douglass, "Annals of the First African Church," 113–14.

74. See, in particular, Kevin K. Gaines, *Uplifting the Race* (Chapel Hill, N.C., 1996), xiv.

75. Tilghman quoted in Allen, "Confession of John Joyce," 12.

76. On Allen's involvement in Barclay's manumission, see "Committee for Improving Free Blacks," August 13 and September 24, 1795, PAS Papers, "Committee for Improving the Condition of Free Blacks," Reel 6. See also David Barclay, "An Account of the Emancipation of the Slaves of Unity Valley Pen, in Jamaica" (London, 1801).

77. See March 1796 entry, "Committee for Improving Free Blacks," PAS Papers, Reel 6.

78. "Committee for Improving Free Blacks," August 13, 1795, PAS Papers, Reel 6.

79. See Barclay, "An Account of the Emancipation of the Slaves," 1–5.

80. Horton and Horton, *In Hope of Liberty,* 221.

81. On this theme, see Newman and Finkenbine, "Black Founders in the New Republic," 93.

82. See, for example, William Hamilton, "An Address to the New York African Society" (New York, 1809).

83. This is Phillip Lapsansky's insight. See Newman, Rael, Lapsansky, *Pamphlets of Protest,* 74.

84. Results of the May 1807 meeting at Bethel Church were reported in the January 1, 1808, edition of *Poulson's Daily Advertiser* (Philadelphia).

85. Absalom Jones, "Thanksgiving sermon, preached January 1, 1808, in St. Thomas's, or the African Episcopal, church, Philadelphia, on account of the abolition of the African slave trade, on that day, by the Congress of the United States" (Philadelphia, 1808), 7–8.

NOTES TO CHAPTER 6

1. Richard Allen's Darby land deals amounted to the following: Lot 1 included six acres and was purchased on October 13, 1808, from Morris Morrison of the Northern Liberties, Pennsylvania, for the sum of $500; Lot 2 included just over seven acres and was purchased on April 6, 1812, from Samuel Shaw of Darby, Pennsylvania, for the sum of $600. The deeds for these transactions were recorded on July 28, 1814. Microfilm copies of the deeds are located in the Historical Society of Pennsylvania, Delaware County, Book L, 527–29.

2. Author interview with Kathryn Dockens, March 5, 2005.

3. *Green v. the African Methodist Episcopal Society,* in John Sergeant and William Rawle, comp., "Cases in the Supreme Court of Pennsylvania" (Philadelphia, 1819), 1:254–55.

4. See the court's wording in ibid.

5. Peter Spencer, a Kent County, Delaware, former slave, founded the Union Church of African Members in 1813 in Wilmington. Though much smaller than the AME would be, it still has rightful claim to the first officially independent black church. See Andrews, *The Methodists,* 152.

6. LEGL, 21.

7. Ibid., 20–21.

8. Payne, *History of the AME Church,* 3–6.

9. Allen and Tapsico, *Doctrines and Discipline of the AME Church.*

10. Ernest, *Liberation Historiography,* 11.

11. See Miller, *Voice of Deliverance,* 158.

12. Most AME historians and ministers retold Bethel's rise vis-à-vis Allen's renderings. See Noah C. Cannon, *A History of the African Methodist Episcopal Church, the Only One in the United States of America, Styled Bethel*

Church (Rochester, 1842); James A. Handy, *Scraps of African Methodist Episcopal History* (Philadelphia, 1902); Benjamin Tucker Tanner, *An Apology for African Methodism* (Baltimore, 1867).

13. LEGL, 20.

14. Cannon, *A History of the AME Church*, 22.

15. Documents pertaining to Methodists' legal intimidation of Allen are arranged neatly in a folder at the Historical Society of Pennsylvania (HSP). Marked simply "African Church," the file contains roughly a dozen documents, including official depositions by Methodist elders, lawyers' opinions, and notes from the sheriff who eventually tried to auction Bethel Church. The fact that the file exists at all testifies to the formidable challenge Allen and his congregants posed to the white establishment. For here one sees not simply the expected bullying of a black man in early national America but rather a group of white figures turning themselves inside and out to figure out a way to defeat a resolute black congregation. That effort translated into money, time, and all sorts of legal and financial wrangling. One lawyer's commentary on the merits of Bethel's claim to sovereignty stretches four pages, and one can barely follow all his citations and allusions to legal precedent. Methodist officials clearly felt that the Bethel congregation posed a serious challenge to their authority. See the "African Church" file in the Edward Carey Gardiner Collection, HSP.

16. Cannon, *A History of the AME Church*, 22, places the date at July 17, 1814.

17. John Emory to Samuel Shoemaker, April 6, 1815, in "African Church" file, HSP.

18. See the legal opinions of Samuel Shoemaker, April 7, 1815, and Joseph Hopkinson, April 24, 1815, in ibid.

19. Legal opinion of Joseph Hopkinson, April 24, 1815, in ibid.

20. Broadside of sheriff's ad, June 12, 1815, in ibid.

21. Allen's deposition is reprinted in "Sword of Truth,"3.

22. Report of Jacob Fitler, June 22, 1815, in "African Church" file, HSP.

23. Robert Burch to Samuel Shoemaker, December 16, 1815, in ibid.

24. Ibid.

25. Ibid.

26. Samuel Shoemaker's notes on Bethel Church case, circa January 1, 1816, in ibid.; emphasis added.

27. Allen to Daniel Coker, January 1816, not extant but reprinted in Cannon, *A History of the AME Church*, 22.

28. Ibid.

29. Ibid.

30. Ibid.

31. Payne, *History of the AME Church*, 6–7.

32. On the Philadelphia Index, see Susan E. Klepp, *"The Swift Progress*

of Population": A Documentary and Bibliographic Study of Philadelphia's Growth, 1642–1859 (Philadelphia, 1988).

33. I am grateful to my brother Eric Newman of Fort Worth, Texas, a math teacher and amateur statistician who compiled these statistics on Bethel Church.

34. See "The Plan of the Philadelphia Dispensary for the Medical Relief of the Poor" (Philadelphia, 1787). See also "An Account of the Philadelphia Dispensary" (Philadelphia, 1802) and "Rules of the Philadelphia Dispensary" (Philadelphia, 1808), which contain references to members, including Allen.

35. U.S. Census records for the state of Pennsylvania culled from federal reports in the years 1790, 1800, 1810, 1820, and 1830. Allen had several apprentices during the 1790s. On Paris's indenture, see PAS "Committee of Guardians" report, February 16, 1793, in PAS Papers, Reel 6.

36. LEGL, 21.

37. Coker, "Dialogue between a Virginian and an African Minister," 53–65.

38. Coker, "Sermon Delivered Extempore in the African Bethel Church in the City of Baltimore, on the 21st of January, 1816 . . . ," in Herbert Aptheker, ed., *A Documentary History of the Negro People* (New York, 1963), 1:67–69.

39. See especially Andrews, *The Methodists*, 123, 150–54, and George, *Segregated Sabbaths*, 87.

40. Payne, *History of the AME Church*, 10.

41. Ibid., 13–14. On black political rhetoric and constitutionalism, see James Oliver Horton's underrated essay, "Weevils in the Wheat: Free Blacks and the Constitution, 1787–1860," reprinted in "This Constitution: A Bicentennial Chronicle" (fall 1985), published by Project '87 of the American Political Science Association and the American Historical Association.

42. Allen and Tapsico, *Doctrines and Discipline of the AME Church*, 8.

43. On Coker, see Christopher Phillips, *Freedom's Port: The African American Community of Baltimore, 1790–1860* (Urbana, Ill., 1997), 131–35.

44. See Payne, *History of the AME Church*, 87.

45. George, *Segregated Sabbaths*, 88; Payne, *History of the AME Church*, 14. Phillips contends that Allen and Coker were designated as dual bishops before Coker's name was removed. See *Freedom's Port*, 131–35.

46. *The Doctrines and Discipline of the African Methodist Episcopal Church* was published by white printer John H. Cunningham, who remained in Allen's orbit for several years. Quotation on women's singing on p. 94.

47. Raboteau, *A Fire in the Bones*, 92.

48. Francis Asbury and Thomas Coke, eds., *The Doctrines and Discipline of the Methodist Episcopal Church* (Philadelphia, 1798). See also Mathews, *Slavery and Methodism*.

49. Allen and Tapsico, *Doctrines and Discipline of the AME Church*, 194.

50. Ibid., 3–4.

51. The opening narrative occupies several pages. See ibid., 3–9.

52. Ibid., 152.

53. Ibid., 63–66.

54. Craig Townsend, *Faith in Their Own Color: Black Episcopalians in Antebellum New York City* (New York, 2005).

55. "Rev. Richard Allen, Founder of the African Methodist Episcopal Church," engraving published by "J. Dainty," Philadelphia, 1813, reprinted in Kaplan, *Black Presence,* 91.

NOTES TO CHAPTER 7

1. Paul Cuffee to Richard Allen, March 8, 1814, reprinted in Rosalind Cobb Wiggins, ed., *Captain Paul Cuffee's Logs and Letters, 1808–1817* (Washington, D.C., 1996), 277. I have chosen the Ashanti spelling, "Cuffee."

2. Neither Charles Wesley's *Richard Allen: Apostle of Freedom,* nor Carol George's *Segregated Sabbaths* examines Allen's colonizationist musings. Other scholars working on Allen, including Albert Raboteau (*A Fire in the Bones*) and James Campbell (*Songs of Zion*), address Allen's international concerns but do not examine closely African colonization. Gary Nash does deal with colonization in Allen's life. See *Forging Freedom,* chap. 7.

3. Although probably written largely by the convention secretary Junius C. Morel, these words clearly reflected Allen's discussions of Canadian resettlement with members of the convention. See Richard Allen, "Address to the Free Persons of Colour of These United States," in "Constitution of the American Society of Free Persons of Colour, for Improving Their Condition in the United States; for Purchasing Lands; and for the Establishment of a Settlement in Upper Canada . . . Also the Proceedings of the Convention, with Their Address to the Free Persons of Colour in the United States" (Philadelphia, 1831), reprinted in Howard Holman Bell, ed., *Minutes of the Proceedings of the National Negro Conventions, 1830–1864* (New York, 1969), 10.

4. Allen and Forten quoted by New Jersey minister and colonizationist Robert Finley in 1817, quoted in William Loren Katz's preface to William Lloyd Garrison's *Thoughts on African Colonization* (New York, 1970), viii.

5. See Wilder, *In the Company of Black Men,* 89–90.

6. James T. Campbell, *Middle Passages: African-American Journeys to Africa, 1787–2005* (New York, 2006), 16.

7. See Nash, *Forging Freedom,* 102–3.

8. Document original in Cox-Parrish-Wharton Collection, Box 9, "Anonymous Folder," HSP. I am indebted to Douglass Mooney, Roy Finkenbine, and Anna Coxe Toogood for information on this petition. For an extended treatment, see Newman, Finkenbine, and Mooney, "Philadelphia Emigrationist Petition," 166.

9. Cuffee to John James and Alexander Wilson, June 10, 1809, reprinted in Wiggins, *Captain Paul Cuffee's Logs and Letters*, 80–81.

10. See Paul Cuffee, "A Brief Account of the Settlement and Present Situation of the Colony of Sierra Leone" (New York, 1812). Winch, *A Gentleman of Color*, 176–92, is particularly insightful on Cuffee's work and appeal to black activists.

11. See Peter Williams, Jr., "A Discourse Delivered on the Death of Capt. Paul Cuffee before the New York African Institution, in the African Methodist Episcopal Zion Church" (New York, 1817), 1–8.

12. Ibid., 10–17.

13. Cuffee congressional petition, March 1813, reprinted in Wiggins, *Captain Paul Cuffee's Logs and Letters*, 252–53.

14. By 1808, Cuffee had regular contact with Quaker merchants and abolitionists in Philadelphia, including James Pemberton, a successful merchant and leading member of the Pennsylvania Abolition Society. By 1812, he was meeting with black leaders in several mid-Atlantic cities. See Wiggins, *Captain Paul Cuffee's Logs and Letters*, 195, 211–18.

15. See Cuffee to Allen, March 8, 1814, June 8, 1814, and March 27, 1815, in Wiggins, *Captain Paul Cuffee's Logs and Letters*, 277, 294–95, 331, respectively.

16. Ibid.

17. On colonization generally, see Eric Burin's recent book, *Slavery's Peculiar Solution* (Gainesville, Fla., 2005).

18. Wilson Moses, *The Wings of Ethiopia* (Ames, Iowa, 1990), 149–54.

19. Cuffee to Nath G. M. Senter, March 7, 1814, in Wiggins, *Captain Paul Cuffee's Logs and Letter*, 276.

20. See James Brewer Stewart's excellent essay, "The Emergence of Racial Modernity and the Rise of the White North, 1790–1840," *Journal of the Early Republic* 18 (summer 1998): 181–217. See also Melish, *Disowning Slavery*.

21. Wesley, *Richard Allen*, 145. For an excellent modern treatment, see Winch, *A Gentleman of Color*, 174–77.

22. Wesley and I have both examined the same central source, the "Minutes of the Committee of Defense of Philadelphia," reprinted in *Memoirs of the Historical Society of Pennsylvania* 8 (Philadelphia, 1867). Although we reach slightly different conclusions, Wesley conceded that Philadelphia's leaders remained wary of black military participation.

23. "A Hint" appeared in *Poulson's Daily Advertiser*, September 3, 1814.

24. See the Philadelphia petition against colonization, hereafter cited as "The Philadelphia Petition," reprinted in Garrison, *Thoughts on African Colonization*, 9.

25. See reports from the PAS board of education's "Visiting Committee" in

1816; for example, report of January 25, 1816. See also the board of education's "Apprenticing Committee" report, May 25, 1815, in PAS Papers, Reel 7.

26. Board of education, "Apprenticing Committee" report, May 25, 1815.

27. Ibid.

28. See Allen et al., "Sword of Truth," 7.

29. Allen, "An Address to Those Who Keep Slaves."

30. See Allen et al., "Sword of Truth, 6.

31. Katz, preface to Garrison, *Thoughts on African Colonization,* vii–ix.

32. Allen, "Address to the Free Persons of Colour," 9–12.

33. Copies of Allen's property deeds are housed in the Bethel Archives, Richard Allen Museum, Philadelphia. See the following purchase documents for Allen's rise to professional man: January 22, 1791, John Willson, Farmer to Richard Allen, Grocer, Tenement and Lot on Spruce between 4th and 5th streets for 250 pounds; October 10, 1791, Mark Wilcox to Allen, Trader, and his wife Flora, Lot at Sixth and Lombard, for 20 Spanish Milled dollars; July 17, 1805, Richard Allen, Dealer, and wife Sarah to AME Church Trustees, Lot on East side of 6th Street, for 550 pounds; January 19, 1818, Joseph Johns (Bricklayer) et al. to Richard Allen, Minister of the Gospel, for an alley six feet wide at the end of Pine Street and Fifth and Sixth streets.

34. See the property deed between Richard Allen and Joseph Lewis, August 10, 1792, for a plot of land at Sixth and Lombard streets, next to Bethel Church, in Bethel Archives.

35. See property deed from John Burk to Richard Allen, April 18, 1795; Robert Green (former AME member) to Richard Allen et al., July 2, 1805; and Joseph Johns to Richard Allen, January 19, 1818, in Bethel Archives.

36. *Freedom's Journal,* November 2, 1827.

37. Allen, "Confession of John Joyce," 5–6.

38. LEGL, 7–10.

39. "The Will of Richard Allen," December 9, 1830, reprinted in Wesley, *Richard Allen,* appendix, 271–74.

40. I am indebted to Phillip Lapsansky of the Library Company, who provided me with a copy of Jones's will from his own collection.

41. LEGL, 10.

42. See land deed between Joseph Murphy et al. and Richard Allen and members of Bethel Church, February 13, 1813, in Bethel Archives.

43. Allen, "Address to the Free Persons of Colour, 9–11.

44. See Allen's commentary to Robert Finley in Katz, preface to Garrison, *Thoughts on African Colonization,* vii–ix.

45. See Allen, "Confession of John Joyce" and "Confession of Peter Matthias." The originals are in the American Antiquarian Society and the Library Company of Philadelphia.

46. Allen, "Confession of John Joyce," 12–16.

47. Ibid., 33–35.

48. Ibid., 23–24.

49. Robert Finley, quoted in Katz, preface to Garrison, *Thoughts on African Colonization*, vii–ix.

50. See, in particular, Nash, *Forging Freedom*, 233–45; Winch, *A Gentleman of Color*, 196–201.

51. On Northern and Southern unanimity on colonization, see Newman, *Transformation of American Abolitionism*, chap. 5. For a dissenting perspective on colonization, see Burin, *Slavery's Peculiar Solution*, introduction.

52. The Philadelphia protest is reprinted in Lawrence B. Goodheart and Hugh Hawkins, eds., *The Abolitionists: Means, Ends, and Motivations* (Boston, 1995), 37–38.

53. On second-wave, or immediate, abolitionism, see Newman, *Transformation of American Abolitionism*, chaps. 5–7.

54. *Freedom's Journal*, November 2, 1827.

55. See "Address to the Humane and Benevolent Inhabitants of the City and County of Philadelphia" (Philadelphia, 1818), 1–5; see also Winch, *A Gentleman of Color*, 196.

56. Nash, *Forging Freedom*, 233–45; Winch, *A Gentleman of Color*, 196–201.

57. Richard Finley, quoted in Katz, preface to Garrison, *Thoughts on African Colonization*, vii–ix.

58. Campbell, *Middle Passages*, 48–53.

NOTES TO CHAPTER 8

1. In other parts of the Quaker State, however, free blacks did occasionally vote, which indicates that social environment dictated the latitude for black suffrage, not lack of desire or will. See Nick Salvatore, *We All Got History: The Memory Books of Archie Webber* (Urbana-Champaign, 2006), part 1.

2. African Supplement, 22.

3. On deliberative citizenship, see Brooke, "Consent, Civil Society, and the Public Sphere," 231–34.

4. "Constitution and Bylaws for the Government of All Official Meetings, Held Under the Charter of the First Colored Wesley Methodist Church, Lombard Street, Philadelphia" (Philadelphia, 1846), 2–3. I am much indebted to Phillip Lapsansky of the Library Company for a copy of this rare document, which he acquired while I was in residence.

5. On Wesley Church's organizational history and affiliations, see in particular the group's account books at the American Philosophical Society, "First Colored Methodist Wesley Church, Minute Book, 1827–1841." See also "Minutes

of the Philadelphia Conference of the Methodist Episcopal Church" (Philadelphia, 1823 and 1839). On church connections to New York City's AME Zion congregation, see Winch, *A Gentleman of Color,* 226.

6. Allen et al., "Sword of Truth," 3–4, 8–9.

7. George, *Segregated Sabbaths,* 94–95.

8. LEGL, 16–17.

9. Tudas's pamphlet is not extant. According to two official depositions before a city clerk, Tudas had carried around copies of a pamphlet entitled "Richard Allen's Journal." Lack of funds prompted the printer to withhold all but a few copies of the pamphlet. See the depositions of James J. Ennis and James Derrickson in "Sword of Truth," 3–4.

10. Joining the initial Bethel secessionists were the following men: James Bird (shoemaker), William Bedford (cartman), Tobias Sipple (dealer), and Allen's old nemesis Robert Green (coachman and dealer). This leadership cadre was identified in "Statement by the Trustees of Wesley," reprinted in Allen et al., "Sword of Truth," 14–16. By August 1820, Josiah Blue was minister. By 1826, many of the original secessionists were gone. See "Constitution and Bylaws . . . of the First Colored Wesley Methodist Church," 2–3, 8–9.

11. Allen reprinted his moral-uplift essay from 1794 in his autobiography. See LEGL, 47–48.

12. For peer trials of Bethel congregants for moral offenses, see "The Records of Mother Bethel AME Church, 1760–1972" (fourteen microfilm vols.), "Minute and Trial Book, 1822–1835," Reel 8.

13. Allen et al., "Sword of Truth," 3.

14. "Constitution and Bylaws . . . of the First Colored Wesley Methodist Church," 2–3, 8–9.

15. Minutes of meeting, August 5, 1822, at Allen's home, in Bethel "Minute and Trial Book, 1822–1835," Reel 8.

16. Minutes of meeting, August 6, 1822, at Allen's home, in Bethel "Minute and Trial Book, 1822–1835," Reel 8.

17. Ibid.

18. Minutes of meeting, August 11, 1822, at Allen's home, in Bethel "Minute and Trial Book, 1822–1835," Reel 8.

19. Ibid.

20. Ibid.

21. Ibid.

22. Bethel trustees meeting, October 3, 1822, in Bethel "Minute and Trial Book, 1822–1835," Reel 8; George, *Segregated Sabbaths,* 99.

23. See the depositions of James J. Ennis and James Derrickson, both taken on March 7, 1823, in Allen et al., "Sword of Truth," 3–4. Because Bethel's membership lists are not extant for this period, it is impossible to know whether these men regularly attended Allen's church.

24. Winch, *A Gentleman of Color,* 226.

25. Allen et al., "Sword of Truth," 4.

26. Ibid, 3.

27. Ibid.

28. Ibid.

29. The deposition of James Derrickson in Allen et al., "Sword of Truth," 3–4.

30. The deposition of James J. Ennis in Allen et al., "Sword of Truth," 3.

31. Allen et al., "Sword of Truth," 4.

32. George, *Segregated Sabbaths,* 98–99.

33. Allen and Jones, "Narrative of the . . . Black People," 33.

34. See Joanne Freeman, *Affairs of Honor* (New Haven, Conn., 2000).

35. See Emma Lapsansky, " 'Since They Got Those Separate Churches,' " *American Quarterly* 32, no. 1 (spring 1980): 54–78. On class divisions in Northern free black communities, see also Leslie Harris, *In the Shadow of Slavery: African Americans in New York City, 1626–1863* (Chicago, 2003). The key primary source remains the PAS's economic and social report, "Report on the Condition of the People of Color" (Philadelphia, 1838).

36. Candy Gunther Brown, *The Word in the World: Evangelical Writing, Publishing, and Reading in America, 1789–1880* (Chapel Hill, N.C., 2004), 208.

37. LEGL, 29.

38. Minutes of meeting, April 6, 1825, in Bethel "Minute and Trial Book, 1822–1835," Reel 8.

39. Winch, *A Gentleman of Color,* 174–75.

40. See Allen et al., "Sword of Truth," 3–6, 11–13.

41. See Wesley's "Receipt Book, 1820–1848" and "Minute Book, 1827–1844," Hare-Willing Family Papers, First Colored Methodist Wesley Church, American Philosophical Society.

42. See the following entries for Perkins's contributions to the church-building effort: September 7 and 15, 1820, and June 21, 1821, in "Receipt Book, 1820–1848," First Colored Methodist Wesley Church, American Philosophical Society.

43. "Statement of the Trustees of Wesley," in Allen et al., "Sword of Truth," 14–16.

44. "Constitution and Bylaws . . . of the First Colored Wesley Methodist Church," 2.

45. Information compiled from extant Philadelphia city directories for the years 1820–30.

46. Ibid.

47. Douglass, "Annals of the First African Church," 115–17.

48. On Gloucester, see Rev. William T. Catto, "A Semi-Centenary Discourse Delivered in the First African Presbyterian Church on the 4th Sabbath of May, 1857" (Philadelphia, 1857), 1–21.

49. See *History of Philadelphia by Thompson Westcott Scrapbooks* (Philadelphia, 1888), 925–26.

50. For results of the referendum at Bethel Church, see the official minutes for a meeting on October 25, 1828, in Bethel "Minute and Trial Book, 1822–1835," Reel 8.

51. Information on Bethel congregants compiled from extant Philadelphia city directories for the years 1820–30.

52. Allen to Daniel Coker, January 1816, not extant but reprinted in Cannon, *A History of the AME Church*, 22.

53. On Bethel signatories and literacy, see Allen, "Articles of Association," 14; Kaplan, *Black Presence*, 238; Wesley, *Richard Allen*, 135.

54. See W. E. B. Du Bois, *The Philadelphia Negro* (Philadelphia, 1899; repr., 1996), 82–96. On black literacy generally, see McHenry, *Forgotten Readers*.

55. On black women's impact on voting during a later period, see in particular Elsa Barkley Brown, "Negotiating and Transforming the Public Sphere: African American Political Life in the Transition from Slavery to Freedom," reprinted in Charles M. Payne and Adam Green, eds., *Time Longer Than Rope: A Century of African American Activism, 1850–1950* (New York, 2003).

56. See Jarena Lee, "Religious Experience and Journal of Mrs. Jarena Lee" (Philadelphia, 1836 and 1849), reprinted in *Spiritual Narratives*, Schomburg Library of Nineteenth-Century Black Women's Narratives (New York, 1988).

57. The most insightful treatments of Lee include Frances Smith Foster, *Written by Herself: Literary Production by African American Women, 1746–1892* (Bloomington, Ind., 1993); and Carla L. Peterson, *"Doers of the Word": African-American Women Speakers and Writers in the North, 1830–1880* (New York, 1995), chap. 3.

58. Lee, "Religious Experience," 11.

59. Ibid., 60.

60. Ibid., 45.

61. Ibid., 96.

62. Ibid., 77.

63. Payne, *History of the AME Church*, 87.

64. Handy, *Scraps of African Methodist Episcopal History*, 343–44.

65. Ibid.

66. Brown, *Homespun Heroines*, 12.

67. Nancy A. Hewitt, *Women's Activism and Social Change: Rochester, New York, 1822–1872* (Ithaca, N.Y., 1984), introduction.

68. See Mary Still's pamphlet, "An Appeal to the Females of the African

Methodist Episcopal Church" (Philadelphia, 1857), and the accompanying headnote (written by Phillip Lapsansky), in Newman, Rael, and Lapsansky, *Pamphlets of Protest,* 254–61.

69. *Freedom's Journal,* February 22, 1828.

70. Mifflin Wistar Gibbs, *Shadow and Light* (Little Rock, Ark., 1902), 1–19. Gibbs (1823–1915), said that his father was a minister in the Wesleyan Methodist Church, which probably meant Wesley Church because his father died in 1831 and AME Wesley was not founded until 1834. Gibbs became, rather ironically, a Presbyterian.

71. Ibid., 8.

72. "The Revd. Richard Allen, Bishop of the First African Methodist Episcopal Church in the U. States" (Philadelphia, 1823). I am indebted to Phillip Lapsansky and my friends at the Library Company for an image of this portrait; in 2006 they secured a rare copy of the original stipple engraving.

NOTES TO CHAPTER 9

1. Richard Allen to "Le President d'Haiti," Jean-Pierre Boyer, August 22, 1824, in Granville, *Biographie de Jonathas Granville,* 224–25. I am much indebted to Julie Winch for making this source known to me.

2. Ibid.

3. For Allen's ministerial outreach, see, for example, Campbell's magnificent book, *Songs of Zion.*

4. Payne, *History of the AME Church,* 2, 4–12, 21–22. See also George, *Segregated Sabbaths,* chaps. 4, 5, 8.

5. Handy, *Scraps of African Methodist Episcopal History,* 5.

6. See Lee, "Religious Experience," 58.

7. A copy of the Joshua P. Eddy preaching certificate is available in the Richard Allen Museum, Bethel Church. I am grateful for permission to quote from it.

8. Payne, *History of the AME Church,* 107.

9. See entry for December 12, 1823, in Bethel "Minute and Trial Book, 1822–1835," Reel 8.

10. Lee, "Religious Experience," 11.

11. Walker, "Appeal," 97–99. On Allen's influence on Walker, see also Peter P. Hinks, *To Awaken My Afflicted Brethren: David Walker and the Problem of Antebellum Slave Resistance* (University Park, Pa., 1997), 38, 65.

12. On Brown's speedy admission to the Mother Bethel board of trustees, see entries for October 2 and 15, 1822, in Bethel "Minute and Trial Book, 1822–1835," Reel 8.

13. On Vesey's international designs, see Douglass R. Egerton's terrific book, *He Shall Go Out Free: The Lives of Denmark Vesey* (Madison, Wis., 2000).

14. See meeting of October 2, 1822, in Bethel "Minute and Trial Book, 1822–1835," Reel 8.

15. The first Allen-Brown meeting may have occurred in 1816. Payne places their first meeting in 1818. See Payne, *History of the AME Church,* 47.

16. See Egerton, *He Shall Go Out Free,* 109–13.

17. Ibid.

18. Jarena Lee noted Brown and Allen preaching together in New York in June 1823; see Lee, "Religious Experience," 29.

19. On Prince Saunders, see Winch, *A Gentleman of Color,* 211–13. See also Arthur O. White, "An Instance of Social Mobility among New England Blacks," *Journal of Negro History* 60 (1975): 526–35.

20. Prince Saunders, "An Address Delivered at Bethel Church" (Philadelphia, 1818).

21. Prince Saunders, *Haytian Papers: A Collection of the Very Interesting Proclamations and Other Official Documents, Together with Some Account of the Rise . . . of Hayti* (Boston, 1818). See the copies bearing Rawle's and Logan's signatures in the Library Company's archives.

22. Ibid., 150–54.

23. Ibid.

24. Allen to Boyer, August 22, 1824, in Granville, *Biographie de Jonathas Granville,* 224–25.

25. On Haiti's impact on black Atlantic society, see Dubois, *Avengers of the New World,* prologue.

26. Benjamin Lundy, in *Genius of Universal Emancipation,* March 1825.

27. Alexander Everett, *America; or, A General Survey of the Political Situation of the Several Powers of the Western Continent* (Philadelphia, 1827), 221–23.

28. William Watkins, in *Genius of Universal Emancipation,* August 1824, 168–69.

29. Granville, *Biographie de Jonathas Granville,* 114; *Philadelphia National Gazette,* June 16, 1824.

30. Meetings between Granville and Allen/Bethel Church members occurred on June 29 and November 2, 21, 22, and 29, 1824; Bethel "Minute and Trial Book, 1822–1835," Reel 8.

31. For those who might need to have housing and other provisions right away, Granville and Boyer offered rental schemes of various sorts.

32. See New Yorker Mahlon Day's pamphlet, which was republished by Afro-Philadelphians (possibly Allen) in 1824, "Society for Promoting the Emigration of Free Persons of Colour to Hayti" (Philadelphia, 1824).

33. Ibid., 16.

34. Mahlon Day, "Information for the Free People of Colour Who Are Inclined to Emigrate to Hayti" (New York, 1824), 1–7.

35. Belfast Burton to Allen, reprinted in *Genius of Universal Emancipation*, July 4, 1825. See also letters to Allen in the *U.S. Gazette*, December 4, 1824; January 11, 1825; February 22, 1825.

36. Ibid.

37. Loring D. Dewey to Allen, reprinted in *Genius of Universal Emancipation*, April 1825.

38. Ibid.

39. See also Loring D. Dewey, "Correspondence Relative to the Emigration to Hayti, of the People of Colour, in the United States" (New York, 1824).

40. Loring D. Dewey, in *Genius of Universal Emancipation*, March 1825.

41. Allen to Boyer, August 22, 1824, in Granville, *Biographie de Jonathas Granville*, 224–25.

42. Day, "Society for Promoting the Emigration of Free Persons of Colour to Hayti"; and Day, "Information for the Free People of Colour Who Are Inclined to Emigrate to Hayti," 3.

43. Allen to Boyer, August 22, 1824, in Granville, *Biographie de Jonathas Granville*, 224–25.

44. *Genius of Universal Emancipation*, July 1825, citing *Petersburg Intelligencer*. For a classic treatment of Southern reaction to Haiti, see Alfred N. Nunt, *Haiti's Influence on Antebellum America* (Baton Rouge, 1988).

45. *Genius of Universal Emancipation*, May 1825, citing Maryland paper.

46. *Philadelphia National Gazette*, June 19, 1824.

47. Allen to Boyer, August 22, 1824, in Granville, *Biographie de Jonathas Granville*, 224–25.

48. For meetings between Bethel trustees and Granville on November 3, 21, 22, and 29, 1824, see Bethel "Minute and Trial Book, 1822–1835," Reel 8.

49. *Freedom's Journal*, November 2, 1827.

50. Walker, "Appeal," 97–99.

51. On the genealogy and meaning of Allen's "Mother Country" address, see Newman and Finkenbine, "Black Founders in the New Republic."

52. See Winch, *A Gentleman of Color*, 219–20.

53. Payne, *History of the AME Church*, 105.

54. Ernest, *Liberation Historiography*, 89.

55. Robin D. G. Kelley, *Freedom Dreams: The Black Radical Imagination* (Boston, 2002), 16.

56. *Freedom's Journal*, November 2, 1827.

NOTES TO CHAPTER 10

1. LEGL, 49, 59–60.

2. *Freedom's Journal*, February 22, 1828.

3. See Andrew Burstein, *America's Jubilee, July 4, 1826: A Generation Remembers the Revolution after Fifty Years of Independence* (New York, 2001).

4. See *Genius of Universal Emancipation,* October, November 1827. On Free Produce generally, see especially Carol Faulkner's fine essay "The Root of the Evil: Free Produce and Radical Antislavery, 1820–1860," *Journal of the Early Republic* 27, no. 3 (fall 2007): 377–405; quotation at 390.

5. See Newman, *Transformation of American Abolitionism,* chap. 2.

6. Wesley, *Richard Allen,* 239–40; see also *Genius of Universal Emancipation,* September 2, 1829.

7. On immediate abolitionism, see James Brewer Stewart, *Holy Warriors* (New York, 1997). See also John Stauffer, *Black Hearts of Men: Radical Abolitionists and the Transformation of Race* (Cambridge, Mass., 2002).

8. Benjamin Lundy, "Free Colored People," *Genius of Universal Emancipation,* May 1830.

9. *Freedom's Journal,* December 19, 1828.

10. According to the (New York) *Weekly Anglo-African Magazine,* Grice "conceived the plan of calling together a meeting or convention of colored men . . . for the purpose of comparing views and of adopting a harmonious movement either of emigration, or of determination to remain in the United States." He sent a circular to black leaders on April 2, 1830. On August 11, Allen summoned Grice to Philadelphia, where he showed the young man a circular from New York City on the same issue. See the *Anglo-African Magazine* 1, no. 10 (October 1859), reprinted in Bell, *Minutes of the Proceedings of the National Negro Conventions,* 2–3.

11. On this founding black national convention, see "Constitution of the American Society of Free Persons of Colour" (Philadelphia, 1830). The constitution was signed and probably coauthored by Allen.

12. The best work on the black convention movement remains Patrick Rael's seminal *Black Identity and Black Protest in the Antebellum North.*

13. William Lloyd Garrison's *Liberator* began publication in January 1831.

14. Allen, "Address to the Free Persons of Colour," 9–12.

15. Ibid.

16. See C. Peter Ripley, Mary Alice Herrle, and Paul A. Cimbala, eds., *The Black Abolitionist Papers,* vol. 2, *Canada, 1830–1865* (Chapel Hill, N.C., 1987), 4.

17. On Morel's interesting career as advocate for voting rights and, later, opponent of the American Moral Reform Society (organized by William Whipper), see Winch, *A Gentleman of Color,* 295.

18. Noah C. Cannon was one such missionary. See Cannon, *A History of the AME Church,* 8.

19. Allen, *Freedom's Journal,* November 2, 1827.

20. Allen, "Address to the Free Persons of Colour," 9–12.

21. Ibid., 10.

22. Ibid.

23. See ibid., iii–iv, 5–8.

24. *Genius of Universal Emancipation,* September 1830.

25. *Genius of Universal Emancipation,* October 1830.

26. On what reformers called "modern" abolitionism, see Newman, *Transformation of American Abolitionism,* introduction.

27. "The Will of Richard Allen" is conveniently reprinted in Wesley, *Richard Allen,* 271–74.

28. Ibid.

29. "Acts of Love," LEGL, 28.

30. LEGL, 4.

31. Ibid., 3, 4.

32. Laymon, *Interpreter's One-Volume Commentary on the Bible,* 258.

33. On autobiographical genres, see, for example, William L. Andrews, ed., *Classic American Autobiographies* (New York, 1992), Vincent Carretta, ed., *Unchained Voices: An Anthology of Black Authors in the English-Speaking World of the Eighteenth Century* (New York, 2003).

34. Joyce Appleby, ed., *Recollections of the Early Republic: Selected Autobiographies* (Boston, 1997).

35. See Valery Smith, *Self-Discovery and Authority in Afro-American Narrative* (Cambridge, Mass., 1987), 153.

36. African Supplement, in LEGL, 22–25.

37. Similarly, Allen changed attribution from the original: where he had once cosigned the original pamphlet with Absalom Jones (and addressed black and white leaders in the hallowed "we"), now Allen took credit for much of the language and content of the pamphlet. On naming debates in black society just after Allen, see esp. Rael, *Black Identity and Black Protest.*

38. LEGL, 42.

39. Allen, "To the People of Colour," LEGL, 48.

40. LEGL, 47.

41. Mathew Carey, "Reflections on the Causes That Led to the Formation of the Colonization Society, with a View of Its Probable Results" (Philadelphia, 1832), 1–37.

42. Ibid., esp. 37.

43. "A Short Address to the Friends of Him Who Hath No Helper," LEGL, 48–49.

44. On interracial abolition, see Newman, *The Transformation of American Abolitionism,* chaps. 4–5; see also Stauffer, *Black Hearts of Men,* introduction.

45. See "Acts of Love," LEGL, 32.

46. See "Acts of Hope," LEGL, 31.

47. LEGL, 56.

48. Ibid., 52.

49. Ibid., 63–64.

50. Ibid., 58.

51. Ibid., 5, 7.

52. On liberation theology in African American religious thought, see Hopkins and Cummings, *Cut Loose Your Stammering Tongue*, introduction.

53. John Stauffer, foreword to Frederick Douglass, *My Bondage and My Freedom* (New York, 2004), xvii.

54. Ibid.

55. "Acts of Hope," LEGL, 27.

56. See meeting of March 29, 1831, in "Minutes of the Union Benevolent Sons of Mother Bethel AME Church, 1826–1844," Bethel Archives, Philadelphia.

57. Wesley, *Richard Allen*, 245.

58. *Poulson's Daily Advertiser,* March 31, 1831; *Philadelphia Gazette and Daily Advertiser,* March 30, 1831.

59. See the *Liberator,* April 9 and May 14, 1831, and *Genius of Universal Emancipation,* September 1830 and March 1831.

60. *Christian Recorder,* October 1, 1870.

NOTES TO THE CONCLUSION

1. *Pennsylvania Freeman,* August 18, 1853. I am indebted to Carol Faulkner of Syracuse University for this citation.

2. Allen, quoted in ibid.

3. McCune Smith wrote as "Communipaw" in *Frederick Douglass's Paper,* May 11, 1855. For a brilliant collection of McCune Smith's writings, see John Stauffer, ed., *The Works of James McCune Smith: Black Intellectual and Abolitionist* (New York, 2006).

4. The bust was briefly unveiled at the exposition before moving to Bethel. Gary Nash is particularly good at detailing the deeper meaning of the Allen statue. See Nash, *First City,* 268–70. See also Wesley, *Richard Allen,* 263–64.

5. See the *Christian Recorder,* February 22, 1894.

6. Douglass, "Richard Allen's Place in History," speech delivered at the Chicago World's Fair Congress of Religions, September 22, 24, and 26, 1893. See the Frederick Douglass Papers, Library of Congress, Box 31, Reel 19, 1, 3, 5, 9.

7. See Du Bois, *The Souls of Black Folk,* ed. Henry Louis Gates, Jr., Norton Critical Edition (New York, 1999), esp. chap. 10, "Of the Faith of the Fathers."

8. See Baldwin's preface to *The Fire Next Time* (New York, 1963).

9. Jesse Jackson, letter to *Time* magazine, May 3, 1976.

10. Ralph Ellison, "Twentieth-Century Fiction and the Black Mask of Humanity," in *Shadow and Act* (New York, 1964), 43.

11. Allen, "An Address to Those Who Keep Slaves," 41.

12. Dawson, *Black Visions,* esp. chap. 1. See also Manning Marable's fine book, *Living Black History: How Re-Imagining the African American Past Can Remake America's Racial Future* (New York, 2006).

13. See Raboteau, *A Fire in the Bones,* 28–30.

14. On black prophecy and prophetic leadership, see David L. Chappell, *A Stone of Hope: Prophetic Religion and the Death of Jim Crow* (Chapel Hill, N.C., 2004). See also Callahan, *Talking Book.*

15. Wilson Moses's admonition that we treat black leaders as dynamic, rather than ideologically rigid, thinkers has influenced my treatment of Allen here. See Moses's own masterful biography, *Alexander Crummell: A Study of Civilization and Discontent* (New York, 1989), esp. the introduction.

16. See King's 1960 speech "Suffering and Faith," in James M. Washington, ed., *A Testament of Hope: The Essential Writings and Speeches of Martin Luther King, Jr.* (New York, 1986), 41–42.

17. Allen, "An Address to Those Who Keep Slaves," 42.

18. David Brion Davis, The Problem of Slavery in the Age of Revolution, 1770–1823 (Ithaca, N.Y., 1975), 564.

Index

Abbott, Benjamin, 47, 145

abolitionism: black conventions, 269–270; black founders, 110; black pamphleteering, 79; concern about union, 268; Delaware, 45; domestic colonization, 194; evangelical antislavery movement, 38; first fugitive-slave law, 106; Free Produce Society of Pennsylvania, 266; Freemasons, 122; gradual abolitionism, 107, 156, 173; Great Britain, 271; Haitian emigration, 261; Haitian rebellion, 112–114; "immediatist" movement, 204–205, 267–268; as a mass movement, 268; "modern" abolitionism, 275; national abolitionism, 112; national meeting (1830), 269–275; Pennsylvania Abolition Society (*see* Pennsylvania Abolition Society); petition (1790), congressional, 112; petition (1799), 147–148, 230; Philadelphia, 54; RA and, 21, 269–270; RA on, 22, 107, 111–112, 144; secular abolitionism, 38; uplift ideology, 57–58, 155; white abolitionists, 284; yellow-fever epidemic (1793), 88–89, 100–101. *See also* emancipation; manumission

Absalom Jones and, Absalom Co., 83–84

"Acts of Faith" (RA), 285

"Acts of Hope" (RA), 285

"Acts of Love" (RA), 285

Adams, Ann (née Allen). *See* Allen, Ann

Adams, John, 14, 16, 127, 266

Adams, Richard Nathaniel (RA's grandson), 275

Adams, Samuel, 16

Addison, Joseph, 150

"Address to Free Persons of Color in the United States" (RA), 270–273

"Address to the People of Colour" (RA), 279, 280–281, 282

"Address to the Public" (RA), 153

"Address to Those Who Keep Slaves and Approve the Practice" (RA), 106–112; abolitionism as national objective, 111–112; authorship, 316n2; black abolitionism, 108–109; black redemption, 194; emancipation, 109; on God, 105; Jefferson in, 107–108; nonviolent call for racial justice, 106–107; racial reconciliation, possibility of, 110; RA's experience with slavery, 111; reprint in RA's autobiography, 279, 284; slaveholder's dilemma, 107–108; transgressions of slaveholders, 194

African Americans: American Colonization Society (ACS), 252; American identity, 261; anti-vice organizations, 154; anti-colonization meetings of, 202–204; arts, rhetoric, 23; black republican mothers, 75–76; black underclass, 194, 199–202, 237; blacks as a nation within a nation, 61; blacks' will to overcome oppression, 295; character formation, 193; class divisions among, 220–222, 227–228, 254; double consciousness of, 149; exclusion from civic participation, 146–148; first copyright by, 78; Haitian rebellion, 185; Jefferson on, 23; as loyal opposition (early 1800s), 149; "mediators" of their political life, 129–130; nation-building efforts, 150; opportunities for advancement, 193; pamphleteering by, 79; patriotism, 191; political power, 210; prophetic leadership, 297–298; RA on, 194; safety valve for, 239, 247, 263; suffrage for, 111;

About the Author

Richard S. Newman is Associate Professor of History at the Rochester Institute of Technology. He is the author of *The Transformation of American Abolitionism: Fighting Slavery in the Early Republic* and coeditor of the series "Race in the Atlantic World, 1700–1900." He has also coedited a book of black abolitionist documents, *Pamphlets of Protest*.

CPSIA information can be obtained at www.ICGtesting.com
Printed in the USA
BVOW08s0638170816

458836BV00006B/3/P